Mesolithic Occupation at Bouldnor Cliff and the Submerged Prehistoric Landscapes of the Solent

Mesolithic Occupation at Bouldnor Cliff and the Submerged Prehistoric Landscapes of the Solent

Garry Momber, David Tomalin, Rob Scaife,
Julie Satchell and Jan Gillespie

With major contributions by
Nigel Nayling, Geoff Bailey, Rachel Bynoe, Mark Robinson,
Jen Heathcote, Derek Hamilton, Anthony Long, Peter Marshall,
Christopher Bronk Ramsey, Gordon Cook and Alison Locker

CBA Research Report 164
Council for British Archaeology
2011

Published in 2011 by the Council for British Archaeology
St Mary's House, 66 Bootham, York, YO30 7BZ

British Library cataloguing in Publication Data
A catalogue record for this book is available from the British Library
ISBN 978-1-902771-84-7

Typeset by Archétype Informatique SARL, www.archetype-it.com
Cover designed by yo-yo.uk.com
Printed and bound by The Charlesworth Group
The publisher acknowledges with gratitude a grant from English Heritage towards the cost of publication

Front cover: Garry Momber diving at BC-V (© Michael Pitts)
Back cover: Garry Momber and Victoria Millership recovering a sample from BC-II (© Michael Pitts).
Insets: Lithics recovered from the seabed (Garry Momber); worked wood from the site (Julian Whitewright)

Contents

Chapter 5   **Rising waters, environmental change, and humans at BC-IV** *by Garry Momber,*
Rob Scaife, Jan Gillespie, Nigel Nayling, Derek Hamilton, Peter Marshall,

Chapter 6   **Dendrochronological and radiocarbon synthesis across the −11m OD peat shelf**
by Nigel Nayling and Derek Hamilton **102**

Chapter 7   **Environmental change in the cultural landscape across the valley**
by Garry Momber, Rob Scaife, and Nigel Nayling **105**

**Section three: Establishing the changing environmental and physical
context of the cultural landscape** **113**

Chapter 8   **The changing vegetation and environment** *by Rob Scaife* 115

List of figures

List of tables

Abbreviations

AMS	Accelerator Mass Spectrometry
BOSCORF	British Ocean Sediment Core Research Facility
CD	Chart Datum
EH	English Heritage
HER	Historic Environment Record
MHWST	mean high water of spring tides
MSL	mean sea level
MTL	mean tide level
NOCS	National Oceanography Centre, Southampton
OD	Ordnance Datum
ORAU	Oxford Radiocarbon Accelerator Unit
PRN	project reference number
RSL	relative sea level
RTK DGPS	Real Time Kinematic Differential Global Positioning System
SMR	Sites and Monuments Record
SUERC	Scottish Universities Environmental Research Centre

Acknowledgements

The Hampshire and Wight Trust for Maritime Archaeology (HWTMA), under the stewardship of Commander Brian Sparks and subsequently Garry Momber, has been investigating the submerged prehistoric landscapes of the Western Solent and Bouldnor Cliff since the mid-1990s. The work built upon an initiative in the 1980s driven by the enthusiasm and knowledge of David Tomalin and Rob Scaife, who knew of the submerged prehistoric landscape at Bouldnor Cliff from local fishermen. The area was searched as part of the Isle of Wight Maritime Heritage Project under the direction of David Tomalin. Credit for locating the submerged forest must be given to John Cross, who found and reported fallen trees during reconnaissance dives. Underwater activities were renewed at the site in 1997, when the underwater cliff was selected for sampling as part of the European LIFE project on 'Coastal Change, Climate and Instability'. The well-preserved trees lying exposed on the seabed at the foot of the cliff prompted the HWTMA to investigate further. In 1998, dozens of volunteers, led by Garry Momber, began systematic surveys: a programme of work that has continued for over ten years. In 1999 Roy Harold and Sophia Exelby recovered the first worked flints from upcast created by the prolific burrowing lobster population at the site. Their finds ensured that the research continued and in 2000 commercial sponsors, including Coastline Surveys, Kongsberg Simrad, Submetrix SEA Ltd, Seaflex Ltd, Analytical Engineering, and Hurst Castle Services, plus a dedicated team of volunteer archaeologists, provided goods and services that made an evaluation excavation possible. Volunteers groups, including the Poole Bay Archaeological Research Group and the Keyhaven Scout Club, facilitated and contributed to the research. A thank you must also go to the National Oceanography Centre for ongoing use of their facilities and Justin Dix of the School of Ocean and Earth Sciences for help in securing geophysical data across the site. The support of the Centre for Maritime Archaeology, University of Southampton, and its Director, Jon Adams, is also acknowledged.

Since the first discoveries of worked flint the HWTMA has been raising funds to extend the investigations at the site. In this regard thanks go in particular to Hampshire County Council, the Isle of Wight Council, Southampton City Council, the Department for Culture, Media and Sport, Isle of Wight Economic Partnership (Leader+), SCOPAC, the Gosling Foundation, Wightlink, the Solent Protection Society, the Herapath Shenton Trust, the Charlotte-Bonham Carter Charitable Trust, John Coates Charitable Trust, Roger Brookes Charitable Trust, Rowan Bentall Charitable Trust, Gale and Company, the Hilton Cheek Charitable Trust, and the Daisie Rich Charitable Trust for their past and ongoing financial support.

English Heritage adopted responsibility for the submerged cultural heritage in English territorial waters in 2002. This enabled the agency to provide substantial support for a new evaluation trench in 2003, from which material was to undergo comprehensive assessment and analysis. It is thanks to this support, and particularly the patience and understanding of Ian Oxley and Helen Keeley, that the work presented here and the publication of this report have been possible. Conclusions drawn from the work have been achievable thanks to the work of the specialists and contributors. Other than those already mentioned, these include Geoff Bailey, Christopher Bronk Ramsey, Rachel Bynoe, Gordon Cook, Jan Gillespie, Derek Hamilton, Jen Heathcote, Alison Locker, Peter Marshall, Nigel Nayling, Mark Robinson, Julie Satchell, Rory Smith, Maisie Taylor, and Julian Whitewright. Their work has formed the core of the investigation around which this publication has been primarily focused. Further thanks should also go to Rachel Bynoe, Julie Satchell, and David Tomalin for helping with the production of the volume.

The three years that followed the 2003 fieldwork saw continued investigations to record the degrading underwater landscape. Thanks must be given for the dedicated endeavours of the core team of HWTMA staff, including Julie Satchell and Jan Gillespie, who maintained a presence at the site while continuing to author this report. Additional support for the ongoing fieldwork was provided in no short measure through the voluntary help of Andy Williams and his team aboard the RIB *Dingle*, by the Defence Diving School and the able seamanship of Dave Wendes in *Wight Spirit*, and by Penny Spikins and Lawrence Moran of the University of York.

In 2007 the final phase of rescue excavation and fieldwork reported here was made possible through the support of the Leverhulme Trust, with funding provided through the offices of Professor Geoff Bailey of the Department of Archaeology, University of York, and the Royal Archaeological Institute. Additional help with funding, enabling the continuation of the work, came from Valerie Fenwick, the Aiken Foundation, and the European Regional Development Fund, who assisted with the final stages of the work through the Archaeological Atlas of the 2 Seas Project. Ongoing storage of the finds at the National Oceanography Centre has been possible thanks to the use of the BOSCORF refrigerated unit, which has been the focus for finds processing with assistance from Jan Gillespie, Rachel Bynoe, Julian Whitewright and Michael Bamforth, who helped with wood technology. In addition, a thank you should be given to the many avocational archaeologists, including members of the Isle of Wight Archaeological Society, who have given their spare time to help process the finds.

The acknowledgements listed above represent a fraction of all those who have been involved. Contributions from other individuals are also mentioned in the text but thanks must be extended to the hundreds of volunteers, including students, professional colleagues, sports divers and interested members of the public, who have made a significant contribution through many hours on the seabed surveying, excavating and recording, and through assistance with post-excavation analysis. The project has provided the opportunity to develop the skills of those involved who were not familiar with submerged prehistoric landscape material; in this way the site is also contributing to an increasing capacity to recognise and investigate such sites in the future.

The submerged prehistoric landscape in the Western Solent is the only such site being investigated by diving archaeologists in the United Kingdom. It is a very rich archaeological resource that is being lost to erosion. Despite two decades of investigation we have examined only a very small proportion of the areas at risk. While sufficient funding for a holistic assessment has not been available through a single source, the HWTMA has been in a position to attract financial and logistical resources from a very broad pantheon. Therefore, a final thank you must be given not only to all those who have generously supported this project but also to those who have ensured the sustainability and advancement of the HWTMA.

Garry Momber

Summary

Interest in the submerged lands of the Solent was first roused in the 1980s, with the discovery of flint tools and chunks of forest floor in the trawler nets of local fishermen. Intermittent diving searches led to the discovery of a submerged woodland plateau with trees embedded in a thick bed of peat. This drowned landscape was dated to the seventh millennium BC. In 1999 flint implements of the Mesolithic period were recovered from a lobster burrow that was still energetically defended by its occupant.

Further investigation demonstrated that the lobster had burrowed into a secure archaeological horizon that was still eroding at the foot of an underwater cliff. With confirmation that this was a stratified assemblage, and the only one of its kind in the UK, the Hampshire and Wight Trust for Maritime Archaeology initiated a multidisciplinary project to evaluate the nature, vulnerability and rate of loss of this archaeological resource. The project design embraced underwater excavation, box sampling and the sawing of trees. The results were subject to archaeological, palaeoenvironmental, dendrochronological, and geomorphological analyses, and calibrated with a suite of radiocarbon dates.

The initial locus of investigation was named Bouldnor Cliff II (BC-II). This was located at the foot of the submerged clay cliff. The seabed here was peat, overlying a clayey sand at a depth of 11m below OD. Dozens of fresh-looking flint flakes and worked flint pieces were scattered where the cliff was actively eroding. The parent deposit from which the lithics were recovered at BC-II represents a streamside environment that had once flourished close to a wetland or lake; the build-up of a freshwater sand bar had occurred between c 6060–5990 cal BC and 6030–5980 cal BC. This was a period of encroaching sea level that, by c 6000–5910 cal BC, had triggered the accrual of brackish water and salt marsh around the fringes of a basin.

While the work on BC-II was proceeding, bathymetric surveys were conducted along Bouldnor Cliff. This revealed a kilometre-long peat terrace at 11–11.5m below OD protruding from the base of a 7m-high cliff. A second, smaller, submerged cliff was recorded at the exposed edge of the terrace. Bathymetric surveys were also conducted in the north-west Solent, where similar, but shallower shelves, of peat were traced between Hurst Spit and Pitts Deeps. Diving investigations identified several sites of interest, including Hawker's Lake, where submerged trees had been growing in a landscape that was now only 2.5–3m below OD by Hurst Spit. Other areas of significance included submerged deposits off Tanners Hard, 6km to the east, where evidence of anthropogenic activity was found associated with two peat horizons at 4m and 6m below sea level. To the south, at –7m OD, Bouldnor Cliff-IV (BC-IV) was the source of several knapped flint flakes that had eroded from the basal deposit, while, 200m to the east at –11m OD, Bouldnor Cliff V (BC-V) was found to be rich in worked organic material.

The discoveries at BC-V were particularly significant as they contained evidence of woodworking and small-scale industry. An archaeological horizon just below the seabed was covered with burnt flints, charcoal, wood chippings, trimmed pieces of wood, and lengths of prepared string. The identification of a tangentially split oak timber suggests the construction of a large structure or possibly a log boat using techniques that do not appear in the British archaeological record for another 2000 years. The site, which was eroding from the exposed edge of the woodland plateau, is 424m west of BC-II.

Analysis of the sediment archive associated with the submerged landscape enabled a reconstruction of events leading to the formation of the Western Solent. The evidence shows that the site had been a lacustrine environment or wetland associated with a river plain. The topography would have been characterised by a sheltered basin fed by the Lymington River and drained by the river Yar to the south. As sea level rose brackish water conditions pushed into the basin, which steadily filled with estuarine silts; these covered and protected the former land surface. The hydrodynamic regime remained depositional until the final protective barrier to the west was breached about 4000 years ago. Once the Western Solent Channel opened the estuarine deposits were steadily eroded. This process is continuing: the isolated pockets of relic land surfaces that remain below Bouldnor Cliff and behind Hurst Spit are succumbing to erosion as they lose their protective silt covering.

This project has evaluated the potential survival of archaeological material within this 8000-year-old landscape. It has identified a rich source of evidence, despite having lifted the cover off only a few square metres of a land surface that is a kilometre wide. The results from this site can be used to help interpret similar submerged geomorphological features in shallow North European coastal waters; indeed, submerged land surfaces with similar characteristics have already been identified. This work has brought us a step closer to identifying the archaeological resource that could lie within them.

Résumé

La découverte d'outils de silex et de fragments de tapis forestier dans les filets des pêcheurs de la région a attiré l'attention sur le paysage submergé du Solent à partir des années 1980. Des sorties de plongée effectuées par intermittence ont permis de localiser un plateau forestier submergé contenant des troncs d'arbres enfouis dans une épaisse couche de tourbe. Ce paysage submergé date du septième millénaire av. J.-C. Un outillage mésolithique fut mis à jour en 1999, dans un trou de homard, lequel défendait son territoire de façon énergique.

Des recherches plus approfondies ont révélé que ce trou de homard avait atteint une couche archéologique en cours d'érosion au pied d'une falaise sous-marine. Après avoir confirmé qu'il s'agissait bien d'un ensemble stratifié, et le seul ensemble de ce genre en Grande Bretagne, le Hampshire and Wight Trust for Maritime Archaeology mit sur pied un programme de recherches multidisciplinaire dans le but d'évaluer la nature, la vulnérabilité et le degré d'érosion de cette ressource unique. Le plan du projet prévoyait des fouilles sous-marines, des prélèvements d'échantillons ainsi que le tronçonnage de troncs d'arbres. Les données obtenues firent l'objet d'études archéologiques, paléo-écologiques, dendrochronologiques et géomorphologiques calibrées par une série de dates obtenues par datation au radiocarbone.

L'emplacement des premières recherches, dénommé Bouldnor Cliff II (BC-II), était au pied de la falaise d'argile submergée. Le fond marin à cet endroit est composé de tourbe recouvrant un sable argileux à une profondeur de 11m au dessous du niveau de la mer. Des éclats et outils de silex jonchaient par dizaines l'emplacement de la falaise en cours d'érosion. La couche-mère produisant ces silex représente un milieu riparien à proximité d'une zone marécageuse ou lacustre; un banc de sable s'était formé entre c. 6060–5990 cal BC et 6030–5980 cal BC. Cette période est marquée par un rehaussement du niveau de la mer qui causa, vers c. 6000–5910 cal BC, l'accumulation d'eau saumâtre et la formation d'un marais salin aux abords d'un bassin.

La falaise de Bouldnor fut l'objet d'un relevé bathymétrique alors que les recherches à BC-II étaient en cours. On découvrit ainsi une terrasse de tourbe longue d'un kilomètre à une profondeur de 11–11.5m au dessous du niveau de la mer au pied d'une falaise de 7m. Une seconde falaise submergée, plus petite, fut identifiée au bord de la terrasse. D'autres relevés bathymétriques dans le Solent Nord-Ouest ont également révélé des bancs de tourbe semblables mais moins importants entre Hurst Spit et Pitts Deeps. Des sorties de plongée ont permis d'identifier plusieurs sites, comme Hawker's Lake où un paysage contenant des troncs d'arbres submergés se trouvait à une faible profondeur de 2.5–3m au dessous du niveau de la mer près de Hurst Spit. D'autres sites d'importance ont été identifiés, tels des gisements submergés au large de Tanners Hard, 6km plus à l'est, où des indices d'activité anthropogénique se trouvaient associés à deux niveaux de tourbe à une profondeur de 4 et 6m au dessous du niveau de la mer. Plus au sud, à –7m, le site de Bouldnor Cliff-IV (BC-IV) a produit plusieurs éclats de silex travaillés provenant de l'érosion d'un gisement de fond, tandis que 200m plus à l'est, à –11m, le site de Bouldnor Cliff V (BC-V) s'est révélé riche en vestiges organiques travaillés.

La découverte de bois travaillé et d'une industrie à petite échelle sur le site de BC-V est exceptionnelle. Un niveau archéologique situé juste en dessous du lit de la mer était jonché de silex brulé, de fragments de charbon de bois, de copeaux, de pièces de bois taillés et de morceaux de liens. Une pièce de chêne fendue en biais laisse envisager la construction d'une structure ou d'une pirogue ; ce n'est que 2000 and plus tard que des vestiges utilisant les techniques utilisées à BC-V réapparaitront en Grande Bretagne. Le site, provenant du bord érodé d'un plateau forestier, se trouve à 424m à l'ouest de BC-II.

L'analyse des sédiments associés à ce paysage submergé a permis de reconstruire la séquence des événements menant à la formation du Solent Ouest. Les données indiquent un milieu lacustre ou associé à une plaine d'origine fluviale. Le terrain aurait été un bassin abrité alimenté par la rivière Lymington et drainé par la rivière Yar au sud. La montée du niveau de la mer remplit le bassin d'eau saumâtre. Des limons estuariens s'y accumulèrent, assurant ainsi la protection du terrain original. Le régime hydrodynamique demeura sédimentaire jusqu' à la brèche d'un banc protecteur situé à l'ouest il ya quelques 4000 ans. Une fois le chenal du Solent Ouest ouvert, les gisements estuariens s'érodèrent progressivement. Ce processus est encore en cours : les rares poches d'anciennes surfaces, telles qu'elles existent sous Bouldnor Cliff et derrière Hurst Spit, sont en train de succomber à l'érosion en perdant leur couche de limon protectrice.

Ce projet nous a permis d'évaluer la survie des vestiges archéologiques contenus dans ce paysage vieux de 8000 ans. Nous avons pu démontrer la richesse des données quoique n'ayant soulevé le voile que de quelques mètres sur une surface large d'un kilomètre. Nos résultats contribuent aux possibilités d'interpréter des éléments géomorphologiques semblables dans les eaux côtières de l'Europe du Nord ; des paysages submergés exhibant ces mêmes caractéristiques ont en effet été identifies ailleurs.

Ainsi nos recherches ont fait un pas de plus dans la caractérisation des ressources archéologiques enfouies dans ces paysages.

Zusammenfassung

Die überschwemmte Landschaft des Solents wurde mit der Entdeckung in den 1980er Jahren in den Netzen von Schleppnetzfischer Booten von Silexgeräten und Stücken eines ehemaligen Waldbodens erkannt. Sporadische Erkundungen durch Tauchen haben bewiesen, dass eine überschwemmte bewaldete Hochebene, die in einer dicken Torfschicht versunkene Baumstämme enthielt, vorhanden war. Diese Unterwasserlandschaft stammt aus dem siebten Jahrtausend v. Chr. Mesolithische Silexgeräte wurden in 1999 in einem Hummerloch gefunden; der Hummer verteidigte sein Gebiet sehr energetisch.

Weitere Untersuchungen haben gezeigt, dass der Hummer in einer sicheren archäologischen Schicht, die vom Fuße einer Unterwasserklippe abgewaschen wird, gewühlt hatte. Nachdem es bewiesen wurde, dass es sich um einen stratifizierten Befund handelte — der einzige dieser Art in Großbritannien —, hat der Hampshire and Wight Trust for Maritime Archaeology ein interdisziplinäres Projekt, dass den Charakter, das Schadenpotenzial und den Umfang des Verlustes dieser archäologischen Quelle auswerten sollte, aufgestellt. Der Projektentwurf enthielt Unterwassergrabungen, das Entnehmen von Proben und das Zersägen von Baumstämmen. Archäologische, paläoökologische, dendrochronologische und geomorphologische Auswertungen, die von einer Serie von kalibrierten ^{14}C Daten unterstützt sind, wurden durchgeführt.

Der Fundort Bouldnor Cliff II (BC-II) am Fuße einer überschwemmten Lehmklippe war der erste Mittelpunkt der Untersuchungen. Der Meeresboden war Torf, der über einem lehmigen Sand lag und 11m unter dem heutigen Meeresspiegel. Dutzende von Silexabschlägen und bearbeiteten Silexstücken waren an der Stelle wo die Klippe verwitterte verstreut. Die ursprüngliche Lage der Silexartefakten von BC-II war das Ufer eines Wasserlaufes, das einstmals in der Nähe eines Sumpfes oder Sees existierte; eine frischwasser Sandbank hatte sich dort zwischen c. 6060–5990 cal BC und 6030 cal BC gebildet. Dies war eine Phase in welcher der Meeresspiegel sich erhöhte, und, bei c. 6000–5910, hatten sich Brackwasser und Salzmarsch am Rande eines Becken gestaut

Als die Untersuchungen in BC-II weiterliefen wurde eine bathymetrische Aufnahme entlang der Bouldnor Klippe durchgeführt. So entdeckte man einen 1km-langen Torfboden, 11–11.5m unter dem heutigen Meeresspiegel, der am Fuße einer 7m-hohen Unterwasserklippe herausragte. Eine zweite, kleinere Wand wurde am Rande des Bodens auch dokumentiert. Bathymetrische Aufnahmen wurden auch im nordöstlichen Solent durchgeführt; dort, zwischen Hurst Spit und Pitts Deep, wurden ähnliche aber geringere Torfflächen festgestellt. Durch Tauchen wurden mehrere Fundorte identifiziert, einschließlich Hawkers' Lake, wo man versunkene Baumstämme einer ursprünglichen Landschaft nur 2.5–3m unter dem heutigen Meeresspiegel bei Hurst Spit fand. Andere bemerkenswerte Fundorte umfassen Ablagerungen 6km östlich von Tanners Hard, wo man Zeichen von menschlicher Aktivität in Zusammenhang mit zwei Torfschichten 2m, jeweils 4m, unter dem Meeresspiegel entdeckte. Weiter südlich und 7m unter dem Meeresspiegel ergab der Fundort Bouldnor Cliff IV (BC-IV) mehrere bearbeitete Silexabschläge die vom Grundboden stammten, und, 200m weiter östlich und 11m unter dem Meeresspiegel, lag der Fundort Bouldnor Cliff V (B-C V), der ein reiches bearbeitetes organisches Fundmaterial lieferte.

Der Befund von BC-V ist besonders bemerkenswert indem er die Anwesenheit von Holzarbeit und Handwerk nachweist. Ein archäologischer Horizont gleich unter dem Meeresboden war mit verbranntem Silex, Holkohle, Holzspänen, Holzstücken und Schnur bedeckt. Ein schräg gespaltenes Stück Eiche lässt darauf schließen, dass eine Struktur oder vielleicht ein Einbaum Boot hergestellt wurde, mit Techniken die erst 2000 Jahre später in Großbritannien wieder auftauchen werden. Der Fundort liegt 424m östlich von BC-II, am Rande der verwitternden bewaldeten Ebene.

Die Analysen der Sedimenten, die mit dieser Unterwasserlandschaft in Verbindung stehen, ermöglichen es, die Ereignisse die zur Entstehung des östlichen Solents führten, zu rekonstruieren. Die Angaben beweisen, dass der Fundort in einem Süßwasser Milieu lag, etwa ein See oder Sumpf in einer Flussebene. Das Gelände wäre ein geschütztes Becken gewesen, von der Lymington River bewässert und von der River Yar im Süden entwässert. Mit der Erhöhung des Meeresspiegels floss Brackwasser ins Becken, das sich stetig mit Flussmündungsschluff füllte. Dieser Schluff verdeckte und schützte die ehemalige Landoberfläche. Das hydrodynamische System blieb von Ablagerungen charakterisiert bis die Sperre, die das Gelände schützte, vor etwa 4000 Jahren im Westen durchbrach. Nach der Öffnung der Rinne des westlichen Solents verwitterten die Schluffablagerungen stetig. Dieser Vorgang geht weiter: die ehemaligen Landoberflächen, die noch vereinzelt unter Bouldnor Cliff und hinter Hurst Spit überleben, erliegen der Verwitterung der schützenden Schluffdecke.

Unser Projekt hat das potenzielle Überleben des archäologischen Befundes in dieser 8000-jährigen

Landschaft bewertet. Es identifizierte eine reiche Datenquelle, obwohl nur sehr wenige Quadratmeter einer ehemaligen Landoberfläche, die 1km breit war, aufgedeckt sein konnte. Unsere Ergebnisse werden hoffentlich die Auswertung von ähnlichen geomorphologischen Vorkommen in den Küstengewässern Nordeuropas unterstützen; Unterwasserlandschaften mit ähnlichen Eigenschaften sind tatsächlich schon identifiziert worden. Unsere Arbeit hat uns einenSchritt näher gebracht, die archäologischen Quellen, die in diesen Landschaften verborgen liegen, zu verstehen.

Preface *by Garry Momber*

i. Report structure

The structure of this report has been formulated to address site-specific questions and to tackle the wider implications of the research. It also endeavours to give a background to what has been an ongoing area of investigation for almost three decades. To achieve this it has been themed within five sections.

The first section (Chapters 1 and 2) summarises the fieldwork investigations in chronological phases. The rationale for assessment of certain sites is presented and their geographical distribution described. This provides an overview of the current marine and topographical characteristics and gives an insight into the circumstances that culminated in the discovery of the archaeology. The different loci are introduced, along with the rationale for their selection and the methods employed during fieldwork.

The second section (Chapters 3 to 7) looks in detail at the locations investigated. Specific investigations are depicted, along with detail on the methods employed to extract palaeoenvironmental and archaeological evidence. The morphological, palaeoenvironmental, dendrochronological and archaeological analyses that have been conducted are presented.

The third section (Chapters 8 to 10) looks collectively at the analysis of the results from across the Western Solent to inform our understanding of the changing palaeoenvironment and the geomorphological evolution of the coast as the sea level rose.

The fourth section (Chapters 11 and 12) applies the results to our knowledge of human occupation in the region and of the geomorphological processes that moulded the prehistoric landscape. This enhanced understanding of the human and physical environment is then used to inform our understanding beyond the confines of the Solent.

The final section (Chapters 13 and 14) concludes by considering questions of management and the research potential housed within this rich archaeological archive.

ii. Solent origins

Over the last 150 years numerous academics have traced the evolution of the 'Solent River' back into the Pleistocene, during which river systems abraded a path through the southern part of the Hampshire Basin (Fox 1862; Everard 1954; Alley *et al* 1993). The primary source of information for these studies has been east–west-tending fluvial deposits laid down in close association with one another as the river

migrated south during successive glacial cycles. Assumptions by early researchers that the river would have flowed along an even more southerly path when sea levels were lower during the last glacial, and extrapolations of the gravel terraces accordingly, led to the proposal of a river running from Poole, through Christchurch Bay, and around the north of the Isle of Wight before it turned towards the Channel. It was suggested that the river was prevented from heading due south after leaving Poole by the chalk monocline that linked the Needles and Handfast Point (see Chapter 10).

In more recent times seismic and coring investigations in Southampton Water and the Eastern Solent have helped to define a channel identified as the Solent River (Hodson and West 1972; Dyer 1975). It has been recorded as running from about 20m below Ordnance Datum (OD) south of Portsmouth down to 45m below OD east of Nab Tower, demonstrating that it would have been a main tributary of the English Channel river system of Pleistocene times. This area is rich in gravel deposits and in peat formed during and preceding the Flandrian Transgression. Many of these deposits correspond with progressive inundation, reflecting the Solent river's clearly defined geomorphological development as sea levels rose (Long and Tooley 1995).

In the Western Solent the course of a 'Solent River' palaeochannel had, until recently, remained unproven. Interrogation of sub-bottom profiles by the School of Ocean and Earth Sciences at the University of Southampton identified a series of south-flowing palaeovalleys which had breached the old submerged chalk monocline prior to the Flandrian Transgression (Velegrakis *et al* 1999; Velegrakis 2000). This evidence refuted the notion of a Solent River passing from west to east to the north of the Isle of Wight during or following the last glacial epoch. The research showed that, rather than there being a single river flowing east, there would have been a number of south-trending channels draining the lands to the north, forming separate waterways east and west of the island.

The loss of the long-postulated 'Solent River' from the Western Solent changed perceptions of the local landscape completely. It now seemed possible that it did not consist of the banks of a mighty river, but, rather, was a sheltered valley which would be more attractive for human occupation. More significantly, however, new questions arose regarding how the Solent *did* form. The processes involved in the formation of the Solent would have had a bearing on the type of material that was deposited during its formation, and would affect the subsequent preservation or erosion of that material, as well as providing insights into the future evolution of the system. This last issue is particularly pertinent, as many of the coastal features continue to erode today: a renewed opportunity now existed, therefore, to question why it appears that the equilibrium between the land and the sea in the Western Solent has not yet been reached.

iii. The submerged and coastal archaeological context

The Hampshire Basin has long been attractive to early hominins. Successive waves of migrants appear to have worked their way north along river systems when conditions were sufficiently clement during previous interglacials, the earliest evidence of this activity coming from Pleistocene river-terrace gravels. Bridgland and D'Olier (2001, 16–19) cite four specific gravel terraces that may be dated by the presence of associated human artefacts, all of which rest on benches on the northern shoulder of the Western Solent valley: the gravels of Setley Plain (*c* 42m OD), Old Milton (*c* 35m OD), Taddiford Farm (*c* 28m OD) and Stanswood Bay (*c* 22m OD). Lower and Middle Palaeolithic handaxes have been discovered in the Solent, but as they have been recovered out of context the amount they can tell us about the hominins who used them is limited.

The termination of the Devensian glaciation saw ingress of modern humans into the south-east some 14,000 years ago. Open-air encampments in the vicinity have been found on Long Island in Langstone Harbour and at Hengistbury Head, overlooking the plains which are now below Christchurch Bay (Barton 1992). Otherwise, evidence remains sparse, despite the fact that sea levels were rising from a low of over 120m below OD, submerging vast tracts of what were once good hunting grounds. The Younger Dryas cold stadial around 11,400 cal BC halted the first pioneering phase of occupation and stalled the rising sea level, which stopped at around 30–40m below that of today. At the end of this glacial event, 2000 years later (*c* 9500 cal BC), Britain warmed between 5°C and 10°C in just a few decades (Alley 2000; Alley *et al* 1993), and once again attracted settlement.

By the time that the sea was approaching the Isle of Wight and Bouldnor Cliff, south-east England had already supported a transient human population for several thousand years, as witnessed by the sites at Thatcham *c* 9150–8600 cal BC (Reynier 2000) and Oakhanger (Rankine 1952). Early Mesolithic sites in the region of our area of research, however, were limited, with some of the nearest being Iping Common and Hengistbury Head (Barton 1992).

Occupation evidence increases as we move further into the Mesolithic. Extensive studies along the coastlines in Langstone Harbour and Wootton Quarr have uncovered numerous flint scatters relating to the later Mesolithic; in the case of Langstone Harbour they suggest temporary camps occupied for only a few days at a time. Amongst the collec-

tion is a tranchet adze and four sharpening flakes. There were fourteen areas of Mesolithic activity recorded in the intertidal zone but there was no evidence of any 'base camp' assemblage or even a site that could have represented a hunting stand (Allen and Gardiner 2000, 203–4). At Wootton Quarr the densities of lithics from the intertidal zone were greater, although they are believed to date to the end of the Mesolithic. Four flint scatters were found and numerous deposits of burnt flint were uncovered in association with sites interpreted as burnt mounds (Tomalin *et al* forthcoming and Section 4, this volume). In addition, 131 axes that were deemed to be coastal were identified in the Isle of Wight SMR.

The evidence being accrued from the Solent coastline showed it to be relatively rich in Mesolithic artefacts. This suggested that further material could lie underwater, a fact that was endorsed when hundreds of lithics were trawled up from the Western Solent by fishermen (see Chapter 1).

iv. The Solent today

The Solent is part of the largest estuarine complex on the south coast of the UK, and forms an open seaway separating the Isle of Wight from mainland Britain. A major feature of the estuary is Southampton Water, which extends north-west from the apex of the Solent and terminates at the confluence of the rivers Test and Itchen (Fig i). The Solent runs east and west from its junction with Southampton Water. Its western arm is relatively narrow, with a predominantly rural surrounding landscape. It begins at the mouth of Southampton Water between Calshot and Cowes and travels south-west before passing through the restrictive channel between Hurst Spit and the cliffs of the Isle of Wight. The exit, into Christchurch Bay, is confined between The Needles and Shingles Bank. By contrast, the Eastern Solent is much wider as it opens out into Bracklesham Bay, and its landscape is heavily urbanised.

Below the woods and fields along the water's edge, the coastal reaches of the Western Solent support areas of sediment accumulation including shingle barrier spits that shelter inter-tidal flats and salt marshes (Figs ii and iii). A key feature is Hurst Spit, which protects Keyhaven Marshes from the open sea. The spit owes its origins to the behaviour of the bedload gravels on Shingles Bank. These gravels have been formed by erosion of the cliff line as sea level has risen, as has Hurst Spit, whose shingle recurves and ridges attest to past behavioural episodes. These features have been attributed to earlier trends in wave action, sea level and wind direction. Recently, the spit has shown notable changes due to an increased rate of transgression and now needs recharging to prevent its breaching. Since 1868 the trend in the configuration of Hurst Spit has been towards retreat, while, in contrast, surveys associated with Hurst Castle which date back to the early eighteenth century suggest that

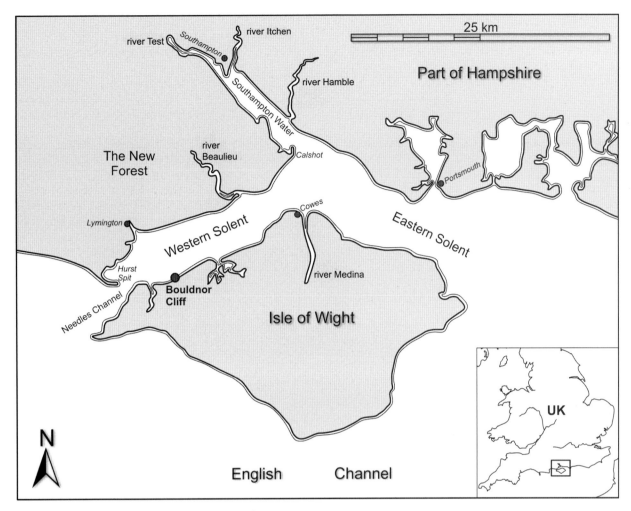

Figure i   The Solent and the Hampshire basin (Julian Whitewright)

the head of the Spit was more stable and even grew (Fig iv), but little is known of longer trends in its behaviour.

On the northern shore of the Western Solent a substantial area of inter-tidal mudflat and salt marsh has accrued along a front approximately 10km long. However, recent studies have shown that these areas, which were once sediment sinks, are diminishing rapidly. Research by Ke and Collins identified areas of mudflats that are being lost by up to 5m per year (2002, 422), while the Channel Coastal Observatory recorded an 83% loss since 1946 (Cope *et al* 2008). Away from the protection of the spits, which are themselves under threat from overtopping (West 2008), erosion is more evident. This is particularly noticeable along the Isle of Wight frontage, where rotational sliding and cliff instability caused by marine erosion regularly results in landslips and topples trees onto the beach (Fig v).

v. Threats to coastal management; the scale and pace of coastal change

The demise of unconsolidated cliffs from around many stretches of the British coastline is not uncommon, but the change from widescale sedimentation to active erosion on the scale seen in the Western Solent is less general and is a worry to coastal managers. The loss of mudflats and rotational sliding along coastal tree-lined hills is causing concern and methods are continually being sought to halt the retreat of the land. However, the factors which lie behind these events are poorly understood. Coastal managers are beginning to look to historical records to understand past trends, but knowledge of longer-term processes is needed if we are to interpret the impacts of future changes.

In the case of the Solent the causes of erosion have not been well understood, making informed management decisions difficult. Fortuitously, the near-shore sediments hold an archive of information that could fill the gaps in our understanding of past events. The survival of a 6000-year-old land surface 4m below OD off Tanners Hard indicated that the landscape had been consistently submerged and protected by silt for thousands of years. Diver survey demonstrated, however, that protective silts had been lost and the ancient land surface was eroding away, a change suggesting long-term stability until recent times. As the seabed erodes and the Western Solent channel deepens wave energies are increasing,

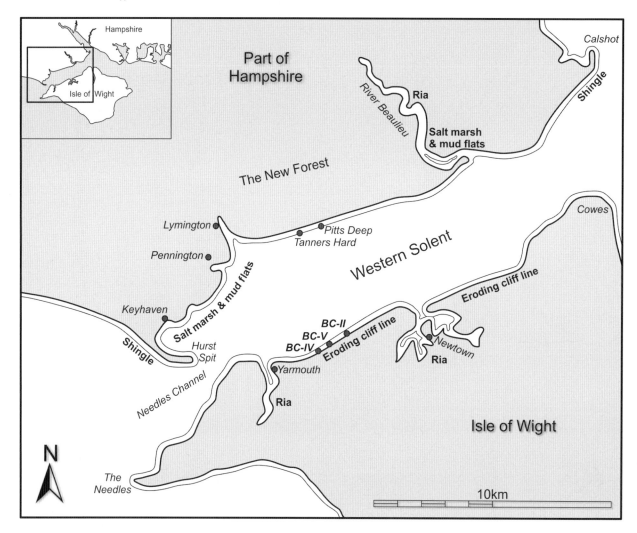

Figure ii   Coastal morphological features along the western Solent (Julian Whitewright)

Figure iii   Threatened salt marsh at Pennington. The expansive salt marsh is under threat from ongoing erosion. This can be clearly seen here along the waterfront off Pennington (Garry Momber)

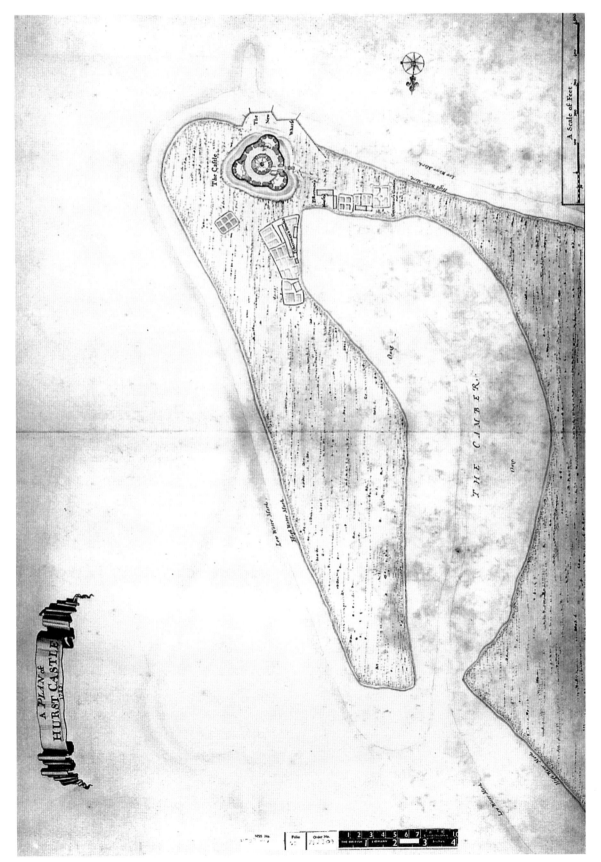

Figure iv   Plan of Hurst Castle in 1735. Images are useful to show changes in gravel migration around the spit

Figure v   Landslips induced by erosion of the cliff's toe and rotational sliding are common along the north-west coast of the Isle of Wight (Garry Momber)

Figure vi   Flint tools collected from the Solent through oyster trawling. They are in the private collection of Michael White (Garry Momber)

putting more pressure on the coastal margins. This raises questions about the long-term stability of the coast and makes an understanding of the cause even more urgent.

Along the south coast of the Solent at Bouldnor Cliff the sediment sequence extends back over 8000 years. The sequences at both Tanners Hard and Bouldnor Cliff tell the story of the Solent's formation, indicating the underlying reason for the current erosive regime (Chapter 10). These deposits are the consequence of coastal geomorphological change and represent the foundations upon which current and future scenarios will unfold (Tomalin 2000c). Such sediment sequences are not restricted just to the Solent, but are found around the coast, where they provide datable archaeological and palaeoenvironmental archives which can offer information on coastal adaptation to the scale and pace of rising sea level. The results can be cali-

brated to provide insights into ongoing processes and future trends.

Coastal realignment is also of concern to the archaeologist, as threats to the heritage are increasing. The results from investigations presented in this report tell of a sheltered landscape that was inundated and covered by protective sediment 8000 years ago. This was not to last, however, as an open marine waterway evolved which is now eating away at the Western Solent and depleting the archaeological deposits. Unravelling the palaeogeomorphological process has told us about the potential for preservation of the drowned land surfaces, but also the rates of loss. The exposure of the old land surfaces has resulted in the recovery of the many lithic discoveries brought up in local fishing trawls (Fulford *et al* 1997; Wessex Archaeology 2004; Sparks *et al* 2001; Glimmerveen *et al* 2004): these have been eroded from drowned soils that were once habitable land (Fig vi).

Section one

Setting the scene

1 The archaeological potential of the Solent submerged landscapes *by David Tomalin, Garry Momber, and Nigel Nayling*

1.1 Sailing into prehistory
David Tomalin

Ever since early speculations had been proffered by Richard Verstegen in 1606 and later scientific observations had been presented by James Geikie (1881), the presence of a submerged landscape linking Britain with its continental homeland was indifferently acknowledged by England's scientific community. The severance of the Isle of Wight had entered the discussion in a similar way, with early investigations – William Fox's seminal paper of 1862 – prompting new scientific observations on the post-glacial inundation of the Solent estuarine system (Tomalin 2000a).

However, it took the discovery of archaeological material to realise the potential of these drowned lands. In 1932 the fishing vessel *Colinda* sailed into history to claim its place in the grey annals of archaeology. At the end of its voyage the skipper, Pilgrim Lockwood, reported the discovery of an object which had been trawled from a submerged early Holocene land surface in the southern sector of the North Sea, some 25 miles (40km) out from the East Anglian coast (Clarke 1954). This proved to be a Mesolithic red deer antler harpoon point now known as the *Colinda* point.

1.2 An unexpected Solent harvest and pioneering investigations during the 1980s

Half a century later, in 1985, Mike Jones, with his Yarmouth fishing vessel *My Pat*, advanced the frontier of archaeological awareness one further step when he brought into harbour a small collection of flint tranchet axes and picks gathered during the process of oyster trawling in the Western Solent. The opportunity was promptly seized (by David Tomalin as Isle of Wight County Archaeologist) to accompany Mr Jones and to examine the results of a typical day's trawling for oysters (Fig 1.1). Soon artefacts of all periods, their frequency and variety truly surprising, were tumbling from the oyster-dredging net.

Mike Jones was anxious to see his discoveries put to good archaeological use. His comment at the time was that archaeologists should have been on hand in the early 1960s, when licensed oyster trawling had first taken off in the Solent region. At that time the quantities of trawled archaeological objects had been truly astonishing: 'You should have been here

then, Nipper, before us lads stirred it all up and scattered it all in a litter for you.'

An agreeable discussion between Mike Jones, David Tomalin and Rob Scaife soon led to questions concerning the underwater contexts from which the tranchet axes were being recovered. Peat and a deeply submerged 'forest bed' were soon mentioned. Rob Scaife, who looked at the pollen within dredged peat in the late 1970s, stressed the importance of these deposits. Consequently, *My Pat* and other Yarmouth fishing vessels were soon helpfully seeking peat samples.

Before the close of 1985 *My Pat* had returned with peat samples recovered 'off Bouldnor', and a new archaeological rapport had been struck up with the Isle of Wight fishing community. At the same

Figure 1.1 David Tomalin searches through shells, cobble and archaeology from the floor of the Solent

time Frank Ball, another Yarmouth fisherman, was reporting scattered fragments of Dressel 1 *amphorae* from a depth of 11–16m in the vicinity of Yarmouth Roads; and from the Hampshire shoreline of the Western Solent further collections of tranchet axes and picks were being assembled by Isle of Wight fishermen Andy Butler and Michael White (see Fig vi).

The year 1987 began as another in which the County Archaeologist's remit necessitated that time was spent focusing on planning-led issues within local authority boundaries set at the Mean High-Water Mark. On the Isle of Wight, however, South Wight Borough Council had become one of just eleven English local authorities to adopt powers under the *Coastal Protection Act* of 1949. This provided certain controls over off-shore activities reaching to a three-mile (4.8km) limit and provided latitude to see beyond the artificial boundary created by sea level. As a registered charity, formed in the mid 1980s to promote greater cultural awareness, the Isle of Wight Archaeological Committee, like the Borough Council, also took a broader view of local territorial waters that covered an earlier prehistoric land surface. Its chairman was Cyril Lucas, then leader of the Isle of Wight County Council and an active fisherman, who had been finding all manner of archaeological objects during his fishing activities.

Coincident with these developments were some exciting opportunities for new archaeological projects through the aegis of government's Manpower Services Commission. On the shore at Bouldnor a defunct nautical school at Eastmore House had recently been acquired for redevelopment. Through the generosity of the new owners Mr and Mrs Trevor Green, of Oxford, the boathouse and schoolroom of this establishment were now made available for an Isle of Wight Maritime Heritage Project, sponsored by the Isle of Wight Archaeological Committee and overseen by David Tomalin and David Motkin of the Isle of Wight County Archaeological Unit. By these means the Isle of Wight County Council was to become the first local authority in England to devise and develop a Maritime Sites and Monuments Record. The first full-time Maritime Sites and Monuments Officer was then appointed with the aid of Manpower Services funds.

By this stage the Council and the Archaeological Committee were convinced that, in the offshore zone, a significant yet unseen heritage was at risk. Soon the Council was lobbying for a change in legislation that might assist the development and use of Sites and Monuments Records in the offshore zone, an issue that was to be debated in parliament.

By the close of 1987 a total of 24 people had found employment on the new maritime project. Underwater 'fieldwalking' now commenced and the Project's diving team was soon in pursuit of Roman anchorage debris as well as a deeply submerged 'forest bed' at Bouldnor. The latter had been identified underwater by John Cross, an active supporter of the Maritime Heritage Project. In this year early pollen analyses were carried out by Rob Scaife and a helpful radiocarbon date was obtained (7230 ± 110 BP or 6380–5840 cal BC (GU-5397) through the good offices of English Heritage Inspector Paul Gosling.

The following year brought some unwelcome changes in fortune for the burgeoning Maritime Heritage Project. A sudden reversal in government policy brought about an abrupt termination of all national funding for Manpower Services schemes. By this time the Project team had assembled some preliminary data on underwater erosion of the 'forest bed', and during a drift dive deer antlers had been reported in the bed, although tangible evidence had yet to be recovered.

Stung by the withdrawal of Manpower Services funds, the Isle of Wight County Council and the Isle of Wight Archaeological Committee recast the Maritime Heritage Project to become the Isle of Wight Trust for Maritime Archaeology. Soon considerable interest was expressed by Hampshire County Council, which was contemplating similar inter-tidal and sub-tidal investigations in Langstone Harbour. The wisdom of a unified approach to the seabed archaeology of the Solent region was quickly recognised and embraced by both County Councils, resulting in the Hampshire and Wight Trust for Maritime Archaeology, which took an active role in the investigation of the submerged archaeological potential.

The 1990s saw a gradual recognition of the national importance of the submerged sector of prehistoric Britain. This was manifest in *England's Coastal Heritage: a statement*, published by English Heritage in 1996. Talk of a 'seamless approach' to the nation's onshore and offshore archaeological resources was persuasively articulated in *England's Coastal Heritage: a survey*, published a year later (Fulford *et al* 1997). Recommendations in this new document were well received, but an anomaly in the wording of the *1979 Ancient Monuments and Archaeological Areas Act* created an impediment to the funding of sub-tidal archaeological work in England. This meant that pioneering work established by the Hampshire and Wight Trust in the Solent region would still be heavily reliant upon the funding from the two County Councils, charitable donations, and contracts for specialist projects. With this ongoing support, however, it was able to facilitate and co-ordinate maritime research.

1.3   Renewed research as the HWTMA takes on the challenge
Garry Momber

In October 1991 the Hampshire and Wight Trust for Maritime Archaeology (HWTMA) held its first Annual General Meeting. Its remit was to promote interest in, research in and knowledge of maritime archaeology and heritage, with its core activities in the counties of Hampshire and the Isle of Wight.

The HWTMA was a new organisation but it

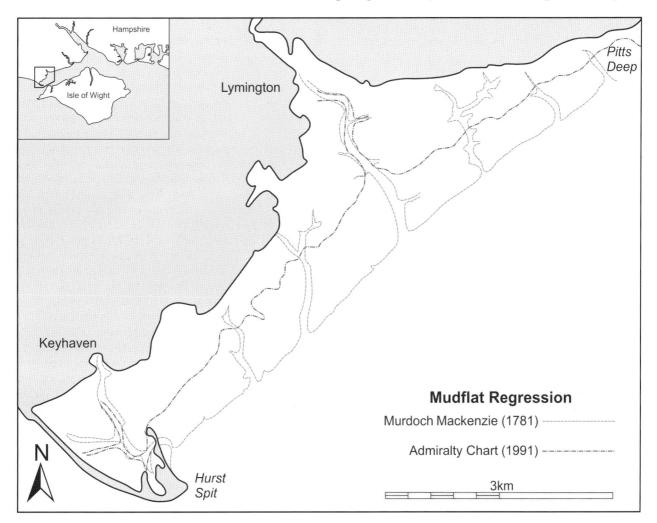

Figure 1.2 Regression of mudflats can be clearly seen when comparing the Murdoch Mackenzie chart of 1781 with the Admiralty chart of 1991. Pitts Deep lies at the western edge of the Murdoch Mackenzie chart (Julian Whitewright after Garry Momber)

inherited many of the aspirations that had developed during the previous decade. A key concern of the county archaeologists, Michael Hughes and David Tomalin, who were instrumental in putting the trust in place, was the need to increase knowledge of the prehistoric surfaces around the coastline. These deposits were proving to be a rich source of archaeological material but their extent below the water was unknown. It was acknowledged from the outset that the HWTMA would work with the local authorities to pursue understanding of the submerged land surfaces within the Solent.

1.3.1 Charting a changing coast in the north-west Solent

One of the first commissions the HWTMA was called on to undertake, in 1993, was a review of the coastal archaeological resource along the New Forest Solent coastline (Momber *et al* 1994). Preliminary assessment from Hurst Spit to Calshot Spit revealed a wealth of prehistoric archaeological artefacts that had been recovered from beneath the

waters of the Solent. The overwhelming majority of these rested in the hands of private collectors. A significant assemblage was that of the aforementioned fisherman Michael White, now retired, who had retained handaxes and worked tools that numbered in the hundreds (Harding *et al* 2004). These had all been trawled from the Solent in his oyster dredge. Discussion with Mr White helped pin down the locations where the majority of the finds were recovered: areas which lay both to the east and west of Lymington River mouth.

Research to identify the source of Mr White's discoveries was then necessary to pinpoint the lithics in relation to submerged landscape features so that the source of the finds could be established. A first step to understanding past change was to review the movement of the coastline over the previous couple of centuries by looking at the regression of coastal features on charts. Inspection revealed a stark reduction in mudflats between Hurst Spit and Sowley during this period. Comparison of the 1991 Admiralty Chart 2040 with the Murdoch MacKenzie chart of 1781 suggested that about half the salt marsh had been lost (Fig 1.2). As the mudflat is

Figure 1.3   View across the shores of Pitts Deep. Historic mudflats have become depleted in this area (Garry Momber)

eroded away, tree-impregnated peat is exposed. The loss is particularly evident off Pitt's Deep, which was once protected by expansive mudflats (Fig 1.3). The results were presented in the *New Forest Coastal Archaeological Resource* report submitted in 1994.

Ongoing liaison with the current Keyhaven fishing community indicated that submerged terrestrial deposits continued beyond the inter-tidal zone underwater. Fishermen were aware that trees and clumps of peat were being trawled up from large tracts of seabed a few hundred metres off the present-day mudflats, and saw occasional 'odd-shaped' flints that came up with the oysters, but which were invariably thrown back. It was becoming clear that a large expanse of relic drowned land lay underwater off Hampshire as well as the Isle of Wight. Evidence from historic charts suggested these deposits had once been below silts but, as the mudflats retreated, the protective covering was being lost and the old land surface revealed. To quantify this hypothesis, divers were deployed to inspect visually the seabed.

1.3.2   *Visual inspection of the drowned land surface*

The latter part of the 1990s saw a series of inspection dives to locate and record the submerged lands. The work was concentrated in areas where many pieces of worked flint had been discovered by fishermen. Large areas of peat inlaid with trees were quickly discovered; notable were the silver birch, the bark of which occasionally retained its silver sheen, indicating the well-preserved nature of the drowned lands. In 1998 and 1999 the searches intensified when a team of 38 volunteer divers and professionals, under the direction of the Hampshire and Wight Trust for Maritime Archaeology, operated from the east wing of Hurst Castle, courtesy of manager Sean Crane and Hurst Castle services. Additional support was provided by Poole Bay Archaeological Group under the guidance of Mike Markey, aboard his boat *Peveril Myth*.

Diving inspections co-ordinated from the castle extended from the reverse end of Hurst Spit in the west to Pitts Deep in the east and along Bouldnor Cliff to the south. The seabed behind the shelter of Hurst Spit was initially examined by drifting with the tide parallel to the shore (Figs 1.4 and 1.5). Here, peat was recorded surviving in patches in a few metres of water. These patches were interspersed with scoured hollows and channels revealing clay beneath. Fallen trees and ancient root systems up to 0.4m high protruded from the sea floor. In areas where the peat was more concentrated the interface between the peat and the edge of the channel formed a sharp drop up to 0.4m high.

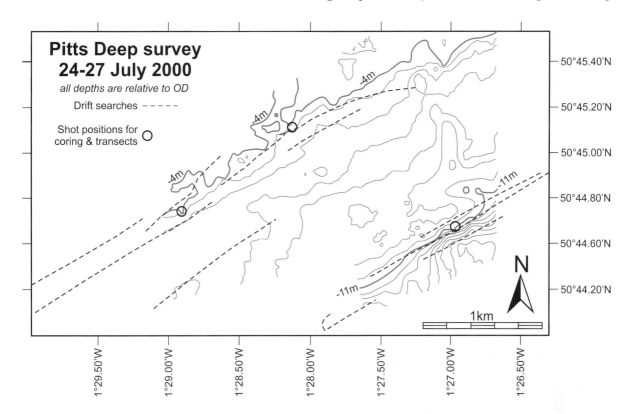

Figure 1.4   Location of initial diver survey from Peveril Myth *off Pitts Deep in the Western Solent (Mike Markey)*

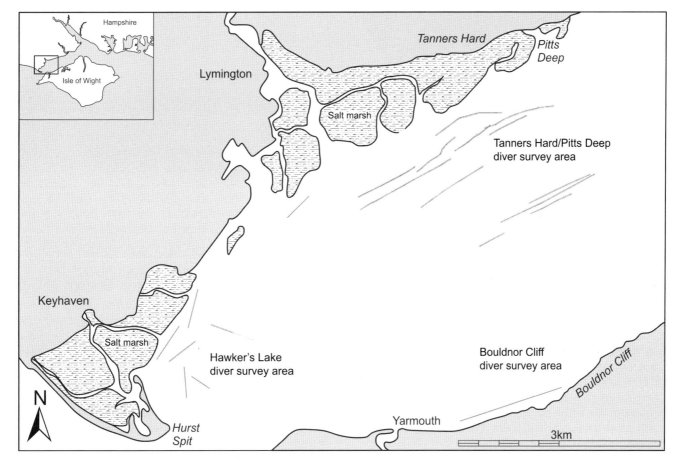

Figure 1.5   Location of drift dives around the Western Solent between 1999 and 2001 (Julian Whitewright after Garry Momber)

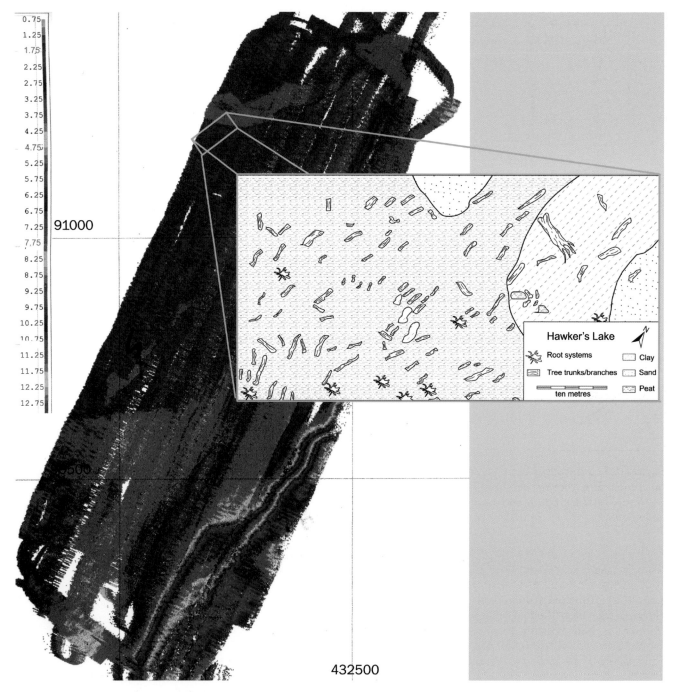

Figure 1.6   Plan of the distribution of trees and peat off Hawker's Lake. The seabed is covered in tree stumps, root systems, tree boles, peat and humic material. Widespread erosion was noted and a channel cuts through the area surveyed. The remains of the tree stump and roots on the floor of the channel suggest that modern currents have caused the erosion and cut into the old land surface (Rachel Bynoe after Garry Momber; Courtesy of SEA Ltd)

A 30m by 60m corridor survey was conducted adjacent to one of the channel features at the mouth of Hawker's Lake. The benthic characteristics and the concentration of surviving wood were recorded, and evidence of human activity looked for. No such remains were identified, but a dense cover of exposed tree boles intercollated with the humic deposits was plotted (Fig 1.6).

To the east of Lymington River the peat deposit was generally thicker and appeared more cohesive.

It was less pitted than in the west and most trees were more deeply embedded. The peat formed a relatively flat and smooth seabed that was occasionally interrupted by wide and deeply incised north–south trending channels. Towards the northern shore the peat was covered by silt which rose above the low water mark to form the mudflats. The plateau-like surface was a metre or two deeper than that seen at Hawker's Lake and the southern limit was terminated by a clearly defined drop-off up to 1.8m high.

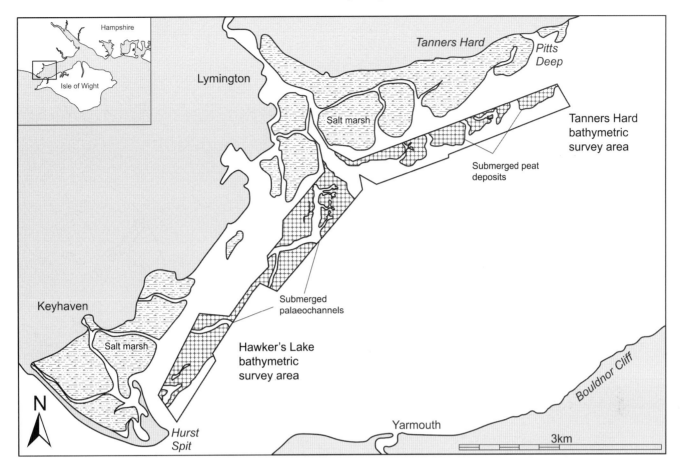

Figure 1.7 Interpretation of bathymetric survey, indicating areas of submerged peat. Hawker's Lake bathymetric survey area (Fig 1.6) is indicated to the right of Hurst Spit. The coloured contoured bathymetry off Tanners Hard can also be seen to the right of Lymington (Fig 7.1) (Julian Whitewright after Garry Momber)

This formed a transition from peat-covered soft clay to a harder clay and gravel seabed. A lower layer of peat that projected from the foot of the small cliff feature was identified; it was in this vicinity that fishermen had recovered worked flint tools and as such was a location that warranted the further investigation presented in Chapter Seven.

1.3.3 Visualisation of the north-west Solent seabed

The diver inspections characterised the detailed nature of the seafloor but the limited visual range inhibited the amount of data that could be gathered. To understand the geomorphological context of the north-west Solent submerged peat deposits, data regarding broader associations on the seabed was required – that is, the spatial relationships, distribution and relative depths of the deposits. To achieve this, a high-resolution multi-beam survey was conducted in conjunction with Submetrix/SEA Ltd in June 2001. The system used was the Interferometric Seabed Inspection Sonar (ISIS) 100 (Momber and Geen 2000). The survey was georeferenced with a Real Time Kinematic Differential Global Position-

ing System (RTK DGPS), courtesy of New Forest District Council, to give highly accurate positioning, and recorded a large expanse of elevated seabed which corresponded to the location of the peat deposits. The interpreted data is shown in Figure 1.7.

The dive surveys could now be integrated with the bathymetric model of the seabed (described above), aiding interpretation and allowing the identification of new areas of interest for further attention. Of great importance was confirmation of the relative depths of the deposit. The peat platform between Pitts Deep and Lymington River lay along a contour with a relatively consistent depth range of 3–4m below OD. Shallower depths were witnessed nearer the shore, where the peat was covered with silt. To the seaward end of Keyhaven Marshes, around Hawker's Lake by Hurst Spit, the top of the peat deposit was recorded at 2.5–2.7m below OD. As noted above, this deposit was heavily degraded, suggesting that it would have been more elevated in the past (see Fig 1.6). The bathymetric information collected during the survey was also evaluated against the historical charts reviewed as part of the map progression: notwithstanding the ongoing erosion witnessed on the seabed, comparison suggested that the submerged

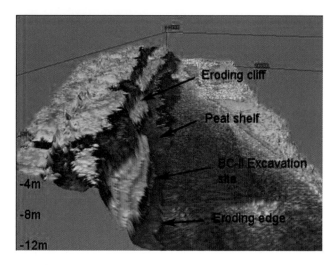

Figure 1.8   SEA Ltd / Submetrix bathymetric image of the submerged Bouldnor Cliff next to the Isle of Wight coastline. The area where samples were excavated from the cliff is indicated. The image is vertically exaggerated (Courtesy of SOES)

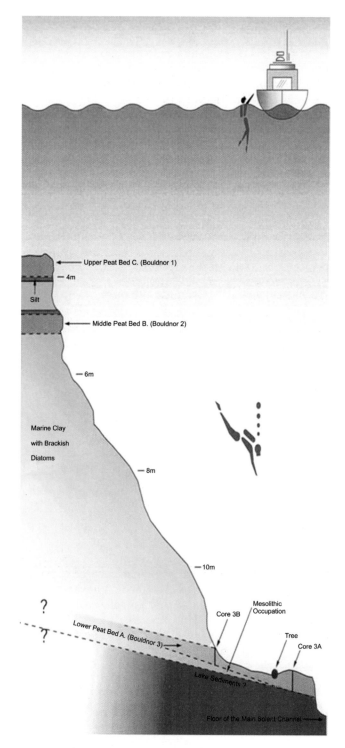

Figure 1.9   Schematic section across the submerged Bouldnor Cliff (Courtesy of Isle of Wight Coastal Centre)

shelf upon which the peat sat mirrored the areas that had once supported mudflats only 200 years previously.

1.3.4   Coastal change, climate and instability at Bouldnor Cliff

During the summer of 1997 the enigmatic submerged forest that lay below the underwater clay cliffs off Bouldnor attracted a renewed surge of attention as part of the European Community L'Instrument Financière pour l'Environment (LIFE) project entitled *Coastal Change, Climate and Instability* (Dix 2000; Scaife 2000a; Tomalin 2000c). One of the three main objectives of the project was to assess the value of archaeological and palaeoenvironmental evidence as a means of measuring the scale and pace of coastal change. Bouldnor Cliff contained a sediment archive with the potential to illuminate past climate change and thus became key to the British underwater component of the project. From 1997 to 1998 the Cliff and its attendant palaeoenvironmental organic deposits were subject to a comprehensive programme of inspection, sampling and recording by the HWTMA. Data collected was analysed to help interpret the Cliff's formation and its relationship with the evolving coastline.

The problems faced when attempting to visualise the underwater features were the same as those faced in the north-west Solent, so, to place the sampling in context, bathymetric modelling was again obtained by a multi-beam survey conducted courtesy of Submetrix/SEA Ltd. The results were processed under the stewardship of Dr Justin Dix of the University of Southampton (Fig 1.8).

The survey showed that, 500m from mean low water to the east of Yarmouth Roads, the sublittoral

bedform falls sharply, dropping from –4m to –13m OD; it stretches parallel to the shore for a kilometre on an approximately east–west alignment. The angle of repose along the cliff varies from a vertical drop to a gentle slope (Fig 1.9). Within the cliff, peat deposits had been recorded by HWTMA divers at –4.1m, –5.1m and –10.5m to –11.5m OD. The top two layers sit on brackish mudflat silts that had accumulated as the Holocene sea level rose (Scaife 2000b;

Momber 2004). This 7m-thick intercalated sediment package of mineragenic silt and organic material sits on a basal peat deposit which protrudes from the foot of the cliff for the length of the exposure. The depth of the basal peat is fairly consistent along its east–west profile but dips across its south–north profile. It measures between 5m and 20m wide and is truncated by a small cliff along its northern edge which averages 2m in height.

The organic and mineragenic sediments seen in the profile of the submerged Bouldnor Cliff proved to be ideal for interpreting changes along the coastline during the Flandrian Transgression, as their deposition was controlled by the rising sea level. Therefore, by recording the depths of the organic layers it has been possible to provide a calibrated marker for the relative positions of land and sea when the deposits formed. This, in turn, provides a temporal framework for the laying-down of the material and the subsequent palaeoenvironmental analysis. The interfaces between the peat outcrops at –4.1m and –5.1m OD were radiocarbon dated to 6475–6280 cal BP (Beta-140102) and 6870–6485 cal BP (Beta-140103) respectively, and the root of an oak tree from the basal peat at –11.3m OD was dated to 8565–8345 cal BP (Beta-140104).

The palaeoenvironmental analysis was carried out by Dr Rob Scaife, who characterised the pollen and diatom sequences within the laminated peat deposits and the intervening brackish alluvial materials. The results have proved to be very valuable in recon-structing the past vegetation environment, sea-level change and the geomorphological evolution of the Western Solent, issues which are explored further in Section three.

1.3.5 Finding archaeology on the old valley floor

The collection and recovery of monolith samples from the underwater cliff during the Coastal Change, Climate and Instability project necessitated prolonged periods underwater which involved close human interaction with the seabed. Despite the difficult working conditions and poor visibility in the Solent, tree remains and exquisitely preserved vegetation compacted onto the old forest floor inevitably drew the attention of the divers. The submerged forest at Bouldnor was of particular interest as it was a basal deposit dated to the ninth millennium BP, suggesting a well-preserved Mesolithic land surface. Time did not permit detailed archaeological investigation of the sea floor during the LIFE project, so the HWTMA, under Director Cdr Brian Sparks and managed by Garry Momber and Julie Satchell, embarked on annual projects to record and map the exposed Mesolithic forest (Momber 2000; Sparks *et al* 2001).

The first phase of fieldwork, in 1998, selected four locations along the submerged cliff. These were named, from east to west respectively, Bouldnor

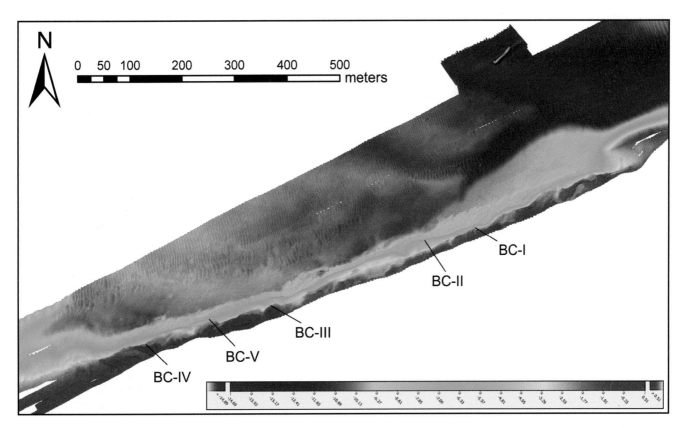

Figure 1.10 Colour-contoured bathymetric image of the submerged cliff at Bouldnor. Variations in angle of repose can be seen along the cliff and positions BC-I, BC-II, BC-III, BC-IV and BC-V are shown (Garry Momber from data provided courtesy of ADUS)

Figure 1.11   Diver inspecting 7m-high wall of clay which sits above the peat terrace at Bouldnor Cliff (Garry Momber)

Cliff I to Bouldnor Cliff IV (BC-I–IV). Profiles were taken across each locus and searches for signs of human activity were begun. Features common to the sites were laterally consistent peat horizons forming terraces and occasional overhangs at the same heights along the length of the cliff. These were recorded at each location and along the intervening sections of cliff face, where they all outcropped at the same depth, despite the large variations of the angle of repose along the cliff face (Fig 1.10).

The cliff profiles at BC-I and BC-III were sheer. The submerged geomorphological features were unexpected and intriguing in their own right but no archaeology was found (Fig 1.11). BC-II was the location sampled during the LIFE project, and BC-IV lay to the western end of the submerged cliff, at the extremity of the Holocene cliff complex where the soft alluvial silts were eroding to leave bare clay geology. It was anticipated that the probability of identifying lithics would be greatest at this point, if they were being exposed as the fine silt degraded. This theory was given added impetus when pieces of knapped flint were seen in a secondary context in gravel accumulations that covered the seabed towards the foot of the slope.

Over the next couple of years the position of BC-IV continued to be refined until the eroding edge of the palaeo-land surface was finally pinpointed by divers. A seam of pre-inundation humic material was exposed protruding from below fine grey silt. The outcropping layer tracked at an angle along the slope which would have once been the side of the old valley wall before it became submerged (Fig 1.12). Dense clay geology sat beneath the humic deposit and fine soft silty clay lay above. The underlying

0.25m

Figure 1.12   BC-IV was on a gentle slope where the land surface was exposed at –6.5m to –10m OD (Garry Momber)

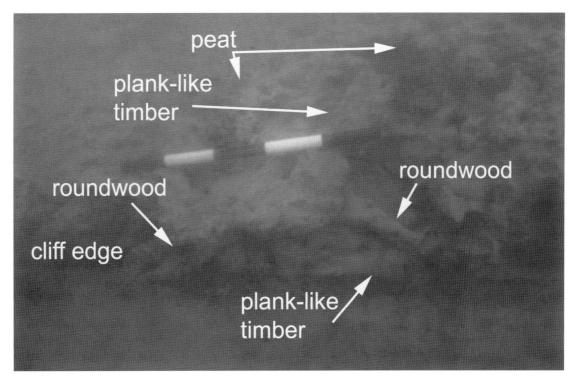

Figure 1.13   The combination of flat timbers lying above roundwood. This feature, subsequently numbered BC-V CF02, was spotted eroding from the edge of the cliff at BC-V (Garry Momber)

harder clay exposures were fragmented, with intermittent pockets of fine sand or gravel suggesting pre-inundation fluvial activity. The location lay at *c* –7.5m OD, being upslope from the 11m-deep peat shelf.

The site dynamics recognised by the dive team during the visual investigations made it apparent that the steady loss of protective sediments was releasing archaeological material onto the seabed. Objects and artefacts were then being moved by the dominant ebb current, which flowed to the west (Sharples 2000; Bruce 1993). Therefore, the thickest sequences of palaeo-land surfaces and, by inference, the areas with the highest potential for primary context archaeological loci were towards the east. These areas also held the densest concentrations of well-preserved trees.

The discovery of the dispersed secondary deposits at BC-IV provided an incentive to continue searching for a less-disturbed location on the tree-riddled platform. During the summer of 1999 the locale at BC-II thus became the focus of archaeological recording. This area was chosen because of its wealth of trees across a relatively wide exposure of peat and because it was familiar to the dive team.

To search the seabed, a survey grid was set up and corridor searches running parallel to the cliff were begun. The strategy was time-consuming and took many dives, but it was amply rewarded when flints were found in a furrow next to a fallen oak tree by Roy Harold and Sophia Exelby. This furrow had been dug by a lobster and its discovery proved to be of crucial importance, because the flints turned out to be humanly worked. The furrow ran through

peat, along the edge of the tree and back into the cliff at the south side of the peat platform. Here it dipped into the deposit below the peat in the foot of the cliff. Observations by the divers recorded not only that the lobster was 'cute' but, more importantly perhaps, that it was pushing sand and cobble out of its burrow. It appeared that the lobster had tunnelled into an underlying cultural deposit and excavated the flints. If this proposition could be substantiated and the source of the lithics traced to their primary context, the find would represent the first such discovery in British waters and would consequently be of national significance. It would also be the first known Mesolithic archaeological excavation by a member of the lobster community.

Over the next five years BC-II became the focus of detailed evaluation and subsequent archaeological and palaeoenvironmental analysis. During this time, however, inspection along the peat shelf revealed another location of human activity on the northern edge where the shelf was terminated by the small cliff. The cliff formed a naturally eroded section cutting through the peat and the underlying humic material associated with the Mesolithic land surface.

During searches between BC-II and BC-IV a cluster of burnt flints sitting precariously within the small cliff face was identified, apparently resting in a pit cut into the old land surface. Many flints had also fallen from the cliff face, to be transported downslope and to the west by the tide, although a few remained on the sea floor below the feature. Another incongruous feature was identified protruding from the cliff edge 1.3m to the west of the flint-filled pit. This was an elevated mound measuring 2.1m across and consisting of various timber elements. The range and variety of the wooden pieces made it unlike any other timber feature recorded within the submerged land surface until that point (Fig 1.13). This discovery precipitated a programme of monitoring which led to excavation and archaeological analysis with support from English Heritage and the Leverhulme Trust. Exquisitely preserved organic artefacts were uncovered as a result (see Chapter 4). The location, BC-V, is 420m west of BC-II and 124m east of BC-IV.

The evidence of anthropogenic activity identified during the diver searches and the archaeological material that was subsequently discovered represents a very small sample of the site's potential, most of which remains on or below the peat plateau or woodland bench. Searches across the whole length of the submerged cliff are not undertaken often and the amount that can be seen during a single pass is limited. The discoveries that have been made were the result of the archaeologist being in the right place at the right time. In addition, once evidence is detected, efforts are concentrated on interpretation of the findings, which also limits the ability to see a bigger area. Despite the lengthy period of work on the site over the years, each dive lasts only around one hour and for the most part divers will need to stay on station at one point for safety reasons. When a diver is tasked to search and record an area they will cover a small patch in a fixed corridor, in which visibility will invariably be limited to a few metres. This means that, following a week's diving, a single diver is unlikely to have seen more than a couple of dozen square metres of the landscape. The divers are rarely in a position to make sense of the surrounding landscape or the archaeological context, the latter remaining buried below the surface unless exposed by erosion or excavation. Therefore, the material that has been discovered should be viewed as a small proportion of what actually remains as extant archaeological evidence within the seabed. This is an unavoidable bias where time is limited and actions have to be prioritised. It should be noted that wherever excavation has been conducted archaeological objects have been found.

1.3.6   Dendrochronological searches and sampling underwater
Nigel Nayling

The discovery of archaeological material was the driver for the exploration of the submerged landscapes, but the association of this material with the landscape was also of the utmost importance. Inlaid

Figure 1.14   Oak tree protruding from the submerged cliff being assessed by Nigel Nayling (Garry Momber)

in the peat and humic deposits were numerous trees, many of which were oak. These were sought as indicators of the past environment and for the development of a dendrochronological sequence.

Tree boles in the basal deposit at Bouldnor Cliff emerged from the foot of the cliff with their full diameter, including the bark, intact. The further the boles extended over the peat platform away from the protective silt the greater their degradation. The same pattern was demonstrated by tree stumps that were fixed to the spot by root systems. Some rose up to 0.5m above the seabed while others, that had been exposed for longer, were all but flattened. This rich resource warranted investigation and examination before it was all irrevocably degraded by the elements. To that end, a programme of tree selection and sampling was progressed at the earliest opportunity. This was initiated in 1999, when Nigel Nayling of the University of Wales Lampeter began a series of dives to identify and recover samples.

Searches were conducted off Tanners Hard and along Bouldnor Cliff. Oak was targeted and different techniques were trialled both to distinguish between trees in the underwater gloom and maximise efficiency when recovering samples with limited time (Fig 1.14). Over the course of five years dozens of samples were collected. Of these, 34 were assessed for inclusion within the local tree-ring chronology and eleven were actually used (see Chapter 3, 3.9, below). The results collated following successful dendrochronological analysis were calibrated by wiggle-match dating against the series radiocarbon dates collected during the project and by cross matching against the Severn Estuary sequence (see Chapter 6, 6.2).

2 Working in a changing environment
by Garry Momber

The voyage of exploration that led to the discovery of the submerged terrestrial deposits in the Western Solent may have begun with chance finds, but they were swiftly followed by targeted exploration, inspection and sampling. Key challenges faced by the archaeologist when investigating underwater relate to survival in hostile, cold, dark, 'gravity-free' surroundings, while the perpetual movement of water attempts to remove anything or anyone that isn't secure from site. In addition, natural as well as anthropogenic erosion causes ongoing changes to the seabed. Working in this environment necessitates well-disciplined practices and techniques that are fit for purpose. During the course of the project new methods had to be developed as the nature of the local setting and material became increasingly well understood. The methods used to overcome the different challenges posed at each location are described in the relevant chapters, but a problem that was common to all sites was the establishment of a fixed and georeferenced baseline on the seabed.

2.1 Positioning and monitoring in a dynamic environment

The need for highly accurate positioning is particularly important for the determination of sea-level index points and for seamless recording between submerged and terrestrial landscapes. It is not possible to use the Global Positioning System (GPS) to position points on the sea floor, unlike on land, as the signal will not pass through water. Vessels which are used for site surveys will have differential GPS to position the ship on the surface, but positioning through the water has to be dealt with as a separate process requiring different tools.

The most effective method to achieve through-water positioning is the use of acoustics. In principle, this works by calculating the time a pulse of sound takes to travel from a source to the sea floor and back. The time is then converted into a distance. In the production of bathymetric plots many thousands of such pulses are recorded and extrapolated together to give a three-dimensional contoured image of the seabed (see Figs 1.8 and 1.10). An acoustic source on a survey vessel can be accurately positioned with GPS and the distances that make up the bathymetric plot can be positioned relative to it. This system can add to the potential for errors, as it relies on the accuracy of the GPS: any inaccuracies in the GPS position will multiply the acoustic errors. The magnitude of these errors will increase with the distance the sound has to travel through water. However, once recognised, these problems can be addressed and, fortunately, in the Solent the accuracy has the potential to be very good and within a matter of centimetres. Even so, the nature of the recording process provides a 'smoothed' image of seabed features, making it very hard to see a true representation of an object unless it is relatively large and distinct. This, in turn, makes it hard for a diver to return to the sea floor in low visibility and find a point that has been recorded on the bathymetric plot. To this end, a repeat bathymetric survey would be beneficial: the first survey would serve to locate the area of interest and the second survey would be conducted after a framework of datums that could be easily imaged with geophysical survey tools had been set up in the area of interest on the seabed.

In the case of this work in the Western Solent, the surveys gifted to the HWTMA were conducted before the locations of interest had been prepared with easily identifiable datums. Consequently, establishing locations of fixed points underwater has been achieved by a range of methods and by cross-referencing the results to seabed features that had already been recorded on the bathymetric survey data (see Chapter 3, 3.1.1).

2.2 Addressing the issue of tides

The tidal currents in the Western Solent can be strong and vary significantly across the channel. A broad indication of the strengths of the current through the tidal cycle is provided by Peter Bruce in the publication *Solent Tides*. However, an understanding of the exact pattern of water movement at Bouldnor Cliff was necessary to inform the positioning of the survey framework underwater, to plan dives, and to maximise dive efficiency. In a first attempt to calculate the current strength of the tides, two industrial RS7 current meters were laid at the established datum points DB (at the bottom of the cliff) and DA (at the top of the cliff) in 1997. The RS7s also contained accurate depth sensors which were calibrated against each other and against a tide gauge at Lymington. The meters were initially deployed for a month to collect data at 15-minute intervals over a series of tidal cycles. However, after several hours seaweed interfered with the devices' mechanical operation, contributing to erratic depth readings. Nevertheless, the short window of tidal data obtained was of value and, although the accuracy of the absolute depths proved questionable, they helped to define tidal rates between high and low tide.

The results from the current meters indicated

that slack water, while the tide changed direction, lasted only a matter of minutes. Prior to the slack, the water flow decelerated relatively quickly. After the tide turned, it increased at an even faster rate. The figures showed that the fastest tidal speeds, and hence the greater volumes of water moved, were skewed towards the falling tide rather than the incoming flood tide. These observations corroborated the work of Sharples (2000), who recorded a net ebb flow through the Western Solent. The velocity of the milder flood tide peaked to almost $1m^3s^{-1}$ about an hour after the local slack water. It then steadily slowed over the next four and a half hours to almost half its speed, before slowing quickly about an hour before high water slack. Detailed knowledge of the tidal flow proved very useful for planning the dive operations, and indicated that the best time to dive was a couple of hours before high water during the incoming flood tide. These conditions are most favourable during the neap tide as at this point the difference between high and low water is minimal and the tides are weaker. When the tidal range is at its lowest, which is normally for a few consecutive days each couple of weeks, diving is possible throughout the incoming flood tide. On spring tides, however, productive dive time is limited to about an hour.

A further impact of the strong tides in the Solent is the stress and resultant erosive forces placed on submerged deposits. Consequently, it was recognised that there was a need to gauge the impact on the underwater archaeology by monitoring its loss.

2.3   Monitoring erosion

The potential for artefact removal by aggressive erosion was witnessed across the whole of the underwater cliff. Where the cliff is steepest, above the *c* –11m OD peat platform, undercuts were evident and large sections of grey alluvium lay at its base where they had fallen. The north edge of the *c* –11m OD platform is truncated by a small cliff, which was also undercut and supported peat overhangs. Large chunks of peat measuring a couple of metres across had fallen to the seabed below. On the sea floor only meagre deposits of fine sediments in protected hollows were found, while organics and soft clays were riddled with holes caused by marine boring organisms. It is these organisms, particularly gribbles (*Limnoria*), that are instrumental in reducing the size and thickness of trees as they emerge from the protective silts (Fig 2.1).

Figure 2.1   Well-preserved tree eroding from the protective silt, showing gribble damage

The evidence suggests that the strongest influence on the submerged landscape is the natural environment. However, human interference was also seen to play a part. Datum point DB was a metre-long galvanised survey pin driven into the peat landscape in 1997. It was located 10m to the east of the evaluation trench that was begun in 2000. The datum remained in place until 2003, when it appeared to have been pulled out and deposited some 8m to the west of its original position. This disturbance had been caused by lobster pots being dragged over the site. Pots were often seen lying on the seabed and have had to be removed from archaeological features after snagging. They are attached to each other and the surface buoy by lines which run for many tens of metres. These stretch across the submerged land surface and are responsible for some cliff falls, as the ropes run over the top of the cliffs and slice through the soft deposits. These human actions accelerate the erosive process and impact on any infrastructure left on the seabed by archaeologists.

The scars caused by erosion were all pervasive and the ability of the currents to disperse material on the seabed was clear. The rate of cliff retreat was, however, unknown, so in 1999 a programme of monitoring was put in place at BC-II (see Chapter 3, 3.1.2).

Section two

Site analysis: palaeoenvironmental
and cultural context within locations of human activity
on Bouldnor Cliff

The submerged landscapes of the Solent were proving to be expansive, rich in archaeology and subject to erosion. The next task was to quantify the significance of the resource and the threats. Four locations were identified as worthy of more detailed study. These were BC-II, BC-IV, BC-V and Tanners Hard. Each site created different challenges and was subject to varying levels of analysis. The first archaeological site identified was BC-II and it was this site that was subject to the most detailed investigations.

3 Bouldnor Cliff II: a window into the Mesolithic landscape *by Garry Momber, Jen Heathcote, Rob Scaife, Jan Gillespie, Mark Robinson, Alison Locker, Nigel Nayling, Derek Hamilton, Peter Marshall, Christopher Bronk Ramsey, and Gordon Cook*

3.1 Bouldnor Cliff II: locating lobsters and lithics

Once the location for investigation at BC-II had been confirmed it was necessary to establish a framework for survey and sampling. The first grid was set up in 1999 and covered an area of 30m by 15m, which was searched and planned. Thirteen tree stumps, extensive scatters of wood and nine substantial boles were recorded within the grid. One of the boles, orientated south–north, measured over 12m in length and was 0.8m wide. This survey was followed by sampling in 2m grid squares in which the cobble was cleared from the surface of the

seabed and recovered for examination. However, no other worked pieces of flint were found on the peat platform until the search was extended another 6m to the west and into the entrance of a second lobster burrow (Fig 3.1), which ran from the base of the cliff and along a gravel-filled groove cut through the peat. Its contents were inspected and more worked flints were identified. This second lobster burrow was located in a similar setting to one that was previously discovered. Both burrows were bordered by trees and worked back through the peat and into the cliff, dipping into the sands and gravels beneath (Fig 3.2).

In total, 50 flints showing signs of human

Figure 3.1 Lobster with collection of flints excavated from the submerged cultural deposit dated to the Mesolithic. The burrow extends below a fallen tree that is eroding from the covering deposits (Garry Momber)

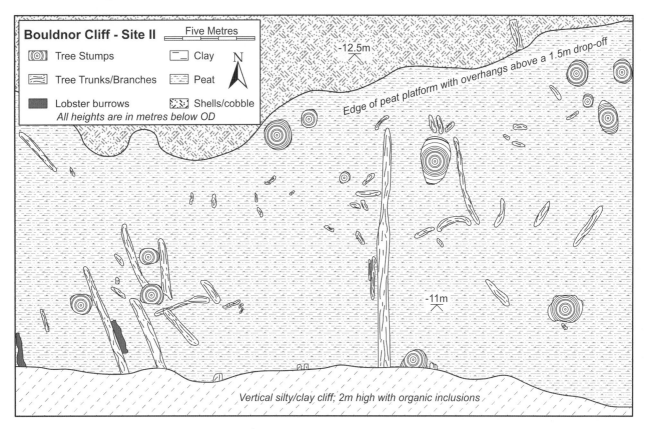

Figure 3.2   Plan of seabed at BC-II with trees and lobster burrows recorded (redrawn by Julian Whitewright after Garry Momber)

Figure 3.3   Examples of lithics recovered from the seabed at BC-II (Garry Momber)

industry were identified from the two lobster burrows, but no worked pieces were found within samples collected from the surface of the peat platform (Loader 1999). Present were 35 humanly struck flints, 8 pieces showing evidence of burning and a further 7 small waste flakes produced by knapping (Fig 3.3). As the flints had not been recovered directly from a stratified sequence (they were found in discrete locations and no flints were identified on the platform nearby) their precise provenance was still open to question, and concern was raised that the lithics had found their way to the seabed from elsewhere. There existed the possibility that the lithics had fallen down the cliff from shallower water, as they did not appear to be covering the old ground surface, as one would expect with a Mesolithic flint scatter. Therefore, a programme of intrusive spot sampling to locate buried archaeology was begun and quickly concluded after two 110mm-wide cores had been sunk 200mm into the sediment adjacent to the first lobster burrow and been found to contain a small amount of flint from a humic deposit at the base of the peat. One piece was a small waste flake, demonstrating that archaeological material lay below the sea floor. It was concluded that the lobsters had excavated the flints from an archaeological horizon below the peat and plans were laid for their eviction the following summer.

3.1.1 Positioning the site for extended survey

The continuation of work at BC-II necessitated more permanent survey points and an associated grid that could be used effectively underwater and related seamlessly to the terrestrial land surface. This was particularly important given that the Holocene sediments that cover the basal land surface relate directly to the rise in sea level. Organic deposits within these could be dated to sea level at given times in the past, thereby enabling the relationship between land and sea to be calculated. There was thus a need to link the underwater survey area to the land and record positions on the seabed to a high degree of accuracy.

The site was initially located by transects against marks from the shore and then with the help of a Global Positioning System (GPS) receiver on a boat. When the boat was on site a buoyed shot was dropped which would land within 10m of the area of interest. This enabled the divers to return to a location, although time was wasted while they searched for the site. This is a level of accuracy commonly accepted by divers investigating wrecks, but more accurate positioning was necessary for the Bouldnor Cliff investigations.

To increase precision above the water the project used an RTK DGPS kindly provided, along with an operator, by New Forest District Council. This enabled centimetric positioning in all three planes at a single point above the water; but, as already noted above, it could not go below the surface. To link the surface position with the seabed a metre-long galvanised surveyor's road pin was hammered into the peat as a benchmark. This point, named datum DB, acted as a fixed datum to which the underwater survey grid could be built. Initial positioning attempts included the use of a marker buoy tethered next to the datum, the position of which was fixed by the boat, while depth was calculated with three dive computers and the high-precision industrial RS7 depth gauge. The depths were calibrated against the tide gauge at Lymington. Unfortunately, the broad variation between the dive computers of more than 1m reduced confidence in this method, making it unacceptable.

In 2000 an attempt was made to improve on the survey positioning, and datum Dp03, a second metre-long galvanised pin, was positioned 8m to the west of DB, next to the area where the flints had been discovered. To increase the accuracy of the depth measurement at this point direct measurements from the surface were taken where a buoyed line, calibrated with a tape measure, was positioned on Dp03 by a diver. The line was pulled taut and the co-ordinates of the buoy were recorded with the RTK DGPS from a boat so the position of the datum could be georeferenced. The vertical component was calculated at 11m by measuring the distance of the line from the pin to a mark on the buoy. These operations were conducted at low water slack, when the weather was calm, to reduce possible errors, and the positions were recorded to the Ordnance Survey Great Britain 1936 reference datum (OSGB36). Dp03 was to be the new control point for any intrusive investigations.

To provide an additional control, a second datum, Dp01, was placed 19.5m to the south on top of the cliff at a depth of –3.2m OD. It was secured to the seabed on a low spring tide when the water was shallow enough for a measuring pole held vertically on the pin by a diver to rise clear of the water, providing a measurable fixed link between the boat and the seabed. The RTK DGPS was used to position the top of the pole. This second point was established to provide a fixed position with the highest possible level of accuracy. Despite care being taken over the positioning of Dp03 the diver had been unable to ensure that the tape remained vertical, as visibility was poor and safe diving practice precluded swimming up and down the tape. Therefore, it could not be assumed that the measurement was totally error-free. Dp01 was used as an extra control against which the site datum Dp03 could be calibrated by direct survey measurements with a tape measure without having to pass through the sea/air interface, thus providing reference points and a baseline that could be used for high-precision survey.

Further calibration was possible by relating topographic features on the seabed to the bathymetric survey conducted by Submetrix/SEA Ltd in the Solent in 2001 (Fig 3.4). The position of the datum was recorded with high precision in relation to points on the seabed which were imaged on the bathymetric plot. The plot had been georeferenced with an RTK DGPS, providing accuracy in the order of 0.1m, which was taken into account when calculating the depth and position for Dp03 as follows: the site of Dp03 was 0.4m from the foot of the cliff on a relative high spot on the linear peat platform. By manipulating the bathymetric data, the seascape could be imaged in three dimensions. The seabed topography in the immediate vicinity undulates slightly in the order of 0.1–0.2m, a feature detectable in the bathymetric data set, which boasted a level of accuracy in the order of 0.025–0.01m (Momber and Geen 2000). The depth at the location of Dp03 was 10.96m. To account for incremental errors associated with the accuracy of the survey equipment and survey process a further 0.1m was introduced, giving a high level of confidence that the depth falls within ± 0.15m of Ordnance Datum. This level of accuracy was supported by the tape measure survey.

3.1.2 Quantifying loss by monitoring change

The fixed points now established on the seabed enabled monitoring of erosion at BC-II. In 1999 steel pins 0.5m long were pushed into the seabed at BC-II with 50mm remaining proud of the peat. They were referred to as datum points (prefixed with Dp on Fig 3.5), and were marked with brightly coloured insulating tape. A year later, in July 2000,

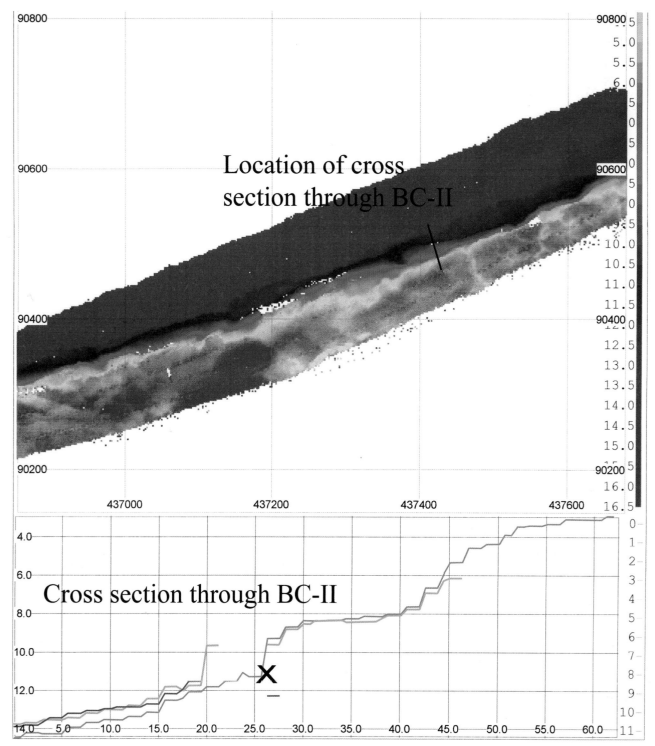

Figure 3.4   Bathymetric image of BC-II conducted by submetrix SEA Ltd in 2001. Colour contouring: the red–orange colour lies at 3.5–4.5m below OD. This is the shallow area that is capped by peat. The variation in colour, and hence depth, is due to erosion of the surface deposit. The band that merges from blue to purple at 11–11.5m below OD is the peat-covered woodland bench that emerges from the base of the cliff. The cross section of the cliff across BC-II has been generated from the same bathymetric data (Garry Momber from data provided by courtesy of Submetrix / Sea)

erosion relative to the pins was recorded, and found to vary considerably, from 160mm to just 2mm. It was greatest at the northernmost point of the peat deposit and on the top of a small clay cliff 2m above the peat to the south.

In 2000, monitoring pins (prefixed with Mp on Fig 3.5), used solely for monitoring purposes, were laid to the west of the datum points (Fig 3.5). In July 2003 searches were conducted for all of the pins. Of the easterly set, only one was located (Dp05). This was found in the middle of the peat platform in the area least susceptible to erosion: here, approximately

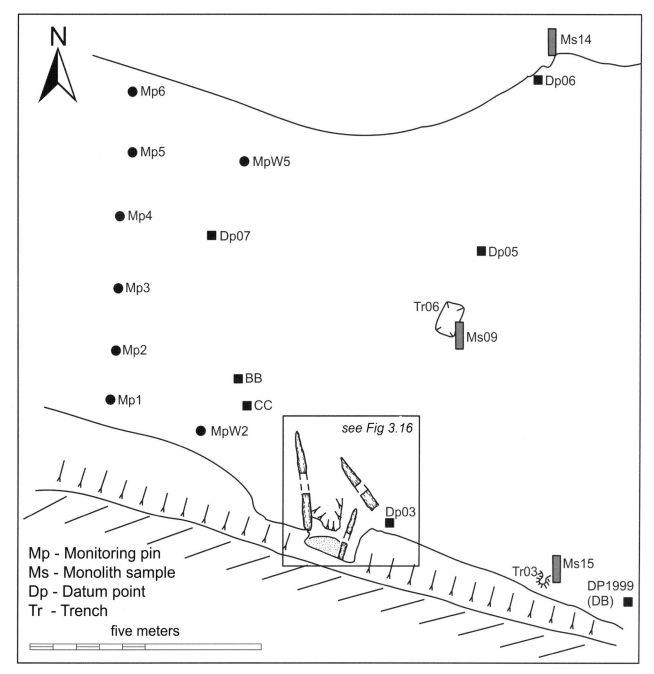

Figure 3.5 Location of monitoring pins and evaluation trench at BC-II (Julian Whitewright after Garry Momber)

70mm of erosion had taken place in four years. To the west, only two pins were located, both from the surface of the peat platform. To the south, Mp2 recorded erosion of 50mm, while the more northerly Mp4 recorded erosion of 80mm. In 2000 Mp4 was 3.1m from the northern edge of the peat platform, but in 2003 it was 1.7m from the edge, showing a regression of 1.4m in three years. Although it is possible that some of the monitoring pins remain to be found, it was clear that many had been lost as deposits eroded beneath them.

Further evidence of erosion was provided by the collection of wood samples for dendrochronological assessment in May 2000 (see 3.9.2, below). Clean sections were revealed once the trees had been sawn, but a repeat visit to the cut-across bole number DS06 in May 2003 showed gribble (*Limnoria lignorum*) infestation had degraded the timber by 60mm.

The monitoring was complemented by observations of tree exposures. The tree associated with the lobster burrow and archaeological finds seen in Figure 3.2 was firmly embedded within the foot of the cliff in 1999, as was a similar tree projecting from the base of the cliff 5m to the west. In 2008 the site was revisited and extensive erosion was noted. Both trees showed signs of degradation and the westernmost tree was now separated from the foot of the cliff by a gap large enough to accommodate a diver. Gravel and sandy clay could be seen among the tree's roots. Immediately to the west, where lobster and crab burrows dug into the base of the cliff, sandy silty clay and coarser fluvial material, as well as flints, had been upcast and exposed on the seabed.

Erosion was likewise recorded in the cliff below the northern edge of the peat platform. Here, the primary exposure is grey lacustrine clay (Scaife 2000a) punctuated with less-consolidated materials, some of which proved to be subject to winnowing. Inspection along the cliff 30m to the west of BC-II uncovered an eroded tunnel leading beneath the peat platform, the entrance of which measured approximately 1m wide by 0.5m tall. It disappeared under the platform for over 2m before narrowing. Pieces of flint were observed on the floor of the tunnel.

3.1.3 Sectioning and sampling underwater

In May 2000 a small evaluation trench 0.45m deep was excavated into and below the basal peat, dropping from *c* –10.75 to –11.20m OD. The objective was to locate the source of the flints and identify whether there was a horizon that contained archaeological material.

The spot chosen was at the location of the small cores which had been taken by the lobster burrow. This lay at the foot of the underwater cliff at the south side of the peat platform, where deposits remained protected. At this point the cliff rises almost vertically to a height of 1.8m immediately behind the lobster burrow. It then levels off to form a small plateau to the south before rising sharply again around a concave slope capped by a layer of peat –4m OD.

In order to provide support for the working divers on the seabed a purpose-built unistrut frame with specially designed brackets was constructed (courtesy of Analytical Engineering Ltd). This enabled work times to be extended and provided a safe anchor point in tidal conditions. An airlift, a trowel and a paintbrush were used to prepare the site by cleaning the sections and removing unwanted overburden.

Preliminary investigations at the foot of the cliff revealed that the peat covered a fine grey sandy silt. This was the material that the lobsters had excavated into, and appeared to be the source of the archaeological artefacts. It was possible that the sandy silt would lose its integrity once it

Figure 3.6 'Box' monolith sample from BC-II being prepared for recovery to the surface for excavation (© Michael Pitts)

Figure 3.7 Archaeologist Julie Satchell excavating a box monolith tin. Controlled excavation took place on board MV Flatholm *(Kester Keighley)*

was exposed to water, so a method to minimise disturbance of the delicate matrix of archaeological and environmental material had to be devised. To address this problem, purpose-built sample boxes were designed by the HWTMA and fabricated by R Bailey Engineering to excavate intact stratified deposits. These were specially constructed marine-grade stainless steel or galvanised steel tins measuring 500mm long, 250mm wide and 150mm deep and 330mm long, 250mm wide and 200mm deep respectively, ensuring that they were not too large for divers to handle but big enough to retain a cohesive sample (HWTMA 2002/2003). They were strengthened so that they would survive being knocked into the fine-grained material, extracted, protected (by being wrapped in industrial-strength cling film by divers) and recovered to the surface with the sample intact (Fig 3.6). Handsaws were used to help separate and remove the boxes from the base of the cliff once they were full. On the surface the samples were excavated and recorded in controlled conditions. They were either dealt with immediately on the back deck (Fig 3.7) or sealed and stored in suitable containers for transportation to cold storage or the laboratory. Three layers of tins were extracted, revealing a section 0.45m in height. Each sample was given a unique number which

enabled the location and information from the units to be reconstructed.

With the samples removed, the back wall of the trench was cleaned for recording (Fig 3.8). The excavated section comprised soft grey marine/salt-marsh clay above a 150–200mm band of humic, detrital fen peat with compacted fibrous wood, occasional flint, fine sand and silt inclusions. This sat above coarse pale grey sandy silt containing archaeological material that appeared to be stratified in its primary context.

The operation was conducted from the Coastline Survey Ltd vessel MV *Flatholm*, which remained moored over the site for seven days (Fig 3.9). This enabled divers to live aboard and work two or three tides a day. The fixed mooring also allowed surface supply operations, in which divers were provided with air via an umbilical which also held a communications cable and a wire to a head-mounted video camera. The communications allowed the reporting of archaeological information directly to the surface, enhancing safety when running power tools – notably an underwater chainsaw used to collect slices of tree trunks for dendrochronological analysis (Fig 3.10) (see Chapters 1, 1.3.6, and 3, 3.9). The efficiency of the auger survey was also improved through direct communications. Auger transects were taken across the site to characterise the subsurface deposits

Figure 3.8 Sketch-plan of section exposed during excavation at BC-II. Stratigraphic layers are well defined and dipping to north (after Dr J Adams)

Figure 3.9 Archaeologists Garry Momber and Steve Campbell-Curtis preparing to dive from MV Flatholm. *Surface-supplied diving was necessary for work with airlifts and a hydraulic chainsaw (Julie Satchell)*

Figure 3.10 Tree section collected with an underwater chainsaw, showing well-preserved tree rings. These were subsequently used for dendrochronological analysis (Garry Momber)

and model the underlying stratigraphy around the archaeological horizon. The work was carried out with a 30mm-gauge auger that was driven vertically through the exposed peat deposits at 5m intervals along the pre-established tape measure baseline. The lobster burrow had provided valuable data on the underlying geomorphology, but the auger samples defined and recorded the depth and strati-

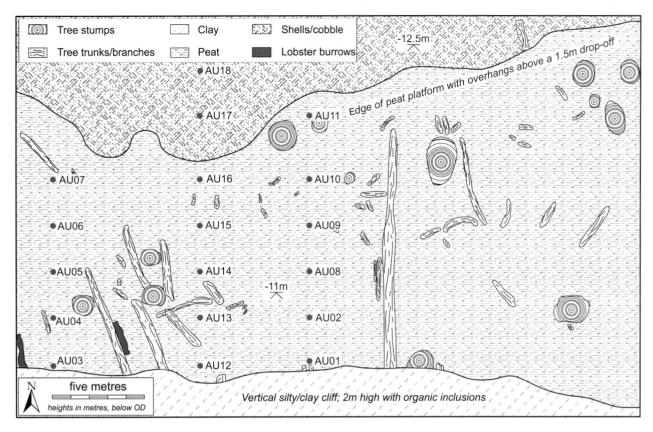

Figure 3.11 Location of auger samples at BC-II (Julian Whitewright after Garry Momber)

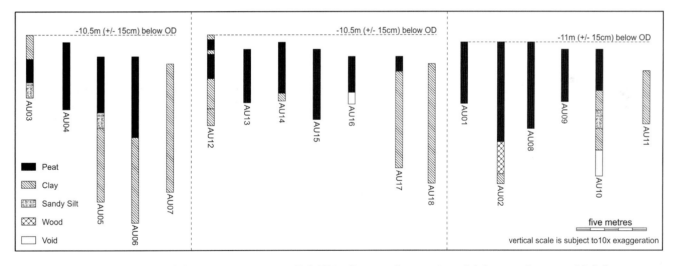

Figure 3.12 The results of the auger survey at BC-II indicates the varying thickness of peat, which has areas where it is separated from the basal clay by a sandy/humic deposit (Julian Whitewright after David Parham)

graphic relationship of the deposits across a much larger area of the site (Figs 3.11 and 3.12).

As the fieldwork progressed, a buried and protected sedimentary sequence containing Mesolithic material was revealed. Lithic material was recovered in the sample boxes from across the 2.5m-wide area sampled along the foot of the Holocene cliff. The distribution of flints initially appeared random and disparate, but following assessment a numerical skew was recorded to the east end of

the area evaluated. This discovery of *in situ* lithics was the first to be made in British waters, but there were many more questions yet to be answered. Specifically, there was a need to understand the nature of the archaeological assemblage in the context of the landscape during its occupation: the potential existed to assess the impact that humans had on the landscape in the Mesolithic and their response to sea-level change resulting in the flooding of the site. However, this was an area of marine archaeology that had yet to be tested in the UK and these questions were being asked against a backdrop of limited skills, expertise and proven methods of analysis. Fortunately, the National Heritage Act 2002 gave English Heritage (EH) curatorial responsibility for the submerged cultural heritage out to the 12-mile (19km) limit, and in the light of the importance of this submerged landscape an application for funding was duly submitted. A year later an EH-funded evaluation trench was opened up, enabling more samples to be recovered and detailed assessment to begin.

3.2   Detailed evaluation in 2003

The delegation of responsibility to English Heritage for maritime archaeology out to the 12-mile limit

enabled the organisation to support the next phase of work at the site. A key driver for EH-funded research, above and beyond the gathering of archaeological data that could enhance understanding of the Mesolithic, was the need to improve understanding of the changing environment in which humans were living (Momber 2004, 39). To recover and interpret these changes the landscape from which the archaeological artefacts were recovered had to be characterised. This included detailed study of sediment and palaeo-environmental samples to allow a consideration of the evolving morphological and environmental conditions before, during and after inundation. To address this, and to collect samples from a section through the archaeological deposits, a larger evaluation trench, that would run across the interfaces between the peat, the covering alluvium and any stratigraphy below, was needed.

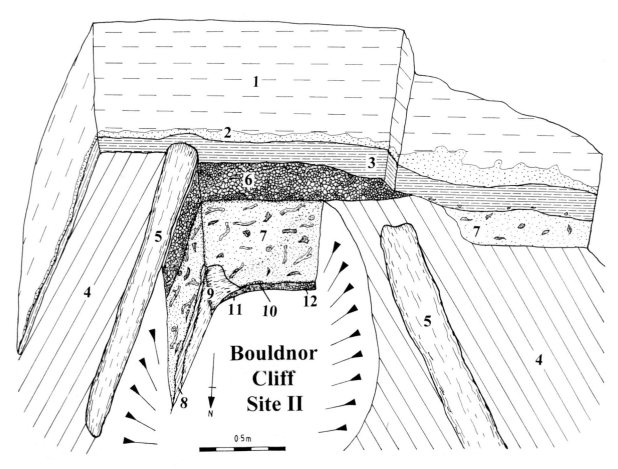

1	Silty grey alluvium	
2	Silty alluvium with dark organic 'staining'	
3	Peat deposit (in section)	
4	Peat deposit covering seabed	
5	Fallen mesolithic oak trees	
6	Gravel with timber inclusions and rolled worked Clint	
7	Fine grey sandy/silt with timber inclusions and freshly knapped flint	
8	Peaty/humic deposit	
9	Lower timber layer	
10	Assemblage of burnt flint	
11	Coarse sand with flint and clastic material	
12	Rounded gravel	

Figure 3.13 Section with three-dimensional relief through BC-II, indicating stratigraphic layers recorded during the excavation (Garry Momber)

3.2.1 The excavation

The location selected for further evaluation and the techniques used to recover material were derived from those tested and developed in 2000. The trenches were extended to reveal a larger section from which the stratigraphy could be better defined and the archaeological sequences tracked deeper into the cliff. It was also necessary to reach an area less contaminated by marine boring organisms, as the clay was heavily inundated with piddock (*Pholas dactylus*) burrows which extended many metres into the cliff face.

The extended excavation began with the removal of the covering alluvial material from above the peat deposit. This was done with saws and spades, the waste being removed with an airlift. When the peat surface was exposed below the alluvium it was cleared, cleaned and recorded. The excavation uncovered an area of peat measuring 1.5m wide by 1.2m deep into the cliff. A fallen oak tree (subsequently sampled for dendrochronological analysis) that was angled slightly downslope and orientated 20 degrees off north lay 200mm from, and parallel to, the eastern wall of the trench. This was one tree of a number that were identified as oak and were used for dendrochronological analysis. The peat was then removed to enlarge the section vertically and to enable sampling beyond the limit of piddock infestation. The piddock were recorded passing through the peat and over a metre into the soft sediment beyond.

Below the peat lay a fan of fluvial gravel that covered the pale grey sand and was known to contain archaeological material. The unconsolidated nature of the gravel made collection of cohesive strati-fied samples impossible, but it was only evident in the east side of the trench so the excavation was extended 0.5m to the west, beyond the poorly consolidated material. Here, the interface between the peat and the deposit of pale grey sand was uninterrupted. The trench was once more deepened, this time for a further 0.7m below the gravel and peat horizon. The underlying section consisted of pale grey sandy clay containing organic inclusions and pieces of flint that were evident at varying depths. Divisions in hue were visible within the deposit, but the limited light and transient submarine conditions made it impossible fully to record all the subtle changes with certainty. Gravel and yellow sand were recorded at the bottom of the trench under the archaeologically rich pale grey sandy material, and burnt flints were recovered from the interface between the two contexts (Fig 3.13).

3.2.2 Maintaining a level in zero gravity

The recovery of the bulk and monolith samples was key to understanding the site. The primary tool in 2003 was the monolith tin. Twenty new monolith tins had been purpose-built by DMR Engineering to a specification designed for ease of handling underwater. They were 600mm long, 80mm wide and 80mm deep, dimensions selected to minimise weight while retaining a large enough mass of material for assessment and analysis. The tins were reinforced to endure robust service underwater and contained vents at the back for escaping water. Handles were incorporated to aid manoeuvrability.

The tins were individually marked top and bottom and pushed into sections excavated in the cliff face. Where necessary, they were encouraged into the deposits with hammers. Saws were used to aid passage into material, particularly fibrous peat, and

Figure 3.14 Monolith tin containing sample from the seabed. Contents have been sub-sampled for palaeoenvironmental analysis across the peat and the covering brackish water sediments (Garry Momber)

Figure 3.15 Garry Momber with spirit level, calibrating depth between samples (Kester Keighley)

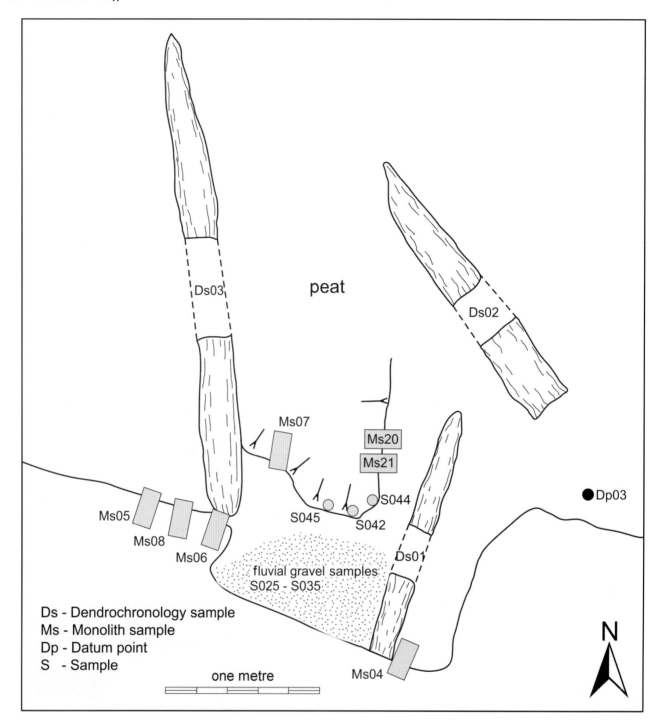

peat

Ds03

Ds02

Ms07

Ms20

Ms21

S044

Ms05

Ms08

S045

S042

Ms06

Ds01

Dp03

fluvial gravel samples
S025 - S035

Ds - Dendrochronology sample
Ms - Monolith sample
Dp - Datum point
S   - Sample

one metre

Ms04

N

Figure 3.16   Plan of BC-II evaluation trench and location of samples (Julian Whitewright after Garry Momber)

where possible they were used to help separate the sample from its sediment (Fig 3.14).

To maintain levels in both the horizontal and vertical and check the relative levels between samples, tools including tape measures, spirit levels, planning frames and depth gauges were used. When collecting monoliths underwater it is often difficult to judge the vertical, a problem resolved by using a spirit level. In general, once one monolith had been taken the next was collected adjacent to it. However, because of the complexity of the stratigraphy, which included the outcrops of gravel, this was not always

possible, and where samples were collected at a distance of perhaps a metre or more from adjacent monoliths the relative heights were calculated by etching a line across the cliff using the spirit level to maintain a constant level (Fig 3.15). The relative heights of monoliths could then be determined successfully with a tape measure.

Where direct measurements were not possible a diver's depth gauge was used. Whenever measurements were taken with a depth gauge underwater it was necessary to cross-reference depths with the fixed datum Dp03 (see 3.1.1). The accuracy of

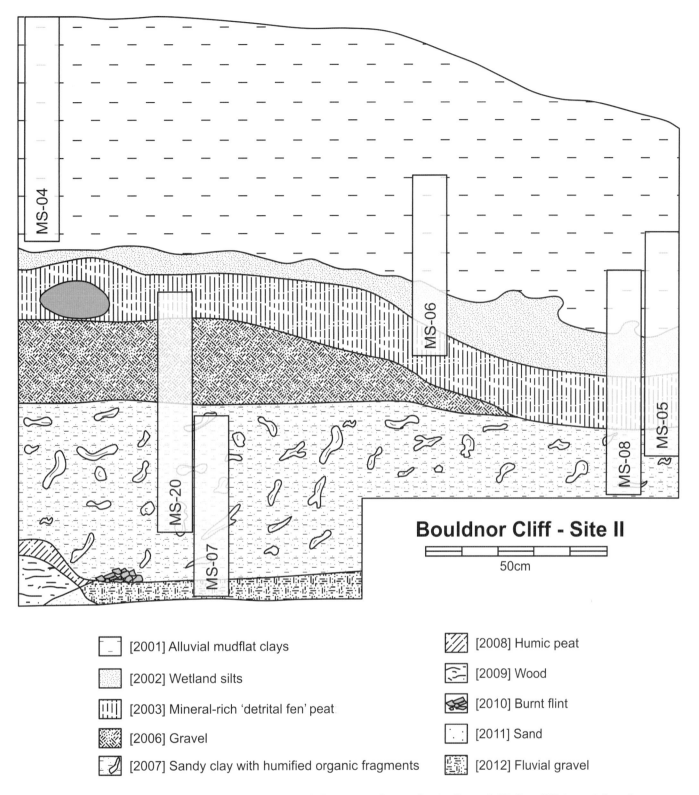

Bouldnor Cliff - Site II

50cm

[2001] Alluvial mudflat clays

[2002] Wetland silts

[2003] Mineral-rich 'detrital fen' peat

[2006] Gravel

[2007] Sandy clay with humified organic fragments

[2008] Humic peat

[2009] Wood

[2010] Burnt flint

[2011] Sand

[2012] Fluvial gravel

Figure 3.17 Stratigraphic section at BC-II with location of samples indicated (Julian Whitewright after Garry Momber)

absolute depths recorded on depth gauges was found to have an error of about 5–10%, a discrepancy which compromised their use for recording absolute depths over large distances, where the error might represent 1m in 10m, but was an acceptable error over a short distance. By cross-referencing with the calibrated Dp03 datum on site and measuring relative depth differences of less than a metre, rather than the total depth, the error was greatly reduced, to within ± 50mm.

Potential errors were also minimised where monoliths cut across stratigraphic units. Here the horizontal interfaces could be used to help calibrate relative depths. This is possible where a horizontal

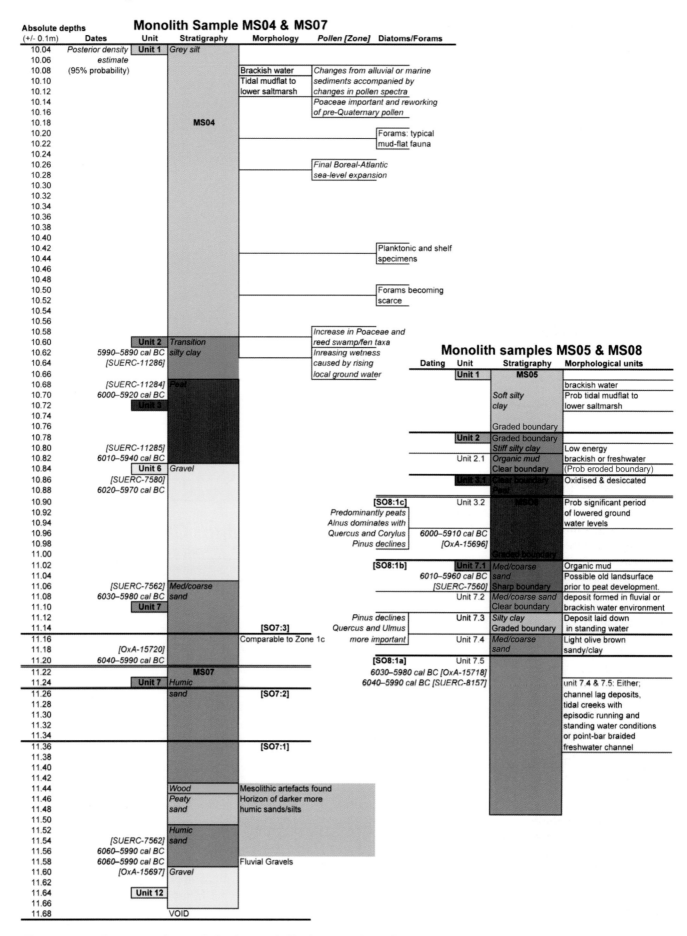

Figure 3.18 Location of monoliths from BC-II, showing their depths and their relationship with their dated stratigraphic units (Julian Whitewright after Garry Momber and Jan Gillespie)

interface is cut across by the bottom of one monolith and the top of the monolith next to it, effectively providing a continual sequence. Where these interfaces varied in the deposit (ie if they dipped), planning frames were used to make a direct record. This increased resolution of relative depths between monolith samples to ± 10mm.

The monolith samples collected from the section in BC-II are shown in Figure 3.16. The well-defined stratigraphy they cut across showed a series of distinct changes in deposited material (Fig 3.14). The stratigraphic units were recorded underwater and in the laboratory, and made available to be sub-sampled for assessment and analysis. The relative positions of the monoliths are shown in Figure 3.17; their depths and their relationship with the stratigraphic horizons are presented in Figure 3.18.

In addition to the monolith samples, block samples were extracted in the purpose-built sampling boxes used in 2000 and bulk environmental samples were collected from fixed points for macrofossil, mammal, insect, foodstuff and other archaeological evidence.

3.3 Introduction to methods of sample collection and analysis

Monolith samples, bulk samples and a large number of lithics were collected from stratigraphic units associated with the archaeology in 2003 and held in cold storage at the National Oceanography Centre in Southampton (NOCS). Here they were sub-sampled by a number of specialists to determine their suitability for full analysis. The most appropriate material was then selected to characterise the stratigraphic units associated with the archaeology. Depositional sequences were scrutinised by Jen Heathcote. Once the monolith samples were described, thin sections were manufactured and inspected at a microscopic scale to identify formation processes that could help unravel the taphonomic evolution in the areas of interest. The detailed analysis was concentrated in the section located in context 2007, where the majority of lithics were found (see Figs 3.17 and 3.18). Scrutiny of palynological material, including pollen (by Rob Scaife) and macrofossils (by Mark Robinson), established the changing vegetation and environment. The presence of charcoal suggests that fire was used for locally opening up the woodland, providing possible evidence for human interaction with the landscape. The chronology of change was determined by radiocarbon measurements obtained from the Oxford Radiocarbon Accelerator Unit and Scottish Universities Environmental Research Centre and interpreted in a Bayesian framework by Derek Hamilton and Peter Marshall. This included radiocarbon dates obtained from material within secure stratigraphic sequences recorded in the monolith tins and wiggle-matching (see 3.10.2, below) of a dendrochonological sequence gathered and interpreted by Nigel Nayling.

Additional environmental information was extracted from insect and mammal remnants by Mark Robinson, while Alison Locker analysed fish remains. Studies of diatoms by Rob Scaife and of foraminifera by Jan Gillespie were conducted to track the introduction of saline conditions as an indicator of sea-level rise.

The results as presented in the following reports have informed our understanding of the adapting patterns of vegetation and the changing environmental conditions around the period of occupation. They also help to identify anthropogenic activity and the steadily growing marine influence within a high-resolution chronological framework. The results are summarised in 3.11 below.

3.4 Micromorphology of the depositional evidence
Jen Heathcote

Of the monolith samples collected from BC-II, seven were initially examined to assess the nature of the sediments they contained and determine whether any further analysis would be useful in suggesting the nature of the depositional environments represented in the sampled sedimentary sequence. The samples were MS04, MS05, MS06, MS07, MS08, MS20 and MS21. Two monoliths, MS05 and MS08, were selected for micromorphological analysis with the aims of assessing whether the provisional interpretations of the depositional environments were correct and refining those interpretations where possible.

3.4.1 Introduction to the analysis

The analysis applied to MS05 and MS08 addressed two key questions:

1. What is the nature of the lower peat contact with the underlying sediment? That is, is it erosive, therefore indicating that part of the sequence has been lost prior to peat formation?
2. Is there any evidence for soil development beneath the peat representing the former land surface (ie that existing prior to peat growth), and what depositional environment is represented by the underlying deposit?

The conclusions of the analysis would make apparent whether the submerged land surface at Bouldnor Cliff represents a pristine land surface, meaning that the associated artefacts are likely to be *in situ*, or an eroded land surface, meaning that the associated artefacts are likely to represent reworked material.

3.4.2 Methods

The monoliths were sampled with Kubiena tins at the NOCS, and the samples processed and thin

34   *Bouldnor Cliff*

sections manufactured at the Laboratorium voor Mineralogie, Petrologie en Micropedologie, University of Ghent, Belgium. Despite dehydrating the samples using a lengthy acetone immersion process, problems were subsequently experienced with partial resin impregnation caused by incomplete dehydration of the samples, probably due to the salt content of the sediments. This meant additional processing stages of re-impregnation were needed before thin sections could be successfully manufactured.

The thin sections were described at a range of magnifications from ×5.8 to ×400 using transmitted polarising light microscopes. Observation at low-powered magnification (×5.8 to ×32) was made using a binocular stereomicroscope (Leica M420 Macroscope) and was used particularly to establish a) the microstructure and b) the relationships of microfabrics within individual sedimentary units or soil horizons. The configuration of many larger pedofeatures is also better understood at this scale of magnification. Examination at higher magnifications (×40 to ×400) was made using compound microscopes. The thin section descriptions were recorded following the terminology and concepts proposed by Bullock *et al* (1985). In addition, the degree of organic decomposition was recorded following the guidelines of FitzPatrick (1993, 156).

3.4.3 *Analysis and interpretation*

The two monolith samples were taken from broadly comparable positions in the submerged sequence at BC-II, although MS08 was slightly lower than MS05 (see Figs 3.17 and 3.18). Both sampled the peat (context 2003) and the underlying mineral deposits (context 2007). They were analysed to provide an indication of the lateral variability of the former land surface and its associated sediments. Tables 3.1 and 3.2 show details of the sequences, including subdivisions of contexts 2003 and 2007 that were recognised in the laboratory description of the sediments, preliminary interpretations of the sedimentary units and the positions from which Kubiena samples were taken for thin section analysis.

Three thin sections, each 100mm in length, were analysed from the following positions: across the boundary at 340mm depth between the organic mud (unit 5/V; context 2007) and the overlying peat (unit 5/IV; context 2003), in order to establish the likelihood of there being an erosive contact at this point (thin section MS05/2); and between 340–540mm depth (units 5/V; context 2007 and 5/VI; context 2007b), where soil development beneath the potential old land surface may be identified (thin sections MS05/2 & MS05/03). In addition, a reference sample was taken from the peat (unit 5/IV; context 2003) to establish whether it showed changing conditions with depth (thin section MS05/1).

Context 2003/1 comprises very mineral-rich peat with very weak horizontal bedding towards the base of the unit indicated by moderately to strongly decomposed vegetation fragments. The underlying mineral component comprises over 95% quartz with accessory grains of glauconite, rare tourmaline and zircon. Occasional fragments of bone <500 m can be found embedded within the fabric, but show no particular distribution.

Secondary mineral formation is evident in the form of pyrite, gypsum and jarosite. Neo-formed pyrite is abundant throughout the unit, within and around decaying vegetation fragments, between mineral grains and embedded within the fine fabric. Pyrite is found as discrete spheres *c* 10μm in diameter, as framboidal accumulations, and as clusters, the last of these particularly within vegetal tissues.

Porosity is low (<10%) and voids are dominated by those associated with organic fragments, small irregular voids (vughs), packing voids between grains, and rare channels. Bioturbation is evident in the form of a vertical root channel, the walls of which exhibit secondary gypsum and jarosite formation, minerals that are likely to have formed through oxidation of pyrite and which are typically found in estuarine and marsh soils (FitzPatrick 1993, 70, 79).

Textural pedofeatures comprising infills of well-sorted skeleton grains of quartz with rare, very thin (<10μm), discontinuous coatings of fine fabric, together with decomposed organic fragments and opaque nodules of a size comparable to the quartz mineral grains, are also found. These are interpreted as features created by material being washed into cracks resulting from peat shrinkage during episodes when the surface of the peat dried out.

In thin section, the boundary between units 5/IV and 5/V (contexts 2003/1 and 2003/2) is transitional, suggesting that there is no hiatus and little or no erosion prior to the peat development. Context 2003/2 is a structureless organic mud containing a higher proportion of degraded vegetation fragments than the underlying layer. The basic mineral component is very poorly sorted and comprises over 98% quartz. There is common secondary pyrite formation, found typically as clusters of spheres (*c* 10μm diameter) in packing voids between mineral grains and embedded in the fine fabric. Occasional organ and tissue fragments of decaying vegetation are randomly distributed throughout the unit and are typically moderately to strongly decomposed; again, these tend to show concentrations of pyrite formation in association. Porosity is very low (<5%) and none is evident without magnification: unlike in the overlying unit, there are no channels.

Occasional textural and fabric pedofeatures occur, taking the form of void infills and areas of well-sorted silt-sized material, the latter embedded within the main fabric. The formation of these is thought to be linked, with the void infills (textural pedofeatures) representing material washed into the pore space by low-energy water when the unit was exposed at the land surface, while the silt-rich zones (fabric pedofeatures) represent the incorporation of these

Table 3.1 Deposit sequence represented in monolith MS05 (Jen Heathcote)

Context	Thickness (mm)	Sediment type	Thin sections	Description: Munsell Chart colour coding	Interpretation
2001	0–130	Minerogenic	(*not to scale*)	5Y 5/1 very soft (buttery) silty clay; homogeneous; few fragmented plant macros (?stems) dispersed throughout; slightly calcareous *Graded boundary*	Deposits laid down in brackish water; probably tidal mudflat to lower salt marsh position
2002/1	130–160	Organic mud		10YR 4/1 stiff silty clay; highly fragmented, unidentifiable humified and fresh plant macros (up to 4mm); non-calcareous *Graded boundary*	Deposits laid down under low-energy (quiet to still water) conditions (brackish or freshwater)
2002/2	160–210	Organic mud		5Y 4/1 more organic than overlying layer and increasingly organic to base of unit; sub-rounded pebble at –200mm (black); increasing content of plant macros that tend to be bedded sub-horizontally and comprise very well-preserved large pieces of plant material (?Phragmites); homogeneous at top and heterogeneous with diffuse lenses of humified organic material at base *Clear boundary*	Deposits laid down under low-energy (quiet to still water) conditions (brackish or freshwater)
2003/1	210–360	Peat	1 / 2	5YR 2.5/2 very dark brown, compact, well-humified peat; roundwood pieces (up to 20mm at –220mm depth) embedded within peat; increasing mineral content (medium sand) with depth but not to the extent that it becomes predominantly minerogenic; rare (<2% rounded and sub-rounded flint pebbles, randomly orientated and distributed towards base of unit); non-calcareous *Graded boundary*	Upper part of unit probably eroded; strongly oxidised and desiccated peat suggestive of significant period of lowered ground water levels
2003/2	360–420	Organic mud	3	5Y 5/1 (medium) sandy clay with fragments of wood and wood ghosts (blackened edges to completely blackened fragments); pocket of humified organic material horizontally bedded at 380mm; non-calcareous *Graded boundary*	?Old landsurface developed prior to peat development?; fluvial or brackish water deposits representing one of the environments listed below
2007	420–600	Minerogenic		5Y 5/1 medium to coarse sandy clay; homogeneous; massive; rare (<2%) rounded pebbles (40mm) and angular granules (2–4mm) of flint; rare woody (twiggy) fragments (poorly preserved and sub-horizontally aligned at 590mm); rare (<2%) sub-rounded flints towards base of unit; highly comminuted humified organic fragments distributed throughout the unit	Either: a) channel lag deposits indicative of low-/medium-energy conditions (eg meander), OR b) tidal creeks with episodic running water and standing water conditions, OR c) part of point-bar within braided freshwater channel

into the body of the fabric through repeated cycles of superficial wetting and drying, and, most probably, bioturbation.

Context 2007 comprises structureless minerogenic sandy clay. The sand grains are poorly sorted sub-rounded to angular and the basic mineralogy is dominated by quartz (>95%) with accessory grains of glauconite, tourmaline and zircon: a single rounded grain of residual (rather than neo-formed) vivianite is also present. Porosity is low (c 10%) and voids are dominated by vughs and irregular curvoplanar cracks partially separating small aggregates.

Table 3.2   Results of micromorphological analysis of monolith MS08 (Jen Heathcote)

Context	Thickness (mm)	Sediment type	Thin sections	Description	Interpretation
2003/3	0–30	Peat	*(not to scale)*	Stiff, silty peat; very dark grey (5Y 3/1); highly humified with no macrofossils visible; non-calcareous	Strongly oxidised and desiccated peat suggestive of significant period of lowered ground water levels
				Graded boundary	
2003/4	30–120	Peat		Heterogeneous colour, predominantly black (5YR 2.5/1) but with patches of very dark reddish-brown (5YR 2.5/2); no plant macros; becoming sandy with depth (medium sand); non-calcareous	As above
				Graded boundary	
2003/5	120–180	—		Missing	Large wood fragment
				Graded boundary	
2002/6	180–210	Peat		Heterogeneous colour, predominantly black (5YR 2.5/1) but with patches of very dark reddish-brown (5YR 2.5/2); no plant macros; becoming sandy with depth (medium sand); non-calcareous	Strongly oxidised and desiccated peat suggestive of significant period of lowered ground water levels
				Sharp boundary	
2007/1	210–255	Organic sand	1	Medium sandy clay; grey (5Y 5/1); occasional sub-rounded flint granules and pebbles; pockets of dark brown highly humified organic detritus; faint streaks rusty brown mottles (20%); slightly calcareous	a) Channel lag deposits indicative of low-/medium-energy conditions OR b) tidal creeks with episodic running water and standing water conditions, OR c) part of point-bar within braided freshwater channel
				Clear boundary	
2007/2	255–260	Minerogenic	2	Very soft (fine sandy) silty clay; olive grey (5Y 5/2); homogeneous; massive; slightly iron concentration (not cemented) developed at contact between this and the underlying unit; non-calcareous	Deposit laid down in standing water conditions, probably reflecting a very small and short-lived micro-environment
				Graded boundary	
2007/3	260–290	Minerogenic		Fine–medium sandy clay; light olive brown (2.5Y 5/4); homogeneous; massive; non-calcareous	a) Channel lag deposits indicative of low-/medium-energy conditions OR b) tidal creeks with episodic running water and standing water conditions, OR c) part of point-bar within braided freshwater channel
				Graded boundary	
2007/4	290–600	Minerogenic		Medium–coarse sand; slightly clayey; clay content increases slightly with depth; fragmented woody and parenchymous plant macros; granules (sub-rounded to angular) of flint; massive; random small pockets of pale grey sandy clay; no preferred orientation; colour grades from pale grey (5Y 5/1) at the top to dark grey (5Y 3/1) at the base; non-calcareous	As above

The organic content appears slightly lower than in the overlying unit, and comprises both large organ and tissue fragments and particulate matter (small dark brown fragments of very strongly decomposed material) randomly distributed throughout the fabric. Again, pyrite spheres and framboids are associated with many fragments, often in localised high concentrations.

While there is no evidence of any diagnostic pedogenic process (eg illuviation, podzolisation), the nature of the fine fabric (organo-mineral), the distribution of the organic and mineral materials and the morphology of the void space suggests that some bioturbation and basic soil formation through weathering has occurred in context 2007.

Two thin sections were taken across the units present between 180mm and 300mm depth to assess whether there was any terrestrial soil development indicated at the top of the organic sand context 2007/1.

Context 2003 as sampled in monolith MS08 comprises peat that has a lower mineral content than the peat sampled in Monolith MS05, although the grain shape and basic mineralogy is comparable. No fragments of bone were identified. Again, there is a high concentration of secondary pyrite present as discrete particles, clusters, and framboids, and many of the vegetation fragments are discontinuously infilled with pyrite spheres ($c10\mu m$).

Although in the monolith tin the boundary between context 2003 and context 2007 appeared sharp, in thin section it is graded, suggesting that there was no hiatus and little or no erosion prior to the peat development. Context 2007/1 comprises an organic sand which shows very strong horizontal and sub-horizontal bedding picked out by vegetation fragments, suggesting that only limited, if any, bioturbation has taken place. Secondary formation of gypsum crystals and jarosite is also evident on void walls, consistent with oxidation of the abundant pyrite component.

Also present in context 2007/1 are textural pedofeatures of two kinds. The first comprises thick (100–500μm) coatings of well-sorted grey silt on void walls, occasionally developing into discontinuous infills within voids. The other comprises very well-sorted fine sand-sized particles of both mineral grains and opaque black/brown particles that are thought to be highly divided and decomposed organic material: all of the particles are sub-rounded to subangular in shape and form discontinuous infills of larger voids. The size of the grains and the morphology of the features do not indicate that they have formed through pedogenic processes. Instead, both types of textural pedofeature are likely to have formed through material washing into surface cracks in the unit when it was exposed at the land surface.

A thin (0.5mm) band of grey silty clay identified within context 2007/2 in the monolith sample was not present in thin section, suggesting that it comprised the edge of a relatively restricted lens of material representing a brief depositional event under low-energy conditions.

Bedded, poorly sorted sand that is gleyed (grey, with no oxidised iron mottling or nodules present), indicating that it is fully reduced, was present within context 2007/3. This is consistent with the deposit having been water-saturated for a prolonged period prior to burial (and submergence by sea water). The organic content is limited to a few rare organ fragments that are moderately decomposed and contain orange-brown amorphous degradation products. There are no features indicative of soil development.

3.4.4 Conclusions

The analysis was carried out to address two key issues, namely: the identification of the nature of the lower peat contact with the underlying sediment; and the identification of any evidence for soil formation associated with the former land surface.

Firstly, analysis has shown that in both MS05 and MS08 the contact between the lower peat and the organic mud beneath is graded, representing a gradual change from one depositional environment to the other, and there has been little or no erosion of the former land surface prior to the initiation of peat formation. Therefore, it appears that the submerged land surface at Bouldnor Cliff represents a pristine land surface and the associated artefacts are thus likely to be *in situ*.

With respect to evidence for soil formation in the pre-peat land surface, the two monoliths show different conditions, despite both comprising organic mud of comparable textures. In MS05 there are signs of bioturbation and soil formation through weathering, seen in the nature and organisation of the fine fabric, although there is no evidence of any diagnostic pedogenic process such as clay translocation or leaching. However, MS08 shows no evidence of bioturbation or soil formation and retains its primary sedimentary structure (bedding), thus indicating that lateral variability exists even over short distances.

The work at Bouldnor Cliff is important as the site represents an apparently *in situ* Mesolithic site with abundant anthropogenic evidence in the form of lithics and contextual evidence that allows landscape change over a very small area to be examined. However, the broader environmental setting of the site is, at present, only partially understood. In the same way that terrestrial sites require contextualising within their contemporary landscapes, so too does Bouldnor Cliff. Future research should concentrate on attempting to refine our understanding of this site through examination of adjacent and associated palaeoenvironmental sequences, as it is only by working at this scale we will be able to address such issues as the specific channel morphology of the river with which this site is apparently associated.

3.5   Pollen evidence for vegetation changes
Rob Scaife

Morphological, sedimentological, and depositional investigations were focused on the relationship between the identified archaeological contexts and the interfaces with adjacent units. The pollen studies, in contrast, extended up the whole excavated section.

After preliminary examination of the range of columns obtained from BC-II in the 2003 season, overlapping monoliths (MS08, MS05, and MS04) (Fig 3.19) and monolith MS07 (Fig 3.20) were chosen

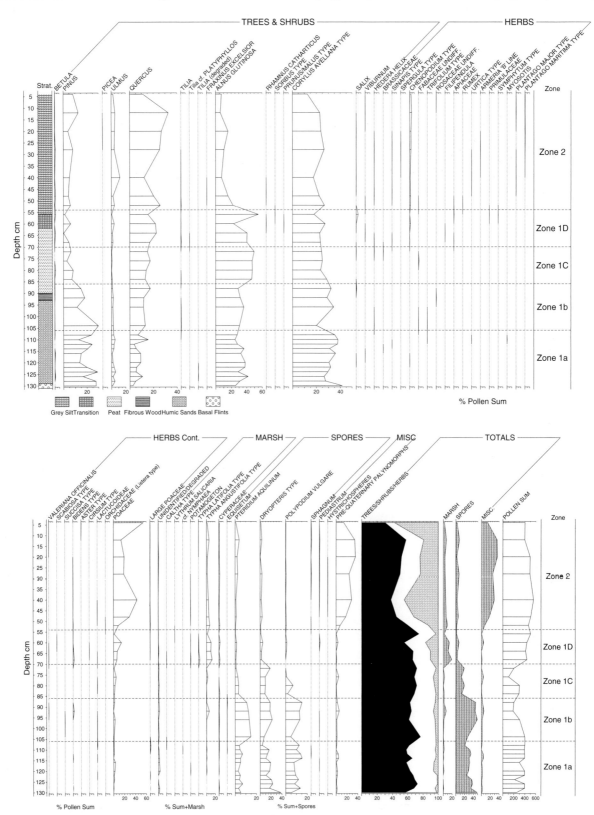

Figure 3.19   Pollen diagram of BC-II/MS04/05/08. The lower diagram follows on from the upper, with the continuation of herb species, marsh species, spores and so on (Rob Scaife)

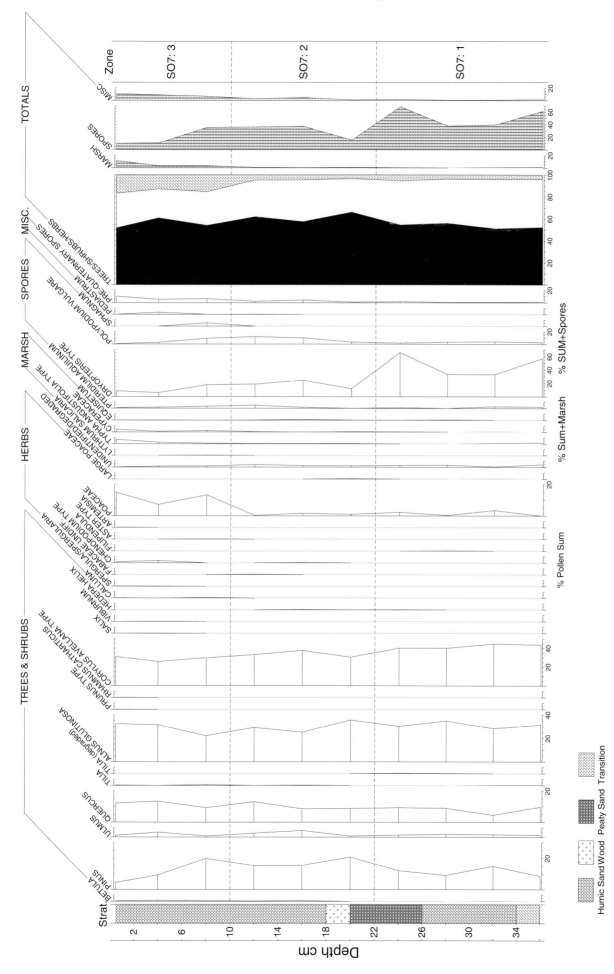

Figure 3.20 Pollen diagram of BC-II MS07 (Rob Scaife)

Table 3.3   Stratigraphy as recorded from the monolith profiles MS04, MS05, and MS08

Depth (mm)	
440–560	Homogeneous grey silty clay with occasional organic clasts. Marine/salt marsh
560–630	Transition to peat – ie peaty silt with oxidisation at the interface and sulphurous sediment. 10YR 5/1 to 10YR 6/1
630–900	Peat. Brown, oxidising rapidly to black. Detrital fen peat containing sand and silt. 10YR 3/1
700	Flint recorded
900–930	Fibrous compacted wood at transition
930–960	Darker. Pale brown silt
960–1080	Coarse grey/white sand
1080–1300	Coarse, grey, but darker humic sand. 10YR 4/1 containing occasional rootlets and twigs (old land surface at 1080mm)
1140–1160	Struck Mesolithic flake and occasional flints in lower part of sequence
1320	Basal gravels

for more detailed pollen analysis (Scaife 2004a). Both of the sequences had the advantages of containing *in situ* Mesolithic artefacts and of spanning the principal contexts of the lower stratigraphy at Bouldnor. The former is a complete sequence which spans the context 2007 (MS08) sand/silt containing Mesolithic struck flints, the overlying fen peat of context 2003 (MS05), and the capping grey alluvial and marine silts and clays (MS04). Monolith MS07 was taken specifically from context 2007 to provide corroborative and specific information on the environment associated with the Mesolithic activity. The results from the analysis of monolith MS07 will be presented following a detailed look at the longer sequence encompassed by monoliths MS04, MS05, and MS08.

3.5.1   Pollen analysis

This pollen analysis forms part of a more extensive research programme analysing the archaeologically related sediment sequences at Bouldnor Cliff. The Hampshire and Wight Trust for Maritime Archaeology took the monolith samples for stratigraphical description, radiocarbon dating, pollen analysis and diatom analysis. The profile was examined and sub-sampled in the laboratory.

3.5.1.1   Pollen method

Standard pollen extraction techniques were used on samples 2ml in volume (Moore and Webb 1978; Moore *et al* 1991). Owing to the high mineral component of the lower sediments, micromesh sieving was also used for the removal of clay. Pollen was mounted on slides in glycerol jelly and was identified and counted using an Olympus BH2 biological research microscope. Total pollen sums of between 150, where preservation is poor (the lowest levels), and 550 grains plus spores per level were identified and counted. A pollen diagram (Fig 3.19) has been constructed and plotted using Tilia and Tilia Graph. Percentages have been calculated as follows:

% total dry land pollen (tdlp)
Marsh/aquatic = % tdlp + sum of marsh/aquatics
Spores = % tdlp + sum of spore
Miscellaneous % tdlp + Miscellaneous
(pre-Quaternary palynomorphs and Pediastrum).

Pollen abundance was calculated for each sample using the addition of markers (Lycopodium spore tablets) to known sample volumes: here 1.5ml for organic/peat and 1.5ml for the minerogenic alluvial sediments (Stockmarr 1971).

Taxonomy, in general, follows that of Moore and Webb (1978), modified according to Bennett *et al* (1994) for pollen types and Stace (1991) for plant descriptions. These preparation procedures were carried out in the Palaeoecology Laboratory of the School of Geography, University of Southampton. An extensive pollen reference collection of modern taxa was available.

3.5.2   Palaeoenvironmental sequence (column SO8) recorded in MS04, MS05, and MS08

This overlapping monolith sequence was examined in detail because it embraces all of the lower stratigraphical units at the location and especially those associated with the late Boreal Mesolithic archaeology. As such, it provided the potential for producing a long record of the vegetation and environment spanning both the Mesolithic archaeology and the environmental changes that ultimately saw submergence of the site by marine transgression. Accordingly, following radiocarbon dating, this represents a key profile with which other sequences examined can be compared.

3.5.2.1 Stratigraphy within column SO8

For the purpose of pollen analysis, samples were taken sequentially downwards from the top of the monolith MS04 through overlaps to the base of column MS08, thus providing a full stratigraphical profile encompassing contexts 2007, 2003 and 2004 (Fig 3.18). The top of the column (2004) lies at a true depth of –10.08m OD ± 0.1m. The bottom of the column at context 2012 lies at –11.40m OD ± 0.1m. The stratigraphy as recorded from the monolith profiles is presented in Table 3.3.

The lower stratigraphical sequences at Bouldnor comprise three principal contexts. To some extent the pollen assemblage zones and sub-zones recognised can be related to these stratigraphical units (Fig 3.18). This may be expected from the changing taphonomy of the sediments and the contained pollen. Two principal local pollen assemblage zones, the lower of which is divided into sub-zones, have been recognised. The environment of deposition of these pollen zones and the stratigraphical units are defined/characterised from the base of the profile upwards. The different units are described below and the heights are presented in Figure 3.18.

3.5.2.2 Pollen zonation across column SO8

Two main zones and four sub-zones have been identified in this column. The zones are characterised from the base upwards.

Zone SO8: 1. 1320mm to 540mm

Overall, this zone is dominated by trees and shrubs. *Pinus* (to 29%), *Quercus* (to c 20%), *Alnus glutinosa* (to 40%) and *Corylus avellana* type (to 40%) are dominant. There are generally few herbs, with only sporadic occurrences. Apart from *Alnus glutinosa*, marsh/fen taxa include small numbers of *Typha/ Sparganium* type, Cyperaceae and individual occurrences of *Nymphaea* and *Potamogeton* type. Spores of Pteridophytes include *Pteridium aquilinum* (Zone 1b), monolete forms (*Dryopteris* type 38% in the basal sample) and *Polypodium aquilinum*.

Zone SO8: 1. Sub-zone 1a; 1320mm to 1060mm (Context 2007)

The lower part of these sediments appears to span an old land surface which developed in the basal gravels and sands. This extends upwards into humic sands. Trees and shrubs are dominant. *Pinus* is marginally more important here than in sub-zone 1b, along with *Quercus* (10–15%) and *Ulmus* (to 5–6%). *Alnus glutinosa* (to 45%) is the dominant fen taxon. *Corylus avellana* type (to 45% at base) is also important. Values of herbs are relatively small (5–9%) and comprise mainly Poaceae with occasional marsh/fen taxa (*Typha angustifolia/Sparganium* type). Spores are important, with *Dryopteris* type (to 38% at base of profile) and *Polypodium vulgare* (to 15%).

Vegetation: *Pinus* was important and probably dominant in surrounding areas, with *Quercus*, *Ulmus* and *Corylus avellana* type. *Alnus glutinosa* was also important and was probably present on or near the sample site. These data are comparable with context 2007 (see below), showing the end of the period of Boreal pine maxima and the progressive expansion to dominance of oak and hazel – that is, early Holocene seral vegetation changes in Flandrian Chronozone Ib and Ic.

Zone SO8: 1. Sub-zone 1b; 1060mm to 850mm (context 2007)

This sub-zone spans the upper humic sands and contains a poorly developed palaeosol and old land surface associated with Mesolithic blades (a possible stabilisation horizon) and the transition into fen carr peat. Trees and shrubs remain dominant. This sub-zone is delimited by the beginning of a decline in *Pinus* from the base of this zone (30% to 15–20%). *Quercus* values start to increase (to 20%), while *Corylus avellana* type and *Alnus glutinosa* remain similar to the preceding zone. Herbs, similarly, remain the same as sub-zone 1a. This sub-zone is also defined by the first, but nevertheless sporadic, occurrences of *Tilia*, and the expansion of *Pteridium aquilinum* (to 20%). *Dryopteris* type and *Polypodium vulgare* remain important.

Vegetation: *Pinus* declines as *Quercus* and *Ulmus* become increasingly important. *Alnus* and *Corylus* maintain importance. *Tilia* occurs sporadically and, as noted for section MS07 (section 3.5.3.2), this probably represents the first evidence of the migration of lime into the region during the late Boreal (Flandrian Ic) prior to the separation of Britain from mainland Europe. *Alnus glutinosa* is important throughout and in sufficient numbers to suggest some on-site and near-local growth, as this taxon also rapidly spread in response to positive sea level (eustatic) change.

The Mesolithic artefacts: context 2007 (Zone 1a and 1b) contains examples of the lithic industry between 1180mm and 1200mm. These are contemporary with the vegetation described above: that is, a predominantly wooded environment of pine, oak, and hazel with some elm. As with section SO7 (see below), the humic sands of context 2007 have an upper, more humic horizon of fibrous wood which may represent the top of a palaeo-land surface. Fern spores, including *Polypodium vulgare*, are important in these lower sub-zones. *Pteridium aquilinum* may suggest disturbed ground associated with human activity, possibly fire. It should be noted, however, that flints within such soils may not relate directly to associated pollen because of their differing taphonomy (see 3.4, above).

Zone SO8: 1. Sub-zone 1c: 860mm to 700mm

This pollen sub-zone falls within the detrital fen peat (context 2003). *Pinus* continues to decline, along with *Ulmus*, to low values. *Quercus* continues to increase in importance. *Corylus avellana* (20%) remains the dominant shrub and maintains the presence of previous levels. The sub-zone is also characterised by the expansion of *Alnus glutinosa* (to 45%) and reductions in percentages of spore taxa. There are few herbs, but Poaceae starts to increase in importance. *Dryopteris* type remains the main spore taxon, while *Pteridium aquilinum* and *Polypodium* decline sharply.

Vegetation: during this phase, predominantly one of peat accretion, *Alnus glutinosa* with *Quercus* and *Corylus avellana* (also macrofossils) were dominant on-site in a damp fen woodland. *Pinus*, however, declined in importance, at least on-site, but may have maintained its importance on less-waterlogged soils.

Zone SO8: 1. Sub-zone 1d; 700mm to 540mm

This sub-zone, the upper peat of context 2003 and the transition to the overlying mineral sediment (contexts 2001 and 2002), is defined by an expansion of herbs (especially Poaceae), including marsh taxa, and the start of *Ulmus* expansion. Trees and shrub, however, remain dominant. *Pinus* values are at their lowest levels in this profile. *Quercus* (23%), *Alnus glutinosa* (peak to 58%) and *Corylus avellana* type (26%) are dominant. *Salix* is also present. Herbs start to become more important and show some increase in diversity with expansions of Poaceae (to 15%), Chenopodiaceae and Asteraceae types. Marsh/fen taxa become important, with *Typha angustifolia/Sparganium* type at their highest values (15%), increased Cyperaceae, and the presence of *Typha latifolia* and *Potamogeton* type. There are few spores, in contrast with their importance in preceding zones.

Vegetation and environment: this was a period of increasing wetness caused by rising local groundwater tables in response to widespread/regional positive eustatic changes. While this was initially freshwater in nature, there are indications of nearby saline/brackish water or marine influences with the incoming of Chenopodiaceae and *Aster* type.

Zone SO8: 2. 540mm to 40mm

This upper zone marks the change from the peats of sub-zones 1c and 1d (context 2003) to the overlying homogeneous grey fluviatile salt-marsh and mudflat sediments, and represents the brackish water/marine transgressive event.

Although trees and shrubs remain important throughout, there is also a substantial increase in the numbers and diversity of the herbs present. Trees and shrubs are dominated by *Quercus* (to 36%) and *Corylus avellana* type (c 30%). *Pinus* remains present at 10–15% while *Alnus glutinosa* declines substantially (to c 10%). Herbs become more important with Poaceae, which is dominant to 55% at the top of the zone. Also becoming more important are halophytes, including Chenopodiaceae (to 5%), along with other *Armeria* types and *Plantago lanceolata*. Marsh and aquatic taxa remain the same as zone 1d, but with reduced values. Particularly diagnostic aspects of this zone are the much increased numbers of derived pre-Quaternary palynomorphs of Tertiary and Cretaceous age, which come from the erosion of local geology and reworking of earlier freshwater and marine sediments.

Vegetation: This phase/zone clearly represents the Boreal–Atlantic expansion of sea level. Changes in sediment source resulted in the erosion and reworking of pre-Quaternary (Cretaceous and Tertiary) pollen and spores from bedrock or earlier Pleistocene or Holocene sediments. *Quercus*, *Corylus avellana*, and *Ulmus* remained the dominant woodland taxa in the region but, along with *Alnus*, these appear less important on-site and nearby owing to fluvial/marine inundation of the site and changing sediment accretion to one of salt marsh or mudflat.

3.5.3   Pollen analysis of column SO7 from sample MS07

As with overlapping monoliths MS04, MS05, and MS08, MS07 (Fig 3.20) was chosen from the 2003 assessment for more detailed pollen analysis. This sequence was selected specifically as it also had the advantages of containing *in situ* Mesolithic blade artefacts (identified at depths of 280–310mm and 200–220mm in the monolith tins) and spanning the principal archaeological contexts of the lower Bouldnor Cliff stratigraphy. It was analysed, therefore, to provide specific and comparative/

Table 3.4   Stratigraphy as recorded in the monolith profile MS07

Depth (mm)	
0–340	Humic sand (context 2007). Dark grey/brown with occasional paler sand lenses, peaty inclusions and small flints
180–260	A darker, more humic unit
NB Struck Mesolithic flints at 200–220mm and 280–310mm	
360	Transition into basal gravels and medium and coarse yellow sand. Flints angular to sub-rounded

corroborative information on the environment associated with Mesolithic activity which has also been described using evidence from MS04, MS05, and MS08. Although absolute numbers were small, pollen was recovered from throughout the humic sands within which a putative palaeosol and an old land surface exist and in which the flints were found.

3.5.3.1 Stratigraphy

The general stratigraphy as recorded in the monolith tin is given in Table 3.4. For detailed sedimentological work see 3.4, above. The whole of the sediment sequence comprises sands of context 2007. It was noted that the sand becomes more humic towards the top of the context, where it is overlain by wood/peat. The transition represents an old land surface of the Mesolithic for which a radiocarbon date of 7170 ± 24 BP (7561–7175 cal BP) (OXA-15697) has been obtained (see 3.10, below).

3.5.3.2 Pollen zonation

Three local pollen assemblage zones have been identified in this sequence. These are characterised from the base of S07 upwards.

Zone SO7: 1. 360mm to 220mm. Pinus–Quercus–Alnus glutinosa–Corylus avellana type–Dryopteris type

This zone spans the lower humic sands (340mm to 220mm) which rest on the basal Devensian gravels. A possible palaeosol is evidenced with Mesolithic blades at depths of 280–310mm and 200–220mm. Tree and shrub pollen is dominant throughout, with few herbs. *Pinus* (to 20%) is dominant, with *Quercus* (10%) *Alnus glutinosa* (40%) and *Corylus avellana* type (43%). There are also small numbers of *Ulmus* (to 3%) and sporadic occurrences of *Tilia* and *Betula*. The few herbs which are present are largely Poaceae with occasional peaks (max 5%) and individual occurrences of marsh/fen types including *Typha angustifolia* type, *Filipendula ulmaria*, and Cyperaceae. Of particular importance, as designated by the high values in this zone, are the high numbers of Pteropsida (monolete, *Dryopteris* forms, peak to 70% sum + spores).

At a depth of 220mm there are indications of an old land surface, or palaeosol. From this level downwards, spores of ferns (*Dryopteris* type) are more abundant. This is also a phenomenon of soil profiles and it seems likely that this was a stand-still horizon which allowed some pedogenesis. Immediately overlying this palaeosol is a thin horizon of wood. This may be a further indication that this was the prehistoric/Mesolithic level of activity which was subsequently colonised by woodland with the onset of a peat-forming habitat.

Zone SO7: 2. 220mm to 100mm. Pinus–Ulmus–Quercus–Alnus glutinosa–Corylus avellana type

Stratigraphically, this zone embraces change from the old land (humic sand) surface of zone 1 to upper humic sands, with wood at the interface. Palynologically, it is characterised by slightly higher values of *Pinus* (22%) and *Ulmus* (to 10%). *Alnus glutinosa* and *Corylus avellana* type decline slightly (to 25% and 35% respectively). Herbs remain similar, with constant but small numbers of Poaceae. Occasional Chenopodiaceae and Fabaceae are present. Spores show a sharp reduction in *Dryopteris* type (10–20%), while *Polypodium* increases (to 10%). With the change to the upper humic sands is some increase in pre-Quaternary palynomorphs.

Zone SO7: 3. 100mm to 0mm. Quercus–Alnus glutinosa–Corylus avellana type–Poaceae

This uppermost zone falls within the upper black/dark brown humic sands and is characterised by a marked expansion of Poaceae. Trees and shrubs, however, remain dominant. *Pinus* declines to its lowest value (5%) from its highest values (in zone S07: 2). *Quercus* (to 43%), *Alnus glutinosa* (30–35%) and *Corylus avellana* type (c 30%) remain as in the preceding zone. Shrubs include occasional fen taxa, with *Rhamnus cathartica*, *Salix* and *Viburnum* present. Herbs become important, with a sharp expansion of Poaceae (15%) and occurrences of Chenopodiaceae (3%) and *Aster* type (cf halophytes). There is also an expansion of marsh taxa with *Typha angustifolia*/*Sparganium* type, *Lythrum salicaria*, and Cyperaceae. There are fewer spores, with declining monolete forms (*Dryopteris* type and *Polypodium*). There is, however, a peak of *Sphagnum* (6%), along with occasional *Pediastrum* and increased numbers of pre-Quaternary palynomorphs.

3.5.4 The vegetation and occupied land surface

The pollen profile that traverses context 2007 is considered to be the most important profile because of the *in situ* Mesolithic artefacts. These occur at c 300mm and 210mm in the monolith profile within a horizon of darker, more humic sands/silts (context 2007). The sediments from context 2007 are also represented in MS05 and MS08 (zone 1a and 1b). The pollen data demonstrate a typical late Boreal (Flandrian Ic) vegetation community showing remaining pine with oak, elm and hazel still of importance. It is thought that this is an old land surface, or at least a stabilisation surface, on which the human activity/occupation occurred.

The vegetation associated with this period of soil formation consisted of pine with oak and hazel forming surrounding woodland. It is not possible to state whether this was a mixed woodland or had areas of differing dominance. Pine was in decline after its earlier period of dominance during the Boreal period at *c* 8250cal BC (9000 BP), but remained important and possibly dominant in the local area on drier interfluve soils, with oak, elm, and hazel. Alder pollen values indicate that, although it was locally present, it did not form dominant carr woodland at this time, but was likely to have been growing close to the site, probably on the edges of a river channel.

Although it is not clear what the on-site vegetation comprised, it seems likely that this was a short-growing herbaceous community, possibly grasses, giving rise to the increased humic component. The presence of a poorly developed soil has also been suggested from analysis of the stratigraphy (see 3.4.4, above). This is pertinent to the interpretation of the archaeology in relation to the pollen in the soils and is further discussed in the various reports in Section Three. It is concluded that the environment was probably a sandy river bar that became stabilised for a short period prior to the rising base levels that caused the peat growth seen in a number of profiles. Here, wood overlies the palaeosol. This may come from stabilised growth on the land surface or from fallen timbers from nearby/adjacent interfluves.

Subsequently, the rising relative sea level caused the demise of this woodland, with back-ponding leading to increasing freshwater conditions which were succeeded by marine/salt-marsh conditions. This is seen in the upper 80–100mm of context 2003 and across the transition to 2002, where a marked change in the record occurs. There is a substantial expansion of Poaceae (grasses), with an increase also of *Typha angustifolia/Sparganium* (bur-reed and reed-mace), *Sphagnum* and *Pediastrum*. This is a manifestation of ecological change caused by local rising relative sea level and increased on-site wetness, causing the development of herb-rich wet fen. This is evidenced in other profiles and is a prelude to full marine incursion early in the middle Holocene (Atlantic) period (Flandrian II). Chenopodiaceae are present in greater numbers in this upper zone and, with *Spergula/Spergularia* type and *Aster* type, probably derive from halophytic communities. There is an increase of derived pre-Quaternary palynomorphs in this upper zone, implying changes in the overall sediment regime, sources, transport, and deposition.

3.5.5   *The dominance of rising sea levels*

Analysing the succession of geomorphological changes within the whole sequence alongside dating evidence confirms that the peat deposits at –11m OD at Bouldnor Cliff date to the late Boreal period (Flandrian chronozone 1b–c) and the Boreal–Atlantic transition between *c* 7150 BP and *c* 6900 BP (see 3.10, below). The evidence demonstrates that the changing sedimentary characteristics and local environmental change that overtook the

archaeological land surface were largely a function of post-glacial sea-level fluctuation. In this region this took the form of a general positive relative rise which caused increasing wetness and peat-formation conditions over the land surface of the now Solent (here a freshwater river sand bar). This ultimately culminated in marine transgression and the formation of salt marsh and mudflat.

Throughout the period of environmental change the vegetation was also undergoing rapid changes as migration and competition took place after the close of the Devensian cold stage. The broader characteristics of these seral changes are now understood, and they contrast with the early ideas of Godwin's zonation based on pollen assemblages (Godwin 1940). It is now accepted, and clearly evidenced from radiocarbon dating, that the seral changes in vegetation communities were asynchronous across the country as the principal trees, initially pioneers, were followed by more competitive dominants extending outwards from their glacial refugia and out-competing the pioneer colonisers. In the south of England the pattern of these changes is evidenced from the Isle of Wight (Scaife 1980; 1982; 1987; 2004a) and from Cranes Moor, New Forest (Clarke and Barber 1987), Testwood Lakes (Scaife 2003a; forthcoming/in press), and Southampton, Mountbatten Park Centre (Scaife 1998), sites with radiocarbon dates that are of value to the understanding of the Bouldnor Cliff sequences. These environmental changes have also been recorded from other Bouldnor Cliff exposures (Scaife 2000a; 2005) and in other local offshore exposures in Sandown Bay (Scaife 2004b) and Tanners Hard (Pitts Deep), Lymington (Scaife 2003b; Chapter 7, 7.3).

3.6   Diatom and foraminifera, and the ingress of seawater
Rob Scaife and Jan Gillespie

The signatures of sea-level change within the Bouldnor Cliff monolith samples were sought by examination of the diatom and foraminifera record. Samples were examined from across the sedimentary units in MS04, MS05, and MS06. The presence of diatoms and foraminifera support other evidence for the marine transgression in which the grey salt-marsh sediments were deposited.

3.6.1   *Diatom analysis*

Diatom frustules, the hard and porous cell wall or external layer of diatoms, were found only in the finer-grained sediments of context 2001. Even here, however, numbers were relatively small. Absence in the other contexts is probably attributable to the unfavourable depositional habitats within the silts and coarse sands of contexts 2002 and 2007 and the very organic/humic peat deposits of context 2003.

Table 3.5 Diatom data from core sample MS04

	Depth mm							
	20	**80**	**160**	**240**	**320**	**400**	**480**	**560**
Achnanthes brevipes		15	21	13	8	2	6	8
Actinoptychus senarius	1	4	1				1	5
Camploneis cf *Grevillei* (frags)	1		2	1	1		2	
Coscinodiscus sp	1	1	2	1		1	1	1
Cocconeis sp			1		3	2		
Cyclotella striata		1						
Cyclotella sp				2	1	2		1
Cymbella sp								1
Diploneis cf *Bombus*		1	4	1				
Diploneis didyma	5	7	10	10	2	9	8	5
Diploneis interupta								
Diploneis sp (frags)		6	6	6	3	5		
Epithemia cf *Hyundmanii*		2						
Epithemia sp			1	1	1		3	
Gomphonema cf *Olivaceum*				1				
Navicula sp	1				1	4	2	2
Nitzschia navicularis	8	27	13	13	12	44	37	53
Nitzschia punctata	6	7	5	7	5	8	19	6
Nitzschia sp	5	1		4				1
Paralia sulcata	19	16	5	12	6	9	4	22
Pinnularia sp	1	1	1	1	1	1		
Pseudopodosira stelligera	1	5	2			2		1
Rhaphoneis amphiceros			4	1	1			1
Cf *Rhopalodia* sp						1	1	
Surirella sp						2	1	
Surirella cf *Bifrons*			1					
Synedra sp	1	4	3	4	2	3	7	3
Thalassiosira sp (frag)					1			
Unidentified centrics		1						
Unidentified	1	2			2		5	2

3.6.1.1 Diatom preparation method

Preparation used digestion of humic/organic material using hydrogen peroxide. Samples were dried on microscope cover-slips and mounted on microscope slides using Naphrax mounting medium. Examination was carried out at high-power magnification ($\times$400 and $\times$1000) using a biological microscope. The floras are referenced following Van der Werff and Huls (1958–1974) and Hartley (1986; 1996).

3.6.1.2 Diatom data

The sequence analysed for diatoms forms forms the upper part of the more continuous pollen column analysed, which embraces all the principal contexts of finer-grained material recorded in monolith samples MS04, MS05, and MS08 – that is, the basal archaeological sand/soil of context 2007, the overlying peat of context 2003, the interface/transition (context 2002), and what have been demonstrated to be overlying salt-marsh and mudflat deposits laid down in brackish and saline conditions (context 2001). This last upper fine-grained clay/silt contained assemblages of diatoms (Table 3.5). The other contexts did not contain diatoms.

Overall, the assemblage is characteristic of brackish water environments and taxa which are frequently found in salt-marsh and mudflat habitats. This confirms the conclusions obtained from both the foraminifera (below) and pollen data. Centrales are present, with *Paralia sulcata*, *Coscinodiscus*, *Camploneis* cf *grevillei*, and *Actinoptychus senarius*. Important taxa include *Nitschia navicularis*, *N. puntata*, *Diploneis* spp, and *Acnanthes brevipes* (var. *parvula*), all of brackish water environments and found in salt-marsh and mudflat sediments. Greater numbers of *Nitzschia navicularis* in the lower samples are indicative of a mudflat environment. This is followed by a reduction in numbers of *N. navicularis* and an expansion of *Paralia sulcata*, which may indicate a change to deeper-water conditions. A peak of the latter in the basal sample (560mm) may have been from a rapid inwash/flooding event. A small number of diatoms may derive from freshwater habitats (eg *Epithemia*) and most probably from rivers and streams exiting into the Solent.

Diatoms were absent in samples analysed from the lower stratigraphical units, which, other environmental evidence suggests, were largely freshwater fen deposits. This is unfortunate, since their presence would help to characterise these depositional habitats.

3.6.1.3 Conclusion

The diatom assemblages confirm that the local environment, characterised by peat deposition, became progressively wetter owing to positive changes in relative sea level, which culminated in transgression and the creation of a marine environment. The diatom assemblages recovered from the finer-grained sediments of context 2001 suggest an initial mudflat environment which, indications suggest, changed to one characterised by deeper water as marine transgression progressed. The formation of this mudflat environment is evidenced by the deposition of fine-grained sediments which overlie transitional silty sands (see Fig 3.18) that had been deposited in a fluvial (riverine) environment or a transgressive littoral or sublittoral marine environment.

3.6.2 *Foraminifera*

Sampling was conducted across the section at BC-II from context 2001, through context 2002, to context 2003. Foraminifera (marine shell-bearing protozoans), like diatoms, were recovered only from the fine grey silts of context 2001.

Planktonic foraminifera live in marine waters of normal salinity and are very rare in brackish waters. The benthonic forms live at or near the sediment–water interface and do occur in brackish to normal marine habitats, and at all depths. Shelf species are benthic and can be found on the continental shelf. Mudflat species differ in that they can live in water that is brackish to marine. Foraminifera are thus ideal for palaeoenvironmental analysis as many species have narrowly defined niches (Murray 1991).

3.6.2.1 Preparation techniques

The samples were washed through a 63µm sieve to remove the clay fraction, then air-dried at 40°C.

Consolidated sediments were soaked in Calgon 10% for 24 hours prior to the washing and drying process in order to break up the clay particles. Samples were then examined and specimens picked using a Leica MZ16 binocular microscope at ×10–×60.

3.6.2.2 Monolith sample MS04 (BC-II)

This sample is the shallowest sample from BC-II. It contains the grey silts from context 2001, which consist of a grey silty clay which is homogenous throughout the core. The pollen evidence from context 2001 shows the first clear inundation of the site. A total of seven samples were taken at 80mm intervals down the core from the top.

Foraminifera, some poorly preserved, were present in most of the samples. They were more abundant in the upper part of the section, becoming quite scarce by 460mm depth (Table 3.6). This possibly indicates the dominance of freshwater being followed by the onset of more tidal conditions. Near the top of the core the assemblage consists of a typical mudflat fauna, *Haynesina germanica*, while further down the section the assemblage is of planktonic and shelf specimens which do not live in the shallow waters of the modern English Channel and North Sea. This could indicate sea-level rise resulting in the relocation of allochthonous marine taxa into this habitat, or a process of resedimentation which brought them in from an adjacent cliff.

3.6.2.3 Monolith sample MS06 (BC-II)

The upper part of this core contains the grey silts of context 2001 with a transitional phase into the silty clay of context 2002, before the lower peats of context 2003. Seven samples were taken from the core (Table 3.7).

Foraminifera were present in samples from the upper 320mm. Within and beneath the transitional stage between 2001 and 2002, and through to the peat at the bottom of the core, no foraminifera were found. The foraminifera found in the grey silts of context 2001 were a typical mudflat fauna of *Ammonia beccarii*, *Elphidium* and *Haynesina germanica*, which is similar to that found in the present-day Hamble Estuary (Alve and Murray 1994).

The evidence from samples immediately above the transitional phase shows an abundance of planktonic species. This is significant and may suggest a sea-level surge which washed the taxa into the system. A change in the environment as the sea level rose is indicated by the presence of the marsh species *Trochammina*, which was dominant before the establishment of the mudflat fauna. Haslett (2001) found in the Severn estuary that *Trochammina* characterises the uppermost foraminifera-bearing zone in high to middle marsh, and is followed by the *Ammonia beccari* and *Haynesina germanica* association.

Table 3.6 Foraminifera from BC-II monolith MS04

Depth	Context	Sediment	Taxon	Habitat
60–80mm	2001	Silty clay	*Haynesina germanica*	Mudflat species
140–160mm	2001	Silty clay	*Haynesina germanica*	Mudflat species
220–240mm	2001	Silty clay	*Nousoa*	Shelf species
			Gavellinopsis	Shelf species
			Inflate, bulloides, glutinata	Planktonic species
300–320mm	2001	Silty clay	*Nousoa*	Shelf species
			Gavellinopsis	Shelf species
			Inflate, bulloides, glutinata	Planktonic species
380–400mm	2001	Silty clay	*Gavellinopsis*	Shelf species
460–480mm	2001	Silty clay	None	
540–560mm	2001	Silty clay	None	

Table 3.7 Foraminifera from BC-II monolith MS06

Depth	Context	Sediment	Taxon	Habitat
60–80mm	2001	Silty clay	*Ammonia beccarii*	Mudflat species
			Elphidium	
			Haynesina germanica	
140–160mm	2001	Silty clay	*Ammonia beccarii*	Mudflat species
			Elphidium	
			Haynesina germanica	
220–240mm	2001	Silty clay	*Trochammina*	Marsh species
300–320mm	2001	Silty clay	*T. cimingodobe*	Planktonic species
			N. pachyderma	
380–400mm	2002	Clay/peat transition	None	
460–480mm	2003	Peat	None	
540–560mm	2003	Peat	None	

3.6.2.4 Monolith sample MS05 (BC-II)

The upper part of the core contains salt-marsh sediments overlying detrital fen peat above coarse sands. Beginning at a depth of 280mm, samples were examined every 20mm down the core (environmental evidence suggests these are freshwater fen deposits – see 3.5.1, above). No foraminifera were found in any of these samples. This demonstrates an absence of marine influence during this period. Diatom evidence from the top of the core demonstrates an assemblage characteristic of brackish water environments and taxa frequently found in salt-marsh habitats.

3.6.2.5 Conclusion

Near the top of the section, in context 2001, the foraminifera assemblage consisted of a typical mudflat fauna (*Haynesina germanica*, *Ammonia beccarii* and *Elphidium? Excavatum*). Below this, the marsh species *Trochammina* was recorded, indicating a transition from marsh to mudflat. Towards the base of context 2001 planktonic and shelf specimens which do not live in the shallow waters of the modern English Channel and North Sea (*Gavellinopsis inflata, Nousoa, bulloides, glutinata*) dominate. These were found towards the base of context 2001 and could indicate a sudden sea-level rise which resulted in the transportation of allochthonous marine taxa into this habitat. This may have occurred during a process of resedimentation from an adjacent cliff or been brought about by a surge which carried the planktonic specimens from deeper water.

3.6.3 Discussion

The peat deposit of context 2003 is shown from

environmental evidence to be detrital fen peat. No forams or diatoms were found in this context. Context 2002 represents a salt-marsh deposit that developed following gradually wetter conditions. This is reflected in the diatom assemblage by a dominance of marsh species followed by a change to typical brackish water/mudflat species.

The final inundation of the sea during the deposition of context 2001 is signified in the diatom record by an expansion of *Paralia sulcata*, which may represent the build-up of deeper water following a flooding event. The ingress of the sea is soon accompanied by an abundance of the planktonic foraminifera *T. cimingodobe* and *N. pachyderm*. This is significant, as these could come either from reworked sediments showing an increasing pre-Quaternary component of resedimentation within the catchment or a sudden influx of seawater.

3.7   Macroscopic plant and insect remains
Mark Robinson

3.7.1   Introduction

Detailed investigations of sediment structure, pollen, diatoms, and foraminifera were accompanied by the analysis, cataloguing, and interpretation of the recovered macrofossil assemblage. This was recovered from bulk samples which also harboured insects and evidence of human activity in the form of flints, charcoal, and burnt hazelnuts. The bulk samples were largely collected from the peat shelf (context 2003) and the grey sandy clay deposit containing the lithics (context 2007).

Assessment established that macroscopic plant and insect remains, including carbonised hazelnut shell fragments, were present. It was decided that detailed analyses of these sediments should be undertaken in order both to establish the environmental setting of the Mesolithic activity and to obtain information on the Mesolithic exploitation of edible plants.

3.7.2   *Marine samples and stratigraphy*

Fourteen samples were analysed from four contexts.

- Context 2007 (organic sandy silt with many tree roots and fresh flint flakes, lowest deposit of sequence): samples S043 base, S043 middle, S043 top, S043 general, S038 bottom, S038 middle, S038 top, S038 general, S042, and S013.
- Context 2006 (flint gravel with some decayed woody roots partly sealing context 2007): two samples reviewed but not analysed.
- Context 2003 (silty peat with some wood and tree roots, above contexts 2006 and 2007): sample S046.
- Context 2002 (slightly organic alluvial silt with some very decayed roots of *Phragmites australis*). Above context 2003: sample reviewed but not analysed.

3.7.3   *Methods*

The bulk samples were collected from the seabed either as cohesive blocks or, where the sediment units could not maintain integrity in the water, as an associated collection. The cohesive units were recovered from contexts 2002 and 2003 using handsaws and trowels. The less-cohesive material was recovered from context 2006 (fluvial gravel) and context 2007 (fine sandy clay). These samples were collected with trowels and put into zip-lock bags that were sealed underwater.

Table 3.8   Charred items and other categories of evidence from BC-II (+ = present)

	Context	2007	2007	2007	2007	2007	2007	2007	2007	2007	2007	2003
	Sample (SO)	43 base	43 middle	43 top	43 general	38 bottom	38 middle	38 top	38	42	13	46
	Sample weight (kg)	4.60	2.50	1.45	1.85	3.35	6.15	4.10	0.76	2.60	4.50	4.00
Corylus avellana L charred nutshell frag	hazel	14	6	2	1	20	28	16	5	9	5	—
Quercus sp charcoal	oak	+	+	+	+	+	+	+	+	+	+	+
Waterlogged macroscopic plant remains		+	+	+	+	+	+	—	+	+	+	+
Insect remains		+	—	—	—	—	—	—	+	+	+	+
Flint flakes		+	+	+	+	+	+	+	+	+	+	—
Burnt flint fragments		+	+	+	—	+	+	+	+	+	+	—

Table 3.9 Waterlogged macroscopic plant remains from BC-II (+ = present)

		Context	2007	2007	2007	2007	2007	2007	2007	2007	2007	2003
		Sample (SO)	43 base	43 middle	43 top	43 general	38 bottom	38 middle	38	42	13	46
		Sample weight (kg)	1.0	1.0	1.0	1.0	1.0	1.0	0.76	1.0	1.0	2.0
Cornus sanguinea L	stone	Dogwood	–	–	–	–	–	–	–	–	1	–
Berula erecta (Huds) Cov	seed	Water parsnip	–	–	–	–	–	–	–	–	–	1
Rumex sp	seed	Dock	–	–	–	–	–	–	–	1	1	–
Alnus glutinosa (L) Gaert	seed	Alder	12	–	–	–	2	–	–	–	1	31
A glutinosa (L) Gaert	male catkin	Alder	1	–	–	–	–	–	–	–	–	1
A glutinosa (L) Gaert	female catkin	Alder	3	–	–	–	–	–	–	–	–	1
A glutinosa (L) Gaert.	bud scale	Alder	3	–	–	–	–	–	–	–	–	1
A glutinosa (L) Gaert	wood	Alder	–	–	–	–	–	–	–	–	–	+
Corylus avellana L	nut	Hazel	–	1	–	–	–	–	–	–	2	1
cf *C avellana* L	male catkin	Hazel	–	–	–	–	–	–	–	1	–	–
Quercus sp	acorn cupule	Oak	–	–	–	–	–	–	–	–	1	1
Quercus sp	bud scale	Oak	–	–	–	–	1	1	–	3	6	2
Quercus sp	*Andricus* sp bud gall	Oak	–	–	–	–	–	–	–	1	–	–
Quercus sp	wood	Oak	+	–	–	–	–	–	–	–	+	–
Valeriana sp	seed	Valerian	–	–	–	–	1	–	–	–	–	–
Eupatorium cannabinum L	seed	Hemp agrimony	–	–	–	–	–	–	–	–	–	2
Alisma sp	seed	Water plantain	–	–	–	–	–	–	–	–	–	4
Luzula sp	seed	Woodrush	1	–	–	–	–	–	–	–	–	–
Sparganium sp	seed	Bur-reed	–	1	–	–	–	–	–	–	–	–
Typha sp	seed	Reedmace	–	–	–	–	–	–	–	–	–	1
Schoenoplectus lacustris (L) Pal	seed	Bulrush	7	–	1	–	2	1	–	2	5	–
Carex sp	seed	Sedge	–	1	–	1	–	–	–	–	–	–
deciduous leaf fragments			–	–	–	–	–	–	+	–	+	+
Bryophyta	leafy stems	Moss	+	–	–	–	–	–	–	–	–	+

The samples were recovered from sealed contexts; even so, some of the samples had holes which had been bored into them by piddocks (*Pholas dactylus*), the shells of which remained. In addition, various other marine organisms had also entered the piddock boring. All the samples were inspected and contaminated areas cut away.

Sub-samples of up to 1kg were weighed, broken down in water and washed over a 0.2mm mesh to concentrate the organic material preserved by waterlogging. In order to recover charred fragments of hazelnut, the heavy residue remaining was sieved over a 0.5mm mesh and dried. The flots and residues were sorted for plant and invertebrate remains under a binocular microscope. The remainder of each sample was washed over a 0.2mm mesh to extract the organic fraction, and the residue sieved over a 0.3mm mesh. The organic fraction was checked under a binocular microscope for charred remains, few of which had floated, and was then subjected to

Table 3.10 Insect remains from BC-II

Context	2007	2007	2007	2007	2003
Sample (SO)	43 base	38 general	42	13	46
Sample weight (kg)	4.60	0.76	2.60	4.50	4.00
COLEOPTERA					
Dyschirius globosus (Hbst)	—	—	—	—	1
Clivina collaris (Hbst) or *fossor* (L)	—	—	1	—	—
Bembidion biguttatum (F)	—	—	—	—	1
Pterostichus strenuus (Pz)	1	—	—	—	—
Agonum sp	—	—	—	—	1
Hydroporus sp	—	—	—	—	1
Agabus sp (not *bipustulatus*)	—	—	—	1	—
Cercyon sp	1	—	—	—	—
Anacaena globulus (Pk)	—	—	1	—	1
Ochthebius cf *bicolon* Germ	—	—	—	—	1
Anthobium sp	1	—	—	1	—
Stenus sp	—	—	—	1	—
Aleocharinae indet	1	—	1	—	—
cf *Cyphon* sp	—	—	—	1	1
Melanotus erythropus (Gml)	1	—	—	—	—
cf *Axinotarsus* sp	—	—	—	1	—
Epuraea sp	—	—	—	—	1
Atomaria sp	1	—	—	—	—
Corylophus cassidoides (Marsh)	—	—	—	—	2
Donacia cf *impressa* Pk	—	—	—	—	1
Plateumaris braccata (Scop)	1	—	1	1	1
Donacia or *Plateumaris* sp	—	—	—	—	1
Prasocuris phellandrii (L)	—	—	—	—	1
Curculio venosus (Grav)	—	1	—	—	—
Rhynchaenus quercus (L)	1	—	—	1	—
Lymantor coryli (Per)	—	—	—	—	1
OTHER INSECTS					
Trichoptera indet	larva	—	—	—	—	5
Formica sp	worker	—	—	—	1	—
Diptera indet	puparium	—	—	1	—	—

paraffin flotation, washed in detergent and sorted under a binocular microscope for insect remains. The dried heavy residue was sorted for charred remains.

3.7.4 Results

Charred plant remains and the other categories of evidence are identified and quantified in Table 3.8. Table 3.9 gives the results for macroscopic plant remains and Table 3.10 gives those for insect remains. Nomenclature follows Clapham *et al* (1987) for macroscopic plant remains and Kloet and Hincks (1977) for Coleoptera.

The only contexts to contain plant remains as sedimentary deposits were 2003 and 2007. Intrusive roots were present in most of the samples. Their presence is of some interest because they grew into the sediments before they experienced marine submergence.

The presentation of organic remains was variable

in the samples from context 2007, where concentration was very low. Organic remains were better preserved in context 2003, although their concentration was again low.

3.7.5 Interpretation

3.7.5.1 Context 2007

The samples from context 2007 included taxa of both woodland and aquatic habitats. Given the high mineral content of the deposit it must be regarded as an alluvial sediment rather than an *in situ* fen on a woodland floor. Possibly context 2007 had been deposited by a stream migrating under woodland conditions. The archaeological material would have been deposited on the site at times when the bank was dry.

The waterlogged remains of trees and shrubs included seeds, catkins and buds of *Alnus glutinosa*, an acorn cupule, bud scales and wood of *Quercus* sp, nut of *Corylus avellana* and a stone of *Cornus sanguinea*. It is likely that alder carr grew in the wettest areas, while dry fen oak/hazel woodland grew elsewhere. The insect fauna was appropriate to such conditions: the Coleoptera included the oak weevil *Rhynchaenus quercus*, the weevil *Curculio venosus*, which develops in acorns, and an elaterid beetle of very rotten wood, *Melanotus erythropus*. There was also an oak bud gall which had been infested by the wasp *Andricus* sp.

The most numerous remains of aquatic plants were seeds of *Schoenoplectus lacustris* (true bulrush). Seeds of *Carex* sp and *Sparganium* sp (bur-reed) were also present. Several of the samples contained the leaf beetle *Plateumaris braccata*, whose host plant is *Phragmites australis* (common reed). It is thought that the sedimentation was occurring in an area of shallow water that received sufficient light for the growth of reedswamp vegetation. There were also remains likely to have been from plants and insects which lived at the interface between the carr woodland and the reedswamp, such as *Valeriana* sp (valerian), *Luzula* sp (woodrush), the amphibious beetle *Anacaena globulus* and the ground beetle *Pterostichus strenuus*.

Evidence for human activity was supplied by carbonised nutshell fragments of *Corylus avellana*, a little *Quercus* charcoal, small fragments of burnt flint and Mesolithic struck flint flakes. Whereas some of the waterlogged hazelnuts had rodent tooth marks, the charred nutshell fragments were certainly human food waste. The fresh state of both the nutshell fragments and the flint flakes, as well as the high concentration of remains, suggested that any reworking of material was slight. The Mesolithic settlement or encampment was likely to have been very close to the place of sedimentation, perhaps on the edge of the area of water.

The occurrence of woody roots in context 2007

suggested that sedimentation eventually created a surface upon which trees or shrubs could become established. It is possible that the roots had grown down from the fen of context 2003.

3.7.5.2 Context 2006

Organic remains, other than some very decayed root fragments, were absent from the samples from context 2006. The coarseness of the deposit implied a relatively high-energy process of sedimentation, probably on a streambed, but unfortunately other evidence is lacking.

3.7.5.3 Context 2003

The remains from the samples from context 2003 included taxa of alder-dominated woodland and of swamp or aquatic habitats. Given that context 2003 was a laminated peat, it probably represented an accumulation of organic material on the floor of a fen woodland. The most numerous remains were from *Alnus glutinosa*, with seeds, catkins, bud scales, and wood all represented. Remains of *Quercus* sp and *Corylus avellana* were also present. The bark beetle *Lymantor coryli* was further evidence for *C. avellana*. While some of the seeds of herbaceous plants were from plants of fen woodland, such as *Eupatorium cannabinum* (hemp agrimony), others were from more light-demanding species of fen or shallow water, such as *Berula erecta* (water parsnip) and *Alisma* sp (water plantain). The phytophagous beetles also suggested such conditions: present were *Prasocuris phellandrii*, which feeds on aquatic Umbelliferae, *Donacia* cf *impressa*, which feeds on *Schoenoplectus lacustris*, and *Plateumaris braccata*, which feeds on *Phragmites australis*. A full range of other fenland habitats was suggested by the insect remains. There were small water beetles such as *Hydroporus* sp and the aquatic larvae of Trichoptera (caddis flies), beetles of wet accumulations of dead plant material such as *Corylophus cassidoides* and beetles of peat surfaces such as *Agonum* sp.

Conditions during the deposition of context 2003 are suggested, therefore, to have been characterised by alder carr with some oak growing on slightly higher areas of peat and some lower, more open, areas with shallow pools in which emergent reedswamp vegetation grew. The only possible evidence for human activity comprised a very few small fragments of *Quercus* sp charcoal. Charred nutshell fragments and flint flakes were absent.

3.7.5.4 Context 2002

Organic remains contemporaneous with the deposition of context 2002 were absent. However, the silt contained rhizomes of *Phragmites australis*, suggesting an episode when the sediments formed the bed beneath fresh or brackish water before full marine submergence.

3.7.6   *Discussion*

The results showed a clear palaeoenvironmental sequence from the deposits: Mesolithic activity including flint-working and the processing of hazelnuts in oak/hazel/alder woodland alongside a stream, the deposition of flint gravel, the development of alder-dominated fen woodland, its replacement (probably as a result of rising water level) by an alluvial reedswamp and, finally, a full marine transgression. Macroscopic plant and insect evidence from earlier Holocene woodland that experienced marine submergence also comes from elsewhere on the Isle of Wight: a mid to late Neolithic peat from the inter-tidal zone at Fishbourne Beach was found to contain fragments of burnt flint that had accumulated on the floor of an oak/yew woodland; there was also a salt-marsh element to the flora, however, suggesting a stronger marine influence on the fen woodland than seen at Bouldnor Cliff.

The discovery of charred hazelnut shell fragments associated with the Mesolithic worked flint in context 2007 was of particular interest. Few Mesolithic food plant remains have been found in southern England and many terrestrial contexts of Mesolithic date have experienced bioturbation to the extent that they are not entirely secure contexts in terms of the charred food plant remains recovered from them. It was disappointing that at Bouldnor Cliff no other charred food remains were discovered bar the hazelnut shell fragments; however, reliable evidence of Mesolithic food plants from southern England is largely restricted to hazelnuts. A large assemblage of hazelnuts was found at a Mesolithic site at Thatcham but, similarly, remains of other edible plants were absent (Scaife 1992). At Westward Ho! a wide range of macroscopic plants of fen woodland had been preserved by waterlogging in a Mesolithic midden now in the intertidal zone (Vaughan 1987), but with the exception of a stone of *Crataegus* cf *monogyna* (hawthorn), hazelnut shell fragments were again the only charred remains of edible plants. Indeed, this pattern seems usual throughout temperate Mesolithic Europe (Zvelebil 1994, 41). The charring of plant remains certainly improves their chance of survival, and at Bouldnor Cliff their prospects were further enhanced by a long history of waterlogging. In these circumstances the absence of other edible food plants may well be significant. These results, along with those from Westward Ho!, are therefore of value in confirming that the predominance of hazelnut shell fragments need not simply be a bias due to the loss of other less robust food plant remains.

3.8   Fish
Alison Locker

A single fish bone was found in the upper part of context 2007. The bone was a precaudal vertebra stained dark brown and in fragile condition. It was identified as pike (*Esox lucius*), an indigenous freshwater species remaining in south-east England after the last Ice Age (Maitland and Campbell 1992, 169). The size of the vertebra – 9.4mm across the widest part of the medio-lateral width of the centrum (after Morales and Rosenlund 1979, 44, cranial view, measurement 2) and 5.7mm in length (Morales and Rosenlund 1979, 44, lateral view, measurement 2) – compares to that of an individual around 600mm+ in total length. This is not an exceptional size; Maitland and Campbell (1992, 167) cite 400–1000mm as the average range for adult pike.

Wheeler (1978, 94) describes the typical habitat for pike as lowland rivers and lakes. A predatory species, it eats other fish as well as birds and small mammals. It was an important food fish until the medieval period in Britain and is still eaten in Eastern Europe. The flesh can be dry and is often described as 'bony' owing to the intramuscular bones in larger fish. This species was also identified from Mesolithic sites at Skipsea (Yorkshire) and Foxhole and Dowell Caves (both Derbyshire) (Simmons *et al* 1981, 119), and in Neolithic and Bronze Age deposits at Runnymede by the Thames on the Surrey/Berkshire border (Serjeantson *et al* 1994, 335).

It is not possible to say whether this vertebral centrum represents human food remains. The vertebra may be a natural part of the aquatic assemblage already described for part of this deposit.

3.9   Addressing the dendrochronological resource
Nigel Nayling

The programme of dendrochronological sampling sought to exploit the potential of tree remains associated with the basal peat exposure at Bouldnor Cliff. Although considerable effort was focused on examining and sampling oaks found in close proximity to numbered loci where direct evidence for human activity had been observed, trees found in intermediate areas of the peat exposure were also sampled (Table 3.11).

This section looks at the analysis of samples from BC-II and the techniques used. The results relevant to the loci BC-V, BC-IV and Tanners Hard are presented in the appropriate chapters.

3.9.1   *Dendrochronology at Bouldnor Cliff*

Throughout the period of the study objectives at the site-specific level sought to improve understanding of the chronology of the exposed deposits and the temporal relationships between the different site

Table 3.11 Dendrochronological samples from BC-II and the immediate vicinity. Total rings = all measured rings, +value means additional rings were only counted. Sapwood rings = +HS heartwood/sapwood boundary, +?HS possible heartwood/sapwood boundary, +B bark edge. ARW = average ring width of the measured rings. Relative date of sequence = dated position in interim site mean Bouldnor_T8, or (if in brackets) in site mean Bouldnor_T3

Sample code	Comments	Total rings	Sapwood rings	ARW mm/year	Relative date of sequence
DS01	Hand-sawn non-oak sample with bark. Identified as *Alnus glutinosa*				
DS02	Chainsaw sample of substantial tree in BC-II. Same tree as DS22	145	+HS	1.59	5–149
DS03	Oak trunk plus alder (?) root	111	+?-HS	1.29	35–145
DS04	Chainsaw sample oak at western extent of BC-II	163+20h	+?HS	1.71	110–272
DS05	Void				
DS06	Chainsaw sample of substantial oak in BC-II. Same tree as DS12	242	3+HS+26s	1.11	24–265
DS07		127	35+Bw	0.65	159–285
DS08	Same tree as DS21	86	–	1.99	28–113
DS09	Hand-sawn non-oak sample				
DS10	Hand-sawn sample	55	–	1.14	undated
DS11	Hand-sawn wedge sample	<50			unmeasured
DS12	C14 wiggle-match sample. Same tree as DS06	220	+?HS	1.14	39–258
DS13	Wedge sample from large, sloping oak bole east of mapped area. Forms part of Bouldnor_T3	212	–	1.12	(54–265)
DS14	Wedge sample from non-oak tree located approximately 150m east of BC-II. Identified as *Alnus glutinosa*				
DS15	Wedge sample from oak tree located approximately 150m east of BC-II	82	+?HS	3.49	15–96
DS16	Wedge sample from oak tree in mapped area. Forms part of Bouldnor_T3	162	+	0.58	(1–162)
DS17	Wedge sample from oak tree west of mapped area	101	–	1.34	96–196
DS18	Half slice of oak tree exposed in 'drop off' to west of mapped area. Difficult to measure – many narrow rings	178	+?HS	0.56	undated
DS19	Wedge sample from oak tree exposed in 'drop off' to west of mapped area. Same tree as DS23. Forms part of Bouldnor_T3	164	+	1.00	(32–195)
DS20	Exposed during excavations in 2003. Non-oak tree bole within peat. Identified as *Alnus glutinosa*?				
DS21	Exposed during excavations in 2003 within peat. Same tree as sample DS08	120	+?HS	1.24	1–120
DS22	Substantial oak tree within peat. Tree previously sampled by chainsaw (see DS02). Wedge sample taken for checking purposes	38	–	2.73	43–80
DS23	Large oak found on drift dive of peat shelf west of BC-II. Same tree as DS19. Forms part of Bouldnor_T3	110	–	1.55	(41–150)

areas through relational dating of oak tree-ring series. Broader objectives included the development of practical methods for the *in situ* dendrochronological assessment of sub-fossil trees in submerged environments and effective sampling techniques that take into account the constraints of different diving configurations and underwater conditions. The construction of well-replicated tree-ring chronologies of Mesolithic date, predating the absolutely dated oak chronologies of Britain and Ireland, formed a wider research goal, with work at Bouldnor running in parallel with similar studies undertaken by the author as part of a Natural Environment Research Council-funded project in the Severn estuary.

The dendrochronological analysis at Bouldnor Cliff was complemented and informed by a substantial programme of radiocarbon dating of deposits and wood from the various site areas (see 3.10, below). The wiggle-match dating of sequential decadal blocks forms one of the building blocks of the Bouldnor Cliff chronology. It provides both absolute dating for the chronology and also an independent test of a proposed correlation between this chronology and those constructed from material in the Severn estuary that has also been subjected to wiggle-match radiocarbon dating (Nayling and Manning 2007).

3.9.2   Tree-ring sampling in the marine environment

The dendrochronological assessment and sampling of the wood at the Bouldnor Cliff exposures has involved a range of techniques utilised in terrestrial and intertidal contexts that were adapted for the underwater environment.

The sampling strategy was focused on the recovery from stratified oak trees of samples with sufficient rings to make them suitable for tree-ring analysis. The samples collected should *not* be considered representative of the full tree assemblage presented in the lower peat exposure at Bouldnor Cliff. A small number of samples were taken to identify non-oak elements within the peat exposure, but the majority of samples reported on here were selected solely for their dendrochronological potential.

The identification of oak underwater is not straightforward. The examination of a clean transverse face of the wood can usually be achieved, but anatomical features characteristic of the genus, such as ring-porous structure and the presence of wide, multiseriate medullary rays, can be difficult to discern in a water-saturated environment. In the case of substantial oak trees with large areas of heartwood exposed on the peat surface the black colour of the heartwood, and a characteristic finely pitted surface (the result of degradation by gribbles, *Limnoria lignorum*), can assist identification. Assessment of ring count is, perversely, made more difficult by a 'gribbled' surface to the wood. Freshly broken sections, especially at the eroding

peat edge, can provide clear cross-section views, although the larger oaks, with their inner core of robust heartwood, rarely sheer in this way, unlike fully waterlogged smaller oaks or species such as alder. In some instances, relatively small wedge samples were taken to allow examination of a part of the ring sequence of trees with apparent potential prior to extraction of a full cross-section slice. Razor blades (to clean transverse sections), a magnifier, and a strong light source help offset some of the complications of carrying out *in situ* assessment.

Once trees had been assessed and selected a variety of sampling techniques was used. Increment coring was employed with only very limited success in early trials, a range of problems being encountered. Of particular importance is the extent to which piddocks (*Pholas dactylus*) have degraded the wood, leaving numerous 'burrows'. Wood heavily damaged in this way is unlikely to provide continuous cores with complete tree-ring sequences, whereas slices normally allow extraction of the tree-ring sequence even if areas of the cross-section have been lost through such marine boring. Both handsaws and chainsaws (hydraulically powered) were therefore used to take cross-sectional slices.

Deployment of a hydraulic chainsaw requires the excavation of sufficient sediment from around the sample site to avoid fouling the chain, and an appropriately trained chainsaw operator diving on surface supply (with associated logistics). Cutting samples in this manner is relatively quick and considerably less-strenuous work for the diver than hand sawing, especially with larger trees. Offset against these advantages are the more limited range of the surface-supplied diver and the attendant costs of such diving practices. Handsaws have thus been employed to take both full cross-sectional samples and less-substantial 'wedge' samples. This approach has been undertaken while diving on SCUBA. This allows for a greater range for sampling on any one dive, and is particularly suited to exploratory surveys and assessment. Hand sawing a full cross-sectional sample from a large tree bole on SCUBA can be very hard work, however, and air consumption was the limiting factor on dive duration on SCUBA at Bouldnor when samples were being taken. The stratigraphic context of each sample taken was recorded using sketches and notes during sampling dives. Where samples were taken in the vicinity of excavations in advance of extraction of monolith samples, scale drawings of these associated features would also have been produced.

3.9.3   Assessment and analysis

Methods employed at the Lampeter Dendrochronology Laboratory in general follow those described in English Heritage 1998. Prior to measurement the samples were cleaned with razor blades to expose the fullest ring sequence. In the case of slice samples which comprised half or more of the complete cross-

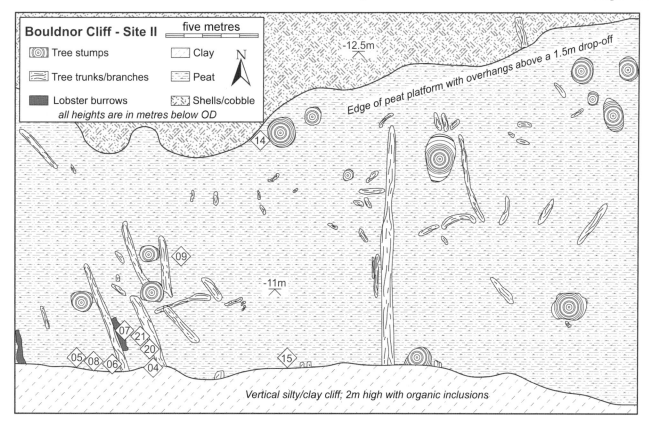

Figure 3.21   Trees on the seabed at BC-II identified by Nigel Nayling. The trees were sampled for dendrochronological analysis (Julian Whitewright after Garry Momber)

section of the parent tree, two radii were usually measured. The complete sequences of growth rings in the samples that were selected for dating purposes were measured to an accuracy of 0.01mm using a micro-computer-based travelling stage (Tyers 1999). Cross-correlation algorithms (Baillie and Pilcher 1973; Munro 1984) were employed to search for positions where the ring sequences were highly correlated. The ring sequences were plotted electronically and exported to a computer graphics software package (Coreldraw™ v.12) to enable visual comparisons to be made between sequences at the positions indicated, and, where these were satisfactory, new mean sequences were constructed from the synchronised sequences. The *t*-values reported below are derived from the original CROS algorithm (Baillie and Pilcher 1973). A *t*-value of 3.5 or over is usually indicative of a good match, although this is with the proviso that high *t*-values at the same relative or absolute position must be obtained from a range of independent sequences, and that satisfactory visual matching supports these positions.

In a few cases, more than one sample was taken from the same tree. Where this became apparent during analysis, new raw 'tree' sequences were constructed using the cross-matched sequences from each sample prior to construction of a site master. All the measured sequences from this assemblage

were then compared with each other and any found to cross-match were combined to form a site master curve.

At this stage, in a dendrochronological study focused on tree-ring dating, measured sequences and calculated site masters would be tested against a range of reference chronologies to attempt to provide calendar dates for the ring-sequences. Most of the samples from Bouldnor Cliff derive from contexts dating to the seventh millennium BC or the very earliest sixth millennium BC (see 3.10, below), but replicated, dated oak chronologies in Britain and Ireland presently extend back to *c* 5200 BC. With no absolutely dated oak chronologies from this region, useful comparison is restricted to undated prehistoric sequences, Mesolithic sequences being developed from the Severn estuary and Continental sequences.

3.9.4   Trees and dendrochronology at BC-II

The presence of a concentration of substantial tree remains on the surface of the basal peat shelf was an abiding characteristic of this area of the seabed at Bouldnor Cliff. During 1999, considerable dive time had been spent mapping these exposures, and both fallen tree boles and root systems in their growth positions were recorded (Fig 3.21).

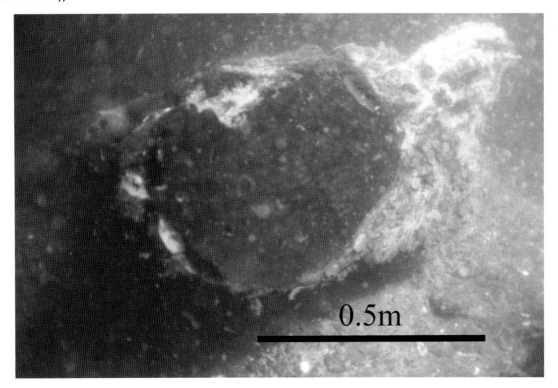

Figure 3.22   Tree on the seabed at BC-II. The tree was sampled for dendrochronological analysis (Garry Momber)

In 2000, the use of the survey vessel MV *Flatholm* allowed the deployment of divers employing surface-supplied diving equipment and a hydraulically powered chainsaw to recover samples from selected trees (see Chapter 2, 2.3). Attention was focused on the dendrochronological potential of the more substantial oak boles, most of which were oriented approximately north–south with a number seen running out from the base of the clay cliff. Trees were assessed *in situ* by the author and marked with numbered labels for sampling by surface-supply-qualified divers. Four large cross-section samples were recovered from the most substantial oaks (Fig 3.22). Additional samples were recovered from less substantial trees, mostly located in the previously mapped area (Fig 3.21), using SCUBA and a handsaw.

In 2001, a more expansive approach was taken using drift diving on SCUBA to locate trees beyond the mapped area. Seven samples were recovered from trees up to approximately 150m east of BC-II.

In 2003 dendrochronology sampling concentrated on resampling trees in the immediate vicinity of the extended evaluation trench to clarify their context and drift diving on SCUBA beyond the area mapped in 1999.

The majority of samples came from oaks, most of which were subjected to dendrochronological analysis. Four samples from the many non-oak trees present on the peat exposure were identified as alder (*Alnus glutinosa*). Ring-width series from eight oak trees were cross-matched and an interim 285-year

mean sequence constructed. Samples from a further three trees (DS13, DS16, and DS19/23) also cross-matched against one another and a further 265-year mean was constructed. The two means did not cross-match against one another.

Hamilton *et al* (see 3.10.4, below) give a date estimate of 6010–5960 cal BC (95% probability) for commencement of peat formation at BC-II. Wiggle-match dating of six successive decadal blocks of annual rings from Tree DS06/12, which forms part of the eight-tree 285-year mean, indicates that this sequence dates from 6280–6240cal BC to 6000–5960 cal BC (95% probability). Considering the assigned dates for peat inception and tree growth, even given the difficulties of interpreting events assigned date ranges of some 40 years, it is clear that this group of trees germinated before peat growth had begun, and at least four of these trees had also probably died before this. This suggests that disturbance factors other than changes in hydrological conditions (such as wind or braded channel migration) had caused the death of these trees. The relative and absolute dates for the deaths of the three latest trees (DS07, winter 285, 6000–5960 cal BC (95% probability); DS06/12, 291–308, 5990–5950 cal BC (95% probability) to 5970–5940 cal BC (95% probability); and DS04, after 302, after 5980–5950 cal BC (95% probability)) could be related to either hydrological changes associated with inception of peat growth or the later marine inundation and linked alluviation which Hamilton *et al* (see 3.10, below) date to 5990–5900 cal BC (95% probability).

3.10 Radiocarbon dating: Bouldnor Cliff

Derek Hamilton, Peter Marshall, Garry Momber, Jan Gillespie, Christopher Bronk Ramsey, and Gordon Cook

A total of 21 waterlogged wood and macrofossil samples from the submerged Mesolithic site at Bouldnor Cliff were submitted for radiocarbon dating by Accelerator Mass Spectrometry (AMS). This was performed at Scottish Universities Environmental Research Centre (SUERC), East Kilbride, and Oxford Radiocarbon Accelerator Unit (ORAU).

The samples submitted to SUERC were prepared using methods outlined in Slota *et al* (1987), and measured as described by Xu *et al* (2004). Those submitted to ORAU were prepared according to methods given in Hedges *et al* (1989) and measured as described in Bronk Ramsey *et al* (2004). Both laboratories maintain continual programmes of quality assurance procedures in addition to participation in international inter-comparisons (Scott 2003). These tests indicate no laboratory offsets and demonstrate the validity of the measurements quoted.

Furthermore, from a large cross-section of timber, six contiguous decadal blocks of wood from a floating tree-ring chronology were subsampled at the Palaeoecology Centre at Queen's University, Belfast. These samples were pretreated to hollocellulose cellulose (Green 1963), graphitised following Slota *et al* (1987), and measured by AMS at ORAU as described in Bronk Ramsey *et al* (2004).

A further two samples from Tanners Hard, two from BC-II and four from BC-V were submitted to Beta Analytic Inc. and processed and analysed according to procedures outlined on their website <http://www.radiocarbon.com>. These samples have been mentioned in the text and are applied to specific artefacts or palaeoenvironmental analysis as appropriate. They were not included in the series of dates listed as part of the analysis in Table 6.1 as they were collected during distinctly different phases of fieldwork.

The results, given in Table 6.1, are conventional radiocarbon ages (Stuiver and Polach 1977), and are quoted in accordance with the international standard known as the Trondheim convention (Stuiver and Kra 1986). The calibration of these results, relating the radiocarbon measurements directly to calendar dates, has been calculated using the calibration curve of Reimer *et al* (2004) and the computer program OxCal (v3.10) (Bronk Ramsey 1995; 1998; 2001). The calibrated date ranges for these samples are given in Table 6.1 and have been calculated using the maximum intercept method (Stuiver and Reimer 1986). They are quoted in the form recommended by Mook (1986), with the end points rounded outwards to ten years. The graphical distributions of the calibrated dates, given in outline in Figures 3.23, 4.11, 5.4 and 6.1 are derived from the probability method (Stuiver and Reimer 1993).

3.10.1 General approach

The Bayesian approach to the interpretation of archaeological chronologies has been described by Buck *et al* (1996). It is based on the principle that although the calibrated age ranges of radiocarbon measurements accurately estimate the calendar ages of the samples themselves it is the dates of archaeological events associated with those samples that are important. Bayesian techniques can provide realistic estimates of the dates of such events by combining absolute dating evidence, such as radiocarbon results, with relative dating evidence, such as stratigraphic relationships between radiocarbon samples. These 'posterior density estimates' (which, by convention, are always expressed in italics) are not absolute. They are interpretative estimates, which will change as additional data become available or as the existing data are modelled from different perspectives.

The technique used is a form of Markov Chain Monte Carlo sampling, and has been applied using the program OxCal (v3.10) <http://c14.arch.ox.ac.uk/embed.php?File=oxcal.html>, which uses a mixture of the Metropolis–Hastings algorithm and the more specific Gibbs sampler (Gilks *et al* 1996; Gelfand and Smith 1990). Details of the algorithms employed by this program are available from the on-line manual or in Bronk Ramsey (1995; 1998; 2001). The algorithms used in the models described below can be derived from the structure shown in Figures 5.4 and 6.1.

3.10.2 Wiggle-matching

Wiggle-matching was also carried out on the samples. This is the process of matching a series of radiocarbon determinations which are separated by a known number of years to the shape of the radiocarbon calibration curve. At its simplest, this can be done visually, although statistical methods are usually employed. Floating tree-ring sequences are particularly suited to this approach as the calendar age separation of different blocks of wood submitted for dating is known precisely by counting the rings in the timber. An excellent summary of the history and variety of approaches employed for wiggle-matching is provided by Galimberti *et al* (2004). A variety of the wiggle-matching approach has also been applied to validate, or choose between, different matching positions of a floating tree-ring sequence against the absolutely dated master chronologies (Bayliss *et al* 1999). The results of the wiggle-match dating are presented here in Chapter 6.

3.10.3 Objectives and sample selection

The primary objectives of the dating programme were to establish a chronology for the defined palaeoenvironmental sequence at the site and determine the chronological relationship between the human occupation and the palaeoenvironmental sequence. More specific aims included the provision of date estimates for peat formation with rising sea level, for the final marine inundation of the site, and for the floating tree-ring chronology.

The first stage in sample selection was to identify short-lived material which was probably not residual in the context from which it was recovered. The taphonomic relationship between a sample and its context is the most hazardous link in this process, since the mechanisms by which a sample came to be in its context are a matter of interpretation rather than fact. All samples consisted of single entities (Ashmore 1999). Nearly all of the material submitted from Bouldnor Cliff was waterlogged

wood remains, although one sample did consist of monocotyledon leaves.

The Bouldnor Cliff site consists of three loci where sampling for radiocarbon dating and chronological modelling took place, in addition to the radiocarbon wiggle-match. Each location has been modelled separately. The results from BC-II are presented below, while those from BC-IV and BC-V have been presented with their relevant sections.

3.10.4 Model development and analysis

BC-II was the most intensively sampled exposure for palaeoenvironmental reconstruction and radiocarbon dating. Five monoliths that had been taken

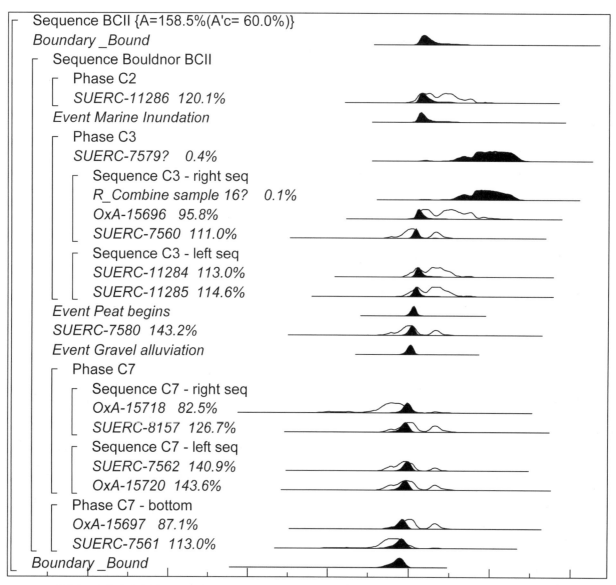

Figure 3.23 Chronological model of Bouldnor Cliff – BC-II. Figures in outline are probability distributions of the simple calibrated dates, following Stuiver and Reimer (1993), while those in solid black are the posterior density estimates *derived from the Bayesian modelling. The brackets down the left side and the OxCal keywords define the model exactly*

Table 3.12 Radiocarbon results from Bouldnor Cliff II

Lab ID	Sample ID	Material	13C (‰)	Radio-carbon age (BP)	Calibrated date (95% confidence)	Posterior density estimate (95% probability)
BC-II						
SUERC-11286	SO70 BCII 06	*Alnus glutinosa*, r/w	−28.0	7030 ± 35	6000–5840 cal BC	*5990–5890 cal BC*
SUERC-11284	SO71 BCII 06	bark, unidentified	−28.0	7060 ± 35	6020–5880 cal BC	*6000–5920 cal BC*
SUERC-7579	MS06 12 BCII	Monocotyledon leaf	−26.8	6925 ± 35	5900–5720 cal BC	–
OxA-15698	MS05 16 BCII	*Betula* sp, 10 years	−26.0	6956 ± 35		–
OxA-15721	MS05 16 BCII	*Betula* sp, 10 years	−26.2	6915 ± 40		–
mean	T'=0.6, =1, T'(5%)=3.8; Ward and Wilson 1978		–	6938 ± 26	5890–5730 cal BC	–
SUERC-11285	SO72 BCII 06	*Prunus* sp, 15mm r/w	−28.6	7065 ± 35	6000–5880 cal BC	*6010–5940 cal BC*
OxA-15696	MS08 14 BCII 03	*Alnus glutinosa*, twig	−24.4	7013 ± 36	6000–5800 cal BC	*6000–5910 cal BC*
SUERC-7560	MS08 08 BCII	*Alnus glutinosa*, r/w	−29.3	7105 ± 35	6050–5910 cal BC	*6010–5960 cal BC (90%) or 5950–5920 cal BC (5%)*
SUERC-7580	SO31 10 BCII	*Alnus glutinosa*, r/w	−22.7	7115 ± 35	6060–5910 cal BC	*6020–5970 cal BC*
SUERC-7562	MS20 03 BCII	*Alnus glutinosa*, r/w	−28.5	7130 ± 35	6070–5920 cal BC	*6030–5980 cal BC*
OxA-15718	MS08 40 BCII 03	*Corylus avellana*, twig	−27.2	7175 ± 45	6100–5980 cal BC	*6030–5980 cal BC*
OxA-15720	MS07 10-12 BCII 03	*Alnus glutinosa*, r/w, 3 years	−24.5	7125 ± 45	6070–5910 cal BC	*6040–5990 cal BC*
SUERC-8157	MS08 05 BCII	*Alnus glutinosa*, r/w	−27.7	7110 ± 40	6060–5900 cal BC	*6040–5990 cal BC*
OxA-15697	MS07 22 BCII 03	cf *Betula* sp, 7 years	−26.9	7110 ± 34	6060–5910 cal BC	*6060–5990 cal BC*
SUERC-7561	MS07 01 BCII	*Alnus glutinosa*, r/w	−29.3	7175 ± 40	6090–5980 cal BC	*6060–5990 cal BC*

from this exposure were utilised for the dating programme. The modelling for this exposure is based on the intra-monolith relationships between samples (ie direct stratigraphic order) and the relationship between samples and the identified contexts from which they were recovered. The stratigraphic section is shown in Figure 3.17, with the approximate sample locations and monolith locations marked.

The model is as follows, moving from the base to the surface. Context 2007 is an organic sand that contains many unabraded knapped flints. Two samples were submitted from the base of this context in monolith MS07 (OxA-15697 and SUERC-7561). Above these two samples, two sequences of samples came from monoliths MS07/20 and MS08. From MS07/20, the sequence is OxA-15720 followed by SUERC-7562, and from MS08 it is SUERC-8157 and OxA-15718.

Above context 2007 is a gravelly alluviation layer, context 2006, which marks the end of human occu-

pation on this land surface. Sample SUERC-7580 (sample SO31 10 BC-II) was taken at the very top of this context as part of a bulk sample.

The next event recorded in the profile is the initiation of peat formation. Six dates were obtained from five samples across three monoliths and one bulk sample from this context. These form two directly relatable sequences, with one sample (SUERC-7579) related only by having come from the same context. In the first sequence SUERC-11285 comes from the base of the peat and SUERC-11284 was taken from the top of the context. The second sequence begins with SUERC-7560 at the base of MS08, followed by OxA-15696 near the middle. At the top of this sequence are two results (OxA-15721 and OxA-15698) from sample MS05 16 BC-II.

Context 2002, overlying context 2003, is a minerogenic deposit with approximately 1mm lenses of horizontally bedded highly humified organics which has been interpreted as signifying the full marine

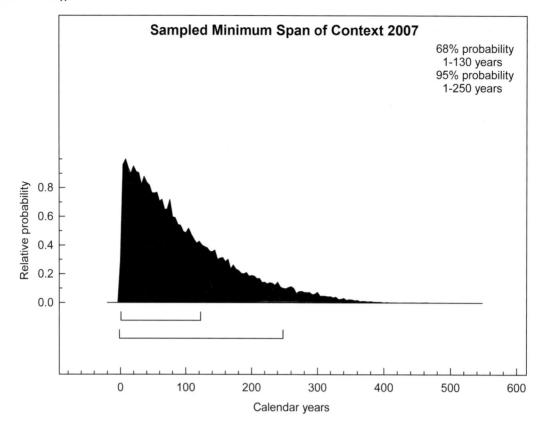

Figure 3.24   Probability distribution showing the minimum span of years between the top and bottom of context 2007, relating to the duration of the accumulation of sand and associated flint artefacts. This distribution is calculated from the model shown in Figure 3.23 (Derek Hamilton)

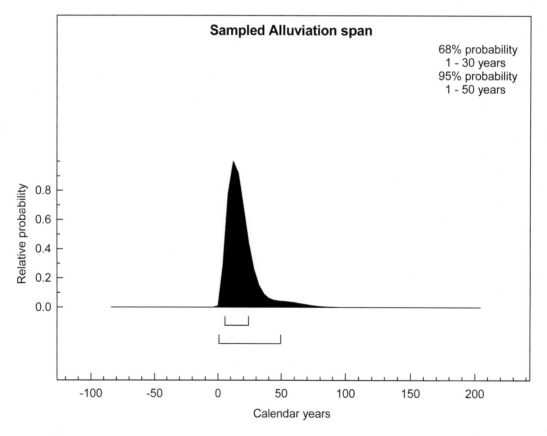

Figure 3.25   Probability distribution showing the maximum span of years between the top of context 2007 and the bottom of context 2003, relating to the accumulation of the gravelly alluvium comprising context 2006. This distribution is calculated from the model shown in Figure 3.23 (Derek Hamilton)

inundation of the site. SUERC-11286 is the only sample taken from this context.

3.10.5 Results from BC-II

The results from the radiocarbon dating models for BC-II are presented below (Table 3.12 and Figs 3.23–3.25). The quality of the results is discussed further alongside the other Bouldnor Cliff sites in Chapter 6, 6.1.

The overall index of agreement between the radiocarbon results and their stratigraphic relationships shown in the model is good ($A_{overall}$=158.5%, Fig 3.23). Three measurements show poor individual indices of agreement with their stratigraphic locations. These (SUERC-7579, OxA-15698, and OxA-15721) are from two samples from the very top of context 2003. The measurements are later than expected by their stratigraphic location. This context predates marine inundation represented by context 2002 and contained piddock burrows, and these samples may represent more recent material that has been brought down the profile through this activity. These measurements have been left out of the model.

The model estimates that alluviation of the site began in 6020–5980 cal BC (95% probability; Fig 3.23, *Gravel alluviation*) and thus provides a *terminus ante quem* for the human activity throughout context 2007. Peat formation is estimated to have begun in 6010–5960 cal BC (95% probability; Fig 3.23, *Peat begins*).

Since no material was available for dating from below context 2007, we cannot assume that the material from the bottom of that context is the oldest, as older material could have been eroded away. However, Figure 3.24 presents an estimate of the minimum time span for the accumulation of the sand and Mesolithic flints of context 2007. The model estimates the minimum duration at 1–250 years (95% probability), but the skewed shape of the probability distribution suggests that the 68% probability of 1–130 years is a more likely representation. The maximum span of years between the top of context 2007 and the bottom of context 2003, related to the accumulation of the gravelly alluvium comprising context 2006, is estimated at 1–50 years (95% probability; Fig 3.25), and more probably at 1–30 years (68% probability). Finally, the model estimates that marine inundation was complete by 5990–5900 cal BC (95% probability; Fig 3.23, *Marine inundation*).

3.11 Summary of stratigraphic layers at BC-II
Garry Momber

The analysis carried out on samples recovered from BC-II between the years 2003 and 2005 has been the most comprehensive of any of the loci investigated and it provides a benchmark for our understanding of the evolving archaeological landscape at Bouldnor Cliff. Therefore, by way of a summary, the following paragraphs selectively précis the results of the studies. The aim is to provide the reader with a summarised interpretation of the phased geomorphological processes at BC-II. The account of the evolving landscape, from the earliest deposit until it was overwhelmed by water, provides a causal framework within which cultural activities could unfold (Fig 3.26).

3.11.1 Phase one

Phase one incorporates contexts 2008, 2009, 2010, 2011, and 2012. The deepest deposit identified was poorly sorted fine to medium fluvial gravel (context 2012). This included rounded to sub-angular flint clasts with little or no matrix. The deposit was associated with a medium–coarse slightly clayey sand with evidence of reworked fine-grained alluvium (context 2011). This has been interpreted as channel lag deposits probably derived from an eroding overbank. The sediment contained randomly scattered fragmented woody and parenchymous plant macros.

A number of burnt flints were discovered in a cluster on the surface of this deposit (context 2010). This suggests human activity from the beginning of the sequence. Wood (context 2009) with a thin covering of humic peaty material (context 2008) may represent a fallen tree on the edge of a waterway that had remained long enough to accumulate organic detritus. The wood lay adjacent to context 2011. A sample of alder collected from immediately above context 2011 and next to the burnt flints is estimated to date to 6060–5990 cal BC (SUERC-7561).

It should be noted that archaeological artefacts were found in the lowermost contexts at the base of the trench. The presence of further archaeological material remaining below this level cannot be ruled out. However, it is an area that is yet to be investigated.

3.11.2 Phase two

A build-up of a fine minerogenic sandy clay above the coarser fluvial deposits marks the beginning of a new phase of deposition (context 2007). Detailed inspection showed the sandy clay to be structureless with highly humified organic fragments; it looks to be the onset of a point bar or channel lag deposit. This fine-grained material would have been associated with a fluvial channel that cut through the landscape. The phases that followed represent the accumulation of fill in the channel.

The remaining vegetation found in the deposit was predominately of woodland origin and comprised pine with oak, elm, and hazel. There was also a strong concentration of alder, which may have been growing near the site, which suggests proximity to fen. The woodland would have been growing adjacent to this fluvial feature and coincident to the build-up of context 2007. The pollen assemblages show

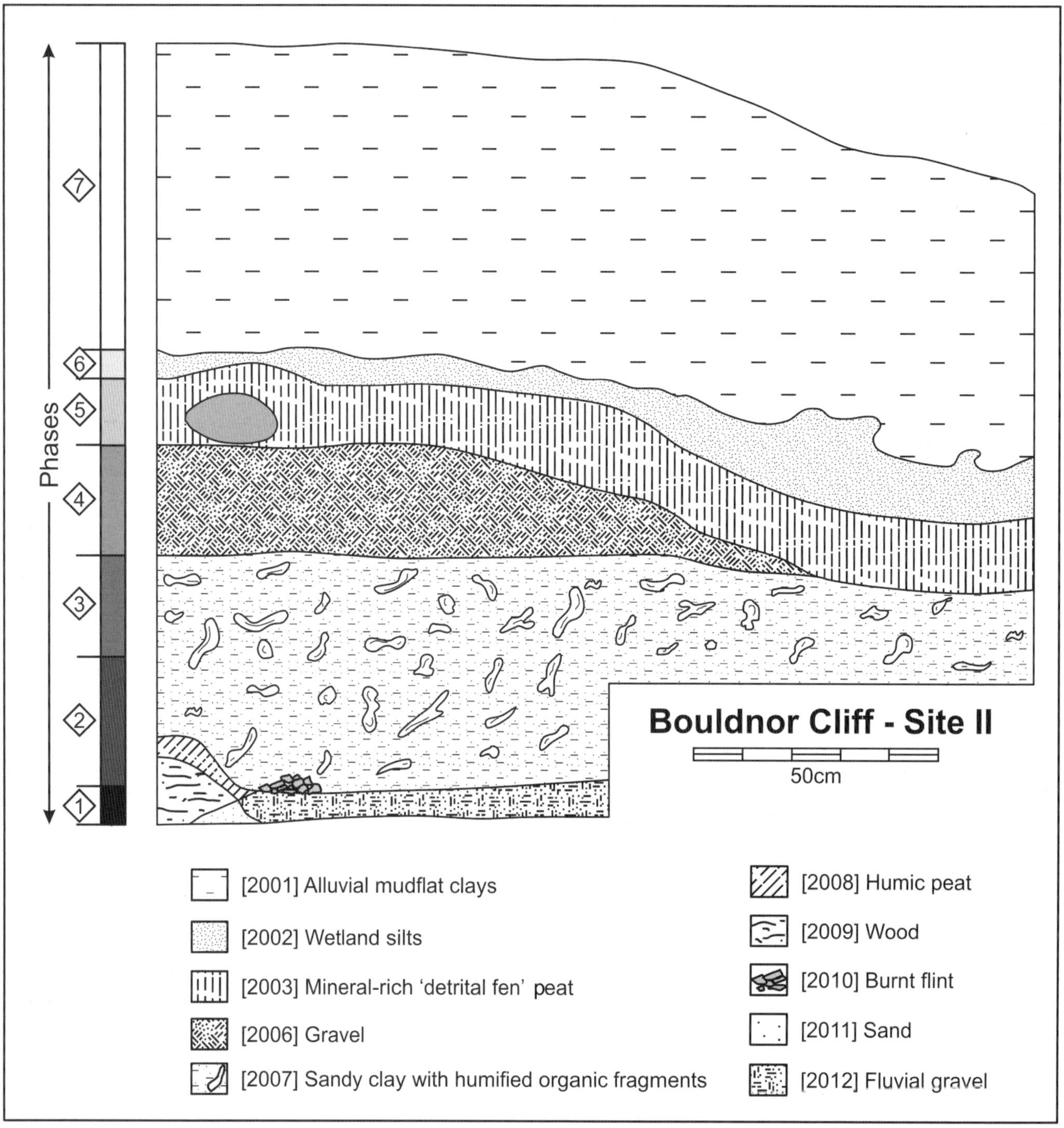

Bouldnor Cliff - Site II

50cm

[2001] Alluvial mudflat clays

[2002] Wetland silts

[2003] Mineral-rich 'detrital fen' peat

[2006] Gravel

[2007] Sandy clay with humified organic fragments

[2008] Humic peat

[2009] Wood

[2010] Burnt flint

[2011] Sand

[2012] Fluvial gravel

Figure 3.26   BC-II section with contexts/phases described (Julian Whitewright after Garry Momber)

the end of the period of Boreal pine maxima and the progressive expansion to dominance of oak and hazel. Spores of ferns were more abundant in this pollen unit than the following phase, while herbs that include Poaceae, inferring nearby grasslands, along with smaller concentrations of marsh/fen taxa, remained consistent.

Sedimentary analysis suggests some bioturbation and basic soil formation through weathering. However, the extent of pedogenic processes varies across very short distances in this localised deposit. The clearest evidence of soil formation was recorded 140mm from the top of context 2007

in MS08, although this distance varies, being doubled in MS07. The period of stabilisation marks the interface between this phase and the next.

Macrofossil samples of alder were taken from directly beneath the soil stabilisation horizon. The assemblage correlated with the pollen analysis and suggested that the deposit was formed in shallow water. The macrofossil samples from just below the soil formation horizon are estimated to date to 6040–5990 cal BC (OxA-15720 and SUERC-8157).

The sedimentation was probably occurring in an area of shallow moving water passing through woodland. The site lies towards the base of the valley, where the waterway may have slowed and levelled before arriving at the valley floor. Evidence of grasses and alder suggest more open areas with wet fen and adjacent carr. Seasonal fluctuations in water level or stream migrations would account for the recorded growth of reedswamp vegetation alongside intermittent periods of soil formation.

Humanly struck flint flakes were recovered from a monolith tin 20mm and 80mm below the layer of soil formation and evidence of charred hazelnuts was found in associated bulk samples. A number of similar flints were recovered from comparable positions within the sandy clay while it was being excavated.

It would appear that the sandy clay material that built up over the coarser fluvial deposits attracted continued human activity. The presence of lithics across the context suggests repeated visits were made to the site as the sand bar feature evolved and consolidated.

3.11.3 Phase three

The third phase was not visible to the naked eye underwater or when being visually recorded in the laboratory. It makes up the upper 150–300mm of context 2007 in the samples inspected and became apparent only following palynological and thin-section sediment analysis. The interface was delineated by a thin soil-forming boundary caused by a hiatus in the development of the sand bar. Stabilisation of the land surface is verified by pedo-features within a humic seam of mud/sand.

This change in the morphology is reinforced by variations in the pollen data. The period of soil formation was superseded by the onset of fen carr peat, and it is at this point that pine starts to decline and oak increases. Lime pollen appears for the first time, while elm, hazel, and alder remain relatively consistent. The significance of spores from ferns and shrubs continues, but this phase is defined by a marked increase in *Pteridium aquilinum*, which grows on deep well-drained soils.

The development of the sand bar continued above the stabilised and weathered soil layer to make up the upper section of context 2007. Macrofossils at the top of the context are estimated to date to 6030–5980 cal BC (OxA-15718 and SUERC-7562), indicating that the weathered soil layer's window of exposure to the atmosphere may have lasted only several years. The period of stability represented by the weathering of the soil occurred within a timeframe between the onset of phase two and the conclusion of phase three, which showed that the total sequence, encompassing both phases, was deposited during a few decades.

Evidence for human activity from context 2007 included carbonised nutshell fragments of hazel, a little oak charcoal, small fragments of burnt flint and Mesolithic struck flint flakes. The charred nutshell

fragments were human food waste. All the artefacts were well preserved, subject to minimal abrasion, and found in high concentrations.

The distribution of macrofossil and insect data associated with the humic sands throughout context 2007 supports a model where sedimentary deposits are associated with a stream migrating under woodland conditions. The result would have been a steady development of sand-bar structures where episodic periods of stabilisation permitted human activity. This was later fixed by vegetation, creating a surface upon which trees or shrubs could become established.

The process accounts for the emergent soil development and the preservation of cultural material below laminations of fluvial sediments. In addition, the fresh state of the flints and organic material suggest that reworking was minimal. Consequently, the Mesolithic activity was likely to have been very close to the place of sedimentation, perhaps on the water's edge. A fish vertebra found in association with this deposit was identified as pike (*Esox lucius*), a fish that is found in lowland rivers or lakes. It is not known whether it was foodstuff, but it can be seen as indicative of local environmental conditions.

The immediacy of water was reaffirmed by the presence of aquatic plant seeds, mainly bulrush. Additional remains of plants, such as the woodrush, and of insects, which included amphibious as well as ground beetles, were diagnostic of carr woodland. A wider human influence on the landscape is suggested by bracken spores. These infer disturbed ground, especially burnt ground, associated with human activity.

3.11.4 Phase four

Phase four is represented by context 2006, which is composed of rounded angular gravel deposited during a high-energy process of sedimentation. It is a localised event and occurs only in the east side of the trench. Similar isolated outcrops have been recorded at other locations below the peat platform. The coarse nature of the deposit and the absence of any discernable stratification within the context suggest that it was formed rapidly. An alder macro-fossil from the top of context 2006 was estimated to date to 6020–5970 cal BC (SUERC-7580).

The fluvial deposits recorded in phases one to four are localised to BC-II, where they cut through the submerged forest of the palaeo-land surface. The relic channel appears to continue to the west, while to the east the woodland bench sits directly on grey lacustrine clay.

3.11.5 Phase five

The phase that followed the high-energy events of phase four was somewhat more sedate, allowing the build-up of vegetation, the remains of which have now become peat (context 2003). The organic layer runs across the surface of the gravel in the east to the west where it dips to marry up with the top of context 2007. Phase five is associated with the development of context 2003 above context 2007.

Context 2003 is a mineral-rich 'detrital fen' peat. The boundary between the top of context 2007 and the base of context 2003 is transitional, suggesting that there was not enough time for erosion to occur before the formation of the peat. Very weak horizontal bedding towards the base of the context is indicated by moderately to strongly decomposed vegetation fragments. The upper part of the context has probably eroded; strongly oxidised and desiccated peat suggests a significant period of lowered groundwater levels. The shrinkage caused by drying resulted in textural pedofeatures in the form of cracks with well-sorted infills.

The pollen record shows an increase in oak, while pine declines. However, alder comes to dominate in the second part of this phase of peat accumulation. The growth in alder coincides with reductions in spore taxa from ferns and an increase in the importance of grasses. Macrofossils confirm the development of an alder-dominated woodland and of swamp or aquatic habitats where the laminated peat probably represented an accumulation of organic material on the floor of a fen woodland. The overall interpretation includes alder carr with some oak growing on slightly higher areas and some lower, more open areas with shallow pools in which emergent reedswamp vegetation grew. The woodland identified at this level appears to have re-established itself once the point bar or channel lag deposit had been covered by the gravels of context 2006 laid down in phase four.

A few small fragments of oak charcoal suggested human activity, although charred nutshell fragments and flint flakes were absent. A macrofossil sample from the middle of the deposit is estimated to date to 6000–5910 cal BC (OxA-15696), and a macrofossil sample from the top of the deposit to 6000–5920 cal BC (SUERC-11284).

3.11.6 *Phase six*

This phase, represented by context 2002, sees an increasingly 'wet' environment, with the development of marsh and salt marsh. Positive eustatic changes were causing local groundwater tables to rise. The wetlands were initially freshwater, although nearby saline brackish water or marine influences are indicated by Chenopodiaceae and *Aster*-type pollen. There is also an increase in grasses and reedswamp/fen taxa with occasional aquatic plants and algal *Pediastrum*. In the surrounding landscape pine continues to decline while oak remains important, as does alder, which peaks in the pollen record.

The appearance of the foraminifera *Trocham-*

mina, the high salt-marsh species, at the interface between context 2002 and the covering grey silt indicates the transition from marsh to brackish water mudflat. Curiously, there is an abundance of planktonic and continental shelf species (*T. cimingodobe* and *N. pachyderma*) within the transitional deposit. There is also an increase in the numbers of the diatom *Paralia sulcata*, which may represent deeper water following a flooding event (see 3.6.1, above). This all suggests a fairly rapid rise in sea level resulting in deeper water and a process of resedimentation from nearby pre-Quaternary cliffs. Alternatively, it could have been a single event causing transportation of allochthonous marine taxa and introducing new diatoms into this habitat.

A macrofossil sample from the top of the deposit is estimated to date to 5990–5890 cal BC (SUERC-11286).

3.11.7 *Phase seven*

The final phase represents the total submergence of the loci under study and, by implication, the whole Bouldnor Cliff peat shelf below *c* –10.5m OD. The sediments in this context (2001) are homogeneous alluvial mudflat clays with a soft 'cream cheese' consistency.

Stratigraphical change caused by alluvial or marine sediments is accompanied by a significant change in the pollen spectra, notably the introduction of saline-tolerant plants (halophytes) such as Chenopodiaceae, or the coastal-growing thrift and/or sea lavender, among others. This reflects both changes in taphonomy (especially transport and pollen sources) and vegetation environment. Changes in sediment source resulted in the introduction of reworked pre-Quaternary (Tertiary) pollen and spores from bedrock or earlier Pleistocene or Holocene sediments. It should also be noted that grasses (Poaceae) were continuing to increase. Oak, hazel and elm remained the dominant woodland taxa but, along with alder, these appear less important in the immediate vicinity owing to inundation and sediment accretion.

Foraminifera found near the top of the monolith, approximately 300mm above the phase six transition, were primarily typical mudflat fauna *Ammonia beccarii*, *Elphidium excavatum*, and *Haynesina germanica*. The planktonic and continental shelf species (*T. cimingodobe* and *N. pachyderma*) were found episodically in this sedimentary unit.

Diatoms were also recovered from the finer-grained sediments within this context. The assemblage is characteristic of brackish water environments and taxa which are frequently found in salt-marsh habitats. Marine and brackish water centrales are present, with *Paralia sulcata*, *Coscinodiscus* and *Actinoptychus senarius*. The presence of *Nitschia navicularis* is diagnostic for salt marshes. A small number of diatoms may derive from freshwater habitats (eg *Epithemia*), probably from rivers and streams exiting into the system.

This phase/zone clearly represents an expansion of sea level that covered the landscape. Total inundation of BC-II occurred shortly after 5990–5890 cal BC.

4 Archaeological, palaeoenvironmental, and morphological investigations at BC-V

by Garry Momber, Rachel Bynoe, Geoff Bailey, Rob Scaife, Nigel Nayling, Derek Hamilton, Peter Marshall, Jan Gillespie, Christopher Bronk Ramsey, Gordon Cook, and Maisie Taylor

4.1 Introduction – the first phase of investigation

Garry Momber, Rachel Bynoe, and Geoff Bailey

Bouldnor Cliff V (BC-V) is being eroded from the northern edge of the basal peat platform. It lies at –11.4 to –11.6m OD 420m west-south-west of BC-II. Here, the deposit has thinned, exposing patches of the relic Mesolithic occupied land. From this location came some of the oldest artefacts recovered from the submerged peat platform to date. The first two archaeological features associated with the area were found in the autumn of 2004 and have since been monitored and sampled by the HWTMA over several years. Both features have been seen to degrade rapidly. The first phase of work at BC-V recorded and sampled these features before, in 2007, a second phase of work began, including the rescue excavation of the remaining elements and the opening up of an evaluation trench across timbers that became exposed as a result of erosion immediately to the south. Further samples were recovered for analysis. This phase of work continued until 2010.

4.2 A pit full of burnt flint

The first composite feature discovered was a pit full of burnt flint (BC-V/CF01). This had been sectioned by erosion and its contents were found spilling out onto the seabed below; an unknown amount was lost. The portion remaining, which measured 450mm wide by 400mm deep, had a clear outline, indicating that it had been dug into the old clay land surface (Fig 4.1). Its uppermost fill, a soft organic humic silty clay, overlay burnt material comprising clay nodules, charcoal, and burnt lithics. The feature was capped by woody peat and a large flat piece of timber. The seabed at this point measures –11.55m (± 0.15m) OD.

Three radiocarbon dates were collected from samples recovered in the monolith MS01, taken through the centre of this pit. They included an unidentified root (at –11.66m ± 0.1m) plus two pieces of alder twig (*Alnus glutinosa*) at –11.74m and –11.83m ± 0.1m. The dates are MS01 31: 6080–

5990 cal BC (OxA-15722); MS01 38.5: 6100–6000 cal BC (OxA-15723); and MS01 48: 6120–6010 cal BC (OxA-15699; 89% probability), respectively.

In 2007 the final section of the pit was removed. It was excavated and transported to the surface in a prepared lifting crate. Examination on shore revealed a few remaining burnt flints embedded in humic material and darkened clay. Burnt layers were evident on the back wall of the pit, which showed signs of repeated heating. It seems that the hollow was used by being filled with heated stones on more than one occasion (Fig 4.2).

4.3 Layered timbers and stratified cultural material

The second composite feature was recorded 1.3m to the west of the pit (see Chapter 1, 1.3.5, Fig 1.13). It comprised a roughly circular mound around 100–150mm in height and 2.1m in width consisting of mixed timber elements of differing shapes and sizes (BC-V/CF02). The range and variety of wooden pieces – flattened pieces of wood above a layer of roundwood – make it unique among timber features recorded in the submerged land surface. It was more resilient than adjacent material and, as such, its western edge protruded from the top of the cliff by over a metre. Unfortunately, this was snagged by lobster pots, which resulted in damage and accelerated degradation. Over the course of two years, weathering and biological attack resulted in the loss of the flat pieces of wood from the surface of the timber structure, revealing the parallel arrangements of roundwood below (Fig 4.3). The feature was recorded both before and after the timber elements were lost to erosion (Figs 4.4 and 4.5).

Stratification was evident within and below the matrix of interwoven timber. The top layer of flat and roundwood timber pieces was set in a fine humic peat (context 5016). Immediately beneath lay a mottled grey clay that felt gritty to the touch. Sampling revealed that this deposit contained burnt flint, burnt flint flakes and blackened organics held within a clayey-silt matrix (context 5017) 150mm thick and apparently resting on a basal horizon of

Figure 4.1 Eroded remains of pit containing burnt flint underwater at BC-V in 2006 (Garry Momber)

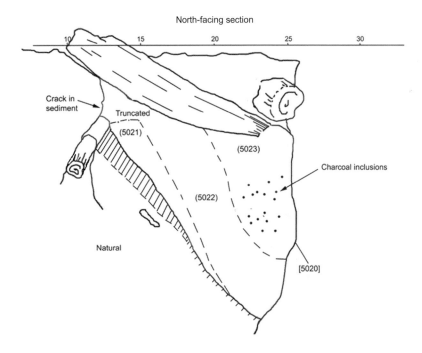

Figure 4.2 Section across feature BC-V CF01. The context numbers show different fill deposits, indicating repeated use. The natural soil on the edge is heat blackened (see Context register, Appendix 1) (Rachel Bynoe after Penny Spikins)

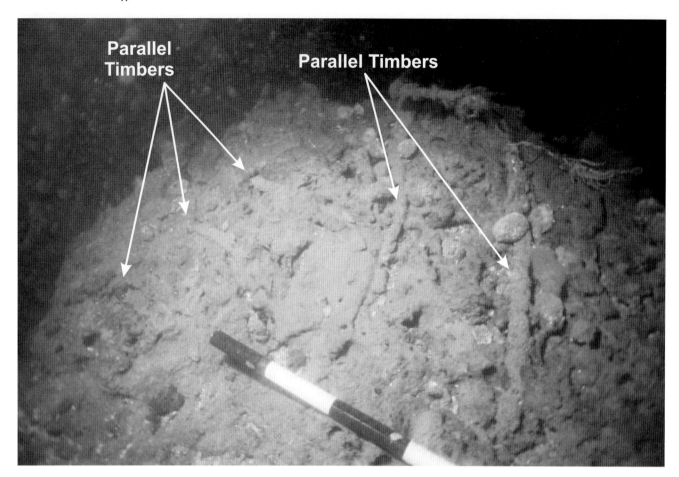

Figure 4.3   This image, taken in 2006, shows the loss of covering sediments and timbers from BC-V (see Fig 1.13 for timber elements before erosion), revealing a platform with regularly orientated pieces of roundwood (Garry Momber)

twigs (context 5018). The whole of this intercalated mixture of sandy silt and cultural remains could be seen in the naturally cut section (Fig 4.6). This was an arrangement not dissimilar to that described by Ole Grøn at the Mesolithic site of Møllegabet II, Denmark (Skaarup & Grøn 2004, 41), where a similar feature was interpreted as an elevated platform associated with a living space.

Protruding from context 5018 in the cliff face were two pieces of roundwood. One of the pieces of wood, which sat 350mm below the top of the peat drop-off (–11.8m OD ± 0.1m), was extracted from the section with a trowel and paintbrush and given the reference BC-V/S06. The lower part of the wood BC-V/S06 formed a fork which, where it extended into the clay below (context 5019), straddled the layer of twigs. The upper part of the wood retained markings suggesting that it was alder or birch, was 50mm in diameter and was impaled with a burnt flint flake (Fig 4.7). It is unclear whether the flint was forced into the wood through natural forces once buried or deliberately by humans; however, the fact that it was humanly struck in the first place provides tangible evidence of anthropogenic activity (Momber and Campbell 2005).

The roundwood sample BC-V/S06 was radiocarbon dated to 6100–5880 cal BC (8060–7830 cal BP) (Beta-209564), and a sample from the layer of twigs

(BC-V 05 S101) to 6240–6000 cal BC (8200 to 7960 cal BP) (Beta-207809). Both samples came from the same depth, although it is probable that the younger sample (BC-V/S06) found its way into the ground at a later date. If this were the case it may have been an integral part of the platform feature BC-V/CF02, which could have been constructed later than the layer of twigs was laid down (see 4.11, below).

In 2006, two years after the discoveries were made, evidence of piddock (*Pholas dactylus*) infestation was abundant and the site had become peppered with holes up to 30mm in diameter. These penetrated for more than 0.5m into the silt. Once timber became exposed it was susceptible to erosion by tidal action and to degradation by the wood-boring gribble *Limnoria lignorum*. Further damage was caused by the dragging of fishing gear and lobster pots across the site (see Chapter 13).

4.4   Pollen analysis across BC-V
Rob Scaife

Two vertical monolith samples (MS01/BC-V and MS02/BC-V) were collected from BC-V/CF01 and BC-V/CF02 respectively (Fig 4.8). Both monoliths had their bases at –11.5m ± 0.15m OD. Pollen analysis

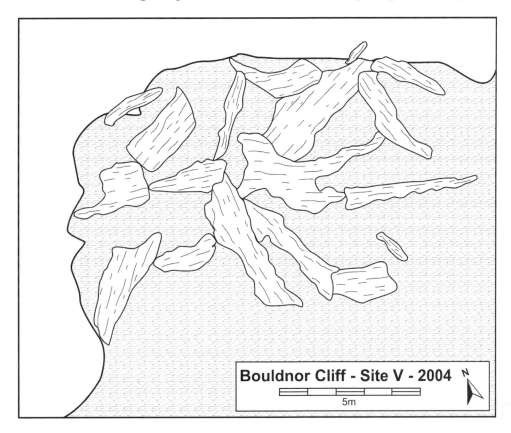

Figure 4.4   BC-V, 2004 survey plan, showing 'plank-like' pieces of timber on a promontory exposed on the top of the eroding cliff. The hatched areas represent peat below the timber (Julian Whitewright after Garry Momber)

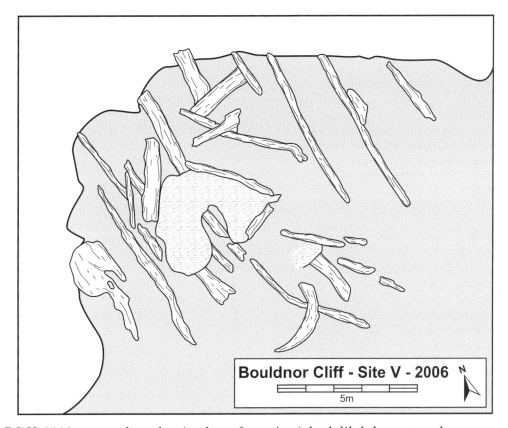

Figure 4.5   BC-V, 2006 survey plan, showing loss of covering 'plank-like' elements and exposure of regularly laid roundwood. The hatched areas represent the remains of peat above the timber (Julian Whitewright after Garry Momber)

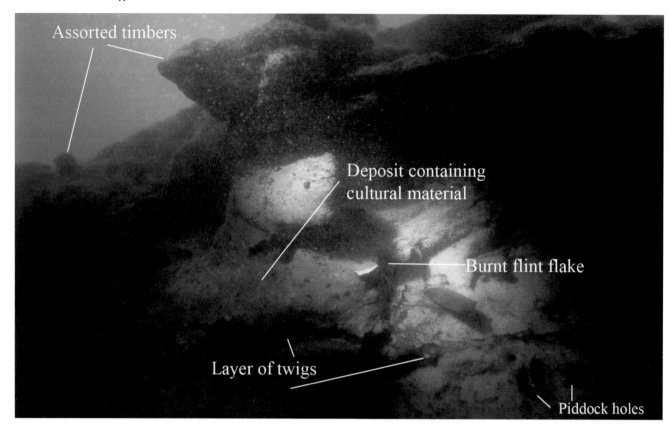

Figure 4.6   Cliff section below platform BC-V/CF02. Anthropogenic features are highlighted (Garry Momber)

was carried out on both pollen profiles (Scaife 2005). Sub-fossil pollen and spores were recovered from the upper, more humic sediments, but are poorly preserved in the lower mineral contexts.

4.4.1   Sample BC-V/CF01/MS01

4.4.1.1   Stratigraphy

The profile comprised 0.4m of wood and humic mineral sediments containing evidence of archaeo-logical activity, charcoal, and burnt flints. The top of the column was recorded at –11.54m ± 0.1m OD; the bottom was at –11.94m ± 0.1m OD (Fig 4.9). The stratigraphy as recorded from the monolith profile is presented in Table 4.1.

4.4.1.2   Pollen zonation

Pollen was absent from the lowest levels (pale grey clay), and above this the assemblages are dominated by trees and shrubs. Few herb taxa are present. Two

Table 4.1   Stratigraphy as recorded in the monolith profile MS01

Depth (mm)	
0–60mm	Large wood (trunk) fragment (*Quercus*)
60–200mm	Grey humic silt with charcoal fragments at 90mm
200–340mm	Massive wood fragment with burnt flint at 220–260mm
340–380mm	Pale grey clay containing branch wood at 360–380mm

Table 4.2   Stratigraphy as recorded in the monolith profile MS02

Depth (mm)	
0–200mm	Void
200–320mm	Trunk wood (*Quercus*)
320–640mm	Fine grey silt and clay containing occasional twigs and root remains. A more distinct horizon of twigs at 440mm

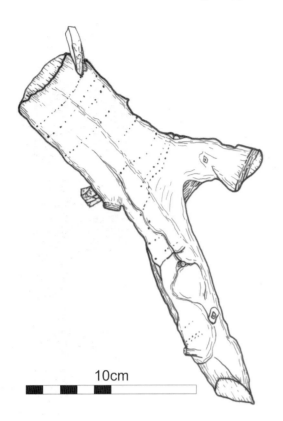

Figure 4.7 Alder impaled with burnt worked flint. Recovered eroding from cliff edge below platform BC-V / CF02 (Garry Momber)

local pollen assemblage zones have been recognised. These are described from the base of the profile upwards (below).

l.p.a.z. BC-V / MS01:1. 320mm Pinus–Corylus avellana *type*

This is a single level but differs from subsequent pollen assemblages in having higher percentages of *Pinus* (20%) and *Corylus avellana* type (52%). There are also higher values of derived pre-Quaternary palynomorphs.

l.p.a.z BC-V / MS01:2. 300mm to 80mm Quercus–Alnus glutinosa–Corylus avellana *type*

Pinus values are reduced (c 10%). *Alnus glutinosa* expands to high values (47% at 240mm) with *Quercus* (20%) and *Corylus avellana* type (45–55%). *Ulmus* is consistently present in small values. *Salix* occurs sporadically. There are few herbs, with only sporadic occurrences of Poaceae, Cyperaceae and *Typha/Sparganium* type. Spores are dominated by *Polypodium vulgare* (to 23%), with monolete (*Dryopteris* type) forms (to 6%).

4.4.2 Sample BC-V/CF02/MS02

4.4.2.1 Stratigraphy

This profile comprises two columns consisting of an upper woody context underlain by humic silts of similar character to those of BC-V/CF01/MS01, described above. The top of the column is recorded at –11.50m ± 0.15m OD, and the bottom at –11.94m ± 0.15m OD (Fig 4.10). The stratigraphy as recorded from the monolith profile is presented in Table 4.2.

4.4.2.2 Pollen zonation

Samples were taken and examined from the base of the upper wood at 320mm downwards to 640mm. Pollen was absent in the basal level. Taxonomic diversity was low; trees and shrubs were dominant, and there were substantial numbers of fern spores in the lower levels. Two local pollen assemblage zones have been identified and are characterised from the base of the profile upwards (below).

Zone BC-V / MS02:1. 600mm to 500mm Pinus–Quercus–Corylus avellana *type*

This zone falls within the lower humic silt. Trees and shrubs are dominated by *Pinus* (to 20%) and

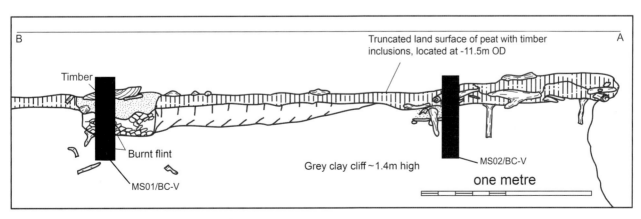

Figure 4.8 Plan of the natural section below platform. The naturally eroded section across the features at BC-V showed elements that appeared very unnatural. Monolith samples were collected and the erosion was monitored (Julian Whitewright after Garry Momber)

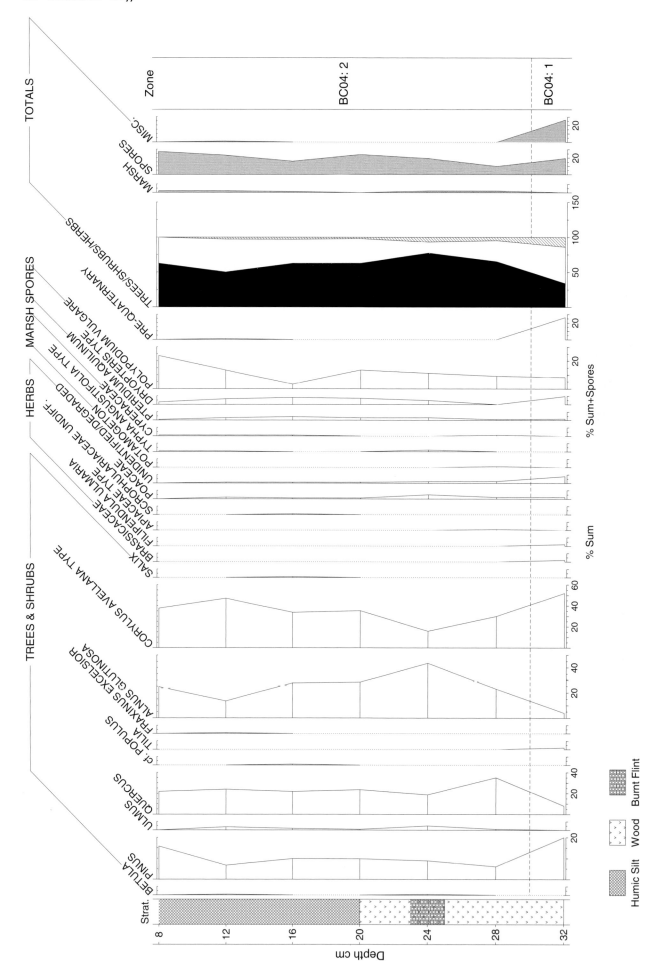

Figure 4.9 Pollen diagram of BC-VMS01 (Rob Scaife)

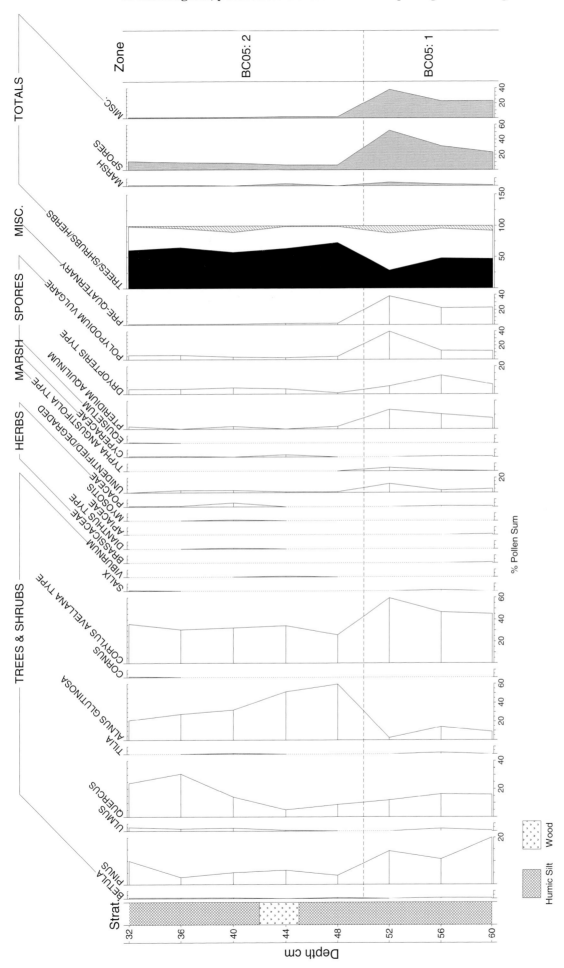

Figure 4.10 Pollen diagram of BC-VMS02 (Rob Scaife)

Corylus avellana type (to 60% at 520mm), with *Quercus* (17%). There are low values of *Alnus glutinosa* (12%), *Ulmus* (<1%), *Salix* (<1%) and *Tilia* (<1% and possibly derived from the local Tertiary basement lithology). There are few herbs, with only sporadic occurrences of grasses and fen/marsh taxa. Spores of ferns are dominated by *Polypodium vulgare* (to 38% sum + spores). Derived/reworked pre-Quaternary microfossils are abundant and include both Cretaceous and Tertiary forms.

Zone BC-V / MS02:2. 500mm to 320 mm Quercus–Alnus glutinosa–Corylus avellana *type*

This zone is characterised by reductions in *Pinus* (5–10%) and *Corylus avellana* type (30–35%), and expansions of *Alnus glutinosa* (peak to 58%) and *Quercus* (to 37% at 360mm). There are few herbs, and the spores and derived palynomorphs of the preceding zone are greatly diminished.

4.4.3   Discussion: the past vegetation and environment

Both pollen sequences have been subdivided into local pollen assemblage zones for the purposes of description and interpretation. Zone MS01:1 is less well defined than MS02:1 and would require additional analysis to confirm differences from overlying levels of zone MS01:2. The pollen-bearing levels appear to extend deeper at the former site (MS01). There are, however, close similarities with this zone and zone MS02:1. The lower levels of both profiles have higher values of pine (*Pinus*) and probably hazel (*Corylus avellana* type). The local and on-site vegetation comprised oak (*Quercus*) and hazel woodland, perhaps with some local pine, although this may have been wind-transported from adjacent regions. Alder (*Alnus glutinosa*) is present only in small quantities, which does not suggest local growth but is, nevertheless, an indication of the progressive migration of alder into the region culminating in its local importance. Dominance of woodland on or close to the site is evidenced by the paucity of herb pollen. Spores of ferns reflect the local ground flora and, in the case of common polypody fern (*Polypodium vulgare*), growth on trees (probably oak).

Change to zone 2 in both profiles is represented by a reduction in pine and hazel woodland and expansions of local alder, oak, and probably elm and ash (*Fraxinus excelsior*, in MS01). The importance of oak and hazel on-site has been evidenced by macrofossils including the substantial oak trunks which overlie both sequences. It is probable that this represents a damp carr-type woodland with oak, hazel, and possibly ash on drier areas of a river floodplain, while alder, which had become relatively more important, colonised wetter areas as carr woodland or growth fringing the rivers and streams. Charcoal and struck flints/artefacts within these upper

humic sediments attest to local and on-site Mesolithic activity/habitation in this environment. It is possible that further analysis may show evidence of localised woodland disturbance.

4.4.4   Dating of the sequences and comparison with other locations

The subdivision of the two pollen profiles into two pollen zones of broadly similar vegetation characteristics and changes is a function of their close spatial proximity. Both profiles demonstrate ecological change from an environment in which pine was an important woodland component to one where oak and alder (and to a lesser extent, other deciduous elements) became locally important. These changes clearly took place at the end of Flandrian Chronozone I (Fl. Ic), the late Boreal period, and this is corroborated by the sequence of radiocarbon dates collected from the site. The changes were a function of two principal factors: first, the demise of pine was caused by the progressive expansion of successional oak and elm, which out-competed pine; and, second, rapidly rising relative sea level during the early Holocene was responsible for the changing depositional environment of the site and was associated with the creation of suitable habitats for migrating alder and ultimately peat formation. The period was one of dynamic vegetation and environmental change immediately prior to the more stable and established environments of the middle Holocene (Atlantic) period (Flandrian Chronozone II).

The reduction of pine and the expansion of alder and oak described here are also seen in profiles from BC-II (Scaife 2004a; Scaife in Chapter 3, 3.5). Lime (*Tilia*) pollen is not present in any quantity in these profiles: this tree became dominant from the very late Boreal and usually from the early Atlantic period (ie after *c* 5900 cal BC) and is clearly seen in the upper levels of profile MS10 from BC-IV (Scaife 2004b) and at Tanners Hard (Chapter 7, 7.3), both sites being middle Holocene in date.

4.5   Dendrochronological samples
Nigel Nayling

Few remains of oak wood potentially suitable for dendrochronological analysis were identified during a number of dives in the vicinity of BC-V (Table 4.3). One medium oak stem from the peat platform close to the pit feature BC-V/CF01 was sampled twice (DS32/3). The combined tree-ring sequences from this piece cross-matched against the interim 285-year area mean for BC-II (Bouldnor_T8) (Chapter 3, 3.9). Wiggle-match dating of the site mean indicates germination of the parent tree in the date span 6244–6204 cal BC (95% probability). With no surviving sapwood or bark edge, a *terminus post quem* of after 6150–6110 cal BC can be given for the death of this tree. As with BC-II, death could have

Table 4.3 Dendrochronological samples from BC-V. Total rings = all measured rings. Sapwood rings = +B bark edge. ARW = average ring width of the measured rings. Relative date of sequence = dated position against interim site mean Bouldnor_T8

Publication sample code	Comments	Total rings	Sapwood rings	ARW mm /year	Relative date of sequence
DS32	Oak roundwood	92	–	1.41	46–137
DS33	Probable repeat of DS32	95	–	1.59	44–138
DS34	Unnumbered sample of upright	119	28+B	0.51	undated

occurred before peat inception, which was linked to the end of use of the pit feature, for which an abandonment date range of 6150–6010 cal BC has been given. The cross-matching of tree-ring sequences from BC-V with those from BC-II points to contemporaneity of some of the material recovered from those two areas, a view which is confirmed by the radiocarbon results (Tables 3.12 and 4.4). The results indicate that oaks growing in the vicinity of BC-II and BC-V in the late seventh millennium BC, during Mesolithic activity in the area, became encapsulated within subsequent peat accretion.

4.6 Radiocarbon dating: model development and analysis
Derek Hamilton, Peter Marshall, Garry Momber, Jan Gillespie, Christopher Bronk Ramsey, and Gordon Cook

This locus contained evidence of *in situ* human activity with datable material from a secure context. In 2004, therefore, three samples were collected from BC-V for radiocarbon dating, and the results were modelled with comparable dates collected as part of the English Heritage contribution to the work at Bouldnor Cliff. The results are presented in Table 4.4.

The dates from both BC-V and BC-II were refined using Bayesian techniques to aid interpretation of archaeological chronologies, and the longer series of dated stratigraphic horizons from BC-II formed a baseline against which the dates collected at BC-V could be compared. A full description of the methods used to select and analyse the samples is presented in Chapter 3, 3.10. The results are discussed in relation to the other radiocarbon dates collected from along Bouldnor Cliff in Chapter 6, 6.1.

The three samples of waterlogged wood used for dating came from the monolith BC-V/CF01/MS01. Relative depths for the samples can be obtained from the base of the monolith, measured to –11.54m OD ± 0.1m. The following sub-samples were extracted from monolith BC-V/MS01 at 0.48m, 0.385m and 0.31m respectively.

• MS01 48 BC-V (7203 ± 36 cal (OxA-15699)) was recovered from the pit at 280mm down the sequence. It came from just above the basal part of feature BC-V/CF01 and was surrounded by burnt flints and fired clay nodules.
• MS01 38.5 BC-V (7170 ± 45 (OxA-15723)) was recovered from the base of the peat that formed over and capped the pit at 185mm depth. This layer of material was deposited after the feature fell into disuse.
• MS01 31 BC-V (7230 ± 45 (OxA-15722)) was also recovered from the peat that capped the feature, but from 75mm further up the profile, 110mm below the surface.

4.6.1 Results

The model for the three dates from monolith MS01 taken at locus BC-V shows good overall agreement between the radiocarbon results and their stratigraphic relationships ($A_{overall}$=105.3%). The model estimates that the pit was no longer in use by 6150–6010 cal BC (95% probability; Figure 4.11; *end hearth use*).

BC-V is 424m away from and 0.7m below BC-II (height taken from the top of the peat in monoliths MS08 and MS01). Figure 4.12 shows that there is a 99.9% probability that the pit at BC-V was out of use before gravel accumulation began at BC-II.

Table 4.4 Radiocarbon dates from BC-V

Lab ID	Sample ID	Material	13C (‰)	Radiocarbon age (BP)	Calibrated date (95% confidence)	Posterior density estimate (95% probability)
OxA-15722	MS17 31 BCV	?root, unidentified	–28.3	7230 ± 45	6220–6010 cal BC	*6080–5990 cal BC*
OxA-15723	MS17 38.5 BCV	*Alnus glutinosa*, twig	–27.2	7170 ± 45	6100–5980 cal BC	*6100–6000 cal BC*
OxA-15699	MS17 48 BCV	*Alnus glutinosa*, twig	–27.4	7203 ± 36	6210–6000 cal BC	*6210–6190 cal BC (2%) or 6180–6140 cal BC (4%) or 6120–6010 cal BC (89%)*

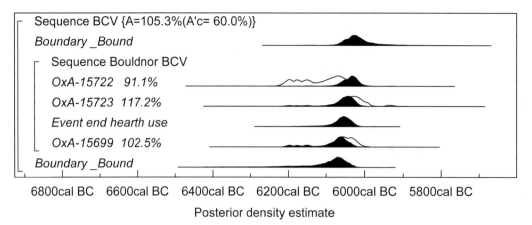

Figure 4.11   Chronological model of Bouldnor Cliff – BC-V. Figures in outline are the probability distributions of the simple calibrated dates, following Stuiver and Reimer (1993), while those in solid black are the posterior density estimates derived from the Bayesian modelling. The brackets down the left side and the OxCal keywords define the model exactly (Derek Hamilton)

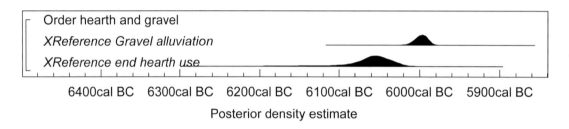

Figure 4.12   Order function that calculates a 99.9% probability that the hearth at BC-V was no longer in use when the gravel was accumulating at BC-II (Derek Hamilton)

4.7   Renewed research at BC-V
Garry Momber, Rachel Bynoe, and Geoff Bailey

In 2006 the base of a roundwood post (SO39) was found 21m to the west of the flint-filled pit (Fig 4.13). It had been trimmed at one end and appeared to have been forced deliberately into the relict land surface. The surviving section was 0.32m long and lay 0.8m below the surface of the peat. It had become exposed as the seabed sediments were eroded from around it and appeared to retain tool marks suggesting that it had been worked. A small piece of wood that had been broken and bent beneath the tip of the post indicated that it had been forced into the ground. The timber was subsequently analysed and the manufacturing marks were characterised (see Chapter 4, 4.8)

In the same year funds were secured from the Leverhulme Trust through the University of York to allow a survey and rescue excavation. Additional funds were provided by the Royal Archaeological Institute and the HWTMA. The main objectives were the planning and recovery of BC-V/CF01 and BC-V/CF02, as well as investigation for more archaeological evidence.

4.7.1   *Methodology*

The 2007 season saw an extended survey grid set up on the seabed to cover an area that encompassed BC-V/CF01, BC-V/CF02 and SO39. Four 30m baselines were laid out on the top of the peat platform parallel with the northern edge of the cliff. They were positioned 1m apart and were held firm with fixed fibreglass pins pushed into the seabed every 5m. The grid was calibrated with a tape measure and subdivided into 1m squares, each of which was given a unique reference number (Fig 4.14). Visual inspections were conducted along the grid and areas were identified for more detailed work.

The survey grid around BC-V/CF02 was subdivided into 12 units (measuring 0.25×0.33m) per square metre, each of which was also given a unique reference number (Fig 4.15). The method used to recover the units was similar to that described in Chapter 3, 3.1.3, although new box sample tins measuring 0.20×0.25×0.33m had been purpose-built. The tins were pushed or knocked into the pre-designated units marked on the old land surface along the northern edge of the feature where a natural section had formed (Fig 4.16). Each successive tin was collected from next to the previous one.

Figure 4.13 End of post that had been torn, trimmed and forced into ground prior to inundation (Garry Momber)

The sample tins were built with detachable lids and fixing points so they could be raised to the vessel on a line or to the surface with a lifting bag (Fig 4.17).

During the survey of the peat platform the end of a flat timber eroding from the peat and clay bank was identified. In front of the bank burnt flint, charcoal, and small pieces of flint were embedded in a dark humic horizon. The area was within the grid and was marked out with pins and string. Box sample tins were used to excavate a small trench (TR02), while the covering and surrounding sediment was removed for processing. Several pieces of timber, including S061, S062, S0102, MS39, MS24, MS20 and S058, were recorded at the bottom of the trench and were recovered individually. Once the samples arrived on the vessel they were removed from their sample boxes ready for processing by excavation, sampling, and recording. This began at a shore base during the course of the fieldwork and continued later at the British Ocean Sediment Core Research

Facility (BOSCORF) refrigeration store and laboratory at the NOCS.

Where features or pieces of timber that were larger than the sampling tins were identified they were wrapped in protective materials underwater and brought individually to the surface. This was the case with BC-V/CF01, S049, and S061, among others.

Sample S049 consisted of an undulating basal surface which had been liberally covered with burnt flints (Fig 4.18). This was covered by a layer of fine clay, the remains of which was approximately 100mm thick and truncated by erosion. A piece of flattened wood 15mm by 50mm in cross section and 105mm long was found within the sample, orientated just off the vertical. It penetrated both the peat and the clay and stopped just above the flint layer (Fig 4.19). It was well preserved and did not appear to be a root, as its end was rounded and showed no evidence of rootlets. It appeared that the timber had been pushed into the ground when the peat was forming and sometime after the burnt flints had been deposited on the initial land surface. It therefore seems likely that it could have been part of a longer piece of wood that has since eroded away.

S061 was the largest piece of timber that was lifted, measuring 0.94m long by 0.41m wide (Fig 4.20). It lay horizontally on the old land surface on a north–south axis, with its north end protruding from the foot of a small step eroded into the peat platform. Less than 50mm of the exposed timber extended from the protection of the seabed, the covering peat and sediment protecting the remainder. S061 was recovered in the autumn of 2007 as a single unit with its underlying sediment, which comprised a matrix of charcoal and twigs, some of which were charred (Fig 4.21). The timber tapers at its southern end, where there are signs of burning, and has a maximum thickness of 25mm. It was initially identified as oak by Dr Scott Timpany through the presence and arrangement of its medullary rays (see Fig 4.22) and had been converted by transverse

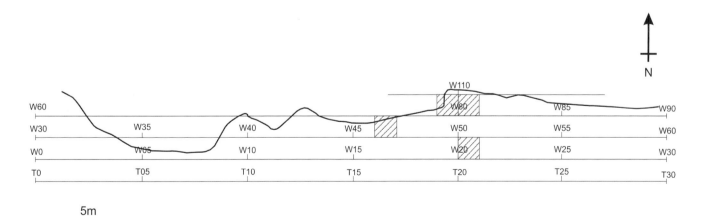

Figure 4.14 Survey grid laid across eroding edge of peat/woodland terrace at locus BC-V. Areas of sampling are marked as hatched squares (Rachel Bynoe after Garry Momber)

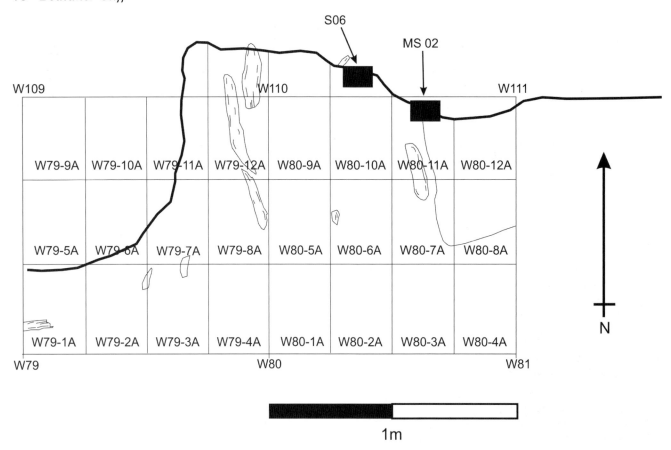

Figure 4.15   *Detail of sub-sectioned survey grid at locus BC-V, showing location of sample numbers from the side of the cliff (Rachel Bynoe after Garry Momber)*

Figure 4.16   *Garry Momber excavates a box sample from the survey area at BC-V (© Michael Pitts)*

splitting from a large oak tree, as evidenced by the tree rings (see 4.8.10, below).

The remains of this large piece of wood, as well as associated timbers, were quite heavily degraded. It was evident that the degradation had occurred at the time the timber was deposited or abandoned; it appeared to have languished for many years before being covered by protective silts. Ongoing research

funded by the Leverhulme Trust has produced a date for the timber of 6240–6000 cal BC (7340 ± 60 BP: Beta 249735). A hazelnut with evidence of charring was found embedded in the surface of the timber and was dated to 6240–6050 cal BC (7240 ± 60 BP: Beta 249736).

The opening of the trench to the south around the timber S061 cut through a sequence that differed

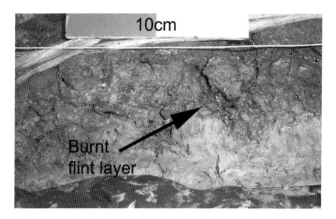

Figure 4.18 (above)   Burnt flints are clearly visible within the archaeological horizon in S049 just after it was recovered (Garry Momber)

Figure 4.17 (left)   Diving archaeologist Dan Pascoe recovers a box sample to the cover boat (Jan Gillespie)

Figure 4.19   Excavation of S049 revealed a layer of burnt flint. A second phase of human activity is represented by the piece of timber that had been pushed through the covering deposit at a later date (Garry Momber)

Figure 4.20   Large flat timber S061 on bed of sediment recorded immediately after being recovered. The piece measured just under a metre long (Garry Momber)

Figure 4.21   Matrix of charcoal, burnt flint and twigs from deposit below S061 (Dan Pascoe)

Figure 4.22   Slice taken from recovered timber S061, showing medullary rays cutting across grain. The medullary rays are almost parallel, as is the grain, suggesting the edge of a large tree (see section 4.8) (Garry Momber)

from that of BC-V/CF01 and BC-V/CF02, so a monolith sample was extracted from the trench wall. This sample, BC-V MS46, was subject to palaeoenvironmental analysis by Dr R Scaife, and the results are presented in 4.10, below.

The evaluation excavation of BC-V confirmed that a large amount of material lay embedded in the palaeo-land surface. Organic material included twigs found with bark, intact hazelnuts with a 'healthy looking sheen' and other delicate macro-fossils retaining exquisite detail. Initial results showed an overlying woody and humic peat horizon (context 5011) above a fine grey silt in the order of 200mm (context 5012). Underlying this was the

organic archaeological material (context 5013) (see Appendix 1 for context descriptions).

The organic timbers and archaeological material are associated with a dark grey humic silt (context 5015) which overlies areas of burnt organic material, charcoal, and burnt flint. These deposits are found below peat that appears to contain timber features with evidence of woodworking and deliberate deposition. Finds include carbonised wood (Fig 4.23), worked flint (Fig 4.24), burnt flint, prepared fibres (Fig 4.25; Fig 4.26 at higher magnification), and worked wood (see 4.8, below).

Figure 4.23 Carbonised timber (MS13), with marks indicating working (Rachel Bynoe)

Figure 4.24 Flint blade from BC-V (Jan Gillespie)

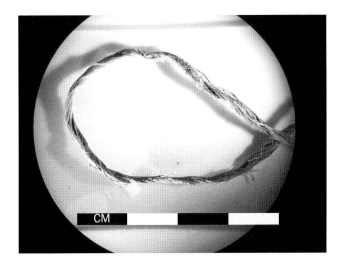

Figure 4.25 Prepared fibre from BC-V (Rory Smith)

Figure 4.26 Prepared fibre at ×35 magnification (Rory Smith)

A plan of the area with the sample trenches is shown in Figure 4.27.

In June 2009 an inspection dive revealed further changes. Natural erosion and trawler damage was seen to have flattened and 'trimmed' the seabed around the area of investigation. The loss of seabed exposed a piece of worked timber from the archaeological horizon beneath a covering of clay and peat. It had been recently uncovered and still retained clearly visible tool marks. A section of the exposed piece of timber 0.2m long was recovered (Figs 4.28 and 4.29). In response to this discovery, further work supported by the Leverhulme Trust through the Department of Archaeology, University of York, uncovered and recorded the threatened timbers. In June the trench (TR02) cut in 2007 was extended to include the area around the newly exposed timber. Removal of the covering sediment revealed a wide array of what appeared to be interconnected trimmed oak pieces measuring between 80mm and 140mm wide (Fig 4.30). The length of the timbers is as yet unknown, as they continue into the bank; however, the complex interplay of worked wood suggests that a substantial Mesolithic structure may have once stood in this location (Fig 4.31).

The concentration of interrelated finds suggested anthropogenic activity. However, the great age of the material and dearth of comparable artefacts warranted detailed analysis of the timber to look for any evidence of working to aid interpretation. This was conducted by Maisie Taylor towards the end of 2009 (see 4.8, below); the wood was identified by Nigel Nayling (see 4.9, below).

4.7.2 Sub-sampling and processing

A total of 110 samples was brought up from the BC-V locality at Bouldnor Cliff: 5 long monolith tins,

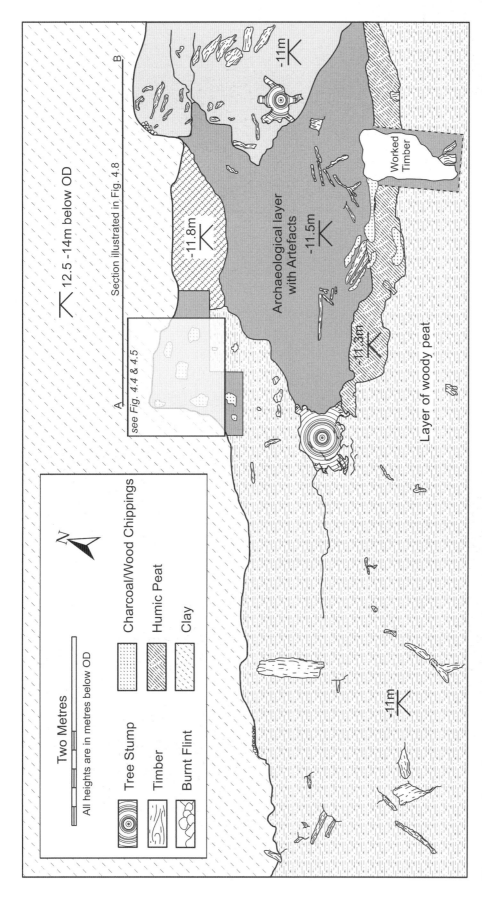

Figure 4.27   *Site plan of BC-V produced following survey in 2007, showing archaeological features and anthropogenic signatures within the matrix of the old land surface (Julian Whitewright after Garry Momber)*

Figure 4.28　Sample S102, sawn from a piece of timber being eroded out of the clay bank. A sharp cut is evident at the end (Rachel Bynoe)

Figure 4.29　A deep groove and a covered channel cut into S102 (Rachel Bynoe)

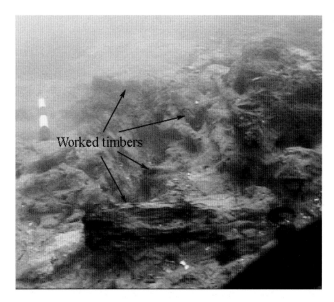

Figure 4.30   The array of timbers remaining on the seabed. They extend back beneath the submerged peat-covered bank (Garry Momber after Trevor Jenkins)

37 box-monolith samples, and 61 grab samples. When processing, both monolith sample types were dealt with in a similar way: they were stored at the BOSCORF laboratory where they were kept at a regulated temperature of 6°C before being excavated in a controlled environment. Each of the samples was first drawn to scale before being excavated by context, recovering finds and taking note of the matrix that was being dealt with. Excavating them in this way, and not underwater,

means that detailed analysis of any stratigraphy can be recorded. After excavation the spoil from each context was wet-sieved through 8mm, 5mm, and 3mm sieve mesh. The residue was then dried and sorted into its various components, such as burnt flint, charcoal, seeds, wood and so on.

4.8   Waterlogged wood
Maisie Taylor

4.8.1   Assessment

The waterlogged wood examined had been recognised as (or was suspected to be) worked, and was lifted. Further material was derived from bulk samples. Detailed wood record sheets were completed for all worked wood regardless of the context, but the two groups of material need to be considered separately because of the different methods of retrieval.

4.8.2   Quantity of material

Seven pieces of wood which had been individually lifted were originally examined and recorded in detail. This material is worked in various ways compatible with prehistoric woodworking techniques. In view of this, it was decided to work through material derived from bulk samples to establish whether there was any woodworking debris previously unrecognised. This material is derived from samples (SO), monoliths (MS) and sieve residues.

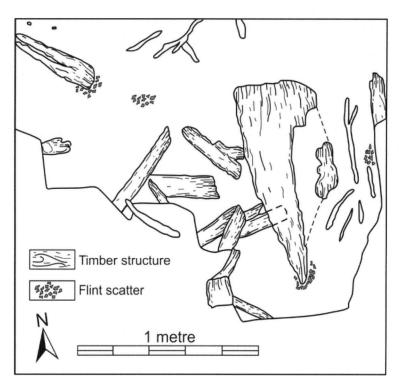

Timber structure

Flint scatter

N

1 metre

Figure 4.31   Plan of trench 02, showing all timbers identified to date. Large timber is S061 (Julian Whitewright after Garry Momber)

**Table 4.5 Table showing criteria for scoring scale, developed by
Humber Wetlands Project (after Van de Noort *et al* 1995, table 15.1)**

	Museum conservation	Technology analysis	Woodland management	Dendro-chronology	Species identification
5	+	+	+	+	+
4	–	+	+	+	+
3	–	+/–	+	+	+
2	–	+/–	+/–	+/–	+
1	–	–	–	–	+/–
0	–	–	–	–	–

4.8.3 *Range and variation*

The seven pieces which had been lifted, examined, and recorded in detail all appear to have been artificially modified in some way. Some pieces show clear and definite signs of working, while others are less clear, but all seem likely to have been modified. The material derived from the samples was more diverse, and it became apparent that some of the samples were simply the woody matrix from wood peat. After initial scanning these were briefly characterised, but where there seemed to be evidence for possible working, however slight, the sample was put to one side for more detailed examination and recording.

4.8.4 *Condition of material*

Using the scoring scale developed by the Humber Wetlands Project (Van de Noort *et al* 1995, table 15.1), most of the material examined in the first session scored 3 or 4. As Table 4.5 shows, a score of 3 or 4 means that almost all the forms of analysis listed there might be suitable, whereas once the score drops to 2 it is less likely that most analyses will be productive. Most of the material examined in the second session scored 2 or 3. This condition scale is based primarily on examination of the surface of the wood and the data recorded from that examination. The condition score reflects whether each type of analysis might be profitably applied – it is not intended as a recommendation for various analyses or treatment. A catalogue of the wood analysed has been presented in Appendix 2 (also see for species identification where available).

Given the great age of the material, some of it is in surprisingly good condition, although there is an inevitable problem with compression. The distortion of the diameters of roundwood through compression is often associated with drying out (Taylor 1998, 141–2), but here it is more likely to be a product of the softening of the wood through time, combined with sustained pressure from the overlying deposits and the depth of water. This distortion can most clearly be seen in the record of the roundwood diameters. Where the diameter is no longer circular, two measurements are taken (eg D 33/50mm). Where, for whatever reason, there is no longer a complete diameter, but there is a complete radius, the diameter is reconstructed and recorded as the 'original diameter' (eg OrigD 110mm).

Damage to the wood, especially the surface, by marine boring molluscs is extensive and this makes some pieces difficult to interpret. Some pieces are also water-worn, although this damage is not necessarily recent. Both the problem of mollusc bore holes and the erosive effects of the water are likely to get worse the longer the material remains unexcavated after exposure.

Where the surface is undamaged, or less water-worn, the wood is generally sufficiently well preserved for indications of ancient woodworking to survive in good condition. The age of the material, combined with the quality of preservation, gives it the potential to produce unique data. Virtually nothing is known about woodworking technology at this time; a small amount of material from the early Mesolithic has been studied at Star Carr (Mellars and Dark 1998), but there is very little other material until the Neolithic. There is, in turn, very little Neolithic material which has been recorded in detail. Significant developments in woodworking technology would presumably have happened at this time as tool types changed and people adapted to a new, more sedentary lifestyle, but at present very little is known about it.

A number of contexts at BC-V produced more than one piece of worked wood; the techniques represented have all previously been associated with Neolithic or earlier woodworking.

4.8.5 *Roundwood*

The worked roundwood is trimmed in a number of ways. MS20 and MS24 (both Pomoideae) are both trimmed at one end from two directions. Diameters vary greatly in these pieces, between 25mm and a mean diameter of 81mm from MS20 (which is heavily compressed). Some roundwood retains all, or part, of the heel where the stem was originally attached to a tree or stump. There are two pieces from S017 and two from S035 (alder). Only one piece of roundwood

Figure 4.32   Underside of timber S061, with indications of burning (Rachel Bynoe)

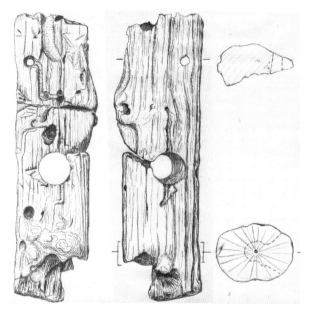

Figure 4.33   Distinct cut marks visible on MS039 (Julian Whitewright)

survived which had both ends modified (SO57): one end is trimmed from all directions and the other is torn. It is 240mm long.

A certain amount of roundwood was split and modified in various ways. MS09 (alder), MS37, and S054 were split in half. They vary in diameter between 35mm and 50mm. S028 is a woodchip which has clearly been removed from a relatively small piece of roundwood. S102 was a piece of roundwood which was modified by being roughly split and squared (see Figs 4.28 and 4.29). It originally had a diameter of *c* 59mm at one end, while the other is trimmed and torn, with a diameter of *c* 41mm. A number of other pieces of roundwood have also been trimmed or modified using a 'chop and tear' technique (eg S039, S058, S102, and S057).

4.8.6   *Woodworking debris*

A number of woodchips were retrieved, examined, and recorded. Four of these are radially aligned. A piece from MS40 appears to have one split surface and another, from MS23, is oak. The lengths of these woodchips range from 35mm to 254mm. A further eleven woodchips are tangentially aligned, two of them across knots. The lengths of these pieces range from 50mm to 125mm.

Among the debris from the site is a certain amount of bark, some of which is extremely thick and obviously derived from large trees. The bark from MS24 ranges from 24mm to 32mm, and there is bark which is 32mm thick from MS40. These pieces are relatively small and cannot therefore be associated with bast production, although there are many others uses for bark. The significance of this material may become clearer if it proves possible to identify the bark to species. The timber S061 is derived from a large tree and there are other

fragments which are also likely to have come from such trees. They are either heavily charred or fragmentary, making further analysis impossible, but do suggest that material from large trees was being worked in the area.

4.8.7   *Timber*

One large timber was lifted (S061). This timber is a tangentially split plank of slow-grown oak which is charred at one end and along one side (Fig 4.32). Tangentially split timbers are more usually taken from large trees, as it is difficult efficiently to split large trees (ie >750mm diameter) radially (Taylor 2010, 90–91). No precise measurements could be taken because of the poor condition of the wood.

4.8.8   *Toolmarks*

Toolmarks which were sufficiently well preserved to show the accurate shape of the tool are rare. Pre-metal tool marks are even rarer, and it seemed unlikely that wood as eroded and damaged as the material here would produce any such marks. One piece of wood (MS39, oak), however, despite its poor condition, seems to have a toolmark preserved in a deep cut. The cut, which is parallel to the grain, is distinctive, as one side is flat and straight while the other is slightly 'crinkled' (Fig 4.33). The cut was made to stop a split from developing further (see 4.8.5, above) and penetrated the wood far enough for it to survive the erosion of the surface. A profile gauge was carefully inserted into the cut and the profile taken. The cut is 31mm long and 2mm deep.

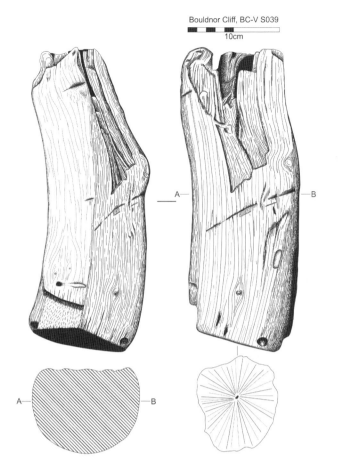

Bouldnor Cliff, BC-V S039

10cm

Figure 4.34 S039, found embedded just off the vertical in the seabed. It contains evidence of tearing, chopping and cutting (Julian Whitewright)

4.8.9 Charring

A proportion of the wood, much of it debris from wood-working, is charred (MS13, for example; Fig 4.23). The Neolithic causewayed enclosure at Etton has similar patterns of charred wood. There, the pattern of the deposits of charred wood in the enclosure ditch (Taylor 1998, fig 140) closely followed the distribution of worked wood and it was suggested that part of the clearing-up process involved burning some or all of the debris from working. It is possible that the distribution at Bouldnor Cliff might represent a similar practice.

4.8.10 Discussion

Mesolithic and early Neolithic worked wood is very rare in this country, and there are virtually no data about stone axe techniques. Recent work on material from Star Carr suggests that the woodworking techniques even at this early date (*c* 8000BC) are neither unsophisticated nor primitive. There are clear indications, however, that the techniques used to get the best out of stone tools were quite different to those employed for metal ones. It is also apparent

that many of these techniques were rapidly lost when early metal tools arrived. A study of the wood-working from the early Bronze Age timber circle at Holme (Brennand and Taylor 2003) shows that, as early as 2049 BC, there is no trace of the distinctive debris generated by woodworking with stone tools.

The development of specialist techniques for stone-tool woodworking technology is an important research topic, which was explored by a group of Danish experimental archaeologists (Jorgensen 1985). The felling of trees with metal tools relies on the fact that metal edges are efficient at cutting, but the Danish archaeologists' experiments with felling trees using polished stone axes indicated that a different approach was used, which did not rely on a sharp cutting edge. The experiments showed that the trees were felled by cutting parallel grooves and splitting out the wood in between. This produced stumps similar to ones which had come out of the north German peatlands and debris which ran at a tangent to the grain and was parallel-sided, like that found associated with the Neolithic long barrow at Stanwick (Harding and Healy 2007). Different, but still closely similar, material came from Star Carr (work in progress), where slight marks of tools were observed on the surfaces of larger pieces in the form of parallel grooves apparently cut to facilitate the splitting-out of sections in a controlled manner. This technique would produce a similar kind of debris to the Neolithic tree-felling technique just discussed.

When the wood from Star Carr was first re-examined (Mellars and Dark 1998) there was clear evidence for the trimming of small roundwood with axes. Early evidence for coppicing had already been found at the causewayed enclosure at Etton, a site which has recently been redated to the mid-fourth millennium BC; the practice at this time was already sophisticated. Ongoing work at Star Carr has also produced a number of pieces with heels and other clear signs of coppicing. The sample from Bouldnor Cliff is not large enough for conclusive evidence for coppicing, but one piece of oak (S039; Fig 4.34) has a straight stem and the curved end characteristic of a coppice piece. The grain suggests, however, that it might be part of the fork from a small tree. Evidence for working came from a running tear which had been stopped with two chops. It was observed infor-mally at Etton that some of the coppiced wood was torn and chopped, and some is illustrated in the report (Taylor 1998, figs 169 and 170), but the signif-icance of this as a possible technique was not fully recognised at the time.

A small piece of roundwood (MS20) from Bouldnor Cliff showed possible but not certain evidence for trimming. A second piece (MS24), which is very similar in shape to MS20, has much clearer evidence for trimming, with one end apparently chopped from two angles on the same side, one of the chops digging in and making an incomplete cut. Other pieces which are torn include S058, a stump with torn side shoots, and S102, a piece of roundwood debris which is either torn or trimmed. S017, S035, and S057

Bouldnor Cliff, BC-V S058

10cm

*Figure 4.35   S058, recovered from immediately
below the S061 piece, where it remained just off the
vertical. It shows clear evidence of coppicing (Julian
Whitewright)*

were also either torn or trimmed and might have
been coppiced.

A technique involving the chopping and tearing
of stems to detach them from coppice stools was
observed when recording the wood from the causewayed enclosure at Etton. It was not discussed in
detail because it was not particularly widespread in
the assemblage and was not a recognised technique
at the time. It is, however, a technique which, once
again, does not rely on the sharp cutting edge of
a metal tool. One piece of wood at Etton, a stump,
shows clear evidence that this technique was used
to detach coppice stems (Taylor 1998, figs 169 and
170), and is closely similar to S058 (Fig 4.35) from
Bouldnor Cliff. Since the publication of the report
on the wood at Etton, it has become more and more
apparent that the use of stone axes required techniques which went out of use quite quickly following
the introduction of metal axes.

Most of the evidence for trimming which has survived
on the roundwood appears to be the working associated with the original cutting or felling. Only one piece
(S057) has been specifically sharpened to a point. The
range of diameters of the worked roundwood varies a
good deal, but most are less than 50mm. Unworked
roundwood is slightly smaller, mostly under 20mm
and all under 40mm. Overall, the quality of the
roundwood and the trimming suggests that, although
the evidence for coppicing is slight, systematic wood
cutting was certainly taking place.

There are some pieces from Star Carr that look
like 'planks' and which could have been produced
using techniques outlined above. Some of the wood
examined for Taylor's 1998 report, as well as pieces
recorded from recent excavations, appeared to have
slight dimpling or faceting on the surface. Similar,
better-preserved faceting caused by hewing has
been recorded on later prehistoric material, and it
seems likely that this technique was already in use
in the earlier Mesolithic. None of the wood retrieved

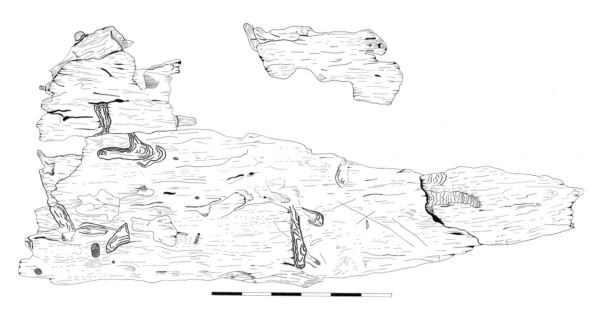

Figure 4.36   The tangentially split timber S061. Scale unit = 50mm (Dan Pascoe)

so far from Bouldnor Cliff has been sufficiently well preserved for this kind of evidence to survive in good condition, although there are intimations of the technique on the timber discussed below.

S061 is the most unexpected piece from Bouldnor Cliff: a large timber of oak which has been tangentially split from a big tree and could have been hewn. These techniques are suitable for, and used on, large oak trees and have been observed in assemblages of timber from the Neolithic to the Bronze Age. Later, the technique continues to be used in boat building. The earliest material of this kind (until now) has been recorded from Neolithic monumental settings (Taylor 2010), but the range of uses for these kinds of timber in the Mesolithic is unknown. They are generally too massive for domestic application and, if not used in monumental contexts, might well be derived from boats. Mesolithic boats are unknown in this country (although many 'dug outs' have never been dated), but occur in Scandinavia, where they are very sophisticated (Coles and Coles 1989, 68). The felling date for an oak tree used to produce massive monumental timbers in the long barrow at Haddenham lies between 3618 and 3573 cal BC (Evans and Hodder 2006, 185–7), and the timber S061 (Fig 4.36) from Bouldnor Cliff must push the date for this technique back a further 2000 years.

A reasonable assemblage of woodworking debris is essential if the woodworking techniques of this period, and this site, are to be understood. A trawl of environmental samples taken from Bouldnor Cliff produced a small quantity of woodworking debris, especially woodchips. Four of the woodchips are radially aligned – the kind of debris often associated with the splitting of wood – and, indeed, one piece from MS40 appears to have a split surface. A further eleven woodchips are tangentially aligned, two of them across knots (MS13, Fig 4.23, and SOW22). Tangentially aligned woodchips are generated by trimming and squaring wood. One piece of oak (MS39) also appears to be some kind of debris. It can only be described as a 'hacked lump' of roundwood with a number of tears and chops, such as the aforementioned 'crinkled' mark (Fig 4.33; see 4.8.8, above). It is an unusual mark which could have being made with a tranchet axe. The side of the axe with the detached rejuvenation flake would have made the clean flat cut and the more heavily worked surface of the other side caused the crinkle effect by crushing rather than cutting. Unfortunately there is no comparative material, but the profile of the cut is quite appropriate for the shape of a tranchet axe.

4.9 Bouldnor Cliff wood identification report
Nigel Nayling

4.9.1 Introduction

This report is the outcome of thin-section sampling and visual examination of a limited number of wood items from excavations at Bouldnor Cliff. Items for sampling were identified in collaboration with Maisie Taylor during February 2010.

4.9.2 Methods

In some cases the recovery of thin sections had to be balanced against maintaining the integrity of the wooden item, which might require either additional recording and or possibly active conservation. In Appendix 2 the site code, object identifying code, comments and wood identification are given. Identifications were made by comparing thin sections observed under transmitted light microscopy at magnifications of up to ×800 with a reference collection of thin sections made from authenticated wood samples from Kew and with descriptions and photomicrographs given in Schweingruber (1978).

The remains of a possible large split timber (BC-V S061, Fig 4.36) were visually examined to confirm the wood species as oak and to examine conversion and average growth rate.

4.9.3 Results

A modern cut on a large fragment from one side of the split timber (S061) allowed the transverse cross-section to be cleaned. In this area, conversion of the parent oak tree was clearly tangential, with the parent tree having slow growth (ie narrow rings). The timber was somewhat compressed and retained 42 heartwood rings with an average ring width of 0.73mm.

4.10 Bouldnor Cliff BC-V: pollen analysis of MS46
Rob Scaife

4.10.1 Introduction

This section presents the results of the stratigraphical examination and pollen analysis of BC-V column MS46 (Fig 4.37). This is the most recent of a number of palaeoenvironmental studies which have been carried out on the lower and archaeologically related peat and minerogenic sediment facies at Bouldnor Cliff. Although pollen was found to be very variably preserved, pollen data have been obtained which suggest that this sequence is possibly of late Boreal, but most probably of early middle Holocene (Atlantic) Age, and as such falls within the more recent age range of the basal peats at Bouldnor.

4.10.2 Stratigraphy

The stratigraphy of column MS46 was described in the laboratory during sub-sampling for other palaeoenvironmental remains. The principal sediment

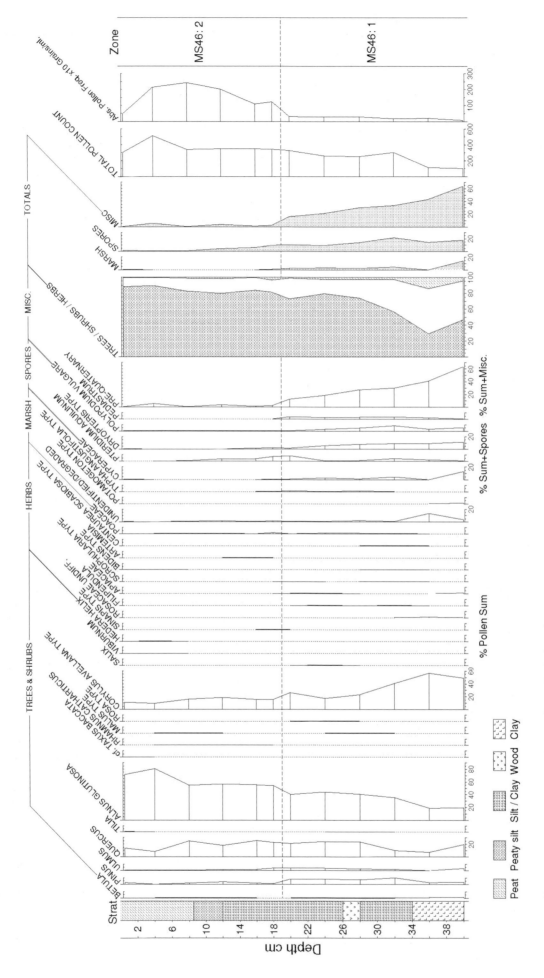

Figure 4.37   Pollen diagram of BC-V MS46 (Rob Scaife)

Table 4.6 Stratigraphy of MS46

Depth (mm)	
0–85	Compacted fibrous, laminated monocot peat with *Alnus* twigs. 10YR 2/1 or 10YR 2/2
85–120	Humic silt with peat inclusions (transition)
120–260	Grey (10YR 4/1) fine silt with rootlet penetration
260–280	Massive wood in column
280–340	Grey (10YR 4/1) fine silt
340–420	Pale, buff-coloured clay with grey mottling. 10YR 6/2

Table 4.7 Details of pollen assemblage zone outlines for MS46

l.p.a.z. MS46: 2 0–190mm	There is a major stratigraphical change from humic silts to pure detritus peat. This has influenced the pollen assemblages. *Alnus* becomes dominant (85%) within the upper peat. *Quercus* remains important (to *c*30%), with *Corylus avellana* type (reduced to 10–15%). *Pinus* and *Ulmus* are reduced. *Rhamnus catharticus* is present. Herb diversity is lower than in the preceding zone with only small numbers of Poaceae. There is a peak of *Pteridium aquilinum* across the zone transition (to 9%). After the very high numbers of pre-Quaternary palynomorphs in zone 1, there are only small numbers in this zone.
l.p.a.z. MS46: 1 190–400mm	Characterised by higher (than above) numbers of pre-Quaternary palynomorphs and Holocene pteridophytes (*Dryopteris* type and *Polypodium*). *Quercus* (to 25%), *Alnus* (increasing upwards to 43%), and *Corylus avellana* type (declining from 60% at 360mm to *c*20% at the top of the zone). *Pinus* (to 10%), *Ulmus* (4%), and a single occurrence of *Tilia* are present in the upper half of the zone. This may be regarded as a sub-zone and is associated with changing sediment character at *c*340mm (ie taphonomic). There are few herbs, although taxonomic diversity is slightly greater than in zone 2 above. There are greater numbers of fen/marsh taxa with Cyperaceae (15% in basal level). *Potamogeton* type and *Typha angustifolia/Sparganium*. Algal *Pediastrum* is more important in this zone (10%). There are large numbers of derived geological palynomorphs in this zone which decline from 64% pollen sum + misc to <10% at the top of the zone.

units are given in Table 4.6. Lower minerogenic (silt and clay) sediments are overlain by a highly humified detrital peat which contains some wood/ twig fragments. The interface between the lower sediment and peat is transitional, but the presence of clasts/inclusions of peat between 260mm and 85mm suggests that some earlier organic/peat material was probably reworked. The stratigraphy of MS46 is comparable with other basal sequences which have been previously described (see 4.4.1 and 4.4.2, above). Lower minerogenic sediments with minimal organic content are overlain by freshwater silts and alluvium prior to stabilisation under on-site damp woodland variously dominated by oak, alder, and hazel. Here, alder was dominant on-site, as attested by wood/twig fragments in the upper peat.

4.10.3 The pollen data

Two local pollen assemblage zones have been recognised in this 0.4m profile. Details are given in Table 4.7.

4.10.4 Discussion: the vegetation and environment

The two local pollen assemblage zones which have been recognised are in large part due to the changing sedimentary environment and the differing taphonomic processes which resulted. This is indicated especially by the very substantial numbers of geological palynomorphs which are present in l.p.a.z. (local pollen assemblage zone) 1. These imply a higher-energy sedimentary environment in which pre-Quaternary sediments and secondary/reworked geological pollen have been deposited on the site. The further implication is that the pollen sources of both the pre-Quaternary palynomorphs and the catchment of the Holocene sub-fossil pollen and spores are different from, and probably come from, a much wider area than that of the more stable overlying peat-forming environment. Furthermore, the pollen can be interpreted in terms of the on-site (autochthonous) and very near-site plant communities as well as more regional sources. If these factors are taken into account, the vegetation is largely consistent throughout the profile. Thus, the changes in the pollen assemblages that occurred were attributable to both the changing local habitat and the vegetation response to these changes.

The on-site vegetation and environment changed in response to base-level fluctuations. These changes, as demonstrated in earlier analyses of the Solent and Bouldnor sites, were initially in response to rising sea level relative to land. This caused local waterlogging of the land surface from which Mesolithic archaeology has been recovered. At first, alluvial sediment was deposited as the fluvial system was ponded back and flooding took place. This process was, however, asynchronous, resulting in diachronous sediment units which were dependent upon local topography and altitude OD. This asynchronism has allowed a picture of the vegetation and environment to be constructed from analyses of a number of diachronous sediment profiles which accumulated from the latter part of the early Holocene (Boreal) period into the middle Holocene (Atlantic) period (Scaife 2008).

Profile MS46 falls within the later age range of sediments overlying the bedrock at Bouldnor – that is, it dates to the very late Boreal and early Atlantic (Fl. I/II). Radiocarbon dating will establish the age, allowing this pollen sequence to be located within the existing model of vegetation and environmental change at Bouldnor.

i: the on-site habitat

This profile shows progressive drying with a change from a freshwater alluvial environment to one of developing woodland. The former was a river floodplain with fen vegetation of Cyperaceae (sedges) and *Typha angustifolia/Sparganium* (reed mace and bur reed). Eroded and redeposited sediment containing large numbers of reworked geological palynomorphs is present, along with the freshwater algae *Pediastrum*. *Alnus* pollen becomes increasingly important, probably representing areas of alder woodland growing on drier areas and fringing the floodplain in near proximity. As conditions became drier, alder colonised the sample site to create dominant floodplain carr woodland (l.p.a.z. 2). This culminated in the formation of the highly humic detrital peat seen in the top 90mm of the profile. From other profiles it is known that continued drying resulted in colonisation by oaks. *Rhamnus catharticus* (buckthorn), a typical fen carr constituent, was also part of this community.

ii: the terrestrial / interfluve zone

The pollen sequence shows the greater importance of hazel in the lower part of the profile (l.p.a.z. 1 sub-zone a). The reduction in percentage values for hazel further up the profile appears to occur as a result of changes in the sediments and environment of deposition and is thus probably a taphonomic phenomenon. However, it is clear that hazel was the dominant or co-dominant (with oak) constituent of areas of woodland on drier ground. Elm is less well represented than oak or hazel, but would also have been a diagnostic component of the woodland. When this assemblage of trees and shrubs is placed within the perspective of the other Bouldnor sites/pollen sequences, this profile falls after a period (the middle to late Boreal) when pine was the dominant woodland with hazel, prior to being ousted by oak and elm. In contrast, the assemblage here, being dominated by oak, elm, and hazel, precedes the very considerable importance of lime (*Tilia*), which became the dominant woodland component after its arrival into southern England at the end of the Boreal period – that is, prior to the full separation of Britain from mainland Europe. The vegetation described here can thus be seen as part of the dynamic post-glacial successional change. Pioneer (juniper and birch) woodland of the early Holocene was replaced by pine and hazel in the early Boreal period, which was in turn replaced by oak, elm, and hazel with remaining pine in the late Boreal; the culmination of this process was the climax lime-dominated woodland of the middle Holocene (Atlantic) period. These seral changes have been detailed at other local and regional sites (Scaife 1980; 1982; 1987; 2003a and 2003b; Haskins 1978; Clarke and Barber 1987), allowing analogies and comparisons to be drawn with monolith MS46. The pollen spectra of MS46 may be compared with the upper section of diagrams from MS05 and pollen zones 1c and 1d from the long pollen profile of MS04, MS05 and MS08 in which there are comparable levels of oak, alder, and hazel (see Fig 3.19).

Pine pollen appears to be more important in zone l.p.a.z. MS46 1. While pine is an important constituent of some profiles from Bouldnor which are of earlier (late Boreal) date (as at MS05), the values here are not sufficient to suggest local importance. Furthermore, it is possible that pine is over-represented here owing to fluvial transport. Over-representation due to this pollen's saccate grains and ability to float over long distances is well known, and also occurs because of copious pollen production and anemophily.

Radiocarbon dating has been undertaken on other Bouldnor profiles. These demonstrate a range of stratigraphical contexts which, at BC-II, are late Boreal (Flandrian Ic) extending into the early part of the middle Holocene (Atlantic) period. In the case of BC-IV and BC-V, the peats are of middle and late Atlantic date. This discrepancy in dating, as noted, reflects the diachronous character of the peat formation in relation to marine transgression. The age span of the sediments associated with the archaeology is only a few centuries, from c 7200 BP to 6900 BP. Although a short time span is represented, this is a critical period in terms of sea-level change and the establishment of the coastline in broadly its present form. It is also eustatic change which was responsible for the changing environment, consequent sediment regime and the final submergence of the old land surface of Mesolithic occupation.

4.11   Conclusions and interpretation
Garry Momber

4.11.1   Summary

Anthropogenic evidence was first identified at BC-V in 2004. Since that time, features have steadily become exposed as natural erosion has taken its course. The sampling and trenching has been a response to the discovery of exposed material following the erosion of protective sediments. However, the ephemeral nature of the artefacts coupled with the absence of comparable material has made definitive identification problematic. This continued to be the case until the evaluation excavation conducted in 2007 confirmed that a large amount of material lay embedded in the palaeo-land surface. Subsequent analysis has demonstrated the presence of sizable pieces of worked material across an area that is at least 22m wide, a few square metres of which have been investigated. The stratigraphy demonstrates that there have been at least two periods of human activity interrupted by the deposition of a layer of silt. These sequences are presented below in the form of three phases.

The first phase of recorded human activity relates to the timbers associated with S061, which was radiocarbon dated to 6240–6000 cal BC (7340 ± 60 BP: Beta 249735); a hazelnut embedded within the upper side of the timber dated to 6240–6050 cal BC (7240 ± 60 BP: Beta 249736). Sample BC-V 05 S101 from feature BC-V CF02 dated to 6240–6000 cal BC (8200 to 7960 cal BP: Beta-207809), and sample MS01 48 from the bottom of the pit full of burnt flints (BC-V CF01) recorded a posterior density estimated date of 6120–6010 cal BC (7203 ± 36 BP: OxA-15699; 89% probability). The lower burnt flint layer from S049 is undated but is identified as from the first phase since it was subsequently covered by the fine silt of the second phase.

A distinct layer of fine silt *c* 220mm thick laid down during the second phase is described in the monolith MS46 as grey (10YR 4/1; see Table 4.6). It was located around the archaeological layer associated with timber S061 in trench TR02, above sample BC-V 05 S101 in BC-V CF02, and above and around the burnt flints in S049. The silt was deposited during a phase of inundation as indicated by the presence of the algae *Pediastrum*, indicating freshwater conditions, while derived geological palynomorphs denote the influx of water containing reworked sediments.

A third phase is characterised by the build-up of humic material above the fine clay. This would have been possible when the waters that deposited the sediment retreated and the land was once again dry. The humic material on the silt was subsequently topped by a woody peat that formed ahead of the marine transgression. Archaeological items associated with this layer include the upright sample from S049 (see 4.7.1, above), MS39 (see 4.8.9, above), and possibly S06 (see 4.3, above), which might also have been pushed into the ground following the second phase. S06 has a radiocarbon date of 6100–5880 cal BC (8060–7830 cal BP: Beta-209564), which is later than the dates from the first phase.

4.11.2 Consideration of the archaeological evidence

The remains recovered to date include burnt flint, charcoal, cordage, wood chippings, and worked timber ranging from a small peg to a large tangentially split oak piece. The vast majority of these artefacts are from the horizon associated with the first phase of activity as defined above, and suggest a site on which woodworking occurred. The archaeological signature remaining suggests an area of industry where structures had been secured to support woodworking and fires had produced flints hot enough to carbonise wood. Carbonisation is a technique that can be used to degrade and weaken the surface of wood before it is stripped or channelled by stone tools. This is a method that has been employed in the construction of log boats, among other things (Vairo 1997, 117; Johnstone 1988, 47; McGrail 1978). At this stage we are not in a position to say exactly what was being built, but the analysis of timbers by Maisie Taylor has identified the technology necessary to split wood tangentially as very sophisticated and approximately 2000 years in advance of similar finds elsewhere (see 4.8.10, above). Where the tree was of sufficient size, the technique could produce a flat plank in the order of 1–2 metres in width and over 10m long. This method uses wedges to separate the plank from the edge of a tree so that the grain runs parallel, or close to parallel, along its width. The resulting timber would be large enough to be used in monumental structures, as was the case with the Neolithic Haddenham long barrow *c* 4000 BC (Evans and Hodder 2006). Removal of the plank also provides access to the rest of the bole, which can be hollowed out to form a log boat. This would produce a larger craft than would be possible if the tree was simply split in half. Log boats constructed by this method had steeper sides and flatter bottoms than typical log boats, which are more rounded, as was seen with the log boats of later periods such as the Bronze Age Appleby boat of *c* 1100 BC or the Brigg Boat of *c* 834 BC (McGrail 1978). These boats were both of oak, which is the material of choice for the many log boats discovered in Britain and northwest Europe (Mowat 1996; Okorokov 1995; McGrail 1978, 117). Only a relatively small fraction of the BC-V loci was explored during the initial evaluation, and the full extent of the material scatter is yet to be defined. The degree of preservation of the discoveries and the extent of the archaeological material suggests that the location has a great deal more to offer, however. Whether people were building log boats or more fixed structures, theirs was an activity that necessitated cooperation and had great potential for skill diversification.

5 Rising waters, environmental change and humans at BC-IV *by Garry Momber, Rob Scaife, Jan Gillespie, Nigel Nayling, Derek Hamilton, Peter Marshall, Christopher Bronk Ramsey, and Gordon Cook*

The location of BC-IV lay to the far west of the submerged archaeological deposits at Bouldnor Cliff (see Fig 1.10). Here the covering alluvium had been eroded and basal humic/peaty material was exposed. This locus was selected for survey and sampling because artefacts were emerging on the seabed.

BC-IV sits on a slope and comprises an archaeological deposit that is at a shallower depth than BC-V and BC-II. It thus presented an opportunity to examine part of the cultural landscape that had been inundated at a later time. Here was an opportunity to determine the rate of sea-level change and the impact on human activity and the environment as the Holocene waters of the West Solent valley continued to rise.

5.1 Surveying the slope and recovering the artefacts

The area of interest was first recognised in 1998 during visual searches. Knapped flints were recovered from secondary deposits at –11 to –12m OD and, in 2000, flakes were found further upslope adjacent to pre-submergence deposits that were actively eroding. BC-IV was relocated in 2003, when English Heritage funded detailed investigations of the submerged land surface. A principal objective was to record the exposed edge of the pre-inundation deposit and plan any samples that were collected or lithics that were discovered.

A georeferenced three-dimensional bathymetric survey produced by Submetrix/SEA Ltd in 2000 was used to image the submerged landscape (see Fig 1.8). This has proved to be a valuable tool for focusing diver effort on the areas with greatest potential, enabling the accurate deployment of divers to inspect the seabed and locate the interface between the eroded palaeo-land surface and the underlying clay bedrock, which had become exposed where the protective Holocene sediment had thinned and been removed by the current.

BC-IV was located around an exposed seam of humic material 30m long running diagonally upslope from east to west and rising from –10m to –6.5m OD. At this point the slope of the underwater cliff dips at an angle of approximately 30° from south to north. A remaining pocket of Holocene sediment protected the exposure towards the base of the slope

in deeper water, while a vertical cliff over 2m high shielded the shallow end of the exposure. This cliff rises from –6.5m to –4.1m OD, where it is capped by a horizontal shelf of peat (see Fig 1.9).

Site selection was followed by the production of a plan (Fig 5.1). This was developed around a baseline (BC-IV B02) between datums Dp03 and Dp04. These datums were, in turn, surveyed to a large concrete sinker that acted as a fixed reference point. The sinker (DpIV01) was positioned on the relatively shallow (–4.1m OD) peat shelf to the south, where it was linked to Ordnance Datum using a RTK Differential GPS via a marker buoy (Chapter 2, 2.2.2). Baseline BC-IV B02 was laid parallel to the exposure, running east-north-east and dipping from –7m OD to –10m OD. It was used to record the position of the main features of interest and the locations from which monolith tins were recovered, and as the reference around which the plan of BC-IV was produced.

Six monolith tins were collected from BC-IV. Monolith MS10 came from the top of the incline, while MS11 and MS12, collected from halfway down the slope, were the lowest samples (Fig 5.2). The samples were collected vertically from outcrops along the exposed seabed or at the base of the covering clay cliff, and were extracted underwater, where they were wrapped in cling film and bagged before being recovered to the surface.

The area adjacent to the exposed edge of the land surface was searched for archaeological evidence via a corridor survey conducted in a 10m² box set up next to baseline BC-IV B02. The box was divided into five corridors that were visually inspected for archaeological material. Four pieces of worked flint were recovered from around the survey area and further flints found eroding from the base of the cliff at –6.5m OD were recorded (see Chapter 11). Small gravel mounds which could represent relic fluvial material were also recorded, and are shown on the site plan (Fig 5.1).

Flints were also recovered in bulk samples from the base of the protected cliff at a depth of –6.5m OD. They came from a fine sandy clay that sat beneath a layer of peat. Sorting and analysis of the recovered samples from BC-IV identified a total of fourteen struck pieces of flint. The base of the cliff from which the bulk samples were recovered was cleaned and monolith MS10 was collected at the point where the flints were found. Following

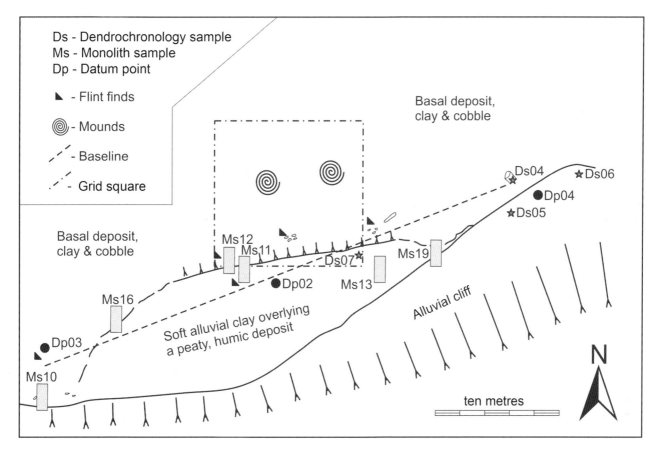

Figure 5.1   Site plan of BC-IV, showing locations of samples and key datums (Julian Whitewright after Garry Momber)

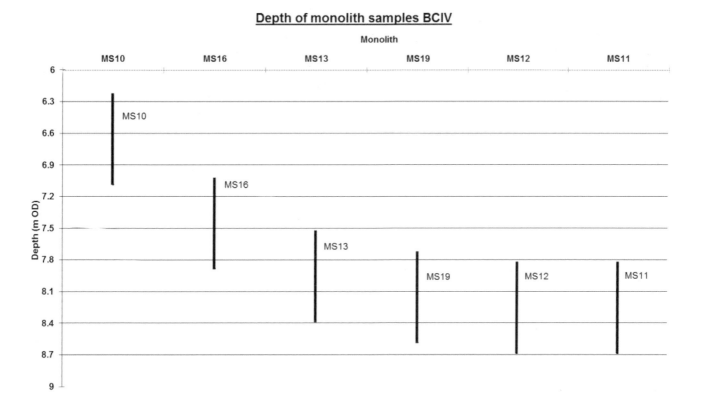

Figure 5.2   Relative depths below OD of monolith tins at BC-IV (Jan Gillespie)

assessment of the monoliths from this locale, MS10 was subject to palaeoenvironmental analysis and radiocarbon dating.

5.2   Palaeoenvironmental analysis of monolith sample MS10
Rob Scaife

The monolith profile at BC-IV is stratigraphically the highest profile inspected in the Bouldnor Cliff sequence (Figs 5.1 and 5.2). The 600mm-long monolith (notwithstanding a void in the top 40mm), was recovered from a depth of –6.8 to –6.2m OD. Three local pollen assemblage zones have been identified in this sequence, and are characterised (below) from the base of the core upwards (Fig 5.3).

5.2.1   Pollen zonation and evidence for vegetation changes

Zone MS10–1: 560mm to 440mm Quercus–Corylus avellana *type*

Sandy lithology. *Quercus* (31%) and *Corylus avellana* type (42%) are the dominant trees, with small numbers of *Ulmus* and *Tilia*. Numbers of *Betula* and *Pinus* are low. *Alnus glutinosa* has its highest values in this profile (peak to 18%), but, given the high pollen productivity of this taxon, these levels are not especially significant. Herbs are dominated by Poaceae (to 18%), although the overall diversity is low. Marsh taxa comprise *Typha angustifolia* type and Cyperaceae. Derived pre-Quaternary palynomorphs are important.

Zone MS10–2: 440mm to 260mm Tilia–Corylus avellana *type*

Old land surface and transition to peat and overlying marine silts. This zone has been defined by the start of increasing *Tilia* percentages. This taxon becomes important (to 33%) in the peat unit. *Quercus* and *Corylus avellana* type appear slightly reduced, but this is due to within sum expansion of *Tilia*. *Fraxinus* is incoming and values of *Ulmus* are increased. Poaceae remains the principal herb (10–15%) and herb diversity is slightly increased. Of note are Chenopodiaceae (to 5%). Spores become more important, with monolete forms (*Dryopteris* type (18%)), especially at the levels of the old land surface. The change to peat from mineral sediment is also manifested by a reduction in pre-Quaternary palynomorphs.

Zone MS10–3: 260mm to 0mm Quercus–Corylus avellana *type–Poaceae*

Transition into silty clay. *Quercus* attains its highest values (to 50%), with reduced *Tilia*. *Corylus*

avellana type remains consistent, at *c* 20% of sum. There is an increase in herbaceous diversity, with the presence of aquatic and probable marsh taxa. Halophytes (including *Plantago maritima*) are present and, although percentages are reduced, Chenopodiaceae remains consistent. The change to mineral sediment is also reflected by increased numbers of pre-Quaternary palynomorphs.

5.2.2   Discussion

Three local pollen assemblage zones have been identified in the pollen sequence (Fig 5.3). Overall, oak and hazel are the most important constituents throughout, with only small numbers of birch and pine, contrasting with the earlier profiles. Lime/linden is especially important in pollen zone 2, marking its arrival and colonisation in the region prior to the separation of Britain from Europe and the Isle of Wight from mainland Britain by rising (relative) sea level (see Chapters 3, 3.5.2, and 7, 7.3.3). Other trees include elm, holly, ash, and yew. These taxa are less well represented in pollen spectra and may have been relatively important constituents of the local woodland. There is little evidence that fen carr woodland was important at the site during this period. However, low-level records of taxa including alder, alder buckthorn (*Frangula alnus*), and wayfaring tree (*Viburnum lantana*) indicate their growth in suitable habitats in the local region.

A poorly developed palaeosol and old land surface is present at *c* 360–420mm in MS10. This developed in alluvial sands and was sealed by development of the overlying peat. At this time, the oak and hazel woodland noted above prevailed on drier soils adjacent to a wet fen or a probably slow-flowing river. However, lime was also starting to colonise this habitat and a peaty humic soil developed. Large numbers of bracken spores in this soil indicate the presence of its local growth on the old land surface.

Increasing rainfall/humidity and increasing relative sea level during the early Atlantic period (Chronozone II) resulted in destruction of the on-site and near-local woodland. Initially, rising sea levels caused conditions suited to peat growth through the raising of the local groundwater table. Cessation of this peat development was caused by final marine/ brackish transgression, which caused a change to deposition of fine-grained sediments under progressively increasing saline conditions. This is also evidenced in column MS04 of BC-II (see Chapter 3, 3.5) although this was a diachronous event. Change to marine conditions is also evidenced in the diatom and foraminifera record. While lime (*Tilia cordata*) probably remained important in nearby areas (of drier soils), its poor pollen dispersal results in less representation in the pollen spectra as growth became more distant from the site. This applies equally to holly (*Ilex aquifolium*), which is also recorded. Oak and hazel remained the dominant woodland types in the local area.

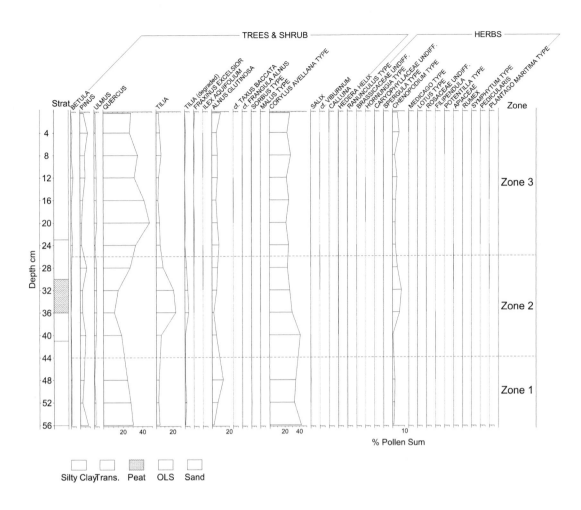

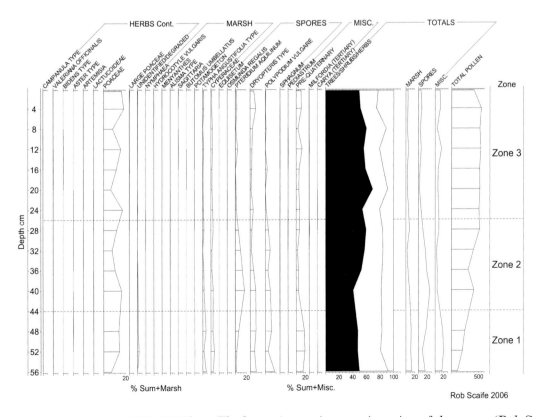

Figure 5.3   Pollen diagram of BC-IV MS10. The lower image is a continuation of the upper (Rob Scaife)

The small values of alder (a very substantial pollen producer) in this profile is unusual for the period. Alnetum was generally a major component of the flora during the Atlantic period and, indeed, Godwin had used the usual sharp expansion at *c* 5900 cal BC (*c* 7000 BP) as the marker for the Boreal–Atlantic transition (Godwin's pollen zones VI/VIIa). Here, alder arrived early along the coastal fringe ahead of the rapidly rising sea-level in this part of the country. Thus, while it is important in the late Boreal peats north-east of the present study area (Scaife 2000a), and from BC-II here, this community appears to have migrated across this zone and onto inland river floodplains where it became and remained dominant. This is clearly seen at Gatcombe Withy Bed in the centre of Isle of Wight and from Borthwood Farm on the Eastern Yar River (Scaife 1980; 1987). It is not clear why there is no apparent peak/wave of its pollen here, marking its expansion across what would appear to have been an ecologically suitable wetland area.

There is no question that continued sea-level change occurred, as indicated by the sedimentology, pollen, diatoms, and foraminifera. This resulted in the submergence of the old land surface at this site in an estimated date range of *5350–5230 cal BC (OxA-15717)*. This change was,

however, progressive and there is clear evidence that the development of mudflat and salt marsh was preceded by a transitional phase in which sands were laid down. This may be interpreted either as a transgressive sand bar that moved across the site prior to development of mudflat and salt marsh in a lower-energy environment, or as ephemeral freshwater/riverine sand caused by the disruption of the fluvial systems. The latter has been suggested in BC-II for the interface of contexts 2003 and 2001 (context 2002), where there is a clear expansion of fen herb taxa.

5.3   Diatom and foraminifera and the ingress of the sea
Rob Scaife and Jan Gillespie

Examination of the diatom and foraminifera assemblage has helped to chart the process that resulted in the flooding of the West Solent valley. The minerogenic unit in MS10 contains clear evidence for the onset of brackish water/marine transgression over the marshlands in which peat accumulated. This dated organic unit, as with BC-II (column MS04), is overlain by the typical grey silty clay. This zone (which appears to be laterally consistent with context 2001) is referred to as 5001 at BC-V and 4001 at BC-IV.

Table 5.1   Diatom data from BC-IV core sample MS10

	Depth mm					
	5	40	120	200	280	320
Achnanthes brevipes	7	9	1	2	9	7
Achnanthes sp				1	1	
Actinoptychus senarius	2		1			
Camploneis cf *Grevillei* (frags)		1		1	2	
Coscinodiscus sp				1	2	1
Cocconeis sp				1		
Cyclotella sp	1				1	1
Diploneis cf *Bombus*				1		
Diploneis didyma	5	3		7	9	5
Diploneis interupta					4	8
Diploneis sp (frags)	1	1	1	4	4	5
Epithemia sp		1				
Melosira sp			1	1	1	
Navicula sp		1		1		1
Nitzschia navicularis	13	17	31	19	9	11
Nitzschia punctata	6	7	2	2	10	2
Paralia sulcata	14	9	10	6	4	
Pseudopodosira stelligera	2			1	2	2
Rhaphoneis amphiceros		1	1			
Synedra sp					1	1
Unidentified	1		2	1		

Table 5.2 Foraminifera from BC-IV monolith MS10 (Jan Gillespie)

Sample depth	*Context*	*Sediment*	*Taxa*	*Habitat*
60–80mm	4001	Soft silty clay	*Ammonia beccarii* *Trochammina inflate* *Gyroidinodes* *Haynesina germanica* *Grodinoides* *Elphidium*	Mudflat species
140–160mm	4001	Soft silty clay	*Ammonia beccarii* *Trochammina inflate* *Gyroidinodes* *Haynesina germanica* *Grodinoides* *Elphidium*	Mudflat species
220–240mm	4001	Soft silty clay	*Ammonia beccarii* *Trochammina inflate* *Gyroidinodes* *Haynesina germanica* *Grodinoides* *Elphidium*	Mudflat species
300–320mm	4001/4002	Transition peat	*Trochammina*	Marsh species
380–400mm		Land surface/peat	None	
460–480mm		Silty clay/coarse sand	None	
540–560mm		Silty clay/coarse sand	None	

5.3.1 The diatom assemblage

In the diatom assemblage brackish water and marine taxa are dominant, as expected. The most important types recovered include *Nitzschia navicularis*, *N. punctata*, *Paralia sulcata*, *Diploneis* spp, and *Achnanthes brevipes* (Table 5.1). There is also a range of other, less abundant, taxa. As with column MS04 (BC-II), there is some stratigraphical variation in the assemblages. Here, *Diploneis* spp, and especially *D. interupta*, are more frequent in the lower sediments, while *Nitzschia navicularis* and then *Paralia sulcata* become more important up the profile. *Diploneis interupta* is suggestive of salt marsh, while the change to *N. navicularis* indicates both a change to mudflat conditions and an increasing depth of water.

These changes in salt marsh and mudflat development were diachronous. Compared with BC-II, at lower elevation, it is tentatively suggested that by the middle Holocene salt marsh had developed over the peat at this elevation, while mudflat probably occurred further seaward. By this period relative sea level was rising at a lesser rate than evidenced for the earlier (Boreal) period. This allowed the gradual development of the more stable salt-marsh habitat (also see pollen in 5.2.1, above). However, relative sea level continued to rise, as demonstrated by the data here, with changing depositional habitats as the site became progressively more inundated – that is, change from fen woodland through herb fen to salt marsh, mudflat and more brackish water sediments.

5.3.2 Foraminifera

Seven samples were taken from MS10 (Table 5.2), revealing brackish water species. This corroborated the diatom results. The lower part of the core, which reaches into the coarse sands of context 4003, was devoid of foraminifera. The transitional phase from context 4002 (sandy/silty humic peat) into context 4001 (grey sediments) showed a very low abundance and the appearance of *Trochammina*, the high salt-marsh species. Beyond this transitional phase there was a gradual increase in abundance of the brackish water species *Ammonia beccarii*, *Gynoidinodes*, *Trochammina inflate*, *Haynesina germanica*, *Grodinoides*, and *Elphidium*. These become abundant towards the top of the core and into context 4001. These foraminifera are of the type found in mudflat habitats. The data thus agree with the diatom evidence for a continued sea-level rise with changing depositional habitats.

5.3.3 Conclusion

The samples from MS10 provide the shallowest and therefore the youngest palaeovegetation data for the basal peats along the submerged land surfaces of Bouldnor Cliff. This is reflected in the remains of flora which is of Atlantic (Flandrian Chronozone II) affinity. This monolith profile represents an old land surface between –6.46m and –6.64m OD with associated Mesolithic archaeology. The land surface

Table 5.3   Dendrochronological samples from BC-IV. Total rings = all measured rings. Sapwood rings = +?HS possible heartwood/sapwood boundary, +B bark edge, +16s number of sapwood rings. ARW = average ring width of the measured rings. Relative date of sequence = dated position against interim site mean Bouldnor_T8 (Nigel Nayling)

Publication sample code	Comments	Total rings	Sapwood rings	ARW mm/year	Relative date of sequence
DS24	Small stem or branch in peat located 15.5m along baseline from DP3 to DP4. Half of stem survived, with possible HS boundary	46	+?HS	1.48	undated
DS25	Wedge sample from oak stem. Insufficient rings – not measured	15		2.6	undated
DS26	Half stem with complete sapwood and bark edge. Compressed with slow-grown rings in sapwood. Cross-match against DS28	85	56+B	0.69	undated
DS27	*Alnus glutinosa* tree stump located 23.5m along baseline between DP3 and DP4				
DS28	Oak stem recovered next to DP2. Slow-grown later rings especially last 16 rings of sapwood, which were not measured. Cross-matches with DS26	78	36+16s	1.13	undated
DS29	Knotty oak branch recovered close to DS24 during excavation of trench dug for monolith sample MS13. Not measured	42	33s+B		undated
DS30	Large oak found on drift dive of peat shelf east of BC-IV. Wedge sample taken. Included in Bouldnor_T11 mean	175	–	1.10	107–281
DS31	East of BC-IV 2003, medium/large oak found on drift dive of peat shelf. Half slice taken. Included in Bouldnor_T11 mean	100	+?HS	1.53	98–197

was subject to increasing wetness, resulting in peat inception and ultimately brackish/marine transgression (see Chapter 8). This is reflected in the diatom and foraminifera assemblage. Radiocarbon measurements estimate the top of the peat/organic unit to date to *5350–5230 BC* (*OxA-15717*) (see 5.5, below).

5.4   Trees and dendrochronology
Nigel Nayling

During 2003, samples of sub-fossil trees were taken from an area of the seabed around BC-IV. No large oak boles were identified in the immediate area, but during a number of drift dives to the east samples were taken, including two from large oaks (DS30 and DS31), which have subsequently been matched against the interim site mean from Bouldnor II (Bouldnor_T8). The results are presented in Table 5.3.

Radiocarbon determinations from alder wood in this peat exposure provide calibrated dates in the last half of the sixth millennium BC, significantly later than those encountered at sites BC-II and BC-V. It is therefore unsurprising that none of the tree-ring sequences from the immediate vicinity have correlated with the mean sequences from BC-II. Sequences from two oak trees, DS26 and

DS28, cross-matched against each other but did not date against existing tree-ring chronologies. These sequences probably date to the sixth millennium BC, later than the 285-year mean (Bouldnor_T11) but predating absolutely dated oak chronologies from Britain and Ireland.

5.5   Radiocarbon dating: model development and analysis

Derek Hamilton, Peter Marshall, Garry Momber, Jan Gillespie, Christopher Bronk Ramsey, and Gordon Cook

Four samples of waterlogged wood remains were submitted from MS10 to provide a chronological framework within which the pollen results could be interpreted. The profile of this monolith is important, as it demonstrates the local establishment of lime (*Tilia*) woodland, which is now considered to have been the dominant or at least co-dominant woodland element throughout the middle and early part of the late Holocene of southern and eastern England.

The samples were taken from the monolith at 200–230mm, 230–260mm, 270–300mm and 300–330mm, and were collected from across the organic deposit which had the land surface at its base to provide a chronological framework within

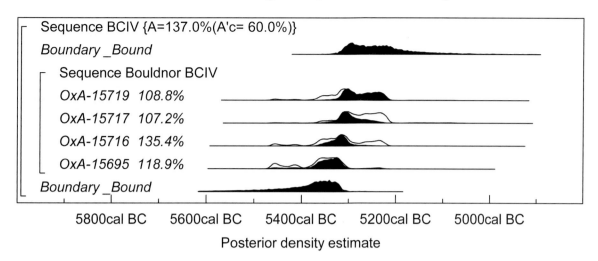

Figure 5.4   Chronological model of Bouldnor Cliff – BC-IV. Figures in outline are probability distributions of the simple calibrated dates, following Stuiver and Reimer (1993), while those in solid black are the posterior density estimates derived from the Bayesian modelling. The brackets down the left side and the OxCal keywords define the model exactly (Derek Hamilton)

Table 5.4   Radiocarbon results from BC-IV

Lab ID	Sample ID	Material	^{13}C (‰)	Radiocarbon age (BP)	Calibrated date (95% confidence)	Posterior density estimate (95% probability)
OxA-15719	MS10 20-23 BCIV 03	Quercus sp, twig	–25.0	6320 ± 40	5380–5210 cal BC	5330–5210 cal BC
OxA-15717	MS10 23-26 BCIV 03	Twig, unidentified	–26.5	6300 ± 40	5370–5210 cal BC	5350–5230 cal BC
OxA-15716	MS10 27-30 BCIV 03	Wood knot, unidentified	–28.1	6335 ± 40	5470–5210 cal BC	5370–5270 cal BC
OxA-15695	MS10 30-33 BCIV 03	Twigs, unidentified	–27.6	6369 ± 34	5470–5300 cal BC	5470–5440 cal BC (2%) or 5430–5300 cal BC (93%)

which the pollen results could be interpreted. The monolith was from a depth of –6.8m to –6.2m OD. The results are presented in Table 5.4. A full description of the methods used to select and analyse the samples is presented in Chapter 3, 3.10, while discussion of the results in relation to the other sites along Bouldnor Cliff can be seen in Chapter 6, 6.1.

Two local pollen zone boundaries were detected in this core at *c* 440mm (Zone 1/2 boundary) and 260mm (Zone 2/3 boundary). Although four samples were submitted in total, owing to the lack of suitable material only the boundary between Zones 2 and 3 could be dated, with the earliest date in this sequence providing a *terminus ante quem* for the arrival of *Tilia* sp.

5.5.1   Results

The model for these four dates shows good overall agreement between the radiocarbon measurements and their stratigraphic order ($A_{overall}$=137.0%). The model represented by Figure 5.4 provides a *terminus ante quem* for the arrival of *Tilia* sp. (Zone 1/2) in *5430–5300 cal BC (OxA-15695; 93% probability)* and estimates its cessation as a dominant/co-dominant species (Zone 2/3) in *5350–5230 cal BC (OxA-15717; 95% probability)*.

Since over 100mm of sediment had accumulated between the arrival of *Tilia* sp. in the pollen record and the earliest date in this sequence, this *terminus ante quem* should be regarded with caution, as it is imprecise.

6 Dendrochronological and radiocarbon synthesis across the –11m OD peat shelf

by Nigel Nayling and Derek Hamilton

The analysis of the dendrochronological and radio-carbon data along Bouldnor Cliff has been described in Chapters 3, 4, and 5. Each area has been looked at individually because they have been subject to specialist analysis that is particular to that locale. However, the three find spots are related across a common submerged land surface that became steadily inundated. The following section compares the dating results, thereby providing a considered temporal framework for occupation in the changing environment while the 'Bouldnor Valley' was being flooded (Table 6.1).

6.1 Radiocarbon dating and depths from across Bouldnor Cliff
Derek Hamilton

The difference in depths between the sites reflects the rising sea level, as the items selected for dating were recovered from the organic peat which sat immediately above the landscape from which archaeological material was recovered.

6.1.1 Discussion of radiocarbon wiggle-matching

The results of wiggle-matching the radiocarbon results on a sequence of six decadal blocks from

a tree-ring sequence at BC-II is given in Figure 6.1. These results can be compared with the dendrochronological results below (6.2). Despite two of the six measurements having low individual indices of agreement (UB-6862 [A=13.5%]; UB-6859 [A=42.0%], A'=60.0%), the model has a good overall index of agreement ($A_{overall}$=32.4%, A_n=28.9%), suggesting that the results are consistent with their relative order. The model estimates the date of the last tree-ring of the sequence to be *6030–5990 cal BC (95% probability*; Fig 6.1; last ring), and probably *6020–6000 cal BC (68% probability)*.

6.2 Synthesis and discussion of dendrochronological results
Nigel Nayling

Sampling and subsequent analysis of those samples from oaks surviving on the seabed at a number of locations at Bouldnor Cliff has led to the cross-matching of eleven samples (eight from BC-II, one from BC-V and two from east of BC-IV) to form a 285-year ring-width site mean (Bouldnor_T11).

Wiggle-match radiocarbon dating of six sequential decadal blocks of samples from tree DS06/12 indicates that the last ring of the wiggle-match sequence dates to *6030–5990 cal BC (95% probability)* (Chapter 6, 6.1.1). The last measured ring of sample DS06/12 equates to ring 258 of the 285-

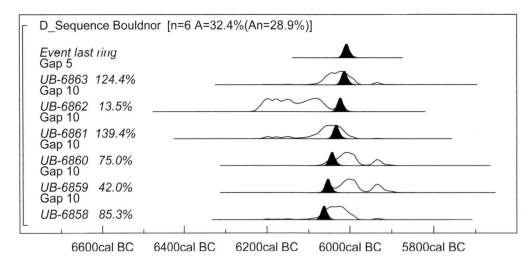

Figure 6.1 Chronological model of the radiocarbon wiggle-match. Figures in outline are the probability distributions of the simple calibrated dates, following Stuiver and Reimer (1993), while those in solid black are the posterior density estimates derived from the Bayesian modelling. The brackets down the left side and the OxCal keywords define the model exactly (Derek Hamilton)

Table 6.1   Combined radiocarbon results from BC–II, BC–IV, and BC–V

Lab ID	Sample ID	Material	¹³C (‰)	Radiocarbon age (BP)	Calibrated date (95% confidence)	Posterior density estimate (95% probability)
BC–II						
SUERC–11286	SO70 BCII 06	*Alnus glutinosa*, r/w	–28.0	7030 ± 35	6000–5840 cal BC	*5990–5890 cal BC*
SUERC-11284	SO71 BCII 06	bark, unidentified	–28.0	7060 ± 35	6020–5880 cal BC	*6000–5920 cal BC*
SUERC-7579	MS06 12 BCII	Monocotyledon leaf	–26.8	6925 ± 35	5900–5720 cal BC	–
OxA-15698	MS05 16 BCII	*Betula* sp, 10 years	–26.0	6956 ± 35		–
OxA-15721	MS05 16 BCII	*Betula* sp, 10 years	–26.2	6915 ± 40		–
mean	T'=0.6, =1, T'(5%)=3.8; Ward and Wilson 1978		–	6938 ± 26	5890–5730 cal BC	–
SUERC-11285	SO72 BCII 06	*Prunus* sp, 15mm r/w	–28.6	7065 ± 35	6000–5880 cal BC	*6010–5940 cal BC*
OxA-15696	MS08 14 BCII 03	*Alnus glutinosa*, twig	–24.4	7013 ± 36	6000–5800 cal BC	*6000–5910 cal BC*
SUERC-7560	MS08 08 BCII	*Alnus glutinosa*, r/w	–29.3	7105 ± 35	6050–5910 cal BC	*6010–5960 cal BC (90%) or 5950–5920 cal BC (5%)*
SUERC-7580	SO31 10 BCII	*Alnus glutinosa*, r/w	–22.7	7115 ± 35	6060–5910 cal BC	*6020–5970 cal BC*
SUERC-7562	MS20 03 BCII	*Alnus glutinosa*, r/w	–28.5	7130 ± 35	6070–5920 cal BC	*6030–5980 cal BC*
OxA-15718	MS08 40 BCII 03	*Corylus avellana*, twig	–27.2	7175 ± 45	6100–5980 cal BC	*6030–5980 cal BC*
OxA-15720	MS07 10-12 BCII 03	*Alnus glutinosa*, r/w, 3 years	–24.5	7125 ± 45	6070–5910 cal BC	*6040–5990 cal BC*
SUERC-8157	MS08 05 BCII	*Alnus glutinosa*, r/w	–27.7	7110 ± 40	6060–5900 cal BC	*6040–5990 cal BC*
OxA-15697	MS07 22 BCII 03	cf. *Betula* sp, 7 years	–26.9	7110 ± 34	6060–5910 cal BC	*6060–5990 cal BC*
SUERC-7561	MS07 01 BCII	*Alnus glutinosa*, r/w	–29.3	7175 ± 40	6090–5980 cal BC	*6060–5990 cal BC*
BC-IV						
OxA-15719	MS10 20-23 BCIV 03	*Quercus* sp, twig	–25.0	6320 ± 40	5380–5210 cal BC	*5330–5210 cal BC*
OxA-15717	MS10 23-26 BCIV 03	twig, unidentified	–26.5	6300 ± 40	5370–5210 cal BC	*5350–5230 cal BC*
OxA-15716	MS10 27-30 BCIV 03	wood knot, unidentified	–28.1	6335 ± 40	5470–5210 cal BC	*5370–5270 cal BC*
OxA-15695	MS10 30-33 BCIV 03	twigs, unidentified	–27.6	6369 ± 34	5470–5300 cal BC	*5470–5440 cal BC (2%) or 5430–5300 cal BC (93%)*
BC-V						
OxA-15722	MS17 31 BCV	?root, unidentified	–28.3	7230 ± 45	6220–6010 cal BC	*6080–5990 cal BC*
OxA-15723	MS17 38.5 BCV	*Alnus glutinosa*, twig	–27.2	7170 ± 45	6100–5980 cal BC	*6100–6000 cal BC*
OxA-15699	MS17 48 BCV	*Alnus glutinosa*, twig	–27.4	7203 ± 36	6210–6000 cal BC	*6210–6190 cal BC (2%) or 6180–6140 cal BC (4%) or 6120–6010 cal BC (89%)*
Wiggle-match						
UB-6863	Q10745F	*Quercus* sp; rings 211–220	–27.0	7156 ± 41	6080–5930 cal BC	*6030–5990 cal BC*
UB-6862	Q10745E	*Quercus* sp; rings 201–210	–25.0	7259 ± 41	6230–6020 cal BC	*6040–6000 cal BC*
UB-6861	Q10745D	*Quercus* sp; rings 191–200	–25.0	7191 ± 41	6210–5990 cal BC	*6050–6010 cal BC*
UB-6860	Q10745C	*Quercus* sp; rings 181–190	–25.0	7127 ± 40	6070–5910 cal BC	*6060–6020 cal BC*
UB-6859	Q10745B	*Quercus* sp; rings 171–180	–27.0	7115 ± 42	6070–5900 cal BC	*6070–6030 cal BC*
UB-6858	Q10745A	*Quercus* sp; rings 161–170	–26.0	7168 ± 42	6090–5980 cal BC	*6080–6040 cal BC*
Tanners Hard						
Beta-166477	TH 01 00A	Organic sediment	–25.0	5510 ± 70	4490–4230 cal BC	–
Beta-166478	TH 01 06A	Organic sediment	–25.0	6170 ± 60	5310–4940 cal BC	–

Table 6.2   Cross-matching dendrochronological sequences. t-values for the 285-year, 11-tree site mean Bouldnor_T11, against Mesolithic oak ring-width chronologies from the Severn Estuary (Nigel Nayling)

Site masters	t-*value*
Redwick, Gwent Levels, Wales (Nayling pers comm)	7.90
Goldcliff, Gwent Levels, Wales (Nayling pers comm)	7.46
Gravel Banks, near Avonmouth, England (Nayling pers comm)	7.91

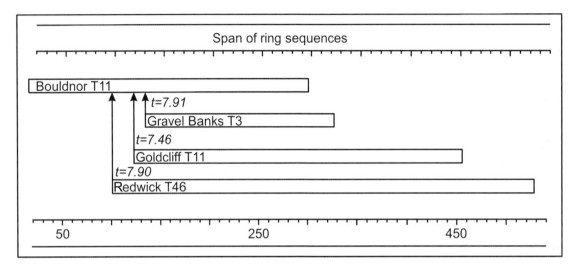

Figure 6.2   Bar diagram showing relative dating positions of site means from Bouldnor Cliff, Gravel Banks (near Avonmouth), Redwick and Goldcliff with computer correlations between sequences given as t-values (Nigel Nayling)

year site mean Bouldnor_T11, hence this site mean is dated from *6280–6240 cal BC to 6000–5960 cal BC (95% probability)*. This predates established calendrically dated tree-ring-width oak series from Britain by some 700 years.

High computer correlations have been identified between the mean Bouldnor_T11 and three cross-matching chronologies constructed independently by the author from intertidally exposed 'submerged forests' at Redwick and Goldcliff off the Welsh Gwent Levels, and Gravel Banks off Chittening Wharf, Avonmouth (Druce 2000). The results are presented in Table 6.2 and Figure 6.2.

Combination of the four cross-matched sites means Mesolithic exposures in the Severn estuary and Bouldnor Cliff produce a 510-year chronology which predates absolutely dated chronologies but can be dated approximately through wiggle-

matching to *c 6280–6240 cal BC to 5780–5740 cal BC (95% probability)*. Radiocarbon models suggest that most of the oak trees studied grew during the period of Mesolithic activity prior to peat development. Some exposures at Bouldnor, such as BC-V, located slightly higher than much of the basal peat shelf, contain trees which were growing during the mid-sixth millennium BC. Continued research at both intertidal and subtidal sites is such that the trees encountered in the Severn and Solent may offer the best way forward in the extension of a well-replicated oak chronology for Britain. This would potentially bridge the gap between calendrically dated tree-ring series beginning in the late sixth millennium BC and the floating chronologies from the Solent and Severn estuary, which span the late seventh and early sixth millennia BC.

7 Environmental change in the cultural landscape across the valley

by Garry Momber, Rob Scaife, and Nigel Nayling

The terrestrial landscape at Bouldnor would have extended across the valley floor into the New Forest. Today the land has been sliced in two, but large tracts of the submerged prehistoric landscape still remain in the north-west Solent. This area has been the source of many artefacts and is therefore an integral part of the old Solent cultural landscape. It has provided essential data for the interpretation of sea-level rise and the geomorphological evolution of this drowned valley system.

7.1 Bathymetry of the submerged land surface at Tanners Hard

Straight out from Tanners Hard on the north-west shore of the Solent the coastline is fringed with mudflat which gently dips below the tidal reach to form a large expanse of shallow water. At a depth of –3.5m OD the muddy silt on the seabed soon gives way to peat. Here lie remnants of a palaeo-land surface that has now been exposed by thinning of the protective mudflats (see Fig 1.3).

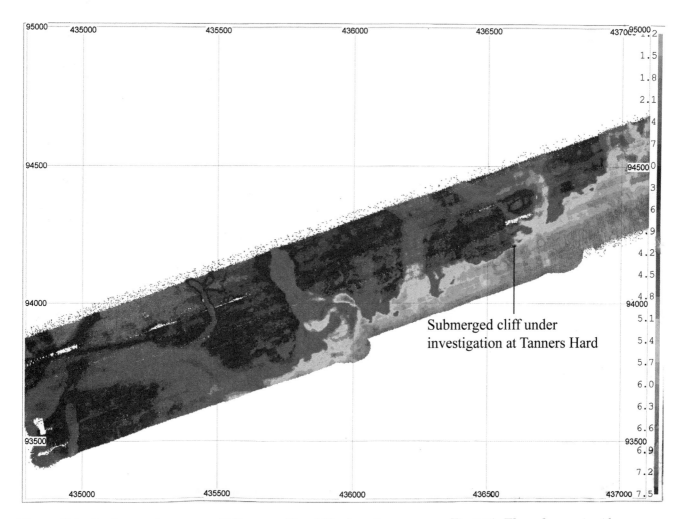

Submerged cliff under investigation at Tanners Hard

Figure 7.1 Bathymetric survey off Tanners Hard (for location map see Fig 1.7). The colours signify different depths. The blue/purple area is peat which lies at 3.5–4m below OD. The bright red channels cut through the peat at a deeper depth of 4–5m below OD. The green is deeper still, at –6m OD. Sharp changes in colour represent steep slopes off vertical drop-offs (Garry Momber from data provided by courtesy of Submatrix/Sea)

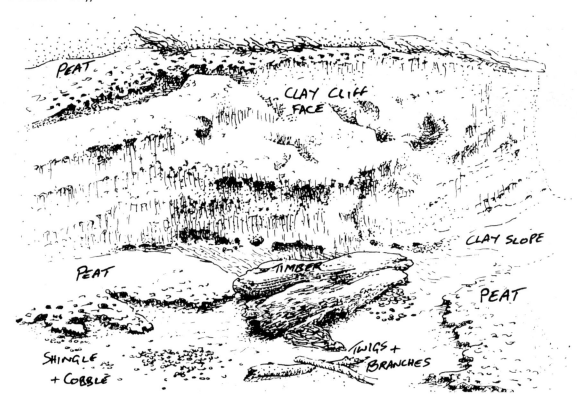

Figure 7.2   Measured sketch of south-facing cliff section in the survey area at Tanners Hard (Courtesy of Paul Cowling)

One kilometre from the beach the bathymetric survey conducted by Submetrix/SEA Ltd shows that the shallows are abruptly truncated by a cliff, the seabed dropping from *c* –4m to *c* –6m OD (Fig 7.1). In the deeper water to the south of the cliff hundreds of lithics have been found by fishermen as they trawl for oysters (see Chapter 1), many of these finds coming from the stretch of water running east of the Lymington River and past Tanners Hard (M White, pers comm).

In 1998 divers were deployed to inspect the area of interest (Chapter 1, 1.3.2). They recorded a seabed that was covered with oyster shells, gravel, and the occasional piece of flint (possibly worked) in 6–7m of water. To the north of the cobble-covered seabed was the distinctive interface with its step of almost 2m. This distinctive profile lent itself to sectioning and was deemed most suitable for further investigation (Fig 7.2).

In the summer of 2000 an evaluation trench was excavated into the cliff at the south of the plateau off Tanners Hard by the Poole Bay Archaeological Group under the guidance of Mike Markey, aboard his boat *Peveril Myth*. A section 1.5m high was cut back into the cliff and monolith samples were collected. The top of the section was capped by peat over soft grey clay (Fig 7.3), at the base of which lay another lens of peat 0.2m thick. This was exposed at the foot of the cliff, from which it extended no more than 2m before being lost to erosion. Fluvial gravels were evident below the peat. The monolith samples have been subject to palaeoenvironmental analysis

by Dr Rob Scaife and radiocarbon dated. The base of the upper peat, which sat at a depth of –4m OD, was dated to 5510 ± 70 BP (2 sig cal BC 4470 to 4240) (cal BP 6420–6190) (Beta-166477), while the lower peat, beneath the silt at a depth of –5.7m, provided a date of 6170 ± 60 BP (2 sig cal BC 5290–4940) (cal BP 7240–6890) (Beta-166478). The results of the pollen analysis are reported in 7.3.1 (below).

Tanners Hard, positioned on the opposite slope of the old valley from Bouldnor Cliff, has the potential to inform our understanding of the rate, scale, and impact of sea-level rise on the previously occupied landscape. It held material comparable with that at Bouldnor, allowing changes that affected the submerged cultural landscape within the Western Solent to be considered over a wider spatial and temporal context.

7.2   Survey and sampling

Prior to the recovery of samples the area of interest on the seabed was surveyed. A large, circular iron sinker was positioned on the seabed to act as a primary datum. This lay on the top of the peat platform at a depth of –4m OD and a distance of 5m from the edge of the south-facing cliff. The sinker was marked by attaching a taut buoyed line and calculating the position of the buoy with a GPS; from this point the survey area could be georeferenced. A grid measuring 20m wide and 10m deep was set up adjacent to the datum. The grid was

Figure 7.3 Termination of the peat plateau at Tanners Hard, showing a capping of peat over fine-grained alluvial sediments (Garry Momber)

Figure 7.4 Diver using an auger to sample the old land surface below the capping of peat (Emmy Kelly)

separated into five corridors for examination by divers.

The remains of fifteen pieces of timber protruding from the peat bed were plotted. They were subject to extensive marine boring but remaining bark on several pieces indicated silver birch. One bole of an unidentified tree measured 0.5m in diameter. The tree rings were not counted, but the relatively large girth suggested a prolonged period of stability prior to submergence.

The seabed surveyed was generally flat, although it had been incised by two small erosion gullies. Such features were commonly seen by divers across the surface of the peat platform. Completion of the survey provided benchmark data that could be revisited to monitor future changes in the seabed at this point; however, no archaeological material was recorded.

Additional seabed inspection was carried out along the foot of the cliff 2–3m south of the lower peat exposure. This was an area covered in shell and cobble. Pieces of flint, one of which was a flake, were found among the cobble.

Following the pre-disturbance survey an additional baseline was laid out for hand augering. A gouge auger 1m long and 30mm in diameter was used. Extensions of 1m were attached underwater, enabling samples to be collected to a depth of 2m. Extra extensions could have been added, but it was not possible for the free-swimming divers to push the auger any further into the seabed (Fig 7.4).

The auger baseline ran north for 20m from the edge of the cliff, bisecting the survey area. A team led by Mike Markey from the Poole Bay Archaeological Research Group collected six auger samples along the transect at 0.5m, 2m, 4m, 10m, 15m, and 20m from the cliff (Fig 7.5). The auger results indicated that the thickness of the covering peat increased with distance from the edge of the cliff, while the underlying clay contained pockets of organic material.

During the same operation a section of the south-facing cliff was cleaned and samples of the peat were collected from the upper and lower peat deposits. A cohesive block of sediment measuring $0.25m^2$ (this sample size being large enough to retain the integrity of the well-consolidated peat) was removed from the top of the cliff face with a handsaw. The leading edge of the peat was 180mm thick, and below it was a soft grey clay similar to the covering Holocene alluvium seen at Bouldnor Cliff. The clay rested on the basal peat at –5.7m ± 0.15m OD.

The lower peat, which was about 100mm thick, was less consolidated than the upper deposit. Below it, sand and gravel were evident. A monolith tin was used to sample this less compact layer. Both samples were sub-sampled by Dr Rob Scaife for palaeo-environmental analysis and radiocarbon dating (see Chapter 7, 7.3).

In 2001 the bathymetry was recorded to decimetric resolution with the Submetrix/SEA Ltd interferrometric ISIS 100 survey system (Momber and Geen 2000) to establish the extent of the deposits. Within a single day this provided a georeferenced image of the seabed that would otherwise have taken divers many years to record. The positions were recorded with an RTK DGPS that enabled accurate three-dimensional mapping. The data has been used to inspect the area remotely, relocate divers, and calculate high-resolution depths in the order of ± 0.15m (see Fig

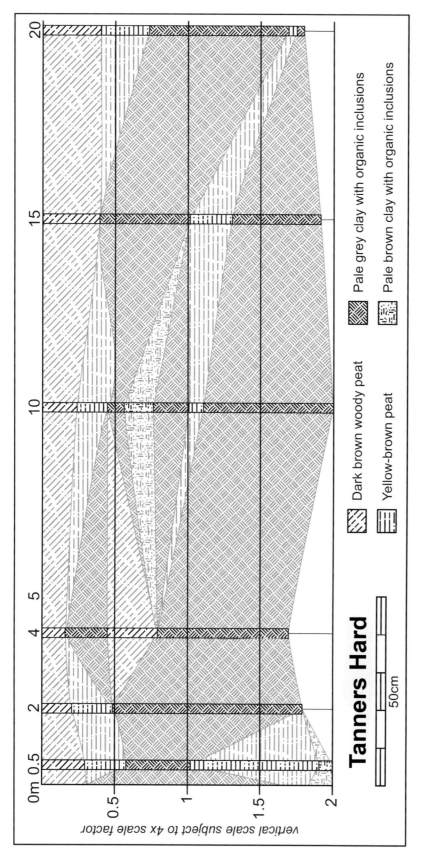

Figure 7.5   Auger transect running south–north at Tanners Hard (Julian Whitewright after Mike Markey)

7.1). The top of the cliff was confirmed to be –4m ± 0.15m OD.

7.3 Tanners Hard: the palaeoenvironment and archaeology
Rob Scaife

Two pollen profiles were obtained from the lower and upper peat deposits. They show significant changes in their pollen spectra and have been assigned to local pollen zones accordingly.

7.3.1 Tanners Hard lower peat (Profile 1)

The lowest peat rests on a sandy substrate (Fig 7.6). Two zones have been recognised in this short basal profile and are characterised below.

Zone 1: 360mm to 310mm Quercus–Tilia

Basal sands. This zone is dominated by trees and shrubs. *Tilia* is dominant, with highest values in the base (63%) subsequently declining sharply. *Quercus* increases to maximum values at the top of this zone (59%). Shrubs comprise *Corylus avellana* type (17%) declining upwards. There are few herbs, with Poaceae most important (to 20%). Wetland taxa include *Alnus glutinosa* (to 20% sum + marsh) with occasional *Salix*, and possibly *Frangula*. Fen herbs comprise Cyperaceae. *Pteridium aquilinum* is the most important fern. *Polypodium* is most important in this zone.

Zone 2: 310mm to 260mm Quercus–Corylus avellana type–Poaceae

This zone is characterised by a sharp expansion of Poaceae (to 68%) and generally increased herb diversity, including increases in Chenopodiaceae (5%). There is a corresponding reduction in trees and shrubs, with only occasional *Tilia* after its previous dominance. *Quercus* is the dominant woodland type (15–30%), with *Corylus avellana* type (peak to 20%). Marsh taxa remain as zone 1 but with some reduction of *Alnus* (5–10%).

7.3.2 Tanners Hard upper peat (Profile 2)

Four pollen assemblage zones have been recognised in this short (180mm) organic unit (Fig 7.7).

Zone 1: 180mm to 150mm Quercus–Corylus avellana type

Quercus (33%) and *Corylus avellana* type (30% at the base of the profile) are the principal shrubs, with occasional records of *Ulmus*, *Tilia*, and *Fraxinus*. There is also some long-distance *Pinus*. Herbs comprise Poaceae, which is increasing in importance (10–45%) to full dominance in the subsequent zone 2. There are few marsh taxa represented, with only small numbers of *Alnus*, *Salix*, and Cyperaceae.

Zone 2: 150mm to 70mm Poaceae

Poaceae are dominant, with high values (peaking to 78%). Trees and shrubs are correspondingly low, with sporadic *Betula*, *Tilia*, and *Ulmus*. *Quercus* and *Corylus avellana* type have highest values (c 10–15% and 5–6% respectively). Other herbs include peaks of Chenopodiaceae, *Aster* type, and *Typha/Sparganium* type.

Zone 3: 70mm to 30mm Quercus–Alnus glutinosa

There is a marked change from a dominance of Poaceae to an expansion of trees and shrubs. *Quercus* peaks to 65%, with *Betula* (5%), *Ulmus* (to 10%), *Tilia* (3%), and *Corylus avellana* type (10%). *Alnus glutinosa* becomes the dominant fen taxon, with high percentage values (peak to 86%).

Zone 4: 30mm to 0mm Quercus–Alnus glutinosa–Cyperaceae–Osmunda regalis

In the upper levels of this peat there is a further change, with a sharp expansion of Cyperaceae (23%), *Osmunda regalis* (40% sum + spores) and some *Salix*. *Quercus* and *Alnus glutinosa* remain important but decline in response to the expansion of herbs. *Corylus avellana* type remains consistent (c 10%).

7.3.3 Radiocarbon dating and the vegetation environment

The lower peat at –5.8m ± 0.15m OD, dated to *5310–4940 cal BC (Beta-166478)*, is placed within the middle Holocene (Atlantic) period (Flandrian II) – the late Mesolithic. The upper peat, from a depth of –4m OD, which falls at the Atlantic/sub-Boreal, dates to *4470–4240 cal BC (Beta-166477)* – the early Neolithic. This sample was recovered from the peat deposit at a depth of –4.1m ± 0.15m OD.

The most diagnostic element of the lower sequence is the presence of dominant lime (*Tilia*) woodland. This was growing on-site on the palaeosols developed in the basal sands and gravels. Lime is considered to be under-represented in most pollen spectra because of its entomophily and because it flowers during summer, when trees are in full leaf, thus inhibiting dissemination (Andersen 1970; 1973). Such high pollen values here attest to its on-site growth and data are comparable with other local

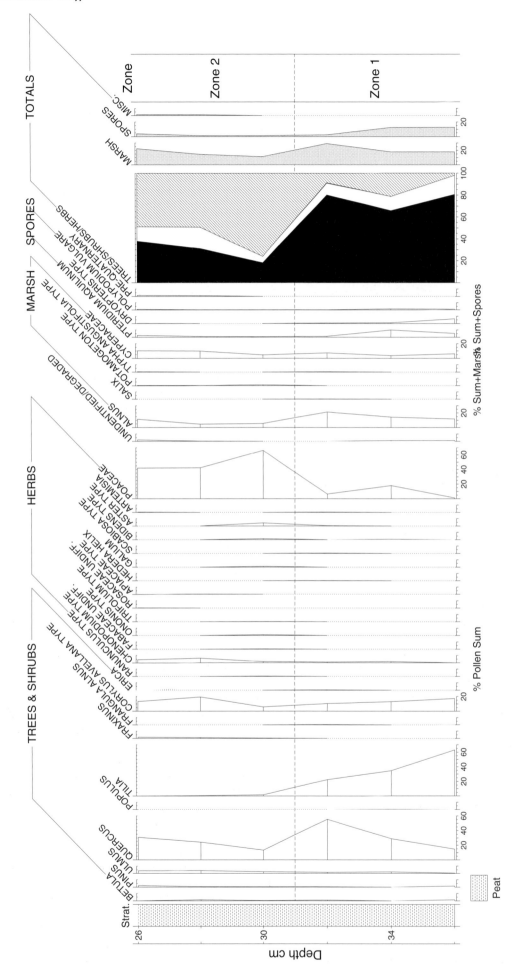

Figure 7.6   Pollen diagram of the lower peat at Tanners Hard (Rob Scaife)

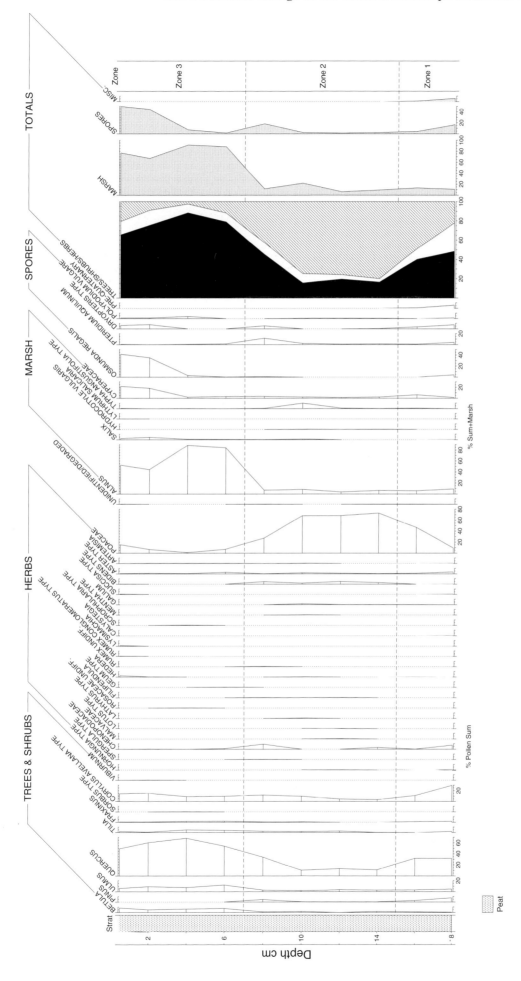

Figure 7.7   Pollen diagram of the upper peat at Tanners Hard (Rob Scaife)

and regional sites, indicating its importance as one of the primary and dominant woodland constituents of the mid-Holocene.

The date here of *5310–4940 cal BC (Beta-166478)* is commensurate with the presence of lime woodland at Gatcombe Withy Bed and Borthwood Farm (Scaife 1980; 1987; 1992). The sandy lithology at this site would have given rise to the well-drained soils which lime favours. With rising relative sea level, however, the hydrology/local groundwater table was affected, causing peat accumulation. As a consequence lime became a less important component of the pollen assemblages locally, although it remained important on adjacent interfluves at greater distance. In addition to lime, oak and hazel were also important woodland elements. Small numbers of alder pollen represent localised growth or more extensive woodland at distance.

The on-site autochthonous vegetation became a grass–sedge fen in which peat formation occurred. The presence of some Chenopodiaceae may derive from halophytes, which are indicative of saline ingress.

The upper peat dated at *4470–4240 cal BC (Beta-166477)* similarly developed under a grass–sedge fen/reedswamp. This was subsequently colonised by alder, forming a carr (Alnetum). Again, owing to rising relative sea level and final inundation there was a retrogressive hydrosere culminating in deposition of sediments in a saline/brackish water environment. An intermediate/transitional phase saw local waterlogging resulting in a change from Alnetum and colonisation by a fen with sedges (Cyperaceae) and, interestingly, royal fern (*Osmunda regalis*). The terrestrial woodland at this time comprised elm, oak, and hazel, and probably ash and lime (NB: the latter are poorly represented in pollen spectra). There are no indications of human activity discernable in this pollen record.

7.3.4   Trees and dendrochronology on the northern shore of the West Solent
Nigel Nayling

During 2001, the dives made to examine oak trees exposed in the vicinity of Tanners Hard found trees most commonly in growth positions on the eroding edge of the upper of two peat shelves or resting on the lower peat shelf in an unstratified state. Only a small number of samples were recovered for analysis and there are no absolute dates for any of the tree-ring sequences generated. Given the quantity of material present along the eroding edge of this extensive exposure, the potential for generating well-replicated chronologies of later Mesolithic to Neolithic date may be high. If these oaks are associated with peat growth, however, they may well have periods of markedly suppressed growth often associated with changes in very local hydrology, which might make chronology-building challenging (Nayling and Manning 2007; Sass-Klaassen *et al* 2004).

Section three

Establishing the changing environmental and physical context of the cultural landscape

The lives of the Mesolithic hunter-gatherer communities that dwelt in and around the Solent basin were dictated in no small part by their natural surroundings. The synthesis of the findings relating to the environmental context of the cultural landscape is outlined in Chapter 8. Here, the backdrop to occupation before, during, and after rising sea levels drowned out the cultural landscape is set out.

Chapter 9 looks at the relative sea-level rise. The radiocarbon dates, gathered as part of the research in the Western Solent over the last decade, are correlated against the palaeoenvironmental deposits to calculate sea-level index points. The research has enabled these dates to be integrated into the regional sea-level curve. The relationship between land and sea had a marked impact on the ecosystems around the Solent, shaping the land and having a direct impact on vegetation adjacent to the coastline.

The final chapter in this section, Chapter 10, builds on the conclusions of Chapters 8 and 9 to look at the reformation of the landscape under the pressure of increasing marine inundation. Palynological, sedimentary, and bathymetric evidence is drawn on to re-create and model the impact of the transgression. The influence of the changing physical and natural environment on the past occupants of Bouldnor is also considered.

8   The changing vegetation and environment
by Rob Scaife

Radiocarbon dating (see Chapter 3, 3.10) shows that the range of basal stratigraphical contexts at BC-II fall within the late Boreal (Flandrian Ic) and early part of the middle Holocene (Atlantic) period. In the cases of BC-IV and Tanners Hard (see Chapter 7, 7.3.1.3), the peats are of middle and late Atlantic date. This discrepancy in dating reflects the diachronous character of the peat formation in relation to marine transgression. Although the age span of the sediments associated with the archaeology that has been uncovered to date along the submerged peat platform is only a few centuries, it is a critical period in terms of sea-level change and the establishment of the coastline in broadly its present form. It is primarily eustatic change that was responsible for the changing environment, consequent sediment regime, and the final submergence of the old land surface of Mesolithic occupation.

8.1   A background to the vegetation and environment

As noted above, radiocarbon dating shows that the pollen sequences, while providing information on the environment of the site and the local area, give only a small window on what was a period of dynamic vegetation initiated at the close of the last cold stage (the Devensian) at c 9500 cal BC (c 10,000 BP). Climatic amelioration at this date set in motion the widespread migration of vegetation types from their glacial refugia. The successional expansion to dominance of pioneer species followed by dominants is well documented. Local pollen data spanning this period come from earlier work further to the northeast at Bouldnor (Scaife 2000a) and from Isle of Wight terrestrial sites at Gatcombe Withy Bed and Munsley Bog (Scaife 1980; 1982; 1987; 2003c). From Hampshire the sites of Cranes Moor, New Forest (Barber and Clarke 1987), and Southampton Water (Godwin and Godwin 1940; Long and Scaife 1996; Scaife in Long et al 2000) are comparable.

Prior to the start of sedimentation at the Bouldnor sites, the immediate post-glacial period was characterised by rapid expansion of juniper and birch on dry ground and willow in wetter valley bottoms at c 9500–9270 cal BC (c 10,000 to 9800 BP). This was followed by a rapid expansion and dominance of pine by c 8250 cal BC (c 9000 BP). Arrival of hazel, oak, and elm into the region shortly after pine dominance provided the principal tree types during the late Boreal period of Mesolithic habitation at this site. Alder and lime were exceptions, arriving during the late Boreal and early Atlantic transition period at c 5900 BC (c 7000 BP) – that is, prior to the separation of Britain from continental sources. The period before Mesolithic occupation at this site was thus a highly dynamic one which culminated in the often-described stable 'climax woodland' environment of mixed oak forest (Quercetum mixtum) of the middle Holocene (Atlantic) period. In reality, such vegetation is now viewed more realistically as a polyclimax, with different ecological niches (soil type, moisture, aspect and so on) giving rise to different dominant taxa and communities. This is clearly the case here, with pollen data providing an insight into the on-site habitats as well as the near-local vegetation of drier land/interfluves away from the river gravel/sand bars on which human activity at BC-II was focused.

The environmental evidence suggests that Mesolithic activity/occupation at BC-II took place on a sandy possible river bar which was semi-stabilised by close-matted vegetation at around c 6200–6000 cal BC (c 7000–7200 BP). This habitat produced the humic sandy soil/old land surface evidenced in monoliths MS07 and MS08 (pollen figures in Chapter 3, 3.5). It is possible that this was colonised by grass, but bracken is also noted at these levels. Such growth would be in accord with the acid sandy (semi-podzolic) soils. In the case of monolith MS07, higher values of monolete fern spores are also indicative of soil formation through differential formation of this robust palynomorph. It was this basal soil profile in which lithics have been recovered, directly from monolith profiles MS07 and MS08 at BC-II and in the proximity of MS10 at BC-IV.

As a result of the faunal and mechanical mixing which has taken place, it is possible that these artefacts predate the radiocarbon dates obtained from the soil. This is also very likely to be the case for the pollen associated with these artefacts in the soil. This problem is well documented for soils from other Mesolithic sites, as at Iping Common (Keefe et al 1965) and Rackham (Dimbleby and Bradley 1975), both Sussex, and relates to the taphonomy of pollen in soils (Dimbleby 1985). Pollen moves progressively down soil profiles through various mechanisms and differentially from larger artefacts such as flint blades, while 'normal' pollen profiles come from vertical stratigraphical peat or sediment accumulation. However, because the Mesolithic environment at Bouldnor Cliff was probably a relatively short-lived and ephemeral feature, it seems unlikely that the age of the artefacts is substantially greater than that of the soils.

Although it is suggested that the the on-site habitat was characterised by herbaceous vegetation, it is clear that alder was an important element of the nearby wetland ecology (in pollen profiles

MS07 and MS08). Whether this was on a floodplain, in fen carr woodland or as growth along the banks of a larger waterway and its tributaries is not clear from the pollen evidence. Its presence locally is, however, also evidenced by its macrofossil remains (Chapter 3, 3.7). Such expansion and importance is typical of the late Boreal to early Atlantic period and is attributed to the increase of suitable habitats caused by extension of the coastline and waterlogging of river valleys through rising relative sea levels and increased precipitation (McVean 1953; 1956; Godwin 1975).

In the immediate vicinity of the site the dry land/terrestrial vegetation was one of dominant coniferous (pine) and deciduous (oak, elm, and hazel) woodland. As noted above, the former was in its descendancy, with oak, elm, and hazel the expanding woodland prior to the rapid expansion of lime to dominance during the middle Holocene. It is not clear, however (there is no definite evidence), whether these formed a mixed woodland environment or whether community stands were associated with different edaphic conditions. The latter would seem the most plausible, with pine retaining its dominance locally on the sandy Headon Beds. Indeed, it has been suggested that some small areas of pine may have remained in these areas until as late as the Neolithic period, at *c* 4350 cal BC (*c* 5500 BP) (Scaife 1980).

It is clear, however, by virtue of the macrofossil remains, that the oak and hazel (and probably elm) were important locally, being able to tolerate the damper and heavier soils at lower altitudes and on the alluvial floodplains of the rivers. Sporadic/occasional occurrences of small-leaved lime (*Tilia cordata*) pollen are the first indications of its late Boreal arrival and local growth prior to middle Holocene dominance in the region. In terms of human occupation, these varied habitats would provide a typical ecotonal range suited to the hunting and foraging existence of the Mesolithic peoples.

8.2 Subsequent environmental changes

Based on the restricted evidence recovered from the small section inspected, the longevity of occupation was limited. This is possibly a factor of the ephemeral character of the river-bar environment or may indicate that evidence of previous occupation has yet to be found. Furthermore, rising relative sea level caused increasing wetness through the ponding back of river systems and probably also higher groundwater tables. The sedimentological response to this was the initiation of peat-forming conditions radiocarbon dated to *c* 6950–7100 BP that would have challenged ongoing activity at this location. This took the form of a humic detrital accumulation from leaf fall and from the ground flora under a damp oak/hazel woodland. In column MS08, this increase in wetness may also be evidenced by some expansion of alder in wetter areas. Some willow is

also in evidence, possibly marking the establishment of more extensive carr woodland.

This phase of peat formation was a short period of transition from low-lying marsh conditions with probable anatomising river systems and river sandbanks and bars to one of full mudflat, fringing salt marsh, and marine conditions. The peat sequence was a diachronous unit, which transgressed the coastal zone in response to rising base levels caused by the regional effects of positive eustatic change change. Thus, for example, the highest (altitude) monolith MS10 from BC-IV and the section at Tanners Hard have peats which are dated to the middle Holocene (Atlantic) period (Flandrian II). Such eustatic and local groundwater changes set in motion a retrogressive hydrosere that culminated in the development of salt marsh and finally marine inundation.

Sedimentologically, this change in fluvial dynamics is evidenced by the very marked change to mineral sediments seen in a number of columns and palynologically described here from columns MS04 and MS10. The first possible indications of marine/saline ingress or approaching coastline is the increase of pollen of Chenopodiaceae (typically halophytes including oraches and glassworts) in BC-II pollen zone 1d (profile MS04–MS08). By zone 2 in BC-II column MS04, other halophytes are also in evidence, with *Spergula* type (spurrey), Plumbaginaceae (*Armeria* B-line type) (sea lavender and thrift), *Plantago maritima* (sea plantain), and Hystrichospheres. This change to marine/salt marsh is also evidenced in these sequences by the foraminifera (Chapter 3, 3.6.2) and diatom (Chapter 3, 3.6.1) assemblages. However, the palynological and sedimentological evidence suggests that this marine transgressive phase occurred after a freshwater/brackish period, as the site became flooded. The lower part of the minerogenic unit contains a greater proportion of fine sands within humic silt which supported a wet fen/reedswamp vegetation with grasses, sedges, and reed mace or bur reed (pollen zone 1d in BC-II; monolith columns MS04–MS08). These changes should be viewed three-dimensionally as a transgressive freshwater fen with an increasing frequency of saline incursion.

Subsequently, full marine/salt-marsh transgression occurred, with the deposition of grey alluvial and salt-marsh silts that contain pollen of salt-marsh plants and halophytic diatoms and foraminifera. Such a major change in sediment deposition would be expected to cause significant changes in the pollen taphonomy, in addition to the taxonomic changes from changing local and on-site vegetation. This was the case and it is probable that the overall pollen catchment was significantly enhanced by the increased fluvially transported pollen component. This could have included material transported via freshwater river systems entering the Solent – as indicated by continued occurrences of fen taxa and cysts of freshwater algal *Pediastrum* – as well as coastal, marine-transported pollen. The change to sediments, by definition derived (allochthonous), is well illustrated by the sharp expansion of derived pre-Quaternary (largely Tertiary) palynomorphs. There are also reductions in alder pollen as its areas of local growth were pushed further inland, while pine, oak, and elm become more important, possibly providing a more regional perspective through the expansion of the pollen catchment via fluvial transport from greater distances.

8.3 The immediate local environs

The transgressive nature of the changing habitats and associated sediments has been noted. The earliest pollen spectra, which come from previous studies to the north-east of the current Bouldnor Cliff sites (Scaife 2000a), contain pine–hazel–oak-dominated peat from slightly earlier in the early Boreal than the Bouldnor Cliff evidence; similarly, it rests on an old land surface. The latter was, unfortunately, devoid of pollen. A causal mechanism similar to that at Bouldnor Cliff was argued by Scaife (2000a) for development of these peats and two higher organic units which are intercalated in salt-marsh and/or mudflat sediments. From this evidence a sea-level change graph was constructed which has been modified here to encompass new sea-level index points (see Chapter 9). This work, combined with data from the Wootton-Quarr Project (Long and Scaife in Tomalin *et al* forthcoming), has shown that there was a progressive sharply rising sea level to around the period of the Bouldnor human occupation. This was at the cusp of change, after which rates of relative rise were reduced. However, even though the coastal outline in its broadest sense may have been established, sea levels were still at around –10m OD at the end of the Boreal period. Subsequently, 7000 years of generally rising sea (relative to land) saw periods of stasis (or even, possibly, sea-level lowering), when further peat accumulations are recorded higher in the Bouldnor profiles (Scaife 2000b and forthcoming/in press).

Such progressive sea-level change resulted in the asynchronous formation of similar sediment sets across the Solent basin. At BC-IV (monolith MS10) and Tanners Hard the lower peat unit occurs at a topographically higher altitude (–6.5m to –5.8m OD ± 0.15m respectively) than at the other sites with peats, and rests on old land surfaces developed in the basal sands and gravels. The peats of the former have been dated to *c* 6400 BP (5470–5300 cal BC) and of the latter to *c* 6200 BP (5290–4940 cal BC), making them broadly contemporaneous with one another and substantially later than those dated for BC-II at *c* 6900–7000 BP (6050–5950 cal BC). The peat, however, started forming in these locations in response to exactly the same mechanisms as at BC-II, as eustatic changes affected higher topo-graphic/altitudinal zones.

Ultimately these higher sites were also inundated and became salt marsh and/or mudflat prior to full marine inundation with deposition of mineral sediments. Although the stratigraphical genesis followed the same route, resulting in similar stratig-raphy, the microfossil content reflects the later age and changed environments of the middle Holocene (Atlantic) period. Significant differences are the absence of pine and, unusually, much lower values of alder than might be expected and a greatly increased importance of lime in the environment. Pine, as noted above, was in its final stages of importance during the late Boreal period and by the middle Atlantic had been generally ousted by the major deciduous trees. Of the latter, oak and elm remained important, but the most diagnostic phe-nomenon was the establishment of small-leaved lime (*Tilia cordata* L.). Godwin (1975) was the first to describe its arrival into Britain just prior to the separation of Britain from continental Europe by the same eustatic changes discussed above.

There are now a very substantial number of records that attest to lime's rise to dominance or at least co-dominance over a larger part of southern and eastern England during the middle Holocene (Birks *et al* 1975; Scaife 1980; Greig 1982). Pollen data from this region demonstrate this trend, showing arrival inland during the early Atlantic period in the Isle of Wight at Gatcombe Withy Bed and at Borthwood Farm; at many sites dominance was attained (eg Bohemia Bog, Sandown) (Scaife 1980; 1987; 1988; 2003c). From adjacent Hampshire a similar pattern has emerged in the New Forest at Cranes Moor (Barber and Clarke 1987), from just after *c* 5900 cal BC (*c* 7000 BP). It is not surprising, therefore, given the middle Holocene age of the peat sequences at both BC-IV and Tanners Hard, that lime was an important element of the woodland at these sites.

At Tanners Hard peat dated at 5310–4940 cal BC (Beta-166478) overlies an old land surface that developed in the basal sands and gravels. This site afforded well-drained soils ideally suited to the growth of lime. The very high pollen values attest to such growth on site, especially as lime pollen is usually under-represented in pollen assem-blages (Andersen 1970; 1973). Here there may be some over-representation due to the robustness of its exine (Keatinge 1982; 1983), but this does not preclude its importance on site. Subsequently, lime does become less important, with oak taking its place in this regard. At BC-IV (MS10) lime is also important, peaking at 5370–5210 cal BC, during the period of peat accumulation. This section is the highest relative to OD of all the samples collected from BC-IV; it is probable that lime was growing in close proximity to the site but on better-drained soils. Increasing wetness of these soils, and thus a less favourable habitat for growth, caused the decline in pollen at these sites, a phenomenon described in detail by Waller (1994). However, lime woodland remained important in the region throughout the late Mesolithic (middle Holocene (Atlantic)) and Neolithic to the middle Bronze Age.

This is evidenced in the long pollen profiles from Isle of Wight sites at Gatcombe Withy Bed and Borthwood Farm (Scaife 1980; 1987; 2004b) prior to late prehistoric clearance for agriculture.

The relative paucity of alder in these later middle Holocene sequences is surprising, as dominance of alder carr woodland is usually a diagnostic phenomenon for the start of the Atlantic period. Its expansion from c 5900cal BC (c 7000 BP) was originally taken by Godwin (1975) as the marker (zone boundary) for the start of the Atlantic (Godwin pollen zone VIIa), with colonisation of river-valley floodplain by alder carr occurring in response to a more humid climate and the effects of the sea-level rise that caused the separation of Britain from continental Europe at this time. Such dominance in the river valleys of the Isle of Wight certainly occurred and is clearly seen at, for example, Gatcombe Withy Bed, where Alnetum became established after c 5900 cal BC (c 7000 BP) and remains today, albeit in a modified form (Scaife 1980; 1987; 1988).

At Bouldnor, alder was most important during the late Boreal and very early Atlantic periods at 6050–5810 cal BC. This certainly reflects the arrival of alder into the region ahead of the sharply rising sea level and most probably represents a wave of vegetation migrating across the lowlands as the environment became increasingly wet and thus more favourable for alder's growth. With the development of the coastline in its present broad outline from c 7000 BP, alder became established and dominant on suitable floodplains as carr woodland. Alder at BC-II (and in the earlier LIFE studies at Bouldnor) (Scaife 2000a) represents this passing local importance of alder. In the later sections of BC-IV MS10 and Tanners Hard, small values of alder come from either occasional growth or more important woodland at some distance (NB: alder is a high pollen producer). Here, fen peat developed over the old land surface and was subsequently followed by salt marsh from brackish water or marine transgression.

8.4   Marine transgression: the change to context/sediment unit 1

From the above discussions it will be clear that at all of the sites the culmination of the sediment sequence was deposition of salt marsh, mudflat, silts and clays. The following characteristics are common to the locations found to date:

- A typical transgressive sequence from the dry land of the probable river bar or interfluve on which Mesolithic activity took place (ie context 2007);
- A phase of increasing wetness caused by regionally rising sea level which initiated peat-forming conditions (ie context 2003) under damp oak and hazel woodland;
- Continued and rapid positive sea-level change which disrupted the freshwater systems, caused further waterlogging and creating freshwater fen

with an increasing frequency of saline incursion (ie context 2002);
- Full marine/salt-marsh and mudflat conditions (ie context 2001). Study of the diatoms from BC-II (MSO4) suggests an initial phase of mudflat development followed by a change to deeper water. In higher (and thus later) sediment records there is evidence from diatoms of salt marsh and subsequent change to mudflat (Chapter 3, 3.6).

Superimposed on this general sequence are probable ephemeral events, including the coarse gravel unit of context 2006, which was formed by a localised high-energy river flood deposit or landslide from the higher-level plateau gravels, of which this context was the toe. The latter are in evidence today along this part of the coastline and are notorious for mass movement (rotational slides); they may themselves have been initiated by destabilisation of the cliff base.

All the principal changes in stratigraphy result from changing sea level (eustatic change). Earlier studies of Bouldnor identified three peat sequences which are intercalated within salt-marsh and fluvial sediments dating from the late Boreal (Flandrian Chronozone Ic) to the late Atlantic/early Neolithic period (late Atlantic, Fl. II and early Sub Boreal, Fl. III). The upper peat/sediment contacts provided sea-level index points from which radiocarbon dates have been obtained and a sea-level graph constructed (Long et al 2000). These data fit within the broader regional model initially established by Long and Tooley (1995) from Stansore Point (at the end of Southampton Water) and from studies associated with the Wootton-Quarr Project (Long and Scaife in Tomalin et al forthcoming).

The development of the Bouldnor Cliff sediment sequence is intricately linked with the progressively rising relative sea level. Importantly, the sediment sequence and Mesolithic site is dated to the very late Boreal period – that is, a time when sea level was still rising sharply (at c 12–10m below OD) but the rate of change was starting to decline. Hence, as noted, this was the period after the very rapid post-glacial rise from c 20–22m below OD during the late-Devensian/Pre-Boreal. Poole (1936) first drew attention to the coastal and riverine distribution of Mesolithic sites, and attributed the growth in numbers of such sites to this period by merit of the fact that at this time such ecotonal environments had expanded sufficiently to make them more attractive for occupation by the hunting and foraging Mesolithic communities.

As the stratigraphy of sites BC-II, BC-IV, and BC-V demonstrates, the effects and timing of this marine transgression were asynchronous and depended on the varying topography of the Solent Basin. However, once sea levels were broadly established during the middle Holocene the development of salt marsh and mudflats occurred along the north-west coast of the Isle of Wight and at Lymington. While the basal peats at Bouldnor reflect the first significant impact of Holocene marine transgression, the upper two peat horizons identified at this site (dated to the Atlantic and early Sub-Boreal periods respectively – 4540–4330 cal BC (5580 ± 60 BP) and 4950–4540 cal BC (5870 ± 80 BP) (LIFE 2000)) must be considered differently. The development of these peats is considered to be associated with periods of stasis, when sea-level change was in balance with sediment input. This may have provided local conditions in which semi-stable salt marsh (the middle peat) and a more important early Sub-Boreal peat associated with freshwater fen and woodland (submerged forest) developed. The latter peats may be found in various other localities around the Solent Basin as, for example, at Langstone (Allen and Gardiner 2000), Southampton Water (Long *et al* 2000), and the north-east coast of the Isle of Wight (Tomalin *et al* forthcoming). This most recent inter-tidal peat appears to represent a longer stand-still phase, or even negative eustatic change, which allowed development of damp woodland after wet fen (hydrosere). These Neolithic–Bronze Age peats were subject to final marine transgression during the Bronze Age. This culminated in the full marine conditions that pertain today. As described for the basal Mesolithic sediments, this final phase also took place with a retrogressive hydrosere that saw change from woodland through wet grass–sedge fen (with royal fern) to salt marsh and mudflat prior to submergence.

9 Sea-level changes and the inundation of Bouldnor Cliff *by Anthony Long and Rob Scaife*

Radiocarbon dating of cultural sediment units as part of the investigations into the submerged archaeology of the Western Solent is providing a chronological framework for human occupation. It is also building substantially on current data sets of sea-level index points for the locality, helping to refine and develop the regional sea-level curve over the last 8000 years. The results from this research are consequently informing our understanding of the Flandrian transgression and its impact along the area's coastline.

9.1 Background to relative sea-level change in the region

The general principals of relative sea-level change in the North Atlantic and North Sea region are reasonably well understood. Relative sea-level (RSL) rise has been reconstructed in a number of local or regional studies that have focused on the Thames estuary (Devoy 1979; 1982), east Kent (Long 1992), Romney Marsh and east Sussex (Jennings and Smythe 1990; Long and Innes 1993; 1995; Long et al 1996). Among the studies in the south-west of England are those of Heyworth and Kidson (1982) and Healey (1995) and, for the Solent, Long and Tooley (1995), Long et al (1999), Long et al (2000), and Long and Scaife (forthcoming). Until recently there has been only very limited systematic analysis of Holocene sea-level change in, and the palaeogeography of, the Solent and Southampton Water region. This is surprising given the available sedimentary archive, the importance of this coastal region, and the role which past sea-level changes have had in shaping the Solent coastal zone. Although the coastal sediments of mainland Hampshire have been a source of interest for over a century, the studies that resulted were largely speculative and were based on little measured data. Many of these early investigations were completed on stratigraphical sections exposed by chance, such as the King George Dock at Southampton (Godwin and Godwin 1940). The earliest studies in the region go back to those of James (1847), Shore and Elves (1889), Shore (1893), and Anderson (1933), with additional information from Clement Reid's account of British submerged forests (Reid 1913). Modern studies have been based on more detailed recorded data and radiocarbon dating (Hodson and West 1972; Nichols and Clarke 1986).

Hodson and West's 1972 study at Fawley and South Hythe was made during the construction of Fawley Power Station in the 1960s. Their work identified unconsolidated mineral sediments and peat between –5.00m and 0m OD which they dated to between 2130–1560 cal BC and 2410–1780 cal BC. An incised palaeochannel at –7.63 to –7.33m OD was dated to 5500–4960 cal BC. Long and Tooley (1995) provided the first detailed RSL graph for the Solent from a sediment sequence at Stansore Point (near Calshot Spit), at the entrance to the Beaulieu River. Samples from a prominent peat layer at c 3.5–0.5m below OD were dated to 4800 BP and 2470–1880 cal BC and 770–200 cal BC. From these dates and altitudinal measurements past sea-level index points were established and a standard age/altitude graph of past sea level was plotted. The data formed the basis for more detailed examinations undertaken during the evaluation of Associated British Ports' Southampton Water sites at Hythe Bay, Bury Farm, and the Hamble estuary relating to the proposed new container ship terminal (Long and Scaife 1996; Long et al 2000). The upper levels of an extensive mid-Holocene peat were dated to 3380–2890 cal BP at –2.33m OD in the Hamble estuary and to 1450–1110 cal BP at –0.11m OD at Bury Farm. Older samples of this peat, dated to 4330–3980 cal BP, occur from Hythe Marshes.

As research on the mainland was progressing, so interest in the sea-level record of the Isle of Wight also grew, building on earlier studies by Devoy (1987) at Yarmouth. Work at Wootton-Quarr (Tomalin et al forthcoming) identified numerous archaeological sites in the inter-tidal zone. Erosion necessitated a fuller understanding of how RSL had changed here during the Holocene, and how changes in palaeogeography influenced human activity in the coast and hinterland zones. As part of the Wootton-Quarr Project an in-depth study of the lithostratigraphy and biostratigraphy of peats and mineral sediments in the Eastern Solent was undertaken. In addition, series of radiocarbon dates enabled the construction of an independent RSL graph for the north-east Isle of Wight/Eastern Solent region (Long and Scaife forthcoming). These sea-level data sets for the Solent region therefore now include observations from both the mainland and the Isle of Wight.

9.2 Methods

For each dated horizon the pollen, diatom, and other sedimentological data is used to make an estimate of the altitudinal relationship between the horizon and a tide level at the time of its formation. The majority of samples formed at, or close to, the former elevation of mean high water of spring tides (MHWST) – that is, in palaeoenvironments which are characterised by vegetation communities transi-

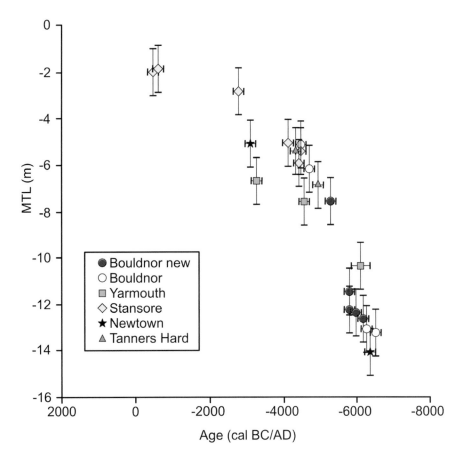

Figure 9.1 Radiocarbon-dated index points depicting changes in mean tide level (MTL) during the last 7000 years cal BC (Anthony Long and Rob Scaife)

tional between semi-terrestrial (freshwater fen and carr woodland) and more open salt-marsh and transitional mudflat communities. The dated samples used as sea-level index points have been corrected for variations in tidal range and plotted as a graph depicting changes in mean tide level (MTL) during the last 7000 years (Fig 9.1). Age errors equal to the two-sigma calibrated age range of the dated sample and an approximate altitude error of ± 1m are shown.

9.3 Sea-level change at Bouldnor

Earlier archaeological and environmental studies carried out at Bouldnor for the LIFE programme (Scaife and Long 2001) produced the first sea-level-change data from the Western Solent region, extending the earlier Wootton-Quarr data (Long and Scaife forthcoming). This work confirmed a pattern of rapidly rising RSL during the Boreal period and a slower rate of rise during the middle Holocene. The record was based on radiocarbon measurements of the three peat sequences sampled from BC-II. Pollen analysis of the peats here demonstrates that organic accumulation was initiated in response to waterlogging of the landscape caused by the ponding-back of water through RSL rise. This process was dia-

chronous, with first lower and then progressively higher sites inundated during the early and then mid-Holocene as RSL rose.

A similar pattern of events is recorded from the more recent dates collected from BC-II, BC-IV, and BC-V. It should be noted that dates obtained on samples of wood found within the lower peats of BC-II and recovered during the fieldwork in 1998 (Scaife 2000b), as well as the more recent samples from the −11m OD platform, may have formed slightly above or slightly below MHWST depending on the coastal configuration at the time of formation. However, the rate of RSL rise was fast at the time of their formation and the altitudinal uncertainty is likely to be of secondary significance in comparison to any possible age errors. Indeed, the lower sequence of samples from Bouldnor Cliff occupy a relatively tight age/altitude space, suggesting that the deposits did indeed form close to the MHWST mark.

The biostratigraphical analysis (pollen and diatom) of the sediments which overlie the basal palaeosol and peats of context 2003 indicate that the grey sediments in which the peat sequences are intercalated were deposited in a brackish water/estuarine environment. The RSL graph (Fig 9.1) depicts mean sea level (MSL) rising steeply from *c* 15m below OD at *c* 6500 cal BC to *c* 6m below OD by 4000 cal BC. The rate of rise then slows, with MSL rising to −2m

OD by *c* 500 BC. No data exist in this analysis for the last 2000 years, but MSL has risen by no more than *c* 2m during this interval at an average long-term rate of 1mm per year.

9.4   Coastal evolution in the Western Solent

The deepest sediments of post-glacial age recorded in the Western Solent comprise freshwater organic sediments recorded immediately above bedrock at Yarmouth (beneath Yarmouth Spit) and in Southampton Water. The biostratigraphy and lithostratigraphy at these sites is consistent in indicating a progressive waterlogging of the landscape, also described for the Bouldnor basal contexts. During the initial phases of this waterlogging the rate of organic accumulation was able to keep pace with RSL rise, but with time these freshwater communities were inundated and shoreline retreat occurred. Today the variation in tidal range within the Western Solent is small (*c* 0.5m). In this analysis it is assumed that the variations seen today have remained constant during the past, but this hypothesis is yet to be tested, and it is likely that the major changes in coastal configuration that have taken place since *c* 7000 cal BC were associated with larger variations in tidal range than are observed at present.

At Bouldnor and at Yarmouth the ensuing period is characterised by the deposition of minerogenic salt-marsh and mudflat sediments. These accumulated as RSL continued its upward trend and near-shore water depths increased. There is a marked lack of radiocarbon dates during the interval between *c* 5800 cal BC and *c* 5200 cal BC, which may reflect inadequacies in the sampling framework to date, but could also signal the real effects of a rapid change in shoreline position forced by RSL rise. After about 5200 cal BC there was a renewed phase of organic accumulation and, at several sites, a thin or more substantial accumulation of peat is recorded. The long-term rate of RSL continued upwards at this time, albeit at a somewhat reduced rate. Phases of organic accumulation are recorded after this time at all four sites analysed here, although the duration of organic

accumulation varies between sites. Despite this variability, the extent of organic sedimentation across salt and freshwater marshes in the Western Solent probably reached its maximum at this time.

The widespread nature of the change in sedimentation reflects the operation of a widespread change in the rate of RSL, but more local factors controlled the duration of peat formation at any single site. Given the probable importance of these local factors, one should be cautious not to over-interpret the wider significance of short-lived phases of organic sedimentation in terms of fluctuations in regional RSL. For example, changes in the availability of sediment supply to the coastal lowlands will have been an important influence on the rate of sediment accretion and hence the ability of coastal marshes to accrete in the face of a prevailing upwards trend in long-term RSL. Other local factors, such as the migration of tidal channels or the breaching and closure of barriers (as at Yarmouth and also at Stansore) may also have controlled short-lived phases of shoreline development.

After about 2500 cal BC, the Isle of Wight coastal sites show a return to coastal minerogenic sedimentation with no further significant organic sediments recorded during the late Holocene. On the mainland, at Stansore Point, the freshwater peats in this protected site are finally inundated by about 1 cal BC. Long *et al* (2000) have argued that this shift to minerogenic sedimentation is recorded throughout the Solent and, though time transgressive, it saw the demise of coastal wetland sedimentation throughout the region by *c* 1 cal BC. The cause of this decline is not certain; it may reflect acceleration in the rate of RSL, a reduction in sediment supply, or perhaps an increase in sediment reworking. It may also signal the collapse of freshwater peats via the process of peat compaction. Whichever the cause, during the late Holocene the coastal environments of the Western Solent were radically different from their mid-Holocene counterparts, with significantly reduced expanses of coastal wetland and salt marsh. One can envisage an associated shift in the floral and faunal diversity of the region from the middle to the late Holocene.

10 Changing landscapes
by Garry Momber

The nature and character of the landscape dictated the availability of resources desired by Mesolithic people. The geology provided the raw materials to fashion stone tools, the natural environment presented essentials for day-to-day living and the topography bestowed varied resources within a range of ecotones that could be opportunistically exploited in a systematic manner. The interpretation of these factors has led to the creation of models that describe prehistoric hunter-gatherer subsistence strategies (Bell 2007).

Models have even been applied to the resource which now lies underwater, and have proved to be very successful where the palaeo-landforms retain a signature on the seabed; the development of these models has resulted in the discovery of underwater archaeological sites in areas such as the sheltered waters of the Storebælt in the Danish archipelago (Fischer 1997). Unfortunately, in the Solent, many of the palaeo-landforms are largely transformed, having been lost or disguised beneath metres of sediment. We must therefore attempt to calculate what has been lost, how the remaining segment relates to what has been lost, and what potential there is for interpreting that which remains of the cultural landscape. This chapter interrogates information that has been gathered during the course of studies at Bouldnor, and across the wider Solent, over the last decade to reconstruct the pre-submergence terrain and unravel the subsequent changes that ultimately created the waterway seen today.

10.1 Geological background

The underlying long-term controlling factor defining the physical characteristics of the Hampshire Basin is geology (Fig 10.1). Deformation of the late Cretaceous chalk and early Tertiary mud, sands, and gravels over many millions of years has seen basal strata folded and manipulated. The most striking feature is the chalk escarpment that runs from the Isle of Purbeck through Christchurch Bay and across the centre of the Isle of Wight before dipping below the waves into the north English Channel off Sussex (West 1980). The chalk, which was once a horizontal lining on the ocean floor, has now been turned through nearly 90° in many places to stand almost vertical. In more recent human timescales the resultant rolling downs and sheer cliffs have been a dominant feature within the landscape as well as a source of high-quality flint nodules.

To the south of the chalk much of the surface-exposed geology is older. It consists of shales, sands, and clays from the Wealden and Lower Greensand groups. These deposits were laid down about 120 million years ago and are from the early to mid-Cretaceous period. Although they predate the chalk they are less consolidated, and are subject to ongoing erosion that causes redistribution of archaic deposits, an issue that will be returned to below (10.5), when discussing the evolution of the Solent.

North of the chalk and Lower Greensand escarpments the sedimentary sequences are younger and generally less consolidated, thereby succumbing more readily to weathering. However, the undulating landscape largely results from deep-rooted basement faults causing moulding of the plastic Mesozoic and Tertiary strata (Nowell 1995) through irregular rates of uplift and down-warping over relatively short distances of the crust. Geological faulting has folded the bedrock up to form an anticline complex that runs along a north-west axis across the Solent from Newtown Creek to the New Forest. Synclines, or downward folds, exist to the east and west; the latter lies below what is now the Yarmouth Roads and the area that hosts the remnants of the submerged landscape. The geology thus underpins the surface morphology, although the latter has been reshaped by fluvial and marine activity cutting into exposed sedimentary sequences.

The most robust bedrock along the north-west coast of the Isle of Wight is Eocene Bembridge limestone. The rock forms a seam of resilient strata with exposures along isolated parts of the coastline, while in other areas soft marls and clays dominate. A significant geological soft spot is the 60m-high cliff at Bouldnor, which fronts a stretch of coastline 2km long a little over 2km east of Yarmouth. It is composed of soft Oligocene Marls that are being steadily pruned by the Solent, resulting in visible rotational sliding (Fig 10.2). The collapsing north-west face contrasts starkly with the gentle south-east-facing slope inland. The cliff is actively receding and would have previously reached further north-west across the Solent towards the New Forest.

To the east of Bouldnor Cliff, finger-like projections of Bembridge Limestone point into the Solent at Hamstead Ledges, while to the west the limestone emerges at Yarmouth near Thorley Street (Reid 1905). Underwater it can be found at Black Rock, which sits at the mouth of the Western Yar. Here it forms a navigational hazard that is exposed during low spring tides. In places the limestone terraces reach up to 1.8km into the Solent (Hamblin and Harrison 1989).

Across the water, to the west of Yarmouth, the geological make-up consists of the Eocene Headon Hill Formation of clays and fine sand. This is less consolidated than the limestone and is more suscep-

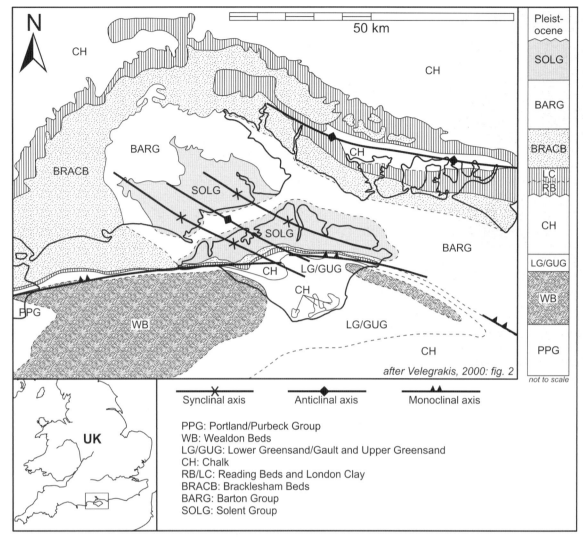

Figure 10.1   Map showing geological features of the Solent, including the surface sediments, gravel deposits, and river terraces (Julian Whitewright after A Velegrakis)

tible to erosion, particularly by the sea. Along one section of coast, behind Fort Victoria Country Park and between Sconce point and Fort Albert at Cliff End, a cliff that rises sharply to a height of 38m has become truncated and is subject to rotational sliding. This north-west-facing tract of foreshore looks directly across the Solent to Hurst Spit and Keyhaven Marshes (Fig 10.3). The Headon Hill Formation continues north under the Solent to the mainland and south back into the island, where the hill behind the cliff rolls gently inland (Fig 10.4).

10.2   River terraces and geomorphological moulding: the evolution of the Solent during the Quaternary

The region's geology has provided a backdrop upon which subsequent morphological changes have been inscribed, notably during the Quaternary, a period characterised by the ice ages of the last two million years. Each ice age lowered the level of the sea (on occasion by up to 130m) and created large ice caps

across the northern hemisphere. The Hampshire Basin witnessed periglacial conditions with freezing temperatures and rock-shattering frost that helped to reshape the land (Lambeck 1995; Murton and Lautridou 2003). When the climate warmed, the glaciers melted and rivers grew to take the run-off across the exposed continental shelf. The vast amount of water held in the upland ice sheets took thousands of years to drain into the low-lying seas, a consequence of which was the creation of deeply incised channels. As sea level rose up the retreating coastline old channels were filled with sediment, covering much of the eroded deposits. On land, the passages of the waterways were marked with gravel and sand deposits. Consequently, one of the most enduring legacies of the post-Ice Age thaw is the remnant drainage system etched into the land surface and seabed of the British coastline, the largest example of which in central southern England is the 'Solent River' (Dix 2001, 7–14).

Gravels along the fluvial pathways left by the migrating Solent River have become uplifted to form a staircase of terraces from Dorset through

Figure 10.2   Rotational sliding is visible along the cliff at Fort Victoria Country Park, on the north-west coast of the Isle of Wight. The retreating cliff is 1.3km from Hurst Castle (Jan Gillespie)

Figure 10.3   The submerged peat deposits extending from the Hampshire coastline reach almost to the end of Hurst Spit. They lie underwater less than 2m below Ordnance Datum. The cliffs opposite Hurst Narrows, on the Isle of Wight, are eroding and receding continually. The gap between the cliff and the peat deposits of the palaeolandsurface is only in the order of 1.5km. This is the area that has been eroded by the sea (Garry Momber)

Hampshire. Detailed investigations between Bournemouth and Calshot have identified twelve distinct gravel beds which are understood to have marked the course of the old waterway (Bridgland

and D'Olier 2001; Allen and Gibbard 1993). The river deposits terminate around the edge of Southampton Water, at which point the drainage patterns take a more south-westerly route (Bridgland and D'Olier 2001; Bates 2001). From here, a palaeovalley system running from about –20m OD in the East Solent down to –45m OD east of Nab Tower has been recorded by geophysical survey (Hodson and West 1972; Dyer 1975). The channels are well defined, being framed by gravel deposits and capped by peat (Long and Tooley 1995).

The old river-gravel terraces cutting through Dorset and Hampshire have proved to be a rich source of Palaeolithic flint tools, reflecting the value of the waterways and surrounding areas as routes for early waves of hominins and as places to subsist. The youngest gravel lens is found across the north shores of the Solent, below the Pennington marshes between Lymington and Milford on Sea. It was laid down c 120,000 years ago towards the end of the Ipswichian (OIS 5e), and sits at a height that equates to current OD. This would appear to continue the established pattern of river migration south, a concept that that has underpinned academic research on the subject throughout the last 150 years. However, unlike the earlier deposits, there is little lateral consistency, making the Pennington gravels less diagnostic. Papers dating as far back as 1862 have discussed the migration and evolution of the 'Solent River' by tracing Pleistocene river systems across the southern part of the Hampshire Basin. It was speculated that the passage of the River ran from

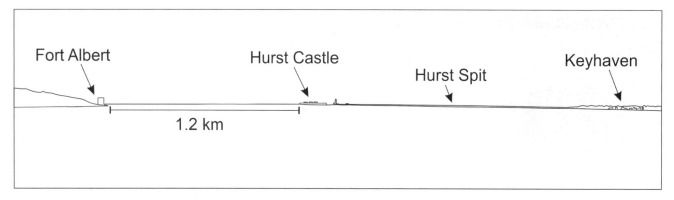

Figure 10.4   View of Hurst Narrows, looking west (Garry Momber)

Figure 10.5   Run of white cliffs from the 'back of the Wight', looking across Freshwater Bay to Old Harry, visible across Christchurch Bay in the distance (Garry Momber)

Poole Harbour, through Christchurch Bay and into the Solent, and was prevented from flowing south by the chalk anticline between the Needles and Old Harry (Fig 10.5) (Fox 1862; Reid 1905; Everard 1954; West 1980; Allen and Gibbard 1993; Wenban Smith and Hosfield 2001). Until recently, it had been believed that the loss of the sediment archive from the floor of the Western Solent made it impossible to resolve the path of the Solent River.

10.3   Challenging the late Quaternary route of the Solent River

The hypothesis that a river passed from Poole to the Solent was ultimately challenged when Velegrakis and others (Velegrakis *et al* 1999; Velegrakis 2000)

conducted a series of sub-bottom surveys across Christchurch Bay and interrogated seismic traces produced for British Petroleum and Total for the Wytch Farm oil field. He observed that a series of palaeovalleys drained Poole and Christchurch Bays, breaching the old 'Needles to Handfast Point' chalk ridge through well-established rivers and reworked channels that were cut prior to the Flandrian transgression. They are recorded at more than –30m OD, suggesting that the Frome, Stour, and Avon would have emptied to the south many kilometres before they reached the Solent (Velegrakis *et al* 1999). Further work on the same data set by the late Ken Thompson delineated the underlying Eocene clay deposits at the approaches to the Solent a few kilometres west of Hurst Spit. Beneath the mobile sediments he recorded the geological base level at 10–15m below CD (12–17m

Figure 10.6 Bathymetric data from the Western Solent. The deep off Hurst Spit drops to almost –60m OD and gets shallower to the north-east and south-west. The shades of white and grey represent contours below Chart Datum (Drawing by Rory Smith with detail from Admiralty Chart 2040, 1991)

below OD). This shallow depth would have equated to a west-facing hill prior to the Flandrian transgression and Thompson agues effectively that it would have acted as a barrier to any river that wished to enter the Solent (Thompson 2006).

The discovery of these river channels and bedrock elevations removes the possibility of a Solent River passing across the north side of the Isle of Wight during the late Quaternary. What it demonstrates is that the rivers of the region trend to the south, carving paths through the land surface. It is worth noting that the channels formed access routes into the hinterland that could also act as conduits for migrations north. The use of waterways for prehistoric people has been indicated by the finds from fluvial terraces that relate to Pleistocene interglacials.

In stark contrast to the elevated submarine geological features identified by Thompson at the entrance to the Western Solent is the Hurst Deep, less than 5km to the east, where the channel narrows (Fig 10.6). This is a furrow that has been excavated to almost –60m OD off the reverse end of Hurst Spit. Tracking another 5km east, beyond the Hurst Narrows, the seabed quickly shallows again, rising to less than –20m OD off Bouldnor Cliff. It is thus plain that the central deep off Hurst Spit is roughly

equidistant from shallow water to its east and west, being confined entirely to where the currents are strongest. It would appear that it is controlled by the morphology of the spit itself, which forces the water into a confined space, causing scour (Dyer 1975). Consequently, the formation of the Hurst Deep can be attributed to recent marine action rather than the effects of fluvial action.

The extensive deepening of the narrows indicates that the seabed is relatively easily eroded. This, in turn, suggests that the shallows identified by Thompson (which are also Eocene clays), would have succumbed to erosion to some degree during and following the last rise in sea level. It is therefore reasonable to infer that the current seabed would have been much shallower prior to the transgression, probably forming a shoulder of land between the Solent and Christchurch Bay. The previous height of this barrier is uncertain, but clues are presented by the remains of old land surfaces in and around Hurst Spit. Three-quarters of the way along the spit from its origins by Sturt Pond a band of peat runs to the west. This peat is exposed during low water spring tides and is covered when the tide is in. It was inspected by HWTMA diving archaeologists in 2000 and found to be compacted, dark, and humic rather than fibrous. It supported large trees with root systems reaching down into the deposit. The peat that has been recorded *in situ* here has yet to be sampled and dated, but provides evidence that a palaeo-land surface rests only a couple of metres below OD. Further along the spit an outcrop of peat was photographed by Ian West when he visited this shore after the winter storms of 1999–2000. Peat was also exposed at the west end of Hurst Castle's west wing after the shingle had been rolled back (West 2008); here it is found within 100m of the Hurst Deep. Behind the eastern or reverse side of the spit large expanses of submerged forest are exposed on the surface of the seabed. These were inspected and recorded by HWTMA divers in 1999 (see Chapter 1, 1.3.2). The submerged peat associated with this forest extends along the east side of Hurst Spit and under Keyhaven Marshes. All three examples examined here demonstrate that former dry land, at an elevation of less than 2–3m below OD, can be found below or behind Hurst Spit.

Where Hurst Spit reaches out in the mouth of the Western Solent it has protected a palaeo-land surface that bridges over half the distance between the mainland and the Isle of Wight. The shortfall is 1.3km between the tip of the spit and the soft eroding cliffs behind Fort Victoria Country Park (see Fig 10.3). To the north of the park, the seabed plunges into the depths of Hurst Narrows and all trace of submerged land has gone (see Fig 10.6). So too, has much of the coastal frontage. Here the Eocene clays and fine sands of the Headon Hill Formation have been washed away by the sea. Prior to coastal erosion the hill would have extended further into the Solent and towards the submerged lands beyond the Narrows.

10.4   The onset of the Holocene and coming of the Mesolithic

The Devensian glacial maximum finished *c* 20,000 cal BC (*c* 18,000 BP). Sea levels were 120–130m lower than today and ice sheets reached south Wales and the English Midlands. The climate then ameliorated until *c* 13,500 cal BC (*c* 13,000 BP), when the Older Dryas cold stadial saw freezing temperatures return to northern Europe. The sea was then 30–40m below current levels. The Holocene began when the Younger Dryas came to an end *c* 11,500 years ago and the climate warmed. Analysis of ice core GISP2 from Greenland shows a rise in temperature of 5–10°C in just a few tens of years (Taylor *et al* 1997; Alley 2000; Alley *et al* 1993), an increase in temperature which caused relatively quick melting of the permafrost and a northward expansion of vegetation. Vast tracts of periglacial Atlantic continental shelf, the British landmass and the North Sea Basin were transformed into open steppe and grasslands. This extension of vegetation away from more temperate refugia attracted grazing herbivores, which in turn attracted predators, including humans. The sequence of vegetation colonisation is described by in this volume by Rob Scaife (Chapter 8).

The Mesolithic people were quick to exploit the resources Britain had to offer as it came out of its deep freeze. Sites at Thatcham (in the south), Star Carr (in the north), and, a little later, at East Barnes in Scotland pay testimony to early arrivals. It is not inconceivable to suppose that where these potential pioneers led the way, a greater number of colonists would follow (see Chapter 12, 12.4). Many may have reached mainland Britain, but it is most probable that concentrations of people would be greater where suitable territories could be established in the resource-rich low-lying riverine hunting grounds on English Channel lands. These lands are now submerged.

10.5   Assessing geomorphological change in the Western Solent Basin

The six millennia that followed the Younger Dryas were formative years for the Western Solent Basin. The glacial run-off that had carved out river valleys now abated, allowing more stable conditions to develop. By the time of the Mesolithic occupation of *c* 8000 BP over 3000 years had passed and the site at Bouldnor now lay on the fringe of a lowland where a wet fen environment was developing (see Chapter 3, 3.5 and 3.7). Pollen from the lower zones of the monoliths show evidence of a marsh, fen or floodplain habitat (Chapter 3, 3.5). Rob Scaife's analysis of a core from Yarmouth Spit shows much the same (Scaife 2000a, V2, 25); a basal Gyttja sediment at –12m OD in this core demonstrates the existence of a freshwater lake or lagoon prior to the development of peat. The extent of the lagoon is not known but its presence suggests a low-energy wetland environment at or near areas attractive to human occupation. The extent of this wetland would depend on available drainage from the Solent valley system.

A major influence in the valley would have been the size of its river or rivers. If we are to set aside the concept of a large Solent River, the prospect exists for a landscape fed by minor waterways in a more sedate wetland on the edge of developing woodland. Such an environment would present different opportunities from those associated with the banks of a large river: it could be relatively easily traversed and would be attractive to mammals, amphibians, and wildfowl. With a wide range of grasses and shrubs and walking access to flint-rich chalk cliffs, it is a setting that has all the attributes to make it attractive to human occupation.

10.5.1   *Drainage of the Mesolithic landscape*

The evidence put forward in 10.3, above, suggests that the western flank of the Solent Basin was formerly bordered by dry land around the position now

Figure 10.7 Fallen trees along the shoreline at Bouldnor Cliff, resulting from cliff erosion and rotational sliding (Garry Momber)

occupied by Hurst Spit (Thompson 2006). Therefore, the Lymington River would have had to exit north-east along the current track of the Solent before joining the large palaeochannel that runs around the east of the Isle of Wight. There is currently no known physical evidence to suggest that a channel left the Western Solent and ran north-east to join the lower course of Southampton Water, despite this appearing to be the most convincing option when relying solely on the bathymetry. The lack of deposits in the base of the channel as a result of erosion, however, makes interpretation problematic. This is an issue raised by Tomalin (2000a and Chapter 12), where he points out that evidence from the centre of the Solent has now been lost to tidal scour, so that any traces of a river that flowed towards Southampton Water are now gone. What does remain is a topographic high on the floor of the Solent immediately off the terrestrial Bouldnor Cliff, but it has yet to be determined whether this is a palaeofeature or more modern seabed loading. North of Gurnard Point, to the east, the seabed drops to below –20m OD, after which it continues to deepen along the Solent palaeochannel. This would provide a drainage route for the Lymington River to the east unless physical barriers of some form held the water back.

At this point the potential loss of land and seabed should be considered. The susceptibility to erosion of the soft Eocene bedrock that lines the Solent has already been noted (see 10.3, above), as has the under-cutting of Bouldnor Cliff by the sea (see 10.1). The latter is an ongoing process: the Bembridge Marls that make up the cliff are prone to fragmentation and rotational sliding, and the exposed cliff-face, which reaches a height of 60m on a slope of some 15–20°, is actively sliding into the Solent, as indicated by fallen trees lying on the beach and expanses of bare rock face caused by mudslides (Fig 10.7). It is also worth noting that the highest point on the hill at Bouldnor lies at the top of the cliff, showing that the hill is still rising at the point where it is severed: prior to erosion, the hill would have been higher, and would, of course, have once extended further across the Western Solent valley towards the New Forest. Indeed, Tomalin (2000a) proposes that the lost watershed or 'final umbilical' bisected the Western Solent between Hamstead Cliff, immediately to the east of Bouldnor, and Pitts Deep. The potential magnitude of a barrier will be addressed in the next chapter, after we have looked in this chapter at a proposition put forward by Tomalin (2000a and Chapter 12) that the Lymington River might have drained along a southerly route via

Figure 10.8   The current origin of the old river Yar at Afton Marshes can be seen in the middle distance. Its elevation is lower than high water spring tides and would be flooded by the sea if this roadway at Freshwater Bay was removed (Garry Momber)

the river Yar and passed through the chalk gap at Freshwater Bay.

The first thing to note when looking at the river Yar is its orientation. The current river runs from south to north, entering the Solent at Yarmouth. For this river to have been an exit point for water from the Solent, the Yar would have had to flow in the opposite direction. This may appear counter-intuitive, as water only goes downhill. However, the gradient along the length of the river is negligible, making it predominately estuarine. The marsh is barely above Ordnance Datum and forms part of a flat alluvial infill deposit that traces a pathway between bluffs all the way from Yarmouth to Freshwater. The marsh would be impacted by the sea from the Solent during high water spring tides if it were not for a causeway built three-quarters of the way along its length. At its southern end the head of the river emanates from Afton Marsh, which lies within 100m of Freshwater Bay. It is separated from the sea by a shingle beach, a road, and a car park. The marsh would be directly attacked by waves at Freshwater if these barriers did not exist (Fig 10.8).

Freshwater Bay is a south-facing cove sitting in the

foot of a deeply incised valley within the chalk hills (Fig 10.9). To the west, white chalk cliffs averaging 100m high run in an unbroken line for over 5km to the Needles. To the east, the cliffs stretch for almost 2km into Compton Bay before the chalk continues into the island to become rolling hills behind the less-consolidated early Cretaceous, Lower Greensand and Wealden formations. The chalk ridge steadily rises to more than 160m to form the backbone of the island. Freshwater Bay is, therefore, a very conspicuous morphological feature that is cut into the chalk cliffs and would have been formed by fluvial action, but, today, no river flows through it.

The evidence presented above suggests that the Western Yar could readily have flowed from north to south and most probably did at some point in the past (Fig 10.10). However, if it were to drain the Solent at the time of Mesolithic occupation, the base of the palaeoriver channel at Freshwater would have to be deeper than that at Yarmouth.

At the mouth of the river Yar a core was taken from the west spit (above, 10.5) and described by Rob Scaife (Scaife 2000a). Bedrock was recorded at –12.25m OD, above which 1.5m of freshwater

Figure 10.9 The valley cut through the chalk cliffs at Freshwater Bay, viewed from the south-east (Garry Momber)

lagoon/lake mire deposits were laid down about *c* 6940–5900 cal BC (*c* 8000 to 7000 BP). The first marine influence is recorded about 5900 cal BC (7000 BP), when ponding back of the river systems led to the development of brackish reedswamp and salt marsh. The development of vegetation associated with this change was dated to 6380–5840 cal BC (7320 ± 110 BP; GU-5397).

The deepest point of a possible palaeochannel in the valley bottom at Freshwater is unknown as no core has yet been taken through the channel fill that remains behind the barrier beach. However, a geophysical survey (98/13-A) conducted by Racal Survey (UK) Ltd in 1990 on behalf of Occidental Petroleum Ltd revealed detail of channels offshore. The survey collected bathymetric and sub-bottom profile data across an area 6km by 4km, 3km due south and to the west of Freshwater. The vertical resolution of the survey data is approximately 0.5m. The survey revealed that the seafloor bedrock lies at around –15m OD (–13m CD) at the nearest point to Freshwater, in the north-west corner of the survey. The bedrock drops gently along a shallow incline towards the south over a submerged wave-cut platform that has eroded into the chalk hills. Within the survey area the seabed changes from chalk to the older, less-consolidated and softer bedrock (see 10.1). Beyond the geological transition the seabed dips more steeply to the south and it is recorded at –27m CD at the point

it emerges from the south side of the survey area. The descent follows broad channels running across the bedrock away from the Isle of Wight.

The dip in elevation of the bedrock from –12.25m to around –15m OD between Yarmouth Harbour and the survey area is almost 3m over a distance of 7km. The southward downslope of the bedrock and the evidence of channels demonstrate that relic watercourses flowed south of Freshwater Bay and could have travelled from as far north as the Solent. It is evident that the chalk, which is more resilient than the surrounding bedrock, acts as a sill, limiting water flow until the water level is high enough to cross it. This could lead to back-ponding where the land was lower than the chalk in the 'West Solent Basin' syncline to the north. Beyond the chalk to the south, the channel dips steeply.

Before leaving the debate on the drainage of the 'Western Solent Basin', the differences between environments resulting from the various scenarios should be considered. If the Lymington River did pass to the north-east along the current passage of the Solent, drainage would have been good, thereby limiting the creation of wetland environments or the deposition of lacustrine deposits. Were the river to drain through the river Yar, where there is a greater potential for back-ponding, wetlands or a lacustrine environment would have been more probable. All the evidence presented in Section Two concurs with the latter scenario.

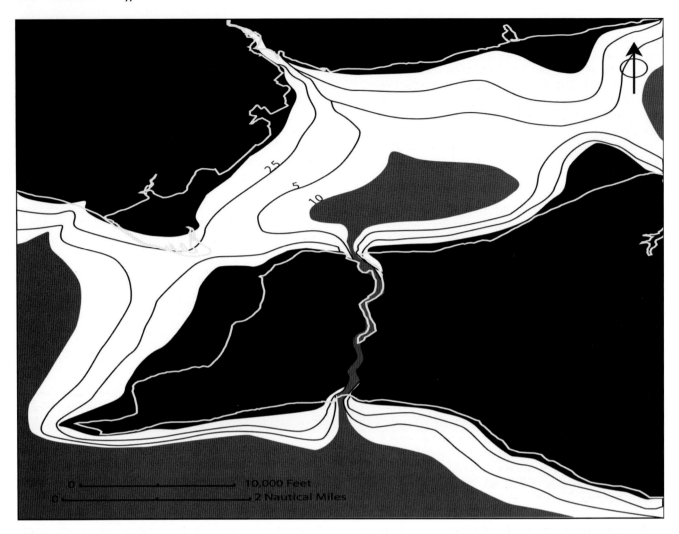

Figure 10.10   Modelled reconstruction of the Western Solent at the time just before the initial ingress by the sea (c 6200 cal BC). The drainage is from north to south. Black represents land above Ordnance Datum (OD) and an approximation of the land prior to the formation of the Solent. White is the land that would have been dry and the contours show levels below OD. Grey is the sea (Drawing by Rory Smith with detail from Admiralty Chart 2040, 1991)

10.5.2   *Sedimentalogical indicators for flooding of the Western Solent*

The water that filled the Solent was laden with minerogenic sediments and remnant biological material. After coming to rest it left a sediment archive containing a record of sequential events. This archive has now become exposed on the seabed in the form of the submerged Bouldnor Cliff, making it accessible to analysis. Sections recovered and linked to the archaeology have been fully reported on in Chapter 2. Other samples from the Bouldnor Cliff profile previously recovered in 1997–1998 were subject to palaeoenvironmental analysis by Rob Scaife and presented in the *Coastal Change, Climate and Instability* project report (2000a). This is a key piece of work that is drawn on in the section below to interpret the pattern of geomorphological change as the water rose.

10.5.2.1   Flooding of the Western Solent

The rising sea level put pressure on the water table and caused ponding along the developing coastal zone. The build-up of vegetable matter in the stagnant water that resulted ultimately became peat. It was these wet anaerobic conditions that preserved the old land surface and its associated organic artefacts (a process described in Chapter 8, 8.2).

Pollen predating the peat in BC-II context 2007 and BC-V contexts 5012/5017 (see Chapters 3, 3.5, and 4, 4.4) shows that the land was dominated by woodland, probably with open glades accompanied by areas of grass–sedge fen. The lower levels of context 2007 show evidence of slow-moving water passing through woodland where the stream gradient levelled near the valley floor. The strong concentration of alder and the presence of grasses suggest fen and carr nearby (Chapter 3, 3.7). Within a few decades, in pollen phase II of context 2007, alder became more prevalent. This seems to accord with a damp carr-type woodland associated with waterways and a river floodplain. At this time there is no indication of marine ingress into this deposit and there is no development of peat. This is the environment directly associated with the Mesolithic habitation.

The transition between a 'well-watered' freshwater fenland to a brackish environment was accompanied by a corresponding increase in alder and grasses, ultimately resulting in colonisation by saline-tolerant plants. By the beginning of context 2001 at BC-II the marine influence on freshwater deposits was completed when marsh turned to salt marsh. Greater reworking of sediments was recorded, with an increased occurrence of earlier pre-Quaternary pollen and spores.

Soon after the formation of salt marsh, marked amounts of deep-water planktonic and continental shelf foraminifera were recorded. Their arrival at the site could have been due to a sea-level surge or to reworking of older deposits (Chapter 3, 3.6.2). This event also coincides with an expansion of the diatom *Paralia sulcata*, which may represent the build-up of deeper water following a flooding event. The salt marsh was soon to give way to mudflat which accrued in a sheltered estuarine environment.

The events outlined above suggest an area of well-watered lowland levelling off at about –12m OD. When marine flooding occurred large quantities of reworked pre-Quaternary deposits were brought into the system and readily deposited in a sheltered sedimentary sink. The most fitting model that would encompass this set of circumstances would be a sheltered basin with an exit channel (such as the Western Yar) cutting through the Tertiary strata (see Fig 10.10). A rise in sea level would reverse the flow in the river channel, transporting sediments north. On reaching an area of open water such as a basin, where the water energy drops, the sediment sinks. Water entering the system from the Lymington River and other tributaries would, similarly, deposit sediments in this basin when the energy in the water was dissipated. It was this build-up of waterborne silts that covered the land surface and created the deposit that is 7m thick at Bouldnor and 2m thick off Tanners Hard. This deposit would have been widespread across the basin before the opening of the Western Solent and the introduction of currents which have steadily removed it and deepened the channel.

10.5.2.2 Sea-level fluctuations and new pollen and sediment inputs to the Western Solent

The next major change in the sedimentary regime occurs between 5.1 and 4.9m below OD (Fig 10.11). Vegetation grew and decayed to leave layers of peat intercalated with grey estuarine sediments. The formation of peat on an alluvial mudflat suggests an interruption or relative still-stand in the rising tendency of the sea.

Scaife's analyses reveal three major taphonomic changes between the peat and the lower and upper silts. The underlying sediment is primarily minerogenic, containing substantial numbers of pre-Quaternary pollen and spores derived from Cretaceous and Tertiary bedrock (Scaife 2000a, 13–23). Pollen from halophytic taxa demonstrate that the sediments were brackish rather than fully marine.

The accumulation of organic peat marks a period when fluvial or marine conditions cease. Initial vegetation consisted largely of monocotyledonous grass including sedges and rushes. The decline in brackish water halophytic taxa such as Goosefoots and Oraches (Chenopodiaceae) shows an absence of saline conditions and it suggests that the sea may have been at some distance. The peat development was followed by re-expansion of Chenopodiaceae and other halophytes in the upper zone when a return to saline conditions occurred. A sample collected near the base of the peat at 5.1m below OD in the middle zone at BC-II was dated at 4920–4535 cal BC (5870 +/- 80 BP, Beta-140103).

This intercalated layer of peat is particularly interesting because it was formed during a hiatus between different marine depositional regimes. The sediment that covers the peat shows a reduction in the numbers of pre-Quaternary pollen and spores. It suggests that input from local fluvial systems or the near-shore erosion of cliffs had diminished. This may be because pathways from the material sources had changed and/or the marine influence has increased. Moreover, higher values of Alder (*Alnus*) and sedges (Cyperaceae) are now occurring. This suggests an increase in waterborne pollen and sediment in rivers entering the Western Solent. Following the earlier still-stand or regression it would appear that the sea returned with an increased marine influence carrying water from a larger geographical catchment.

The resurgence of alluvial sediments containing reworked material from local Tertiary bedrock represents a further phase of deposition. Material from Cretaceous formations is no longer present. Rob Scaife recorded that the diatoms in the grey minerogenic sediments reveal marine or brackish water and salt marsh conditions (Scaife 2000a).

At –4.1m ± 0.15m below OD, alluvial deposition diminished and the spread of vegetation resumed across these areas. Another relative fall, or perhaps a still-stand, in sea level enabled the development of grass–sedge fen on the salt marsh (Scaife 2000a). The top of the peat has since degraded or has been lost to erosion but sufficient remains to show that oak and hazel woodland had established on the drier areas of the mire habitat (Scaife 2000s). A sample collected from the base of the upper peat deposit was dated to 4540–4330 cal BC (5580 ± 60 BP, Beta-140102).

The influx of Cretaceous and Tertiary pollen spores in the sediments below the middle intercalated peat accord with an input of marine sediments

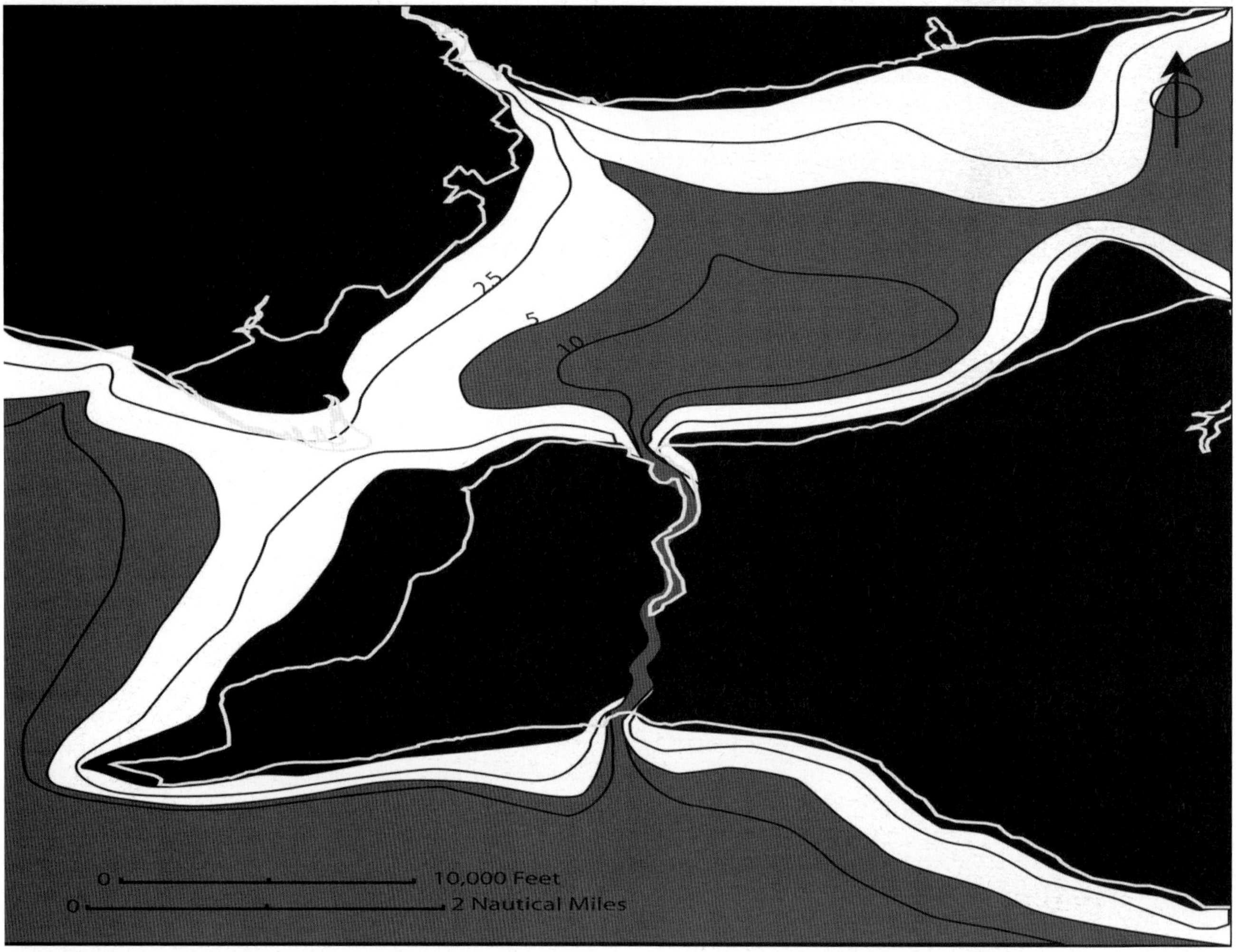

Figure 10.11   Modelled reconstruction of the Western Solent at 5m OD, when a breach of the basin is hypothesised to the east (c 4920–4535 cal BC). From this point in time the river Yar would not have been necessary to drain the Solent. Black represents an approximation of the land above OD that would have existed before being eroded during the formation of the Solent. White is the area below OD that would have been dry land when sea level was lower. Contours indicate levels below OD. Grey is the sea (Drawing by Rory Smith with detail from Admiralty Chart 2040, 1991)

via the river Yar (see model proposed in 10.5.2.1). Cretaceous material would be derived from the unconsolidated Wealden and Greensand formations that would have framed the mouth of the Yar while the Tertiary material would come from more local sources around the Western Solent Basin.

The colonisation of the mudflats coincides with a change in the drainage system. When marine conditions returned, Cretaceous sediments were no longer present. This suggests that the previous pathway from the south of the chalk had been neutralised, while reworked Tertiary material which dominates the geological record to the north of the Isle of Wight increases. For this to happen, another opening into the Western Solent Basin is needed. The most probable route would be to the east over the top of the land that was once an extension of Bouldnor Cliff. Access from the larger Southampton Water/East Solent drainage network would account for the increase in diversity of the pollen spectra.

The dramatic change in hydrodynamic regime and sediment redistribution around the Western Solent may account, in some part, for the dominance of the land over the sea at 4920–4535 cal BC (5870 +/- 80 BP, Beta-140103) as plants took hold. This would account for the peat at –5m below OD. In addition, the opening of a new channel to the east allows the introduction of water with sediment from Bembridge Marls which would explain the dominance of reworked Tertiary material that covered the –5m peat.

10.5.2.3   The final breakthrough and formation of the Solent

Several submerged peats on the fringes of the Western Solent suggest that semi-stable freshwater or brackish conditions existed prior to the formation of the open seaway. At Bouldnor and Tanners Hard, peat occurs at –4m OD. At Hurst Spit, peat-forming

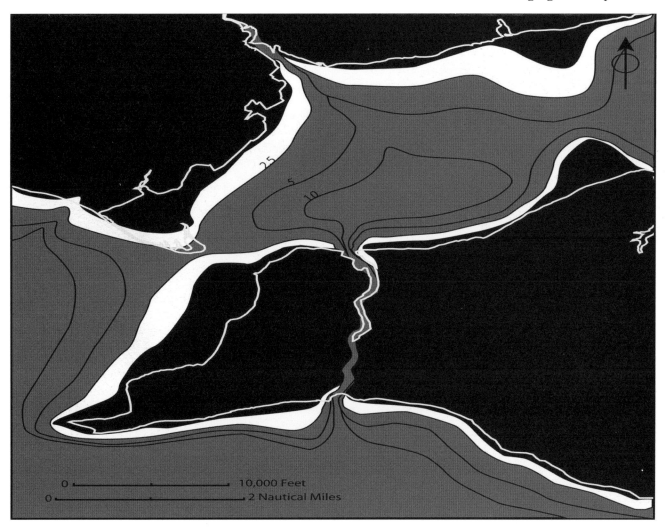

Figure 10.12 Modelled reconstruction of the Western Solent at –2.5m OD, when a second entrance to the system is hypothesised to the west. This would have opened the Solent to new erosive currents. Black represents an approximation of the land above OD that would have existed before being eroded during the formation of the Solent. White is the area below OD that would have been dry land when sea level was lower. Contours indicate levels below OD. Grey is the sea (Drawing by Rory Smith with detail from Admiralty Chart 2040, 1991)

conditions persisted until they were eventually terminated at –2 or –3m OD (Fig 10.12).

Studies conducted through the University of Southampton looking at the morphodynamics and evolution of the salt marshes have concluded that these peats formed within an inner estuarine or bayhead deposit in the Western Solent. Furthermore, a date has been speculated for the final submergence of the peat and the opening of the Solent to Christchurch Bay at somewhere before 2500 years BP (Ke & Collins 2002, 435). The figure is based on the assessment of dated peat samples from similar heights in the region (Devoy 1982; Dean 1995; Hampshire County Council 1995).

The data presented in 10.1 and 10.3 above refutes the concept of an early fluvially cut channel from the west. The extensive erosion of the soft Eocene deposits wherever the land is exposed to marine tidal action also supports the case for extensive geomorphological remodelling during the late

Holocene. The deep cut through Hurst Narrows when compared to the relatively shallow seabed to the east and west demonstrate how the sea has readily excavated the soft Eocene clays where the tides are strongest. The submerged terrestrial deposits lying just below CD, beneath Hurst Spit, show that land existed in the western passage which could have extended to the Isle of Wight. The capacity clearly exists for the marine channel to have been excavated quickly and fully once tidal scour was of sufficient strength towards the end of the transgression. All this evidence gives support to a relatively recent breach of the western entrance to the Solent.

10.6   Conclusions and discussion

The model put forward in this chapter describes a Mesolithic landscape in a basin that sits within an anticline and is associated with a river floodplain. The river, being an amalgam of the Lymington River and the Western Yar, runs from north to south and is attended by various feeder streams that serve the surrounding upland. The strip of submerged land remaining off Bouldnor Cliff indicates that the depth of dry land within the river basin would have been about 12m below OD. Drainage from the basin would have been controlled by the maximum depth of the Western Yar river channel. A confirmed depth has currently been identified as 12.25m by direct coring although the deepest part of the channel may exceed this (see Tomalin, Chapter 12). The evidence presented shows that the difference between the level of the land in the palaeochannel and the level of the river is only in the order of 1m. Land lying below the river within the basin would be drowned and only a small rise in water levels would be necessary to flood large areas. This includes the lower reaches of the submerged hillside that remains at Bouldnor Cliff.

The basin offered a range of habitats in which hunter-gather communities of the Middle Stone Age could fish and roam. This landscape included broadleaf woodland, alder carr, fen, open grassland, reed swamp, and a variety of watercourses set amongst low interfluve benches and mobile sand bars. The basin was surrounded by a varied and undulating landscape that was drained along the course of the Western Yar through a gap in the chalk hills to the south. The sea lay within a few kilometres of the chalk although the positive eustatic trend during the Flandrian transgression brought the sea closer until it ultimately flooded the basin. The sea would have first entered via the Western Yar although it was encroaching along the Solent from the east and through Christchurch Bay to the west. Estuarine conditions and the open sea could have been readily accessed by travelling overland or along the Western Yar.

The sedate inundation of the basin through the Western Yar resulted in excellent preservation of a Mesolithic landscape and artefactual remains. The most promising conditions are to be found in and below the thicker peats that have accrued near the basin floor. It is clear from the archaeological evaluations that there is a varied land surface blanketed by peat that supports geomorphological and archaeological features. Diver observations have traced fluvial gravel outcrops and humic horizons across this terrain. Results from the current work, and the ongoing recovery of human artefacts as they emerge from this fast-degrading seabed, indicate that much may yet to be revealed if the palaeomorphology of this submerged landscape can be further charted and sampled.

The palaeoenvironmental evidence from this location shows a landscape eventually turning to salt marsh when the sea enters and the freshwater basin changes to a brackish estuary. The ongoing process of inundation saw the coastal fringes retreat to be covered and protected by mudflat as sedimentation continued. Human adaptation to these changes has yet to be fully understood but the cultural remains found on other margins of the Solent estuarine system suggest that the entire basin may have been a theatre of human activity. Here, the unpredictable character of a coastal wetland environment would have been resource rich attraction that while the environmental changes demanded innovation and an ability to adapt (see Chapters 11 and 12).

Following inundation, the whole landscape was buried below metres of silt and would be today if it were not for the transformation from a depositional regime to one of persistent erosion. This change was brought about with the formation of the Western Solent when the sea finally breached the protective arms of land to the east of Bouldnor and then to the west across the 'Hurst Ridge'. Attrition of the final barrier that defended the estuary would have been gradual at first, then steadily accelerating as the channel grew and the volume of water through it increased. The process continues today and is demonstrated by the ongoing loss of seabed deposits in the Western Solent and in particular the submerged cultural landscape of Bouldnor Cliff.

Section four

The lithic assemblage from Bouldnor Cliff and its broader Mesolithic context

11 The assemblage of lithic artefacts from the Mesolithic occupation features on the sea floor at Bouldnor Cliff *by David Tomalin*

Worked flint tools remain the most frequently located of Mesolithic artefacts, and as such provide indicators with which to compare the material at Bouldnor with other known collections. It is through such comparison that initial interpretations of the type of site and activity represented at Bouldnor have been derived. This report examines 187 pieces of humanly struck flint that were found in association with the submerged forest deposit at the foot of the underwater cliff at Bouldnor. A collection of 79 fire-crazed flint fragments was also examined. The flint artefacts illustrated or photographed in this report are cited in this text by an examination number in bold.

11.1 Background to the recovery of lithic material

The recovery of this material covers the years 1999 to 2005. Most of this collection (200 pieces) comes from a single feature (BC-II) lying some 11–12m below OD. Fifteen struck flint pieces were recovered from BC-IV. A minor presence was also noted at BC-V, where two small tri-planar blades were recovered. In 2006 the presence of another submerged site was detected in the Western Solent when minor fragments of burnt flint were found off-shore from the Hampshire coast at Pitts Deep. This site awaits further study.

The flint recovered in 1999 was gathered from the disturbed upcast of the lobster burrows among the roots, boles, and trunks protruding from the base of the submerged cliff. The material recovered in 2000 came from within a small evaluation trench. In 2003 further stratified lithics were recovered from BC-II when a sondage section was cut back at the foot of the cliff. During the subsequent field season a further feature was recognised some 670m to the west: this was BC-IV, and produced fifteen further pieces of humanly struck flint (see Chapter 1).

11.1.1 The seabed context of the assemblage

With the exception of that from BC-IV and BC-V, which are spatially distinct sites, all of the lithic material described in this report comes from a single deposit that is sited at the base of the under-water cliff at BC-II. The source of this material lies in a sandy silt that contains numerous fragments of woodland trunks and branches (context 2007). This stratum appears to rest on the bed of a minor stream or creek where the basal deposit varies from sand (context 2011) to gravel (context 2012). The 'lithics bed' is partially overlain by a further deposit of gravel (context 2006) that seems to represent a minor episode of fluvial deposition before this location was blanketed in silty peat (context 2003). This is overlain by a silty grey alluvium (context 2002) that gives way to marine silt (context 2001). See Chapter 3 for a detailed analysis of BC-II's morphology.

It has since become apparent that the deposit at BC-II is just one component among a group of features clustered around the pre-inundation course of the present Bouldnor Brook. Other features or activity points within the complex have been identified at BC-V, 420m to the west, and BC-IV, 670m to the west and upslope at –6.5m OD.

Observations since 1986 had shown that the platform or 'woodland bench' had been formed by progressive recession of the cliff and by the process of current attack on the protective peat bed overlying context 2007, which had produced an exposed bench of woody and silty material. Lithic artefacts recovered from the furrows created by lobsters are commonly encrusted with marine growth and some have clearly been subject to erosion, showing differential patination and erosion where some of their surfaces have protruded from the surrounding deposit (Figs 11.1 and 11.2). An excavation in the summer of 2000 left no doubt that those flint artefacts excavated by the lobsters and those found by exposures at the foot of the cliff came from BC-II's context 2007.

The tidal scour of the Solent removes falls of material from the foot of the underwater cliff but, despite this, it seems that the clastic qualities of the peat and waterlogged timber do offer prolonged resistance to the processes of erosion. These unusual conditions have allowed a few precious seasons during which exposed archaeological features can be recognised and investigated before they are removed by tidal scour. An outstanding question concerns the number of lithic clusters that have already been removed by erosion and the number yet to be revealed during the ongoing retreat of the underwater cliff. Only sustained monitoring can resolve this latter issue.

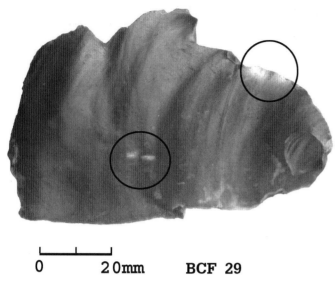

0   20mm   **BCF 29**

Figure 11.1   Gloss on BCF 29 (Patrick McGrorty)

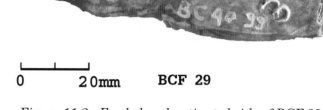

0   20mm   **BCF 29**

Figure 11.2   Eroded and patinated side of BCF 29 (Patrick McGrorty)

11.2   Samples and stratigraphy

11.2.1   The samples

The lithic material recovered between 1999 and 2005 is listed in Table 11.1. The 'lobster lithics' recovered from the localised upcasts of 1999 can be safely reconciled with the assemblages gathered at BC-II in 2000 and 2003. All of this material can be attributed to a parent deposit of grey sandy silt (context 2007) lying immediately below the forest bed (context 2003).

General conclusions concerning the lithic industry at this site can be drawn from all of the flint artefacts recovered at BC-II between 1999 and 2005. The precise location of each stone artefact should nevertheless be borne in mind. This caveat is particularly applicable to the flint artefact **120** (shown in Fig 11.8) from location 1051. This is a tranchet flake that has detached the blade end of a bifacially retouched flint axe. Prior to reworking, the blade of this tool displayed a remarkably uniform cutting

edge that is surprisingly similar to axes of Neolithic type. Its occurrence in a British Mesolithic context is certainly unusual.

11.2.2   Reviewing the stratigraphy and geomorphology of the submerged archaeological contexts

It is important to recognise that the location occupied by the BC-II lithic site is very different from a conventional inundation context where a submerged occupation site might sit on the floor of a risen sea. In such 'conventional' circumstances the location might be concealed by silts and sediments that had accrued on a relatively even and shallowly inclined plane.

In contrast, the Mesolithic features at BC-II, BC-V and BC-IV have been deeply entombed by channel deposits accruing to the substantial depth of some 7m (see Chapter 10, 10.5). These archaeological loci would still be completely buried were it not for the action of those Solent sub-surface currents that are now re-excavating and removing the submerged mid-Holocene channel deposits on this part of the coast. The outcome of this process is the formation and retreat of an underwater cliff, which is discussed in greater detail in Chapter 10, 10.5. It seems that it is the retreat of this cliff that is exposing a longitudinal section of the inundation fills of the former Western Solent valley or lowland. The geology and the Pleistocene geomorphology of this valley system have been reviewed by Tomalin (2000a), Dix (2001), and Hosfield (2001).

Currently the line of the underwater cliff bisects just three Mesolithic occupation features, but it is not unreasonable to suspect that a larger area of human occupation may still be entombed within the body of the underwater cliff. The rate of cliff retreat

Table 11.1   Summary of lithic material recovered between 1999 and 2005

Year	Site	Number
1999	BC-II	50
2000	BC-II	224
2001	BC-II	1
2002	BC-II	1
2003	BC-II	75
2003	BC-IV	15
2005	BC-V	2
Examination total		368

Table 11.2 Summary of lithic types from BC-II and BC-IV

Artefact type no	Artefact type	Quantity	
		BC-II	BC-IV
1	Hammerstone	1	
2	Core	5	
3	Core rejuvenation flake		4
4	Axe	0	
5	Tranchet flake from axe	3	
6	Non-microlithic tools	11	3
7	Micro-burin technique		1?
8	Microliths	2	
9	Flake	78	8
10	Blade	30	1
11	Bladelet	26	
12	Spall	7	1
13	Debitage – irregular waste	15	
14	Thermal	62	1
Total		240	19
Combined total			259

seems relatively rapid; general observations since 1986 suggest that it can be up to 0.5m per year.

11.3 Methods of recording and analysis

Before examination each lithic artefact was washed and placed in an individual polythene bag. An Access database was compiled using five descriptive fields to record site locational and find-processing information. A unique 'examination number' in the database was used as the primary record number for each artefact and this was marked on each find bag. The same number was inked on artefacts where appropriate, although many lithic items were too small to receive them without severely disfiguring and obscuring their surfaces.

A further eighteen fields in the database were used to record formal attributes, including metrical data concerning length, breadth, thickness, length–breadth ratio, butt length, and butt width. A free descriptive field was also provided, and for general quantification a summary field was used to record artefact type, using the categories outlined in Table 11.2. Further information was provided by the addition of lower-case suffixes as shown in Table 11.3.

11.3.1 Examination of the lithic assemblage

All lithic artefacts were first assessed with a hand lens before being examined as necessary with a binocular microscope at ×20 and ×35. Pieces

selected by this method were then examined with a Wilde M3C microscope at magnifications of up to ×120. Select photomicrographs of edge fractures, fine retouch and use-wear gloss were made, and many of these photographs appear in this section. The incidence of cores, flakes, tools, and burnt flint pieces was noted, and some 200 pieces of angular flint gravel were removed. Some material that had been suspect yet retained at the assessment stage was also discounted.

Attention was given to the qualitative properties of the lithics, including their colour, surface texture, and cortical or weathered surfaces. Their method of manufacture, their relative freshness or erosion,

Table 11.3 Suffixes and abbreviations used within the lithic recording database

p	prismatic
s	segmented
t	tri-planar
uf	utilised flake
nf	notched flake
ub	utilised blade
ubt	utilised bladelet
seg	snapped segment

General abbreviations in the database	
n	natural item
mg	marine growth (encrustation)

Figure 11.3   BCF 27 clean side (Patrick McGrorty)

Figure 11.4   Intense marine growth on BCF 27 (Patrick McGrorty)

and the presence of marine encrustation were also noted. Occasionally, marine growth would fully encrust one surface of a flint artefact, but colonisation of the under-face was extremely rare (Figs 11.3 and 11.4).

11.3.2   The nature of the raw material

Caution and objectivity in the characterisation of the flint prevented 75% of the material from being classified beyond a simple description of either 'burnt' or 'indeterminate'. This meant that, owing to the absence of cortex, no objective distinction could be made between nodular flint (1) and beach pebble/boulder flint (2). The remaining 25% of the collection nevertheless offered a sufficient sample to characterise the principal lithic materials used at this site. These comprised four types of raw flint and one example of quartzitic stone that was intrusive to the region (Fig 11.5 and Table 11.4).

Where nodular flint could be identified most of the examples (53%) were flakes on which cortex could survive over as much as 50% of the artefact surface. The remaining examples of chalky cortex were found on some cores, core rejuvenation flakes, tranchet flakes, microliths, blades, and bladelets.

Where beach flint had been employed it, too, was mostly detected on primary and secondary flakes; these amounted to 47% of the examples. The remaining examples were found in a few cores, core rejuvenation flakes, and microliths. Perhaps not surprisingly, traces of beach pebble surfaces were also observed on small spalls. Arguably, these spalls may have been detached from hammerstones. In three minor instances beach pebbles were found to be burnt.

Where gravel flint could be identified it appeared

Figure 11.5   Quartzite hammerstone BCF 63 (Patrick McGrorty)

that it had been used solely for heating and boiling. The gravel pebbles of the neighbourhood seldom exceed 30mm in diameter; they are poorly suited to knapping purposes and it is not surprising that these pebbles were not selected for the tool-making industry. Whitened fire-crazed flint amounted to 14% of the entire collection of flint recovered from the site. It seems likely that much of this heavily altered material may have come from gravel pebbles that had lost their outer surface.

A glossy sandy-white flint observed in flake **231** was particularly distinct. This material has been

Table 11.4 Summary of flint and stone raw material from Bouldnor Cliff

Ref	Percentage	Description
1	55%	Nodular flint with white chalky cortex
2	36%	Beach or 'cobble' flint struck from well-rounded shingle pebbles or boulders
3	7%	Pleistocene gravel flint comprising small rounded pebbles with thin grey cortex and grey or buff core and coarse irregular fracture
4	1%	Distinctive sandy-white glossy flint possibly from a particular source
5	1%	Purple-tinged quartzite

observed in some tranchet axes and Neolithic axes in the Isle of Wight, and may come from a particular source that was favoured for axe production. Alternatively, it might have been a rare and favoured material gathered among beach boulders. The transportation and sorting processes of the Solent shoreline can certainly offer a discerning flint-knapper a wide variety of choices.

A single quartzitic pebble (**63**) was identified as a split hammerstone subsequently used for some experimental core preparation (Fig 11.5). This stone resembles some south Devon quartzites and there remains the possibility that it was gathered from marine-transported material such as that which has been noted 70km west of Bouldnor in the composition of Chesil Beach (Durrance and Laming 1982, 168–9; West and Harvey 2005). Some large naturally transported pebbles of quartzite and indurated sandstone are also to be found in the shingle of Hurst Spit. This potential source lies only 6km west of Bouldnor, but its presence during the seventh and sixth millennia BC seems unlikely. Nevertheless, sub-bottom geophysical survey in the mouth of the Western Solent has revealed the presence of an earlier Holocene beach that is now submerged at –12m OD (Velegrakis 1994). It seems likely that this west-facing feature and its successors could have readily received alien quartzitic material from the Bournemouth region, where derived pebbles from more distant sources are present in the Boscombe Sands. It is also possible that one of these sources was the Triassic pebble beds of Budleigh Salterton, examples from which were found in the shingle of Chesil Beach.

11.3.3 The sources of raw material

While struck flint can be notoriously variable and difficult to characterise, the material at Bouldnor conveniently displays a simple range of textures and types. All of the struck flint is of good quality and it generally varies from grey to dark grey in colour. In some cases the darker shade approaches black. The texture or 'glassiness' increases in quality in the darker shades but all is of good knapping quality and there can be no doubt that all had been gathered with care and discrimination.

Where flakes and blades are devoid of cortex they have been assigned in the descriptive catalogue to an 'indeterminate' source because, objectively, this must be the case. It is this writer's suspicion, however, that all of the struck flint was obtained from no more than two local sources: the chalk cliffs of West Wight and beach supplies from the past shoreline of the Western Solent.

Whether or not virgin flint nodules were actually prised from the cliffs, it should be observed that some cortical flakes, such as fragment 17, show traces of deep nodular cavities or holes that are characteristic of undisturbed nodule beds in the Upper Chalk of the cliff face. Cortical flake 103 carries a fresh fossil cast in its cortex, indicating that the parent nodule was not subject to marine erosion at the base of a cliff.

The chalk cliffs of West Wight are accessible within 5km of Bouldnor at Freshwater Bay and at a distance of 7km at Alum Bay. These cliffs rise to a maximum height of 90m and their steeply dipping beds of nodular flint offer the knapper a rewarding choice of sizes and textures. Alternatively, the beach and wave-cut platform at the foot of these cliffs provides an array of dislodged, rolled, and semi-rolled material that still offers excellent knapping quality. It is uncertain how much of this southerly chalk cliff line was under wave attack during the sixth and seventh millennia cal BC, but some of the more westward tracts of Tennyson Down were surely exposed.

That raw material was certainly gathered from the beach is evident in the surface of many of the cortical fragments. Where the white cortex is accompanied by traces of nobbly protrusions or concavities the flint has been described in the catalogue as nodular, but this does not preclude the likelihood that it was gathered after it had come to rest on a beach. Moreover, where white chalky cortex survives it has commonly been 'thinned' in a manner that can be attributed to sea action and beach processes, while some cortical fragments show the water-worn and abrasion-impacted surface of well-rounded beach pebbles. Large and small pebbles of good-quality flint can be readily obtained from mature over-top beaches in the vicinity of the West Wight cliffs and possibly from other beaches closer to Bouldnor.

The last category of flint to be identified at Bouldnor is that used in burning/cooking processes. The total quantity of burnt flint is relatively modest

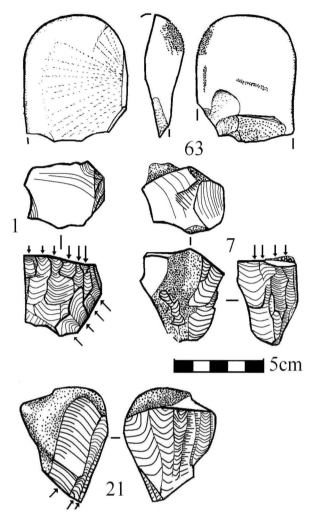

5cm

Figure 11.6   Hammerstone and cores. 1: Type D bi-directional core with obliquely set platforms; 7: uni-directional core struck from nodular flint; 21: Type E bi-polar core with parallel platforms. Beach pebble flint; 63: fragmentary quartzitic hammerstone pebble with bruising (David Tomalin)

(79 pieces), but it would not be surprising to find that this sample comes from the periphery of a much larger deposit of burnt flint that still remains *in situ* within the body of the underwater cliff. Most of these pieces can be readily attributed to the rounded pebbles of coarse oxidised flint that are otherwise to be found in the Plio/Pleistocene 'Plateau' gravels of North Wight. In fracture, the colour of this flint is commonly reddish or pinkish. The remaining pieces are small broken, non-cortical fragments that seem

likely to have originated as further pebbles of this same gravel.

A neighbouring deposit of this gravel flint is to be found no more than 2km away on the crest of the present sea cliff at Bouldnor. It seems likely, however, that minor streams such as the Bouldnor Brook could have carried these pebbles much closer to the site. Indeed, the stream gravel in context 2012 might well represent an on-site source of this material.

11.4. The components of the lithic industry

11.4.1 Hammerstones

Only one hammerstone (**63**) was recovered from the site (Fig 11.6). This was a cleaved and slightly reworked fragment of a quartzite beach boulder, and now weighs 112g. Prior to cleaving an original weight of at least 500g seems likely, based of the shape of the surviving portion. An original length of some 120mm might be postulated.

A well-rounded edge on this boulder has been bruised and whitened by pounding. This suggests former use as a hard hammer or pestle. The cleaving blow has been delivered some 20mm from the bruised point, perhaps as the result of careless use. After breakage and before rejection this heavy detached fragment received several edge-trimming flakes, seemingly to evaluate its knapping qualities. This item is of purplish colour and its lithology is alien to the solid geology of the Hampshire–Wight region (Fig 11.5).

11.4.2   Cores

Five cores were recovered (artefact nos **1, 3, 7, 21 & 171** (Figs 11.6 and 11.7 and Table 11.5)). Core types generally accord with those of Alexander and Ozanne (1960).

The survival of cortex on these cores ranges from 15% to 30% of the surface area. The raw material in this very small collection is made up of 60% beach pebbles and 40% nodular flint from the chalk cliffs, but this sample is really too small to be significant, and contrasts with percentages of 36% beach pebbles and 55% nodular flint in the larger sample of all classifiable cortical fragments from the site.

The lengths of the cores range between 30mm and 61mm, with a mean length of 46.8mm, and the breadths range from 22mm to 53mm, with a mean

Table 11.5   Summary of the five cores recovered from Bouldnor Cliff

Type	Description	No	Artefact no(s)
A	Single platform partially used	2 cores	3, 7
D	Two platforms obliquely set	2 cores	1, 171
E	Two parallel platforms	1 core	21

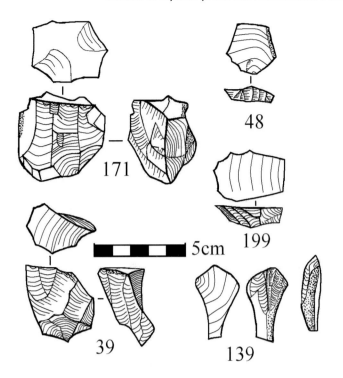

Figure 11.7 Cores and core rejuvenation. 39: core rejuvenation flake; 48: core rejuvenation flake; 139: core rejuvenation flake; 171: Core; 199: core rejuvenation flake (David Tomalin)

of 46.8mm. These are cores of relatively small proportions and they compare well with those from the Powell assemblage at Hengistbury Head, where the mean length of bladelet cores was 49.84mm and the mean breadth was 31.6mm (Barton 1992, 209).

11.4.3 Core rejuvenation flakes

Four core rejuvenation flakes were identified (artefact nos **39**, **48**, **139** & **199**) (Fig 11.7).

11.4.4 The proxy representation of axes through the production of tranchet flakes

At least two tranchet flakes (artefact nos **120** and **27**; Fig 11.8) could be attributed to the sharpening of tranchet axes or adzes. Flakes **95** (Figs 11.10 and 11.16) and **272** (Fig 11.16) offer further evidence. These items provide evidence for the use of complete examples of these tools. Flake **272** shows that the axe acquired slight wear gloss before resharpening. Item **27** may be the truncated cutting edge of a further axe, but its lateral break is ambiguous and the whole could be a complete chopping tool.

11.4.5 Non-microlithic tools

Sixteen non-microlithic tools were present (Table 11.6). A few flakes and blades bearing minor traces

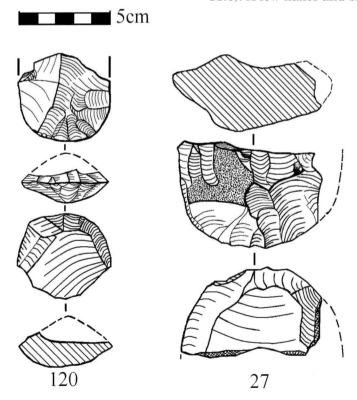

Figure 11.8 Tranchet-axe-sharpening flake and axe or chopper fragment. 27: tranchet flake from axe or adze; 120: axe-sharpening flake (David Tomalin)

Table 11.6   Summary of retouched and unretouched tools from Bouldnor Cliff

Code	Description	Artefact no
A	Pièce tronquée	188
B	Utilised flakes	85, 107, 222, 303
C	Notched flake	291
D	Utilised blade	275
E	Utilised bladelet	180
C	Hollow scraper	304
D	Burin?	262

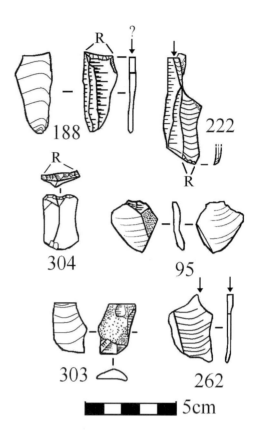

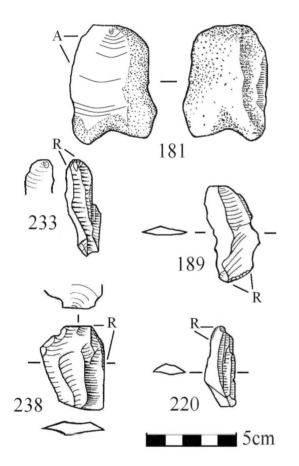

Figure 11.9   Retouched tools. 181: utilised cortical flake with abraded edge; 189: utilised blade with distal retouch; 220: blade with side retouch near proximal end; 233: tri-planar blade with proximal retouch; 238: utilised flake with side retouch (David Tomalin)

Figure 11.10   Tools and microliths. 95: sharpening flake(?) bearing truncated wear gloss; 188: tool. obliquely retouched piece or 'pièce tronquée'; 222: blade; 262: flake possibly modified as burin; 303: utilised flake; 304: steeped hollow scraper (fire-whitened flint) (David Tomalin)

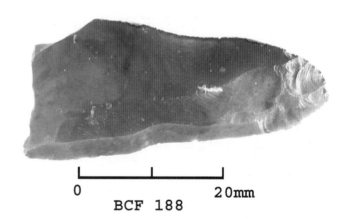

Figure 11.11   Pièce tronquée BCF 188 (Patrick McGrorty)

of utilisation are included here but have otherwise been counted in their parent artefact category in Table 11.6. Two unretouched flakes bear traces of use/wear gloss (nos **51** & **107**) and some edge abrasion (Figs 11.17 and 11.19 below). Other flakes had acquired minor edge damage or incidental retouch as the result of utilisation (nos **85, 181, 220, 222, 233, 238** & **303**). Two blades (**189** & **275**) and

a bladelet (**180**) also bore traces of edge utilisation. Tools referred to in this paragraph are illustrated in Figures 11.9, 11.10, 11.15, 11.17 and 11.19.

Only item **188** (Figs 11.10 and 11.11) bore heavy and deliberate retouch. This is a truncated piece bearing steep retouch at the blunted distal end and some shallow retouch at the bulbar tip. The blunted

Figure 11.12   Microlith BCF 126 (Patrick McGrorty)

Figure 11.13   Detail of retouch on microlith BCF 126 (Patrick McGrorty)

Figure 11.14   BCF 271 (Patrick McGrorty)

end is slightly concave and may have been 'twin-pronged' before losing one tip to a burin-type blow or fracture. This tool may claim an early Mesolithic ancestry among *les pièces tronquée* of the Azilian of the Paris Basin (Valentin *et al* 2004, 179, fig 4). In the Solent region this form persists in a local example at the Powell site at Hengistbury Head (Barton 1992, 229, fig 5.22 no 7). The Bouldnor example also resembles an item in the assemblage from Mother Siller's Channel at Christchurch (Palmer 1972, 22, fig 12 no 11).

11.4.6   The micro-burin technique

Item **291** (Fig 11.15), which is a non-bulbar segment of blade bearing a deep notch, was recovered from BC-IV. The notch may have survived a mis-snap of the blade during the micro-burin blade-snapping process. Item **253** was considered as a potential snapped 'micro-burin' bearing a residual trace of its notch. Its prismatic surfaces are, however, irregularly striated and are inconclusive of knapping. For this reason it has been excluded from the count.

11.4.7   Microliths

Only two items, artefacts **126** and **271**, fulfilled the definition of microlith. Item **126** is a backed blade with continuous abrupt retouch applied to one side. It is extremely small – no more than 23mm long (Figs 11.12 and 11.13). Item **271** is an obliquely blunted point which has been laterally snapped at its bulbar end, where there are some arguable traces of a micro-burin notch (Fig 11.14). This point is 18mm long.

11.4.8   Flakes

A total of 76 flakes from loci BC-II (Table 11.7) and BC-IV was examined. Just 9% were primary flakes and 10% were secondary flakes (these were defined, respectively, by more than 75% cortex and 25–75% cortex on the outer face). The remainder showed less than 25% cortex or nil.

The 65 flakes from BC-II and eleven flakes from BC-IV were all used for statistical analyses. A total of sixteen primary flakes could be attributed to nodular flint and then to beach pebbles. The remaining 50 bore no trace of cortex. The length of the flakes ranged from 4mm to 88mm and their breadth ranged from 9mm to 65.4mm.

Analysis shows a preponderance of flakes below 46mm in length and below 38mm in breadth. The mean length was 35.2mm, the mean breadth was 25.2mm, and the mean thickness was 6mm. When these dimensions are expressed as standard deviations these provide respective figures of 15.7mm, 12.5mm and 4.2mm.

After 23 flakes were found to be non-bulbar there remained 42 flakes of which the butts could be examined. They showed a high incidence of plain platforms (57%). A further nine flakes (21%) displayed minimal butts and only four (10%) were dihedral; five were unclassified. Where minimal butts were observed, these mostly occurred on thin skimming flakes. Flake **35** was an exception, being a thick fragment bearing some 40% cortex. One other flake bore 4% cortex. The remaining examples were thin, non-cortical flakes. These flakes hint at the possible use of a punch to deliver finely targeted impacts on the virtual brink of the striking platform. The mean thickness of these flakes, with the exclusion of flake **35**, was 3.7mm.

In total, 55% of the flakes could be attributed to early stages of core use, when remnants of cortex were still being detached. Where dorsal scars could be examined, the direction of flaking could be detected in 45 cases. Here, uni-directional flaking occurred

Table 11.7   Quantitative measurements of flakes from BC-II

Main dimensions	Length	Breadth	Thickness
Total	65	65	65
Range	4–88mm	9–65.4mm	1–18mm
Mean	35.215	25.246	6.051
Standard deviation	15.794	12.536	4.243

Butt dimensions	Length	Breadth
Total	31	30
Range	1–8.7	1–65mm
Mean	10.690	4.197
Standard deviation	5.908	2.443

Butt types on flakes at BC-II

Type	No	Percentage
Non-bulbar	23	35%
Minimal	9	14%
Plain	24	37%
Dihedral	4	6%
Other	5	8%

Dorsal scars on flakes from BC-II

Type	No	Percentage
Uni-directional	31	69%
Multi-directional	5	11%
Crossed	4	9%
Bi-directional	1	2%
Unclassified/indeterminate	4	9%

Distal terminations on flakes from BC-II

Type	No	Percentage
Hinged	7	11%
Carinated	5	8%
Blunt	10	15%
Snapped	8	12%
Feathered	35	54%

in 31 examples (69%). Only a single instance of bi-directional flaking was observed. Multi-directional flaking occurred in five cases (11%), and four examples of cross-directional flaking were observed (9%). A further 9% (four flakes) of dorsal scars were classified as 'other'.

Given the relatively small sample of flakes, little can be safely postulated from these measurements other than the possibility that the generous incidence of uni-directional flaking could accord with a generous supply of good-quality flint which reduced the need to hoard or 'curate' cores. The large

numbers of uni-directional flake scars might also accord with the selection of nodules and pebbles of relatively modest size. In this case a minimal amount of primary trimming would be required before blade production could commence.

The distal termination of a flake must surely reflect both the intention of the flint-knapper and his or her level of accomplishment. The terminations of Bouldnor flakes were classified in five classes: *hinged, carinated, blunt, snapped,* and *feathered.* Hinged terminations generally reflect failure, inexperience or carelessness on the part of the knapper, although they may also reflect difficulty in removing inconvenient protrusions during core preparation. The poor choice of raw material implied by the latter may also reflect inexperience, although it can be a product of a meagre flint-bearing environment.

At Bouldnor, where flint supplies were plentiful, only 11% of flakes had produced a hinged fracture. More than half of these occurred on cortical flakes that were attributable to the primary preparation of cores. Where carinated terminations were noted, these too are best attributed to core preparation. These accounted for just 8% of the flake sample. Blunt terminations were found in 15% of the flake assemblage, and virtually all of these examples bore cortical surfaces that were also typical of core preparation. The snapped or broken pieces that were observed seemed attributable to post-manufacture breakages that had removed the original end of the flake. Given the general thinness of these flakes it is unlikely that their original distal ends were anything other than feathered. Barton (1992) reminds us that breakages of this kind can be readily produced by trampling over flint-working debitage. At Bouldnor, snapping amounted to no more than 12% of the flake sample, and this modest breakage rate may reflect the soft ground that is suspected to have been present during the occupation of this site.

In *toto*, analysis of flake terminations at Bouldnor leads to a conclusion that some 34% of flakes, comprising hinged, carinated, and blunt-ended products, were generally produced during core preparation. The remaining 66% of flakes can be mostly attributed to the working of cores and tools where shallow feather-ended flakes could be detached with skill and precision.

11.4.9 Blades

Twenty-nine blades were used for statistical analysis (Table 11.8 and Fig 11.15). These included blades otherwise considered to be utilised pieces. The blades ranged in length from 16.6mm to 64.5mm, the mean length being 38.5mm. Eight blades were fully tri-planar in cross section and five were fully prismatic. Two segmental fragments were excluded from length calculations. The remainder lacked symmetry throughout their length and were unable to offer a consistent cross section.

Where butts were examined on these blades, non-bulbar features were found in ten instances (36% of this very modest sample). Where bulbar butts were observed, a further 36% of the sample showed no more than a minimal presence, while 21% showed simple plain butts and just two examples (7%) took a dihedral form. If the dihedral butt is a reflection of an irregular platform then some incidences of dihedral facets must inevitably occur unless the platform was excessively scalloped by horizontal scars.

More interesting is the notable incidence of

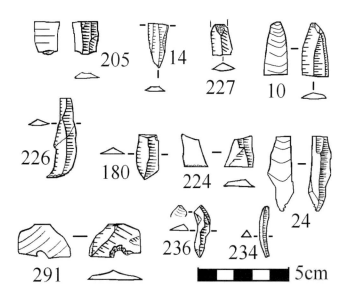

Figure 11.15 Blades and bladelets. 10: snapped tri-planar blade; 14: tri-planar bladelet; 24: bi-planar bladelet; 180: utilised bladelet; 205: blade segment; 224: blade segment; 226: retouched blade; 227: blade segment; 234: triangular-sectioned bladelet; 236: bladelet; 291: notched flake (David Tomalin)

minimal butts struck with a soft blow from a hammer or punch. It seems unlikely that anything other than a punch could reduce platform sizes to the subliminal scale seen in this assemblage.

Cortex occurs on just eight blades at Bouldnor (27%), accounting for no more than 5.6% of the total surface area of all the blades. Nevertheless, one exceptional blade displayed cortex over 60% of its surface.

An examination of the dorsal scars on the blades revealed consistent evidence of uni-directional flaking. The distal ends of the flakes showed a high incidence of feathering. Rare exceptions were one blunt-ended flake and one flake with a carinated tip. Two flakes with snapped tips could also be confidently attributed to the feathered class.

11.4.10 Bladelets

Bladelets are defined by a width of less than 12mm (Butler 2005, 35). A total of 26 bladelets was recovered, of which 24 were used for statistical analyses (Table 11.9). Their length ranged from 10.6mm to 33.1mm, their breadth range was 5mm to 11mm, and their maximum thickness varied between 0.6mm and 4.9mm.

Only five bladelets were noted as being consistently tri-planar and only two were prismatic throughout their length. Cortex survived on seven bladelets (24%) in proportions ranging from 8% to 30% of the artefact surface: throughout the full collection of bladelets this amounted to no more than 4% of the

Table 11.8 Quantitative measurements of blades from BC-II

Main dimensions	Length	Breadth	Thickness
Total	29	29	293
Range	16.4–64.5mm	12–50mm	1–6.2mm
Mean	38.5	17.6	3.8
Standard deviation	16.37	8.5	1.77

Butt dimensions	Length	Breadth
Total	23	23
Range	2–17.7mm	1–4.7mm
Mean	7.2	3.05
Standard deviation	1.8	4.3

Butt types on blades from BC-II		
Type	No	Percentage
Non-bulbar	10	36%
Minimal	10	36%
Plain	6	21%
Dihedral	2	7%

Dorsal scars on blades from BC-II		
Type	No	Percentage
Uni-directional	25	89%
Multi-directional	0	
Crossed	0	
Bi-directional	0	
Unclassified/indeterminate	3	11%

Distal terminations on blades from BC-II		
Type	No	Percentage
Hinged	2	7%
Carinated	2	7%
Blunt	2	7%
Snapped	3	11%
Feathered	17	61%
Unclassified	2	7%

total surface area. The butts of the bladelets showed that 44% were of non-bulbar form, while a further 44% showed minimal butts incapable of measurement. Two examples showed bruised butts that were probably the product of the same method of striking that had produced the minimal butts. The use of a punch, as with the Bouldnor blades, must be suspected. Only one plain butt was noted. It seems likely that those blades that were devoid of butts had been snapped in the course of tool production. Three examples that were devoid of bulbs and butts showed further snapping at the distal end.

The dorsal scars on the Bouldnor bladelets were very largely uni-directional (88%). A few exceptions showed single examples of crossed, bi-directional, and multi-directional striking. The dominance of uni-directional examples suggests that few bladelet cores were rejuvenated by reversal or driven to complete exhaustion. This may well reflect the ease with which good raw material could be obtained in this locality. It is also compatible with the suspected selection of small nodules or pebbles of the raw material.

The distal terminations showed a dominance of feathered edges (56% of the bladelet sample). It

Table 11.9 Quantitative measurements of bladelets from BC-II

Main dimensions	Length	Breadth	Thickness
Total	24	24	24
Range	10.6–33.1mm	5–11mm	0.6–4.9mm
Mean	19	8.4	2.1
Standard deviation	8.6	2.8	1.26

Butt dimensions	Length	Breadth	
Total	2	2	
Range	3–5.4mm	2–2.2mm	
Mean	4.2	2.1	
Standard deviation	0.14	1.69	

Distal terminations on bladelets from BC-II

Type	No	Percentage
Hinged	3	13%
Carinated	1	4%
Blunt	3	12%
Snapped	4	17%
Feathered	13	54%

appears that these were bladelets that had been discarded without further attention. Other discards probably included the three bladelets with hinged terminations. Snapped terminations accounted for 16% of the bladelet sample and blunt-ended examples comprised a further 12%. All of these pieces seem to have received some further attention after their initial striking.

11.4.11 Chips/spalls

Seven chips/spalls were noted in the assemblage. This was a heterogeneous collection offering little to the general characterisation of the assemblage. One example (**239**) displayed a minimal bulb that appeared to be the product of hard percussion. The means of percussion in the production of the remainder was indeterminate. Item **177** was a flake of minimal proportions seemingly struck as a result of a failed blow for blade production. Item **30** had been detached from a nodular beach boulder with thinned chalky cortex. Battering at its proximal end had removed the bulb to produce a short pyramidal tip that may have been utilised as a graver. The remaining pieces were of diminutive size and probably the products of smash waste.

11.4.12 Debitage – irregular waste

Fifteen small sharp pieces of flint were considered to be unclassifiable examples of smash waste.

11.4.13 Flint altered by thermal fracturing and fire-crazing

Thermal fracturing was evident in 75 pieces in the flint sample. Some 82% were intensely fire-crazed pieces typically whitened throughout. Many had lost their cortical surfaces and may have been reduced to their current diminished and irregular appearance by several firings. The intense crazing of these pieces and their small size is consistent with a cooking process. The remaining flints were portions of small pebbles that had been subject to alteration by mild heat. This had commonly produced cracked or spalled surfaces where reddening might be seen. These pebbles were composed of inferior-quality flint of the type that could be gathered or derived from the local outcrop of Plio/Pleistocene gravel.

11.5 General observations

The assemblage excavated in 2000 contained just eight discernable tools and three cores. Together with debitage, this was mostly recovered from eroding sediments on the scoured 'bench' at the base of the underwater cliff.

The assemblage from the 2003 excavation is well recorded. After natural flint items have been discounted it comprises some 75 pieces, of which 8 are burnt pebbles or pebble fragments, 47 are struck flakes, mostly of prismatic or tri-planar form, and 3 are minor spalls; a single core is present which displays two platforms set at right-angles.

It is also evident from the repetition of shallow bulbs that the knapping process was carried out with the aid of an antler or bone hammer. This technique has been replicated in a knapping experiment by Phil Harding and in further experiments with Isle of Wight flint by John Winch.

11.5.1   Axes and axe production

Several discoveries of tranchet axes have been recorded in the Solent coastal area of West Wight, including beach finds made within some 300m of the current underwater site at Bouldnor. A notable number of tranchet axes, adzes, and picks have also been recovered by fishermen from the seabed of the Western Solent (Harding *et al* 2004).

Although tranchet axes have been recovered from the beach at Bouldnor (Poole 1936) and from the seabed in adjacent areas of the Western Solent, no axe has yet been recovered from the underwater site. Given the modest size of the lithic sample recovered by underwater investigation this hardly seems surprising: at Gatcombe, Isle of Wight, where 292 plough-scattered flint pieces were collected from a Mesolithic and early Neolithic site, just one tranchet axe was recovered. It was also observed at Gatcombe that there can be an element of absurdity in attempting to quantify the presence of axes at a site where damaged examples of these heavy implements can be so readily reworked into cores, flakes and smaller tools (Tomalin and Scaife 1979, 27–9).

The contemporary use of axes in the Bouldnor assemblage is attested by proxy evidence provided by tranchet flakes that were detached during axe sharpening (see Fig 11.8). Item **120**, from the upper part of context 2007, is a detached cutting tip of a bifacially prepared flint axe with a blade width of 42mm. The regular blade edge, with its weak S-shaped profile, had been carefully formed with shallow skimming flakes. It would seem that the cross section of the axe was a shallow regular ellipse. The care and symmetry displayed in this work are usually associated with Neolithic craftsmanship. Occurrence in a Mesolithic context is certainly unusual, but perhaps not without continental analogy.

Item **27** may have been mis-struck during axe or adze rejuvenation or breakage. Its original post-fracture outline is conjectured in Figure 11.8. The cutting edge of this item bears unifacial retouch. Other flakes were driven off after the main butt end fracture had occurred, leading to the suspicion that this item may have been used or utilised as a chopping tool.

11.5.2   Retouched tools

Only four items claimed status as retouched tools. They are too few to be equated with a definitive industry. Item **188**, a distinctive obliquely blunted blade (Figs 11.10 and 11.11), is also one of the few

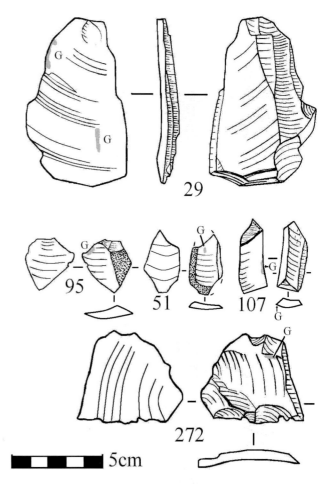

Figure 11.16   Lithic pieces with gloss (G). 29: semi-tri-planar flake with wear gloss on edge;
51: tri-planar flake with wear gloss; 95: sharpening flake(?) bearing truncated wear gloss;
107: utilised flake bearing edge wear gloss;
272: tranchet flake with slight wear gloss near former cutting edge (David Tomalin)

items to bear marine encrustation and evidence of marine erosion. This is attributed to exposure among the peat and timbers of the submerged forest. This form of tool claims a long ancestry, for it can be found in the Azilian of the Paris basin, where it falls within the description of *'une pièce tronquée'* (Valentin *et al* 2004). The same form is also to be found at the Powell site at Hengistbury Head (Barton 1992, 229, fig 5.22 no 7). Item **222** (Fig 11.10) is a long tri-planar flake with retouched nose. Item **262** (Fig 11.10) is the distal end of a flake that appears to have been mis-snapped close to a retouched notch.

11.5.3   Utilised blades and flakes without retouch

The reuse of sharp-edged blades and flakes could be detected by minor edge damage and by occasional snappings. The most revealing evidence was found on heavy flake **29** (described below), where the edge

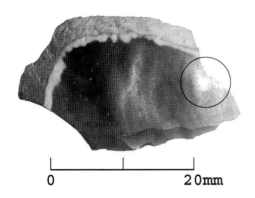

Figure 11.17   Gloss on BCF 51 (Patrick McGrorty)

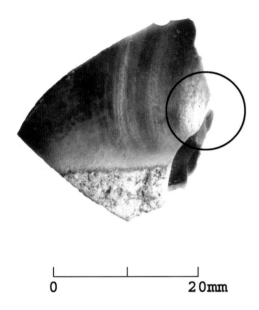

Figure 11.18   Gloss on BCF 95 (Patrick McGrorty)

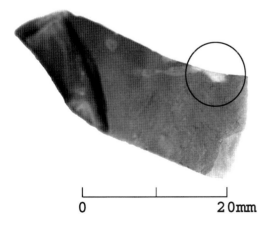

Figure 11.19   Gloss on BCF 107 (Patrick McGrorty)

showed minor abrasions yet edge gloss signified repetitive use (Fig 11.16; see Fig 11.1).

11.5.4   Use-wear gloss

Small areas of incidental polishing or gloss have been detected in five instances (artefact nos **29**, **51**, **95**, **107** and **272**; 1.6% of the assemblage). This seems to be a noteworthy proportion of the assemblage and is particularly interesting because the environmental history of the site precludes any prolonged processes of groundwater movement or sub-aerial erosion that might offer alternative circumstances in which glossed surfaces could, arguably, be created by natural means. At Bouldnor it seems unlikely that the lithic assemblage could have remained in a dry terrestrial environment for more than some 200 years.

Butler (2005) comments that general use-wear analyses have highlighted that it is not only the formal implement types but also many unretouched flakes that were used for all manner of cutting and scraping tasks in prehistory. In his view, the possible uses of unretouched flakes 'may have been vastly understated'. The examples of wear gloss observed at Bouldnor certainly support Butler's hypothesis.

Artefact **29** is a large, heavy tertiary flake with long fluted scars on its dorsal surface. There is no retouch, but one lateral edge near the butt has a sharp and usable cutting edge. Utilisation of this part of the flake is attested by edge gloss on the ventral surface (Figs 11.1 and 11.16). Less explicable is a second area of gloss near the centre of the ventral face. This is a small linear strip some 10mm by 2mm aligned parallel to the main axis of the flake. Semenov (1964, 14) has commented that some gloss in unusual positions on implements may be the result of repeated gripping by hands. This seems an unlikely explanation for a narrow band such as this. A more likely explanation is that this second area may have been produced by chafing when the flake was mounted in a haft. The fact that this glossed strip lies parallel to the glossed cutting edge seems to support this hypothesis.

Artefact **51** (Figs 11.16 and 11.17) is a small secondary flake bearing some cortex on its dorsal face. When the cortical face is included it is triplanar in cross section with a small area of gloss on its central face. This small flake is devoid of its bulbar end and its distal has been snapped off at the point where use or retouch may once have been applied. It seems likely that the gloss on this item may also be the result of chafing when the flake was mounted in a haft.

Artefact **95** (Figs 11.16 and 11.18) is a short prismatic and partially cortical flake bearing edge gloss on its ventral surface close to a useable spur or bec, although this thin protrusion shows no obvious signs of use. The fact that the distal tip has been rejected perhaps in favour of a lateral point might be explained by the fact that the flake might be more readily gripped or mounted for use from its lateral side. The breaks at the bulbar and distal ends of this flake, shown in the illustration, might be the result of failure during use. Given the short, spall-like character of this specimen, it is also possible that this small area of gloss is a residual portion of a larger area on a parent item from which this flake has been detached.

Artefact **107** (Figs 11.16 and 11.19) is tri-planar flake that is essentially triangular in cross section. It is devoid of its bulbar end and bears no retouch. Its steeper lateral side bears edge gloss on the dorsal surface which extends 7mm along the cutting edge and advances just 2mm across the face. The utilised cutting edge of this flake has been naturally formed at 40°. This seems to have offered the toolmaker the steep edge that precluded the need for modification.

12 The Bouldnor Cliff Mesolithic site in its geographic and cultural setting *by David Tomalin*

12.1 The location and significance of the Bouldnor Cliff Mesolithic assemblage within the environs of the Western Yar

Analysis of the lithic assemblage provides a glimpse of a Mesolithic culture set in the submerged and lost basin of the Western Solent. The environmental context of this lithic assemblage lies somewhere on the valley margin of a former riverine/estuarine configuration of the Western Yar river. The former character and catchment of this river has been addressed in Chapter 10, above. Today, much of the river is occupied by a post-Flandrian ria inlet (Fig 12.1). This is entered from the Solent at the modest ferry port and natural harbour at Yarmouth. Beneath this inlet lies a deep sequence of palaeovalley sediments that are testimony to the Holocene history of the river. These sediments have been cored at Yar Bridge and Norton Spit, both close to the river mouth at Yarmouth. Here they have been explored to a depth of –14m OD (Devoy 1987; Tomalin *et al* forthcoming). At Norton Spit a series of helpful radiocarbon dates has also been obtained (Tomalin 2000b) and some informative palynological assessments have been made (Scaife 2000a).

To the north of Yarmouth the course of the Western Yar and its associated floodplain, palaeovalley or wetland basin lies somewhere beneath the bed of the Western Solent. It is possible that here it was once fed by an eastern tributary which would include in its catchment a tertiary feeder channel conveying the waters of the Bouldnor Brook.

It is unfortunate that this former portion of the Western Yar catchment has been so extensively drowned by the formation of the Western Solent seaway. The full marine breakthrough of this seaway as described above seems to have been responsible for the genesis of a process of powerful ebb tidal

Figure 12.1 Ria drowning of the Western Yar (David Tomalin)

155

Figure 12.2   Reedswamp margin of Western Yar (David Tomalin)

downcutting which has since entrenched Hurst Narrows to a depth of 56m. It would appear that headward erosion of this trench has since advanced eastward as far as Hamstead, where it may have been slowed by the former presence of an early Holocene watershed and land bridge that has now submerged (Tomalin 2000a, 15, fig 3).

A further question concerning the nature of the early Holocene Yar has been its past direction of flow in earlier Holocene times. This ria-drowned river has gained a northerly exit, but it has been proposed that it flowed south prior to marine invasion (Tomalin 2000a, 16). The evidence put forward in Chapter 10 supports this model, which conforms to the general drainage pattern demonstrated by palaeovalleys west of Wight, where the earlier courses of Dorset rivers can be seen to pass through the former Wight–Purbeck chalk ridge (Velegrakis 1994; Velegrakis *et al* 1999). Empirical data in the form of dated palaeoenvironmental sequences from the river Yar sediment archive should confirm this hypothesis.

This tentative reconstruction of the palaeogeomorphology of the Western Yar allows us to position our Mesolithic occupation at Bouldnor in a wooded environment adjacent to the floodplain of a mature river with associated wetlands. By 6000 BC some central portions of the catchment and floodplain of this river were surely experiencing the effects of the marine encroachment. Assessment of recent evidence would suggest ingress via the river Yar. It seems that the effects of this advance would include the back-ponding of certain freshwater drainage routes, a decline of alder-dominated fen woodland, and the advance of alluvial reedswamp over the floodplain. Around 6000 cal BC these conditions had reached our site and are attested in the palaeo-environmental evidence recovered from context 2002 (see Chapter 3, 3.5).

Our interpretation of the site is governed by the degree to which the flint industry at Bouldnor best befitted a woodland, riverine, or coastal habitat. South of Yarmouth, in the vicinity of Mill Copse, some modern environmental analogues can be found where mixed deciduous woodland descends the valley slope and gives way to a mixture of brackish back-ponded water, residual alder carr, and open reedswamp on the eastern margin of the *ria* inlet (Figs 12.2–12.4). A natural 'forest fence' at the junction between the woodland and the

Figure 12.3   Emponded freshwater wetland near Mill Copse (David Tomalin)

Figure 12.4   Emponded alder carr on margin of Western Yar (David Tomalin)

reedswamp/open water environment is particularly well suited for hunting and fowling activities. Open corridors such as these, beyond the tree line, offer an annual attraction to substantial flocks of Brent and Canada geese, which are still habitually locked into a migration route that is essentially dependent upon the Solent and, presumably, was also dependent upon the proto-Solent.

It was suggested that notable levels of fern pollen recorded in the palynological record from context 2007 represented open or disturbed areas created as a result of human activity. If human impact was sufficient to create fern-dominated clearings, it seems reasonable to suspect that the small archaeological features so far detected at Bouldnor may be repeated over a larger area at this locality.

The localised human impact on the environment at Bouldnor makes an interesting comparison with other evidence gathered some 1.8km to the west on the eastern margin of the Western Yar valley at Norton Spit (Scaife in archive). Preliminary analysis of a deep core at this location has revealed charcoal flecks in sediment units 15 and 13. The charcoal represents adjacent human activities contemporary with an environment of brackish water and *Phragmites* reedswamp located at a level of –8.5 to –7.2m OD (Scaife, pers comm).

While no direct dating is available for these deep sediment units their position in the Norton Spit core lies between samples dated 6380–5840 cal BC 6370–5890 cal BC (GU5397) at –9.4m OD) and 4780–4350 cal BC (GU5383), (5680 ± 100 BP, 4770–4330 cal BC, GU5382). When combined with the evidence recovered at Bouldnor it is difficult to resist the suspicion that Mesolithic activity on the floodplain margins of the ancient Yar may have been common and perhaps seasonal.

12.2   The significance of the Bouldnor Cliff Mesolithic assemblage within the Solent and Isle of Wight region

In its 'near coast' setting, the Bouldnor Cliff lithic assemblage appears to be characteristic of an array of similarly situated Mesolithic occupation sites occupying comparable positions throughout much of the Solent estuarine system. This estuarine system owes its nature to the process of post-glacial down-warping and rising sea level. This process has been responsible for a crenellated coastline of drowned creeks, or rias, which can be traced from Hurst Spit to Pagham Harbour – a direct east–west distance of 55km. Within this sector of the southern English coast the convolution of creeks and estuaries provides a total shoreline length of some 300km, virtually all of which is very sheltered.

An outstanding question concerns the degree to which the past geography of this coastline may have nurtured or induced a pattern of Mesolithic activity that was driven by the onshore and offshore resources of the coastline. Present investigations at Bouldnor are unable to answer this question, yet there are undoubted hints that Mesolithic activities in this region were commonly drawn towards near-coast, near-creek, or river-mouth environments.

Hubert Poole, writing in 1929, was the first to give serious thought to a Solent coastal Mesolithic culture, his ideas driven by the notable numbers of picks and axes of Mesolithic type that had been recovered from the Isle of Wight shore of the Solent. During the 1950s further scatters of picks, axes, and other Mesolithic lithic products came to light on the Hampshire shore at Rainbow Bar, Portsmouth Harbour, and Langstone Harbour (Rankine 1953; 1956; Draper 1951; 1968). Poole used the insular geography of the Isle of Wight as a closed sample in which to explore the possibility that the sandy uplands and the crenellated coast of the Isle of Wight had nurtured their own separate Mesolithic communities. Could these be distinguished by their lithic industries?

Poole chose the pick and the tranchet axe as the distinguishing tools of his coastal communities. When the number of inland find-spots for these tools is noted, however, the argument cannot be readily sustained (Loader forthcoming). The number of coastal find-spots in the Isle of Wight amounts to 66% of the total find-spots for these tools, and it is thus true that the actual number of picks and axes recovered from the coastal locations is substantially larger than that from the terrestrial zone, but this is probably due to the manner in which these items are so readily exposed by tidal action (see Appendix 3 for details of tranchet axe/adze and pick find-spots recorded in the Isle of Wight Historic Environment Record (HER)). Conversely, in beach environments small lithic items such as blades and bladelets are extremely difficult to see and on pebble beaches their threshold of survival is hopelessly low. In ploughsoil, however, the numerical superiority of small flint debitage provides for a greater chance of discovery over the incidental axes and picks.

It should be no surprise that the tranchet axes and picks of the Isle of Wight are not an exclusive hallmark for coastal Mesolithic communities of the region. Owing to their bulk and robustness they are, however, a principal means by which Mesolithic sites can be identified on the inter-tidal margins of the Solent.

At the time of writing the distribution of find-spots for tranchet axes in south Hampshire shows little more than an incidental association with the coast. The coastal find-spots currently noted in the county HER are Rainbow Bar, Portsmouth Harbour, Fareham, Langstone Harbour, and Hayling Island (Hants HER nos 20888, 19698, 19708, 19703, 19719, and 37223: see Appendix 4 for further details of submerged and potentially submerged Mesolithic sites on the English Channel coast of Wessex and Devon). Recent research into fishermen's finds (Harding *et al* 2004) drastically changes this picture, however, adding a further 24 find-spots in the near-shore zone of the Hampshire coast (see Appendix

5 for details of find-spots of tranchet axes, adzes, and picks in the West Solent region). A particular lacuna that can now be adjusted, therefore, is the Hampshire shoreline of the Western Solent. Here, no coastal Mesolithic sites can, so far, be detected through the HER, and it is also interesting to see from the evidence in the HER that, despite the apparent suitability of its sandy and wooded terrain, the New Forest appears to contain few Mesolithic tranchet axes, there being no more than six in total. The addition of the fishermen's finds compels us to readdress the possibility that a particular Mesolithic subsistence strategy had once focused upon the changing coastal habitats of the Solent estuarine system. It is unfortunate that, despite some profuse scatters of tell-tale axes and picks in the preservative environment of the inter-tidal and sub-tidal zones, the archaeological characterisation and dating of these coastal sites is so inadequate. In many respects we have seen little progression since the first hypotheses were proffered more than half a century ago by Poole (1929; 1936; 1938), Godwin (1940), and Oakley (1943).

At Langstone Harbour, Allen and Gardiner (2000) have suggested a landscape of the 'Earlier Mesolithic' period in which a dry-land basin was dissected by an entrenched drainage system reaching to a depth of −14m OD. At this time estuarine waters would have lain at least 6km to the south, where the rising sea was steadily advancing up the course of the 'Solent River', and the open coast of the Channel lay some 30km to the south. At Bouldnor we can postulate a somewhat similar advance, with the rising sea beginning to impinge upon into the catchment of the Western Yar. In around 7000–6000 BC the environment at Langstone changed when the general 'Flandrian' increase in sea-level rise prompted back-ponding and peat formation on the narrow floors of the two deep incised channels. This was followed by continued accretion of fine-grained over-bank and channel alluvium. The burial of the peat beds and the steady infilling of the incised river courses then ensued.

Allen and Gardiner postulated that the incised channels at Langstone may have served as 'routeways to the coast' for communities of the earlier Mesolithic but, owing to their inaccessibility, no evidence could be won from the deeply buried floors of the river channels. This ravine-like environment makes an interesting comparison with Bouldnor, where the adjacent onshore topography of Bouldnor Cliff, and the infill sediments exposed in the underwater cliff, show that the Mesolithic occupation at this location was surely on the old valley floor, which has now become covered by deep infill deposits.

At both Langstone and Bouldnor it is later Mesolithic communities, employing tranchet axe/adzes and picks, for which we have evidence. At Langstone there is no absolute dating for the Mesolithic occupation. A relative date is inferred by the position of the lithic scatters above the upper sediments of the infilled valleys. At both sites it is evident that locations had been chosen where watercourses gave access to not-too-distant estuarine waters. At both sites, too, it appears that the flint assemblage does not match the range of tool types that is typical of many contemporary late Mesolithic assemblages in this region (Jacobi 1981; Allen and Gardiner 2000, 204).

The incidence of primary flakes and blades at Bouldnor is notably low (as is also the case in the Mesolithic assemblages from both Langstone and Hengistbury), amounting to no more than 9%. At Langstone most of the Mesolithic lithic finds were concentrated on Bakers Island, where the incidence of primary flakes varied from 15% to 23% in the gathered samples (Gardiner 2000). This proportion has also been considered to be low, and Gardiner attributes this to extensive core trimming and core rejuvenation. Both of these processes would maximise blade production and inhibit the production of primary flakes. At Bouldnor there is little evidence of core trimming, but good evidence to suggest the careful selection of good-quality material with a preference for small-sized cores.

12.3 The significance of the Bouldnor Cliff site in relation to the floor of the English Channel

The recognition of the Bouldnor site comes at a time when a new image of *sous Manche* Mesolithic activity is beginning to emerge. In 1972 the French oceanographer Claude Larsonneur produced his sub-bottom plan of the great braided river systems lying on the pre-Flandrian floor of the English Channel (Fig 12.5). In 1977 Susanne Palmer was cautiously postulating a 'maritime' Mesolithic culture in the English Channel region where a high incidence of heavy flint picks seemed discernible along the southern English coastline from Portland to Hastings. This claim was never effectively substantiated, but the publication of late glacial and early Mesolithic occupation sites at Hengistbury Head in 1992 has drawn further attention to the possibility that Mesolithic sites on the central and eastern sections of the English Channel coastline may reflect a lost theatre of hunting and gathering activity that was once concentrated in a broad riverine landscape that is now submerged offshore. This has brought attention to bear on the vast alluvial grazing lands that have been lost to post-glacial sea rise.

A remarkable archaeological feature of the Solent estuarine system is the incidence of Mesolithic picks and axes found both on its floor and at its coastal margins. As most of these implements have been recovered either by trawling offshore or by beachcombing in the inter-tidal zone they have seldom been reported in contexts, where the smaller components of a flint assemblage might be sought. The result of this skewed sampling has been a persistently poor understanding of the broader cultural context to which these heavy tools and their associated industry belong.

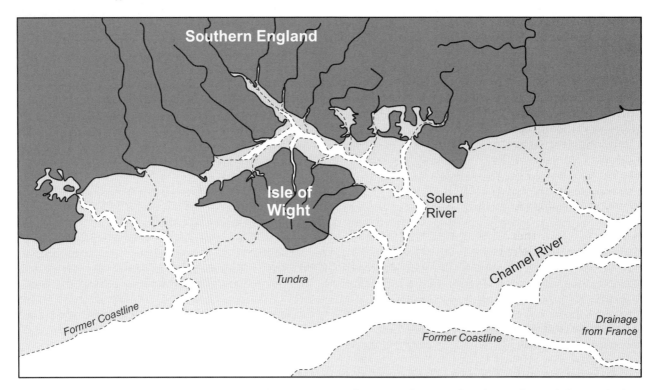

Figure 12.5   Sub-bottom plan of the braided river systems lying on the pre-Flandrian floor of the English Channel (Julian Whitewright after BMAPA)

Identification of the vast braided network of river channels on the floor of La Manche has demonstrated a physical link between northern France and England when the sea level was lower. It is therefore necessary for archaeological thought to be turned to some of the Mesolithic industries discovered in France that have been responsible for the production of analogous picks and axes beyond the southern margin of the English Channel. The production of picks was certainly underway in the Lower Seine before the close of the Boreal period, as these items are to be found at the Mesolithic site at Acquiny (Eure) in a context dated to 7940–7070 cal BC (8460 ± 170 BP; Gif-89337) (Verron 2000). South of the Seine, analogies can be sought among the *pics a crosse* which are present in certain Sauveterrian contexts. A helpful absolute date is that of 7120 ± 110 BP (Gif-5820) for the Middle Sauveterrian site Grotte de Larchant (Hinout 1989a). After the opening of the Atlantic period, around 6400 cal BC (7500 BP), picks can also be detected in small numbers in the Final Tardenoisian. This has been dated to around 5330–4800 cal BC (6150 ± 100BP; Gif-6318) at Ferme de Chinchy, Villenueve-sur-Fere, on the valley gravels of the Aisne (Hinout 1989b, 347).

The tranchet picks and axes from Britain are clearly embedded in the Maglemosian culture, which is to be found in southern central and eastern England as well as in its Danish homeland. Early examples occur at Star Carr, where tranchet axes and adzes are in use during an episode of occupation that opened around 8970 BC and persisted for some 200 years (Dark 2000, 304). Thereafter it appears that the heavy axes developed in the Maglemosian were probably extensively deployed in the wooded environment of lowland England as well as 'Northsealand' or 'Doggerland' (Clarke 1954; Coles 1998; Bridgland and D'Olier 1995).

The cultural phenomenon of the Montmorencian in the Ile de la France and la Foret de Montmorency produced a lithics industry which was capable of fabricating heavy Mesolithic tranchet axes of the *pic a crosse* and *pic a crochet* type. An absence of absolute dates makes the chronological position of the industry insecure (Tarrête 1977; 1989): a general bracket of fifth–fourth millennia BC with a possibility of later survival (Guyot 1998). Westwards, in eastern Armorica, heavy Mesolithic axes and picks are to be found in the Organais assemblage at St Reine de Bretagne. Here the axes are associated with microliths of scalene and triangular form as well as with petit tranchet arrowheads (Kayser 1989). At Dissignac this industry was succeeded by an early megalithic horizon which might otherwise be attributed to the mid-fifth millennium cal BC. Kayser (1989) has raised doubts over the persistence of the Organais industry into the Neolithic of this region, while similar questions have been advanced by Tarrête (1989) for the Montmorencian and its axes in the environs of the Seine.

At Wootton-Quarr 7% of the axes/picks were composed of Greensand chert, a material characteristic of the cliffs of south Wight. The quality of these tools is too poor to merit trade or exchange, so we may assume that they were carried by the communities that made them some 15km north for use on the Solent coast. Such journeys, which were perhaps seasonal in nature, must signify certain territorial interests or rivalries if practised in the company of other social groups.

If territorial sensitivities were beginning to be stirred in the late Mesolithic, then the confined insular geography of the Isle of Wight would seem to be one of the natural points of genesis. The dates gleaned for the inception of the Neolithic in the British Isles now suggest that the first environmental impacts of agriculture were occurring around 4000 BC (Brown 2007). Interpretation of some of the earliest evidence supporting these dates has been put forward by Woodman (2000) and Innes *et al* (2003).

Around this time there is evidence from the Lower Schelde area of the Belgian coast that ceramics were being adopted by perpetrators of the 'Doel assemblage', a Mesolithic culture that was otherwise immune to all other aspects of the Neolithic lifestyle. Passing westwards, further lithic variations have now been recognised among Mesolithic communities on the north-west European seaboard (Crombé *et al* 2000).

It has been recently suggested that a marked dietary change can be detected in some late Mesolithic coastal communities, whereby a traditional dependency on 'the wet and wild' has been redirected by Neolithic influence towards 'the dry and the tame' (Andersen *et al* 2004). This argument offers new substance to earlier propositions that have sought recognition of specific Mesolithic coastal cultures or subsistence strategies by suggesting that some Mesolithic coastal cultures were complemented by Neolithic-type practices that had an influence on their territories (Yesner 1980; Larsson 1983; Palmer 1977; Milner *et al* 2003).

For southern Sweden, Larsson (1980) has proposed that Mesolithic social organisation might be characterised by a social distinction between self-sufficient groups each of 25–50 members in the maritime zone and smaller groups of 1–2 families apiece operating seasonally in the terrestrial interior. More recently, a particular example of a maritime subsistence preference has been detected in southern Sweden in which the interception and exploitation of herring shoals played an important role (Lidén *et al* 2004). This is a maritime resource that could have been equally attractive in the advancing coastal waters of the Solent region.

All of these opportunities and adaptations remind us of the drastic changes in human subsistence that were inevitably tied to the environmental transformation of the early Holocene floodplain in the lost lowlands of La Manche. The date of these changes was surely tied to marked inundation between *c* 5470 cal BC (*c* 6500 and 6000 BP) and *c* 4890 cal BC (*c* 6000 BP), by which time the submergence of Doggerland had been completed (Ward *et al* 2006).

In the Solent region there certainly arises the suggestion that Mesolithic subsistence strategies pursued in the coastal zone might be carried over or further developed during the Neolithic period.

On the Solent shore and in Langstone Harbour picks have been recovered among disturbed scatters of Neolithic flint waste and tools. Moreover, in the inter-tidal zone at Wootton-Quarr, generous scatters of fire-crazed flint were apparent in creek-side locations close to the Neolithic shoreline. At Wootton-Quarr site Q99, tranchet axes and profuse flint debitage were recovered at a point where very large quantities of fire-crazed flint had been dumped into the silts of a freshwater creek. The bulk of fire-crazed flint on the Wootton-Quarr shoreline suggests the involvement of larger social groups operating in this coastal zone in the fourth millennium cal BC. It is possible that some of these activities could have involved the capture of stream water for use in a cooking trough, or *fulachta fiadh*. This would facilitate the boiling of food with the aid of fire-heated flint nodules or pebbles. At BC-II and BC-IV the modest quantities of fire-crazed flint pebbles seem to have been sufficient for no more than a few episodes of cooking. It may not be unreasonable to suppose that more of these features remain to be exposed during the retreat of the underwater cliff.

Recent investigations and experiments at the Belgian coastal Mesolithic site on the Schelde at Verrebroek show that more than twenty non-structured hearths can occur or accrue at a favoured location. Here the hearths are generally around 8–12m apart (Sergant *et al* 2006), and have produced burnt hazelnuts, shell, and bone, as well as evidence for the production and discard of flint tools. Some of this lithic material appears in discrete scatters around the periphery of the fires. It may be safely assumed that spatially dispersed evidence of this kind still remains to be investigated as the underwater cliff continues to retreat at Bouldnor.

Whatever the former resources of this inundated valley may have been, its attraction to human communities seems to have increased by the Neolithic. At the mouths of the Western Yar, Newtown River and the Quarr Stream, utilisation of this environment would eventually progress to the determined construction of Neolithic wooden trackways in the late fourth millennium BC (Tomalin *et al* 1998; Tomalin *et al* forthcoming). This was a melding of woodland, wetland, salt marsh, and tidal inlets where opportunities for human exploitation were clearly irresistible. It is subsequent to these major geographic changes that Neolithic coastal activities can be detected in the upper peats that hug the low tide boundary of the present Solent shoreline.

12.4 Conclusion

The Bouldnor assemblage and its environmental setting provide a glimpse of a coastal Mesolithic flint industry some two millennia before the Neolithic revolution in southern Britain. The onset of British cereal agriculture is now set at the opening of the fourth millennium BC. This comprehends evidence offered by such sites as

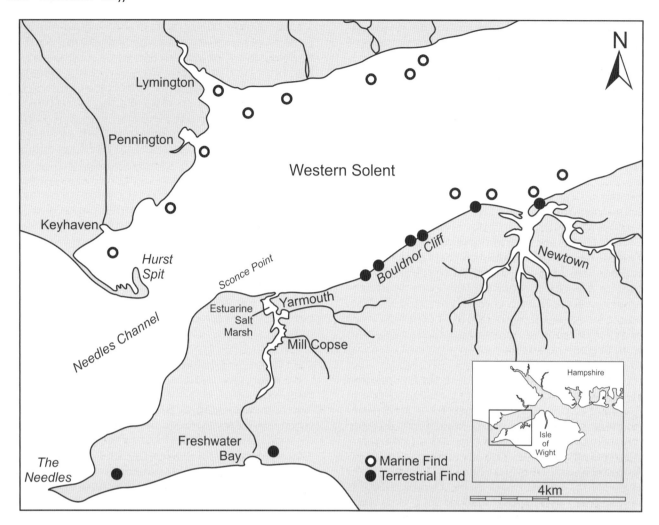

Figure 12.6   Distribution of find-spots for tranchet axes, adzes and picks (David Tomalin)

Flea Moss Wood, Bidston Moss, Soyland Moor, and Cashelkeelty (Cowell and Innes 1994; Williams 1985; Lynch 1981).

Might some transitional traits of semi-sedentary behaviour already be falling into place, however? At present the assemblage has been too small and the investigation too limited to say, but when it is combined with the large timber elements found from BC-V (see Chapter 4) some enticing possibilities deserve attention. It seems that the flint-knapping site at BC-II was set at a streamside where ready access could be gained to a sheltered coast. Indeed, the site is situated at a point where the stream water was destined to become brackish around the close of the seventh millennium BC. By 5900 cal BC the bed of the stream at this point was accruing marine sediment.

With ready access to a wooded shoreline, what were the opportunities to secure an advantageous subsistence from the natural resources of the sea and the coast? There are hints at the use of tranchet axes and possibly the clearing of trees, which could lead to the creation of the fern-rich areas that have been noted in the contemporary pollen record from this site. Further possibilities involving the use of the heavy adze/axe elements might also include

boat-building and the construction of log walkways through rising water levels in the inter-tidal reed swamp.

Mellars and Reinhardt (1978) and Care (1979) observe that an examination of the general distribution of tranchet axes in southern Britain shows that most of the higher densities of finds correspond with those areas where good material for axe production is available. This has some interesting implications for the West Wight study area, because while it is the chalk cliffs that offer the prime source of flint in the region, it is the West Solent basin that seems to have attracted the greatest use and discard of axes and picks. The lithic assemblage at Bouldnor is dominated by beach flint and cliff flint. These materials accord with the principal theatre for human activity at this location. There is a heavy flaking element to the flint industry as well as the production of blades and bladelets from small curated cores. Soft hammer techniques predominate and there is a notable absence of hammerstones. The assemblage attests to the accomplished production of blades and bladelets, but there is a relatively weak contingent of microlithic products. Perhaps the exploitation of marine food sources reduced demand for those lithic tools, which may have been more commonly used in a terrestrial hunting environment, particularly in the exploitation of the ecotonal zone.

There is an implicit use of axes or adzes at the Bouldnor site although these heavy tools are only represented by detached sharpening flakes. Such implements accord with other finds of axes, adzes, and 'picks' that have been noted in some quantity at other and neighbouring locations along the Solent coast (Poole 1929; 1936; Fig 12.6). These heavy tools have also been found on the beach at Bouldnor where they may have been cast-up from offshore.

There remains a need to recover larger samples of tools and debitage from the Mesolithic hearths and activity points at Bouldnor so that a clearer vision of the lithic industry can be obtained. Similarly, this report frequently refers to axes, adzes, and picks in local assemblages that have not been systemically recorded or described. This is another essential requirement before the true nature of Mesolithic activity in Solent lowland can be better understood.

Around 4000 cal BC inter-tidal fish traps were being erected on the east Solent coast at Wootton-Quarr, and notable quantities of tranchet axes and picks have been found scattered here in the inter-tidal zone. They come from disturbed positions near cooking places where much burnt flint is now being found. By this time Solent sea level had risen to approximately –6m OD (Long and Scaife 1996; Scaife 2000a, fig 3.1) and in the eastern Solent back-ponding was again taking place, leading to the formation of a higher level of coastal peat. These deposits may not be dissimilar to the upper peat horizon at –3.72m OD in the Bouldnor Cliff section which has been dated at 5580 ± 60 BP (Beta 140102). An earlier episode of minor peat formation at –5m OD occurs at Bouldnor at 4525–4330 cal BC (Beta 140103) 5870 ± 60 BP, 4900–4550cal BC (Beta-140103).

It is unfortunate that evidence of molluscs, crustaceans, and fish has not, so far, been recovered from the Bouldnor site. Nevertheless, it is pertinent to ask whether the marine resources of this coastline might have been sufficient to nurture a particular littoral subsistence strategy that might betray its identity through aspects of a material culture that would include its flint industry. A particular dependence on marine food could also lead to a pattern of strand-looping and an early and incipient interest in territorial claims over propitious sections of the coastline.

In summary, therefore, there remains the possibility that, owing to its broad mesh of low-lying river systems, the land of the English Channel floor and its adjacent feeder river systems once offered a particular focus for Mesolithic communities of the sub-Boreal period. It may be several decades before our technology and our legislation are sufficient advanced to pursue and resolve this intriguing archaeological possibility. At present it seems that we must endure a considerable time lapse before we equip ourselves to record and protect that prehistoric landscape which is truly at sea in the English Channel.

As a peripheral glimpse of this larger picture, the submerged site at Bouldnor now offers our very best hope of pursuing answers to this question. The next steps must be to monitor and record the full spatial extent of this particular site while the window of opportunity is ajar. In parallel with this challenge, there is a need to quantify and characterise those other submerged sites on the floor of the Solent where a Mesolithic presence has already been indicated by the axes, adzes, and picks recovered by fishermen. It can only be through the survey and quantification of this Solent phenomenon that we can hope to move towards an estimate of the size and nature of that Mesolithic culture that once wedded the land of Britain to its European neighbour.

Section five

Review of research, investigation, and management of the submerged landscapes of the Western Solent

13 Threats, management, and protection
by Julie Satchell

13.1 Introduction

The investigations at Bouldnor Cliff undertaken over the past ten years were initially prompted by recognition of the potential of the palaeoenvironmental resource present on the seabed. However, this potential quickly multiplied through the discovery of evidence ranging from lithic artefacts to *in situ* features demonstrating Mesolithic occupation. The unusual nature of the site, in terms of its location underwater, the extensive preservation of Mesolithic organic remains, and the associated sedimentary sequence all provide challenges for management and protection.

This report has demonstrated that Bouldnor Cliff represents a set of exceptional circumstances in terms of the survival and investigation of submerged prehistoric landscapes which is further enhanced by by its rarity in a UK context. The site must, therefore, be considered to be of high national, and indeed international, importance.

Bouldnor Cliff has further relevance in terms of contemporary debates about environmental change and the impacts of sea-level rise on coastal communities. These are phenomena that have been witnessed on multiple occasions during the past, as demonstrated by the three levels of prehistoric landscape represented at Bouldnor Cliff. The study of the physical processes and human responses (if it is possible to interpret these) involved in the past has much to add to modern debates regarding and management of these phenomena.

Despite the importance of the site it remains outside the current heritage protection regime. This assessment has demonstrated the need to consider future management requirements; however, in order to develop effective approaches there is a need to first understand the range and impact of threats to the resource.

13.2 Threats to the site and the need for protection

The work at Bouldnor Cliff has helped to raise awareness of the submerged prehistoric cultural heritage, which has increased significantly over the past five years. Results from Bouldnor have combined with investigations in the southern North Sea (Gaffney *et al* 2007) and to the east of the Solent in the Arun Valley (Gupta *et al* 2004) to demonstrate the huge potential that the submerged resource holds to add significantly to knowledge of the environment inhabited by early human populations.

The recent publication *Selection Guide: Prehis-toric Landsurfaces and Deposits* states that 'For a prehistoric landsurface to be of special interest, the remains must be capable of making such a distinctive contribution to our understanding or awareness of people's actions or environment in the past that the remains themselves should be protected from uncontrolled damage' (Wessex Archaeology 2008, 6). In the light of the development of draft legislation to allow the protection and management of such sites (DCMS 2008), Bouldnor Cliff, which clearly represents such a site of special interest, presents an important case study for the testing of the development of effective protection in such cases. There is, in fact, an urgent requirement for the development of a suitable management and protection strategy for this site which is underlined by the threats to the site which come from both natural processes and human impact.

13.2.1 Natural threats to the site

There is a range of natural threats to the features, finds, and deposits at Bouldnor. In Chapter 10, above, the over-riding geomorphological changes and associated forces of erosion were presented; with the formation of the Solent not yet complete, it is inevitable that degradation will continue and could increase with rising sea levels. In general, natural mechanisms threatening the site include the detrimental effects of weathering, erosion from tidal and wave action, and damage from burrowing macrofauna. In addition, modern fishing practices have been shown to have damaging effects on exposed timbers.

13.2.1.1 Physical processes

The hydrodynamic regime at Bouldnor Cliff has been discussed in earlier chapters in terms of both the challenges it poses to diving archaeological work on the site and the impact it has on the archaeological material. Through the detailed study of the palaeoenvironmental evidence and the geoarchaeology, further insights have been gained into the physical and environmental processes at work on the site: the deposits are, therefore, helping to throw light on the development of the Solent and the severance of the Isle of Wight from the mainland UK, but it is the continued development of the Solent as a tidal channel (see Chapter 10) that presents the most significant threat to the site.

This development is impacting the site in a variety of ways. Most significantly, the sediments along the cliff are subject to ongoing erosion, with the less-resistant clays succumbing first and thus exposing sections of the peat deposits, which are generally more resistant. The trees embedded within the peat also help it to stand up to the erosion more effectively than the upper sediments. However, once exposed the peat does begin to recede, albeit at a slower rate than surrounding sediments, and the trees themselves are also affected as their exposure leaves them open to attack from piddocks and gribbles (see below). On a more localised scale the effects of tidal movement causes scour around specific features and outcrops. The result is a constant removal of material throughout the tidal cycle. Finer sediments go into suspension in the water and are carried away, while heavier sediment and blocks of deposit frequently end up at the foot of the cliff. Inevitably, artefacts such as flints are dislodged and hence are also found at the foot of the cliff, meaning that some flint finds have been recovered from a secondary context. However, when recovered from the base of the cliff the flint is often in a good condition, implying that it has not been rolling around on the seabed for any length of time.

The effects of tidal action have been recognised from the early years of study at Bouldnor by the HWTMA and in response monitoring mechanisms have been put in place and trialled (see Chapter 3, 3.1.2). The measuring of the depth of sediment via pins and the measurement of the degradation of timber over time has provided empirical evidence regarding the net loss of material, which occurs at up to 0.5m per year. While such observations demonstrate the loss of sediments, the loss of archaeological material over such a long period is not so well understood; however, recent work involving the recording of features as they become exposed is beginning to address this omission.

Inevitably, there has also been some impact from excavations carried out at the site. When periods of investigation have been concluded every effort has been made to reinstate the trenches using sandbags to prevent erosion of exposed sections.

13.2.1.2   Macrofauna damage

As mentioned above, the actions of macrofauna have a significant impact on the site and deposits, mostly through their burrowing activities. While their actions are more localised than the erosive processes the effects can be equally damaging. The three principal species affecting Bouldnor Cliff are lobster, piddock and gribble.

*Lobsters (*Homarus gammarus*)*

The burrowing action of lobsters can be witnessed along the length of Bouldnor Cliff. The relatively hard peat deposit and associated trees form a ledge under which the lobsters can burrow into the softer sediment of the prehistoric land surface (Fig 3.1). This phenomenon was witnessed from the early diving seasons when survey of the submerged forest and peat platform was being undertaken, and divers became familiar with the presence of individual lobsters and their burrows, which were included on early survey drawings (Fig 3.2). It was the actions of lobsters which revealed the first worked flints from the site, which were found in the 'spoil' deposited outside the entrance to the burrows.

In the early seasons the large lobsters that were seen at Bouldnor had dug burrows of correspondingly large sizes into the deposits (up to 0.5m across and 0.3m high). However, in later years, smaller lobsters have taken up occupation; it is assumed that lobster potting has captured the larger individuals. The presence of smaller individuals is no less damaging, as burrows are continually being dug into the prehistoric landscape deposits in a range of locations, often in close conjunction with one of the fallen oak trees. Also burrowers, but less frequent occupants of Bouldnor, are crabs, which exploit the same environment but generally do not create such large burrows.

The resulting impact on Bouldnor Cliff is physical damage to, and disturbance of, the stratified sequence. As the lobsters particularly target the prehistoric land surface, the peat shelf above it can be undermined; although this is also occurring as a result of tidal actions, it is exacerbated by the lobsters' activities. The resulting destabilisation of the deposits not only hastens the pace of erosion but also removes *in situ* Mesolithic material, leading to the disturbance of the primary contexts.

*Piddock (*Pholas dactylus*)*

The actions of piddocks are very visible within the Bouldnor material. These bivalve molluscs have the ability to burrow significant distances into a range of materials, including sandstone and rock. Their presence can be observed within the peat deposits as their burrows, which measure up to 30mm in diameter, show up clearly in the box sections of excavated material (Fig 13.1). Piddocks' ability to burrow into solid material means they are also capable of infesting the fallen oak trees, the effects of which can be seen within slices of trees taken for dendrochronological analysis.

The damage caused by the piddocks has a range of effects on the archaeological and palaeoenvironmental deposits. Burrows through trees can make the selection and/or analysis of dendrochronological samples difficult, as a 30mm burrow winding its way across a tree sample can obliterate ring sequences. As outlined in Chapter 3 (3.9.2), the presence of burrows was one of the main factors behind the limited success of increment coring. Site stratigraphy can also be compromised as the burrows, which can reach more than a metre in length, provide a route for material from higher contexts into those

Figure 13.1 Image showing piddock damage to organics such as wood. Piddock damage has been seen to penetrate beyond a metre into the seabed (Garry Momber)

below. When working with the larger box samples the presence of piddock burrows are usually distinct and thus possible disturbance can be identified. However, when taking auger and monolith samples the burrows' presence may not be apparent until after extraction. It has also been suggested in Chapter 3 (3.10.4) that piddock burrows may have affected the radiocarbon dating of some of the samples at BC-II, as intrusive material brought down through the sequence via the burrows would have resulted in some dates being slightly younger than expected in relation to their stratigraphic location.

*Gribble (*Limnoria *sp)*

The burrows created by individual gribbles are much smaller than those of the piddock, at around 1–2mm in diameter; however, as they target any exposed wood their attack is much more widespread. The effect of gribble attack is the degradation of the whole surface of exposed organic materials. This is particularly noticeable with the large oak trees which have been exposed for some time (see Fig 2.1). While gribble activity occasionally helped in the identification of oak specimens (Chapter 3, 3.9.2), in

general their indiscriminate attack is detrimental to any exposed organics.

While the loss of the surface of oak trees measuring up to 0.6m in diameter may not have too much of a detrimental effect in terms of sampling and analysis, the effect of gribbles on the surface of delicate worked Mesolithic wood can mean the loss of significant amounts of information and surface detail. After the exposure of timbers through sediment erosion they quickly become infested with gribbles; as long as some of the timber remains covered by sediment there is a chance that only a limited part will be affected, but where there is more extensive exposure the threat of loss is significant. This highlights the need for regular inspection of the underwater cliff to identify areas of erosion and the potential exposure of features which are then at high risk of damage.

13.2.1.3 Addressing the effects of marine boring macrofauna

The rate and extent of the activities of boring macrofauna at the site is a management problem which needs urgent attention. While the monitoring and environmental assessment of wreck sites has received attention in recent years (Cederland 2004; Johns *et al* 2007; HWTMA 2006), approaches have yet to be developed for submerged prehistoric sites. The effects of burrowing macrofauna have also been recognised in terms of threats to more modern structures such as piers and jetties (Crossman and Simm 2004), but to date work in this area has concentrated on challenges to engineering rather than threats to the historic environment.

Of the main species that threaten the material at Bouldnor Cliff, only the gribble has been studied in any depth (Palma 2005). These studies appear to show the infiltration of more damaging gribble species into UK waters, which underlines the need to assess the rates of damage to the Mesolithic material. Gribbles target wood specifically and hence are a threat to exposed organics; however, the larger burrowing macrofauna can cause significant damage via the destabilisation of deposits and features, and so can present a more significant threat to the archaeology. Very little research has been undertaken on the threats posed by lobsters and piddocks. Ferrari and Adams (1990) highlight threats from a range of species including these, but very little data have been gathered to quantify impacts since this date.

Over the past sixteen years the HWTMA has gathered an archive of information related to the incidental recording of damage from burrowing macrofauna to a range of site types, but most of this material has been recorded incidentally, and has not been part of a structured research programme. It is of prime importance that such research and associated monitoring is carried out at Bouldnor Cliff, as this site provides a unique opportunity to gauge increasing levels of threat to those as yet uninvestigated submerged prehistoric sites in other areas as offshore research and industrial activity expands.

13.2.2 Human impacts and threat

There is a range of ways in which human actions are also contributing to the damage of the submerged site and the sediment archive. While these activities are not as constant as those of the natural environment they can nevertheless have a detrimental effect on features and deposits.

13.2.2.1   Lobster fishing

The principal human activity on the site at Bouldnor is lobster fishing. The practice of placing strings of lobster pots which are marked at either end on the surface by a buoy involves the laying of lines along the seabed. Lobster is a lucrative catch and, understandably, local fishermen are keen to exploit the resource. While the practice of lobster potting often has a limited impact on flat seabed or near low reefs, at Bouldnor Cliff the presence of the submerged cliff and the fallen oak trees present different circum-

stances. During the recovery of the pots they may become tangled in the trees and the lines between them may be dragged across the exposed deposits and features of the underwater cliff with a 'sawing' action which can be made worse if pots become tangled, further increasing both the strain on the lines and the displacement of features. Such damage has been witnessed along Bouldnor Cliff (Chapters 3 and 4), and includes the removal and displacement of survey pins installed at the site. One datum point, DB, a galvanised pin 1m long, remained in place on the site for six years before it was ripped from the seabed, to be discovered by archaeologists along with pots snagged against archaeological features and lying on the seabed.

13.2.2.2   Diving

The majority of diving undertaken at Bouldnor Cliff is for archaeological purposes; however, the site is open to sport divers and is advertised as a dive site by one local dive boat skipper. The principal impacts of archaeological diving on the site have been quite substantial due to the intrusive sampling and excavation that has been undertaken. However, this work has been carried out within a planned research framework and in the face of imminent erosion.

There has been no visible evidence of impact upon the site by sport divers to date. However, as the site is effectively open access there is the potential for such impacts to occur, whether directly through disturbance of the site in search of Mesolithic material or indirectly through the careless placing of boat anchors.

13.2.3 A site at risk

As has been demonstrated, the site at Bouldnor Cliff is under threat from both human and natural agencies. The threats to the site include medium-term erosive forces causing constant attrition of features and sediments, alongside the more immediate impacts of burrowing macrofauna and lobster-fishing practices. In summary, the opportunity to study such well-preserved Mesolithic occupation evidence within its environmental setting will be available for only a limited number of years.

While it can be argued that many archaeological sites are under threat from erosive forces, and that there is a degree of inevitability implicit in these processes, there is an urgent need to consider the impact of all these processes in combination with the significance of the site and associated landscape at Bouldnor Cliff. To date, the assessment of risk in relation to archaeological sites and monuments has been concentrated largely in the terrestrial zone, although the recently published *Heritage At Risk* summary (English Heritage 2008a) and *Protected Wreck Sites at Risk* (English Heritage 2008b) demonstrate a growing awareness of marine heritage assets. As policy, EH supports the use or reuse of heritage assets where possible, but it does acknowledge that for some sites 'the only long-term solution is one of managed decline once the historic significance of the asset has been carefully recorded'. The historic significance of the site at Bouldnor Cliff has now been recognised, while the challenge to record the archaeology present before it declines is being continually addressed.

14 Project overview and conclusions *by Garry Momber and Geoff Bailey*

14.1 Introduction

Our understanding of the Western Solent today is built on decades of endeavour. It is based on the steady accumulation of data primarily through diver investigation and the analysis of recovered empirical evidence. A key feature of the analysis has been the ability of the archaeologist to read the seabed and, in particular, the sediment history and cultural material it contains.

The fragmentary nature of Mesolithic structures and the scarcity of associated organic remains of Mesolithic date make archaeological interpretation difficult. To date, investigations at Bouldnor have been prompted by opportunistic identification of anomalous signals on the seabed. Most of these are incongruous features which have stood out from the rich palaeo-vegetation that covers the old land surface. Even so, archaeological signatures have been hard to detect in this submarine environment, especially after the removal of surface detail by marine organisms and the perpetual abrasion of the sea. Loss of detail can also be inflicted by boring organisms that can damage objects even before they are exposed to the water column. As a result, archaeological features are easily overlooked.

The obstructive forces of nature and the difficult working conditions have led to the development of special working practices and strategies. Ten years after the first archaeological discoveries, methods to extract information have become more refined. The project has now reached a stage where investigators know what they are looking for and the potential of what they may find on the seabed. In recent years their understanding has been aided by new bathymetric imaging tools that can be used to great effect when mapping and interpreting the submerged landscape. Methods have also been developed to recover material from the seabed with divers in order to interpret the submerged landscape as efficiently and effectively as possible (see Chapter 3).

Long-term work on Bouldnor Cliff has helped the dive team gain experience of the variable conditions of weather and tidal changes that affect working conditions under water, primarily with regard to the visibility and accessibility of evidence. The constraints imposed by natural conditions necessitate experience and training, and archaeological divers need sufficient time and supervision to adjust their skills to a site like Bouldnor. There has been a scarcity of trained personnel to perform this work, which has dramatically constrained progress and frustrated the quest for knowledge.

Work on the submerged landscape is still pushing new boundaries and this continually demands pioneering methodologies that can deal with new tasks and challenges. Skills are more readily taught as methods develop and tasks can be broken down into manageable components that can be accomplished by individual diving archaeologists. The refinement of tasks allows us to build on current understanding and deliver against wide-ranging research and development agendas.

The challenges encountered and overcome during the course of the work in the Western Solent were thus extensive, and a great deal was learnt. In many ways, the investigations form part of the evaluation necessary to identify the potential prehistoric and palaeoenvironmental resource that remains around the coastline. This evaluation, however, has also produced a rich variety of well-preserved artefacts from a number of locations that contribute to our knowledge of the Mesolithic in the region. It has also addressed the formation of the Western Solent, the context that this process provides for the archaeological material, and the threats to the material's survival.

This concluding section contains an overview of the work with reflections on some of the central issues, and considers how future studies can build on the results of this research.

14.2 Cultural divergence and sea-level rise

At the outset of the Mesolithic in north-west Europe cultural traits appeared fairly uniform across a vast territory from Estonia to Scotland (Bailey and Spikins 2008). The warming that followed the last glaciation saw humans follow migrating herds of megafauna onto the productive northern European plains. The widespread evidence for dwelling structures in open-air locations vividly demonstrates how people adapted to the new opportunities (Bjerck 2008; Casati and Sorensen 2009; Waddington 2007a; 2007b; Bang-Anderson 2003; Crombé et al 2003). The vast open ranges of the habitable lowlands were soon to be fragmented by forestation and rising sea levels, restricting migration routes on land and slowing the passage of people (Bailey 2004; Flemming 2004; Lambeck and Chapell 2001; Shennan et al 2000; Coles 1998; Reid 1913). Access routes along waterways became more favourable and the growing resource-rich wetland and lacustrine environments provided an attractive focus for human settlement in a changing environment. The reliance on fixed places in the landscape would have become more pronounced and led to a more regionally focused lifestyle. This is seen when comparing differences between structures and burial practices across Europe (Conneller 2009; Schulting 2009; Grøn 2003). Variations in the exploitation of marine resources also provide indications of local adaptations. In Scotland, for example, substantial midden sites at Oronsay, Oban, and the Forth Valley, among others, indicate a specialised lifestyle and the development of tools without parallel on mainland Europe (Wickham-Jones 2009; Mithen 2004). The variability of the deposits suggests an element of regionalisation, and Richards and Schulting (2003, 123) have used stable isotope analysis data to support an argument for sedentism in some cases.

Elsewhere in Britain, later Mesolithic sites exploiting marine resources are few. In England, they include Portland (Palmer 1977; Mannino and Thomas 2009) and Westward Ho! (Churchill 1965). At Wootton-Quarr, Isle of Wight (Loader *et al* 1997; Tomalin *et al* forthcoming), and Langstone Harbour (Allen and Gardiner 2000) a multitude of worked flint tools have come to light in coastal locations, although evidence for the exploitation of marine resources is limited. In Wales, activity is recorded in association with a range of coastal and intertidal sites, notably at Goldcliff on the Severn estuary and Prestatyn (Bell 2007). The remains indicate temporary seasonal encampments rather than a permanent presence. In Britain, coastal exploitation appears to have been important for some but not significant for most.

The record of British later Mesolithic coastal exploitation contrasts markedly with the European evidence. In north-west Europe, as later Mesolithic cultures appear to be drawn to the coast, there is increased coastal sedentism and social development. The result is social and technological advancement (Åstveit 2009; Fischer 2004; Skaarup & Grøn 2004; Grøn 2003). This is particularly true of the Ertebølle culture of the Baltic, whose hunting, gathering and fishing lifestyle continued for around a thousand years after the arrival of farming (Lübke 2009; Pedersen 1997), although the movement to the coast had begun in the Baltic with the Kongemose people as soon as marine conditions arrived. The timing (*c* 6400–7400 BC) compares favourably with the occupation at Bouldnor Cliff. The quality of the Kongemose worked flint has been justifiably referred to by Anders Fischer (1997, 70) as representing 'some of the finest blades from the Mesolithic in Denmark'.

Much of this variability within Britain and between Britain and southern Scandinavia may reflect differences in the visibility and preservation of evidence resulting from geographical variations in relative sea-level histories. Northern Britain, for example, has undergone isostatic rebound since deglaciation, and it is probably no coincidence that some of the earliest British coastal and estuarine sites, dating from between 9000 and 8000 years ago, occur in northern Britain, as at Howick in North-umberland (Waddington 2007b), Mount Sandel in northern Ireland (Woodman 1985), and Kinloch in Scotland (Wickham-Jones 1990). Coastlines of this period in most of Wales and southern England are now below present sea level. Even after the stabilisation of sea level after about 6000 years ago, much of southern England has continued to sink relative to present sea level, and this may well account for the relative rarity here of substantial coastal sites and shell mounds of later Mesolithic date compared with the situation in Scotland (Tolan-Smith 2008). Similar effects are apparent in Scandinavia, with early dated coastal sites on the uplifted shorelines of Norway (Bjerck 2008), and substantial shell mounds of the later Mesolithic Ertebølle culture in northern Denmark, which has undergone some degree of isostatic rebound. Sites of comparable date in southern Denmark and along the Baltic shorelines of northern Germany are now under water as a result of the sinking coastline, and have been recovered only as a result of underwater investigations (Fischer 2004; Harff *et al* 2007). It is probable that similar conditions apply in many regions of southern Britain, and that productive and sheltered bays and estuaries capable of supporting substantial sedentary settlements and the formation of shell mounds in the later Mesolithic existed on many parts of the shoreline, but these will have been inundated and submerged, removing the archaeological record from view. These factors underline the need for underwater exploration in search of now-submerged Mesolithic shorelines, and highlight the importance of the Bouldnor investigations in providing just one glimpse of the sorts of evidence that may await discovery in other submerged locations.

Despite the loss of terrestrial living space, the encroaching waters increased the number of estuaries and multiplied the length of intertidal coastline as islands were carved out of the higher ground. A positive outcome of sea-level rise, when the sea reached optimum levels in relation to the land, was the development of more protein-rich ecosystems such as estuaries at coastal locations. These conditions would have been as enticing for other north-west European hunter-gatherers as they were in the Baltic. The negative impact was coastal squeeze, with the loss of land and rivers, curtailment of hunter-gatherer territories, displacement of populations, disruption of lines of communication, and ultimately the segmentation of the European peninsula.

The archaeological record during the Mesolithic suggests that there were initially strong similarities with continental Europe and that similar cultural influences were widely diffused over large territories. It appears that 'cultural drift' in Britain relative to Europe was caused by the increased degree of separation resulting from sea-level rise. The processes that led to the formation of Britain as an island were mirrored in the Western Solent with the separation of the Isle of Wight from mainland UK.

14.3 Climate change, coastal geomorphological adaptations and impact on human activity

Towards the end of the Boreal the Western Solent basin would have been a sheltered wetland that provided a rich array of resources (see Chapter 8). The geomorphological evolution presented in Chapter 10 suggests a single outlet to the open sea via the river Yar when people were first recorded in the area. This would provide easy access to the coastline of Freshwater Bay which could be travelled by watercraft or on foot. The evolving bay west of the current Hurst Spit provided another supply of marine resources in what would have been a sheltered bay. Inland, the varying geographical and ecological zones across a range of altitudes and soil types allowed foraging groups to gather a wide range of materials.

An underlying driver for hunting and gathering would have been the need to access these resources. Depending on the local habitat this could be quite an extensive task; studies of Mesolithic territories suggest ranges of 30km to 100km (Schulting 2009; Coles 2000; Woodman *et al* 1999; Louwe Kooijmans 2003). Where possible, a reduction in effort would undoubtedly be sought and this may have been possible in the Western Solent, where a basin presented a natural hub surrounded by ecologically diverse environments. This could have reduced the need for Mesolithic people to stretch their boundaries and may have allowed for extended periods of occupation at preferred locations near a central place. If water transport was available, a lake or wetland in the basin would provide routes in all directions. Water transport is quite likely, given that the use of dug-out canoes or log boats is well attested during the Mesolithic in wetland contexts (Christensen 1997; Skaarup and Grøn 2004; McGrail 1998). For more extended journeys to outlying resources, small and consequently less-evident temporary bases would suffice. This could explain both the relative dearth of substantial Mesolithic sites yet discovered within the Hampshire Basin and on the Isle of Wight, and why the pattern of evidence contrasts with established models showing patterns of movement between large seasonal base camps (Clark 1972; Jacobi 1980; Bell 2007, 332; Binford 1980; Palmer 1990; Simmons 1996).

Shortly after 6000 cal BC the encroaching waters of the Flandrian transgression brought seawater into the Western Solent basin, turning the lowland lake or wetland into an estuary. Areas that were land now became covered by water and terrestrial access routes were interrupted, limiting the opportunities for exploitation on foot. As the water rose the resources in the estuary would have changed, but adaptations to hunting strategies could be made to exploit new marine species (Rowley-Conwy 1983; Pedersen 1997). Initially, these adaptations would have enabled occupants to remain in the same locality, although ultimately the wetlands and estuarine lagoon were lost and replaced by a more open coastline. Terrestrial subsistence patterns would have needed to evolve as hunting grounds were steadily forced back inland along the estuaries and the linear territories defined by rivers. The foraging routes that would initially have fanned out in any direction around the basin would now be limited to the waterways that fed the estuary. Accordingly, ranges would need to extend further into the hinterland and more effort would have to be expended to gather equivalent resources. These effects may have been more acute in isolated regions and it is possible that the growing disruption occasioned by the loss of land may have had an impact on technical advancement.

An alternative approach to the problems caused by rising sea level would be the complete abandonment of territories by populations as they were flooded, followed by a search for new lands. This approach was unavoidable for the occupants of islands such as parts of Doggerland, which were ultimately lost as sea level rose further (Coles 1998), and may have been seen as a viable alternative elsewhere. It is interesting to note that the wood technology used to fashion the tangentially split timber S061 is not seen again in the British archaeological record until the hunter-gatherer lifestyle gave way to agricultural settlement (Chapter 4, 4.8), and the care taken to prepare the bifacial flint axe **120** (Chapter 11, 11.5) is, again, not witnessed until the Neolithic. This would suggest either that the technologies employed to make these objects were lost or forgotten when the area was overwhelmed by the sea or that the people who harnessed these skills moved away from the region, and Britain, as the UK became separated from mainland Europe by the sea.

The waters that flooded the Solent and formed the surrounding seas appear now to be on the rise again. The separation of Britain from the Continent is a demonstrable example of sea-level rise in the past and the unfortunate consequences – coastal erosion and land loss – that followed. The sediments laid down in the Solent are datable markers which indicate the scale and pace of rising water and the resulting coastal adaptations. Any future changes to the coastline will be influenced by past geomorphological alterations. The evolution of any coastline may not be what it appears to be, as has been demonstrated in this study of the Solent. Knowing and understanding these past changes would forearm coastal managers when assessing the impact of rising sea levels in their regions, thereby enabling informed decision-making.

14.4 The rich archaeological resource within the landscape

The survival of the land and archaeology therein is due to inundation of the lower peat platform, which was buried by protective silt 8000 years ago. As the silt is removed the protection goes, but an undisturbed archaeological time capsule is revealed.

This report has identified individual find-spots and locations of differing activity across the palaeo-land surface. These were visually identified after artefacts had become exposed by erosion. Preservation of material before it is exposed can be very good, and includes fine organic matter and details of tool marks conserved in worked wood. Unfortunately, this quickly degrades or is washed away once uncovered. A great deal has already been lost but the continuing exposures indicate there may be much more still buried. It is worth noting that wherever excavation has been conducted archaeological objects have been found. The submerged deposits thus offer a great opportunity to research Mesolithic activity across a landscape that has been undamaged by subsequent human impact.

The potential for further work, however, should not detract from the importance of the discoveries that have already been made. The review of the lithics by David Tomalin in Section Four has contributed to the growing understanding of Mesolithic activity in the region. Along with the work by Allen and Gardiner in Langston Harbour (Allen and Gardiner 2000) and the intertidal surveys at Wootton-Quarr (Tomalin *et al* forthcoming), the new evidence pushes forward our knowledge of regional occupation at a time when the sea level was lower. With this enhanced data set David Tomalin has been able to draw parallels with other coastal assemblages and to raise the possibility of a semi-sedentary lifestyle focused around the region's watercourses that fed the encroaching estuaries as sea level rose (Chapter 12).

Discoveries from occupation areas with differing functions across Bouldnor Cliff emphasise the importance of viewing the landscape as a single entity rather than seeing the different locales as individual sites of activity. BC-II is rich in lithics that were deposited at a waterside location where resources could have been gathered, while BC-V is an area where material was worked. Both locales served different purposes while also being contemporary.

The discovery of an array of associated worked timber pieces at BC-V hints at a sizable structure, and potentially a permanent one, fixed in the landscape (Chapter 4, 4.7). Timber S061, in particular, was tangentially split from a large slow-grown oak with a bole that could have been a metre or two wide and in the order of 10–15m long. Such timbers are associated with monumental structures in the Neolithic and are not pieces that would have readily been moved (Chapter 4, 4.8). It is possible that S061 was a piece discarded following the construction of a dug-out canoe. If a dug-out canoe had been built at the site, the method of construction suggests it would have been a large boat on a par with the Bronze Age Appleby boats of *c*1100 BC or

the 15m-long Brigg Boat *c* 834 BC (Johnstone 1988, 47; McGrail 1998). Such boats would have needed a sizable crew and hence a large enough hunting group to provide sufficient oarsmen. This, in turn, would potentially require a base to operate from and return to. Both possibilities – the boat and the structure – suggest an element of sedentism or a least a fixed place in the landscape that would have attracted repeat visits. The local palaeotopography and palaeoenvironment during the late Boreal/early Atlantic would have supported opportunities for a semi-sedentary lifestyle.

14.5 Management and risk

In the Western Solent, the research is highlighting the potential existence of a rich source of Mesolithic archaeological material associated with the period of severance from Europe. This was a time when terrestrial, lacustrine, and estuarine environments would have offered a rich and varied range of resources within accessible territories. Unfortunately, the whole of this palaeo-landscape is now under water and mostly covered beneath sediment. To the east side of the Isle of Wight, detailed bathymetric survey across the Arun Palaeovalley has revealed deep fluvial systems with submerged geomorphological features which would suggest that sheltered lakes and estuaries existed (Gupta *et al* 2004; Wessex Archaeology 2004). More recent studies in the North Sea by the University of Birmingham have identified extensive buried morphological features (Gaffney *et al* 2007). These are comparable to the basin in the Western Solent and imply that similar processes that led to the severance of the Wight from the English mainland would have occurred in the North Sea and English Channel.

There is every reason to suspect that many more prehistoric archaeological sites exist in British coastal waters, but this resource is acknowledged as a very difficult one to interpret and more data of higher resolution is necessary before effective management will be possible (Peeters 2007, 231; Maarleveld and Peeters 2004, 109). The sites in the Western Solent, and particularly Bouldnor Cliff, present one opportunity to develop a larger data set. The ongoing erosion that has sliced through the old valley floor, the sheltered conditions, the accessibility of the Mesolithic land surface with its exquisite preservation, and the recent development in archaeological methodologies now provide the chance to gather essential baseline data. Paradoxically, the ultimate loss of the site to erosion provides the greatest archaeological opportunities.

Appendix 1   Contexts at BC-V

Context	Type	Description
5010	Deposit	Alluvial silty clay above peat (5011)
5011	Deposit	Overlying peat deposit in area of significant timber finds such as S061
5012	Deposit	Clay with inclusions, overlain by (5011) and overlying (5013)
5013	Deposit	Wood and timber layer containing archaeology, overlain by (5012) and overlying (in the area of S061) deposit (5032)
5014	Deposit	Organic, burnt flint, and charcoal inclusions. Overlain by (5034) and overlying (5026)
5015	Deposit	Dark grey humic silt below wood (5013) in MS46 and grey area on plan. Not yet identified within samples
5016	Deposit	Timber and peat layer in area of platform. Overlies (5017)
5017	Deposit	Sandy clay with organic inclusions. Overlain by (5016) and overlying (5018)
5018	Deposit	Layer of twigs and charcoal seen in section of platform. Overlain by (5017) and overlying (5019)
5019	Deposit	Pale grey deposit underlying (5018)
5020	Cut	Cut of the burnt pit east of the platform. Cuts clay deposit (5025)
5021	Fill	Primary fill of [5020]. Burnt layer
5022	Fill	Secondary fill of [5020]. Contains burnt flints
5023	Fill	Upper fill of [5020] overlain by burnt wood F142 (initially S026)
5024	Deposit	Peat which caps fills from [5020] and surrounding area
5025	Deposit	Grey clay cut by [5020]
5026	Deposit	Pale grey clay underlying deposits in area of S061
5027	Deposit	Greyish-brown silty clay with organic inclusions overlain by (5031) and overlying (5028)
5028	Deposit	Burnt flint layer from S049. Overlain by (5027) and overlying (5029)
5029	Layer	Grey clay underlying (5028)
5030	Deposit	Gravel from palaeochannel west of main site area
5031	Layer	Peat deposit overlying platform 2 (to the west of site W76 area)
5032	Deposit	Unburnt twigs underlying log boat. Overlain by (5013) and overlying (5033)
5033	Deposit	Charcoal layer which underlies (5032) and overlies (5034)
5034	Deposit	Layer of unburnt twigs underlying charcoal (5033) and overlying (5014)

Appendix 2 Catalogue of wood examined and recorded for evidence of working, plus wood identification table

BC-V – Worked wood, lifted and recorded in detail

MS20 Roundwood, ?trimmed similar to MS24 Orig D 63/100mm
MS24 Roundwood, trimmed 1 end/2 directions Orig D 20/30mm
MS39 Debris, oak (*Quercus* sp), torn and trimmed L 284 × 70 × 50mm
S039 Roundwood, oak (*Quercus* sp), slow grown, torn and trimmed Orig D 110mm
S058 Roundwood, ?stump, torn Orig D 145/75mm
S061 Timber, oak (*Quercus* sp), tangentially split
S102 Roundwood, ?torn and ?trimmed Orig D 33/50mm

BC-V – Worked wood from monoliths and samples recorded in detail

Not numbered
 Debris, woodchip, radial L 60 × 38 × 7mm
 Debris, woodchip, tangential L 58 × 28 × 12mm
 Debris, woodchip, radial L 35 × 25 × 7mm
 Debris, woodchip, tangential L 58 × 21 × 10mm
 Debris, woodchip, tangential, L 50 × 27 × 9mm
 Bark fragments, compressed roundwood and further debris too dry for analysis
Not numbered
 Roundwood, side branch trimmed and 1 end/2 directions L 1200 D 60mm
BC-V Trench D
 Debris, woodchip, tangential L 80 × 40 × 8mm
 Debris, woodchip, tangential L 82 × 42 × 10mm
 Roundwood, very compressed
 Bark fragments
 Compressed wood peat
BC-V Level 2
 Large fragments (Th min 12mm) heavily carbonised slow-grown oak
BC-V Square 1
 Debris, tangential woodchip, heavily charred L 85 × 30 × 8mm
 Fragments of very slow-grown oak
MS03 Roundwood, ?root, L 205 D 28/40mm
MS04 Debris, woodchip, tangential, oak L 60 × 30 × 17mm
 Roundwood, D 10mm
 Small fragments
 Debris, woodchip, tangential, charred one edge, oak L 100 × 73 × 17mm
 Debris, woodchip, tangential, heavily charred, oak L 125 *c* 76 × 40mm
MS09 Debris, ½ split roundwood L 100 × 35 × 17mm

Roundwood D 32mm
 Fragments roundwood <10mm
MS13 Debris, woodchip, tangential across knot, surface charred deeply 1 side L 102 × 42 × 25mm
MS16 Debris, woodchip, radial L 70 × 18 × 4mm
 Fragments, very dry
MS23 Debris, woodchip, ?radial, piddock damage and water-worn, oak L 254 × 50 × 30mm
MS24 Bark L 200 × 36 × 24mm
 Bark L 345 × 40 × 32mm
 Bark L 370 × 56 × 30mm
MS37 Debris, ?½ split, very dry L 243 × 50 × 30mm
MS40 Debris, woodchip, radial, one surface ?split L 130 × 72 × 28mm
 Bark L 220 × 48 × 32mm
SO16 Debris, heavily charred L 117 × 43 × 34mm
 Knobbly root fragment
SO17 Roundwood, heel L 55 D 10mm
 Roundwood, possible fragment of heel L 105+ D 30/42mm
SO28 Debris, ?roundwood chip L 55+ × 24 × 6mm
 Roundwood D 24/36mm
 Roundwood D 16/20mm
 Roundwood D 14/17mm
SO35 Roundwood, heel, torn L 87+ × 27 × 13 D 10/13mm
 Roundwood fragment D 12/14mm
 Roundwood fragment D 7/10mm
 Roundwood fragment with heel attached D 13/16mm
SO54/ADebris, ½ split, but too dry for analysis L 275 × 40 × 26mm Orig D *c* 40mm
SO57 Roundwood, trimmed 1 end/all directions, 1 end/torn L 240 D 37/42mm
S102 Roundwood debris, 2 faces ?split but badly damaged (piddock), squared L 245 × 59 × 39mm
SOW22 Debris, tangential across knot, dry L 50 × 25 × 11mm
 Roundwood fragments

BC-V – sub-sampled wood from monoliths and samples

MS03 Roundwood, small dry fragments, D *c* 3–7mm, also possible woodchips *c* 40 × 30 × 3mm
MS04 Roundwood, ×8 heavily compressed, max 30 × 19 × 9mm, min 25 × 16 × 6mm
 Roundwood, charred, compressed L 120 D 10/25mm
MS07 Roundwood, D *c* 5–20mm, also ×3 bark, max Th 5mm
 Peat – very compressed
MS11 Roundwood ×2, L 105 D 8/20mm and L 76 D 11/20mm Condition 3

Wood identification table

Site Code	Object Code	Comment	Species
BC-V	S054/A	Dried out, diffuse porous, non-oak	UNID
BC-V	S055	'Assorted pine bark'. Diffuse porous, scalariform perforation plates 20 bars	*Alnus*
BC-V	S102	'Meso structure', semi ring-porous, 4–5 seriate rays	*Prunus*?
BC-V	MS39	'Worked'	*Quercus*
BC-V	MS37	Dried out, diffuse porous, non-oak	UNID
BC-V	S026		*Quercus*
BC-V	S039	'Wood stake', sampled *in situ* for dendro?	*Quercus*
BC-V	S058	Slide made up but poor preservation. 1–3 seriate rays, diffuse porous	*Betula*?
BC-V	MS24B	Small roundwood, diffuse porous, 1–3 seriate rays	Pomoideae
BC-V	MS20	Diffuse porous, 1–3 seriate rays	Pomoideae
BC-V	S035	Compressed immature roundwood. Fine pits on pores with scalariform plates *c* 20 bars	*Alnus*
BC-V	MS13	F149 Level 1. Worked wood. Charred. Ring porous, uniseriate rays but immature	*Quercus*
BC-V		'Trench D Cross beam end'	*Quercus*
BC-V	MS09	'W79–7A'	*Alnus*

MS16 Roundwood ×5, D 5–20mm Condition 3
MS32 Roundwood, compressed, *c* 15 × 20mm Condition 3
MS36 Charcoal, roundwood and timber, max 20mm
MS37 Roundwood, D 3–8mm
MS38 Roundwood, small, twiggy *c* 2–10mm Condition 3
MS41 Roundwood, dry fragments, D *c* 2–8mm Condition 2
SO2(2) Fragments, roundwood, 5 × 30mm and 30 × 10mm. Condition 2
SO5(98)Bark fragments ×15 (dry), min 25 × 20 × 4mm, max 40 × 35 × 5mm
SO17 Gnarled root. Condition 3
SO28 Roundwood, *c* 10 × 3mm. Condition 2
SO29 Bark fragments, *c* 20 × 10mm thick
SO38 Roundwood, charred L 120 D 15mm Condition 2
SO45(1) Roundwood, 3 × 5mm + bark Condition 3
   Roundwood *c* 3mm, bark *c* 30mm and natural debris – wood peat?

SO46 Fragments, fine sieved material, *c* 200mm. Condition 2
   Roundwood, *c* 15 × 10mm, gnarled, some charred Condition 2
   Roundwood, *c* 200 × 3mm Condition 3
SO50 Fragments from fine sieve
   Compressed wood peat
   Roundwood, D 3–11mm also bark fragments, max D 11mm
   Roundwood, D 2mm and fragments from sieve
SO51 Roundwood, D *c* 1mm Condition 3
SO51/B Fragments, dry, from fine sieve
SO53 Roundwood, dry D 8–15mm Condition 2
SO54/BL2 Roundwood ×10, D 5–15mm Condition 3
SO56 Roundwood ×*c* 15, compressed, D 5–12mm Condition 3
SO60 Roundwood, D 2–12mm also bark fragments, max Th 9mm

Appendix 3   Tranchet axe/adze and pick find-spots recorded in the Isle of Wight HER

Basford 1980 fig 3, no:	I of W HER PRN	Description
1	43	High Down (Poole 1929)
2	101	Afton Down (Poole 1929)
3	103	Afton Down (Poole 1929)
4	179	Hamstead. 3 axes (Poole 1929)
5	180	Bouldnor. Axe on beach (Poole 1929)
6	181	Bouldnor. Axe on beach
7	186	Bouldnor. 2 axes in inter-tidal mud
8	189	Bouldnor. 4 or 5 axes in creek marsh sediment
9	228	Atherfield. 0.4m below cliff top
10	229	Atherfield. Near edge of palaeochannel N of Whale Chine
11	359	Stone Place. Axe on farmland (Hookey 1952)
12	376	Loverston Farm
13	510	Gatcombe Mill. From stream bed
14	563	Elmsworth. 3 axes on beach (Poole 1929)
15	564	Saltmead 8 axes from coastal area. 2 were in brickearth (Poole 1929; 1940)
16	574	Off Newtown. Dredged find
17	578/1414	Thorness Bay. Axe from beach (Poole 1929)
18	606	Gurnard Bay. 5 axes from beach (Poole 1929)
19	752	St Boniface Down. Surface find (Poole 1929)
20	793	Blackpan Farm. Tranchet axe with microliths (Poole 1928)
21	878	Great Pan 1 or 2 axes from gravel workings (Poole 1929; 1936)
22	882	St Georges Down. Small axe from gravel workings
23	919?	Whitecroft. From Meso–Neo field scatter
24	929?	Blackwater. Axe from ploughed field
25	1002	Newchurch. 2 axes (Poole 1929)
26	947	Kings Quay. 6 axes from beach (Poole 1929)
27	948?	Woodside Bay. Large axe from beach (Poole 1929)
28	948?	Woodside Bay Axe from beach (Poole 1929)
29	952	Werrar. Axe and other lithics from shore of Medina estuary
30	976	Medina estuary. North of Binfield Luck
31	1069	Chapelcorner Copse. 4 axes on beach (Poole 1929)
32	1083	Wootton Creek. 3 axes (Poole 1929). Now many more
33	1083	Binstead Point. Axe (Poole 1929). Now many more from inter-tidal zone (Tomalin *et al* forthcoming)
34	1109	Yaverland. 4 tranchet axes and transverse flaked axes and microliths (Poole 1938)
35	1100	Yaverland. Axe from slope of cliff (Poole 1929)

Appendix 4   Submerged and potentially submerged Mesolithic sites on the English Channel coast of Wessex and Devon

Beaulieu, Boarman's Lodge, Hampshire (SU 380 020)

Mesolithic finds near the estuarine head of the Beaulieu River (Trowbridge 1936; Rankine 1940). Elevation uncertain.

Bouldnor, Solent coast, Isle of Wight (SZ 375 902)

Flint pick recovered from the beach by the geologist G W Colenutt (Poole 1929, 655). Two more picks or axes were found in the 1960s but sold by the finder. The latter were stratified in the tidally exposed sediment of Rush Creek.

Chichester Channel, West Sussex (SU 830 020 general)

Lithic artefacts from the inter-tidal zone have been reported by Arthur Mack.

Fareham, Wicor Shore, Cams Hall, Hampshire (SU 587 056)

Flint artefacts including two picks found on submerged land surface exposed only at low tide (Wymer 1977, 113; Jacobi 1981).

Gurnard Bay, Isle of Wight (SZ 473 955 approx)

Four flint picks recovered from the beach by Mr Acourt Smith and another found by him in the neighbouring cliff face (Poole 1929, 655). The bay is entered by the valley of the Luck stream.

Hamstead, Solent coast, Isle of Wight (SU 395 916 approx)

Three picks found on the beach by G W Colenutt (Poole 1929, 655).

Kings Quay, Solent coast, Isle of Wight (SZ 538 933 approx)

Six picks recovered by G W Colenutt from the beach where Flowers Brook enters the Western Solent (Poole 1929, 655).

Langstone Harbour, Hampshire

Various scatters of Mesolithic lithic material have been recovered from the inter-tidal margins of the diminishing islands in the interior of this drowned basin. A more detailed account of the various sites on these islands has been compiled by Allen and Gardiner (2000, 252–6).

> North Binness Island (SU 6913 046)
> South Binness Island (SU 699 029)
> Bakers Island (SU 695 035 etc)
> Long Island (SU 701 041)

Newtown Harbour, Solent coast, Isle of Wight (SZ 418 922)

Picks, tranchet axe, and microlith reported from estuarine clay in inter-tidal zone on the east of the mouth of this ria inlet. Neolithic flint artefacts have also been reported from brickearth in a low cliff (Poole 1940, 235). Submerged Neolithic trackway structures also survive in the inter-tidal zone.

Poole Harbour, Dorset (SY 940 880)

Microlith reported from Swineham marshes on the margin of the harbour. Dorset SMR 6 002 142.

Portchester, Seabanks, Portsmouth Harbour (SU 627 050)

Flint artefacts noted *in situ* in inter-tidal mud (Palmer 1977, 109). They include a micro-burin.

Rainbow Bar, Hill Head, Southampton Water (SU 530 022)

At the entrance to Tichfield Haven. Pick, graver, and unclassified flakes recovered from submerged surface that is accessible only at extreme low tide (Draper 1951; Hack 1998; 1999; 2000).

Saltmead, Solent coast, Isle of Wight (SZ 440 930 approx)

Three picks recovered from the beach by G W Colenutt (Poole 1929, 655).

Southampton

George V Graving Dock (SU)

Ocean Dock (SU 424 105)

Lithic artefacts reported from a depth of approximately –20ft OD. They include a quartzite pebble with hour-glass perforation.

Corporation baths (SU 416 120)

Waste flake recovered from a depth of –18ft in a peat bed with oak, beech, hazel remains attributed to pollen zones VII to VI.

New Dock, Millbrook (SU 385 129)

Convex scraper reported from New Dock reclamation.

South Wallington (SU 586 065)

Lithic finds reported from the bank of the tidal course of the Wallington river.

Thurlestone Sands, Bigbury Bay, South Devon (SX 660 440)

A submerged forest was examined by Winder (1924). Later noted as a possible Mesolithic site by Palmer (1977, 163).

Werrar, Medina river, Isle of Wight (SU 506 927)

A submerged land surface with a scatter of lithic finds was reported here by Poole (1936).

Weymouth, Dorset (SY 6705 7692)

Worked flint, apparently Mesolithic, reported from the shore. Dorset SMR 4 002 616.

Weymouth, Dorset (SY 6700 8000)

Two picks retrieved from river-bed contexts in 1865 and 1874. Dorset SMR 4 002 635.

Wootton Haven (Fishbourne Creek), Isle of Wight (SU 555 931 approx)

Picks and axes have been found on both the eastern and western shores of the haven mouth. An early report by Poole (1936) recorded a total of six. The Wootton-Quarr inter-tidal survey has pressed inter-tidal survey 4km eastwards, as far as Players Beach, Ryde, increasing the number of picks and axes from the inter-tidal zone to more than 100. The distribution of these finds shows clustering around the mouths of Wootton Haven, Quarr Stream and the Binstead Brook. All of these finds come from submerged contexts now being denudated by wave action.

Appendix 5 Find-spots of tranchet axes, adzes, and picks in the West Solent region

Items dredged from the seabed by Michael White to which an approximate location can be attributed (see Harding *et al* 2004)

1. River Itchen, off Corral's Wharf
4. Off Lymington River
5. Southampton Water. Perforated mace
6. Stanswood Bay. Unspec core tool
7. Off Stone Point. Lepe
8. Off Cables. Lepe
9. Off Sowley. East side of boom
10. Off Pitts Deep
11. Off Sowley Boom
12. Off Hamstead Ledge
13. East of Newtown River. Large pebble mace
15. Off Newtown River
16. Off Hamstead Point and Newtown River
18. West side of Newtown River mouth
19. Off Netley. Southampton Water
20. Sowley. Off Pitts Deep
23. Between Pennington Sewer and Lymington River
24. Off Oxey Lake and Mystery Lake
29. Between Hawker's Lake and Pennington sewer
30. Pennington Creek
31. Off Pennington
34. Marsh at Keyhaven
42. Milford on Sea. Field at Taddiford
44. Off Pylewell
45. Off Tanners Lane
46. Tanners Lane. Close inshore
48. Fawley. West side of hot water outlet
49. In mouth of Lymington River
50. Just outside Starting Box in Lymington River
52. By Bourne Gap. Stanswood Bay

Bibliography

Alexander, J & Ozanne, P C & A, 1960 The excavation of a round barrow on Arreton Down, Isle of Wight, *Proc Prehistoric Society*, **26**, 263–302

Allen, L C & Gibbard, P L, 1993 Pleistocene evolution of the Solent River of Southern England, *Quaternary Science Reviews*, **12**, 503–28

Allen, M J & Gardiner, J (eds), 2000 *Our changing coast: a survey of Langstone Harbour, Hampshire*, CBA Res Rep **124**. York: Council for British Archaeology

Alley, R B, 2000 The Younger Dryas cold interval as viewed from central Greenland, *Quaternary Science Reviews*, **19**, 213–26

Alley, R B, Meese, D A, Shuman, C A, Gow, A J, Taylor, K C, Grootes, P M, White, J W C, Ram, M, Waddington, E D, Mayewski, P A & Zieginski, G A, 1993 Abrupt increase in Greenland snow accumulation at the end of the Younger Dryas event, *Nature*, **362**, 527–9

Alve, E & Murray, J W, 1994 Ecology and Taphonomy of Benthic Foraminifera in a Temperate Mesotidal inlet, *Journal of Foraminiferal Research*, **24**(1), 18–27

Andersen, S, 1970 The relative pollen productivity and pollen representation of north European trees and correction factors for tree pollen spectra, *Danmarks Geologiske Undersogelse* R.II, **96**, 1–99

Andersen, S, 1973 The differential pollen productivity of trees and its significance for the interpretation of a pollen diagram from a forested region, in H J B Birks & R G West *Quaternary Plant Ecology*. Oxford: Blackwell, 109–115

Andersen, S, Bailey, G N, Craig, O E, Milner, M & Pedersen K, 2004 Change of diet in Northern Europe's Mesolithic–Neolithic transition; a new critique, *Antiquity*, **78**, 9–37

Anderson, F W, 1933 The new dock excavations, Southampton, *Proc Hampshire Fld Club Archaeol Soc*, **12**, 169–76

Ashmore, P, 1999 Radiocarbon dating: avoiding errors by avoiding mixed samples, *Antiquity*, **73**, 124–30

Åstveit, L, 2009 Different ways of building, different ways of living: Mesolithic house structures in western Norway, in S B McCartan, R Schulting, G Warren & P Woodman (eds) *Mesolithic Horizons*. Oxford: Oxbow Books, 414–21

Bailey, G N, 2004 The wider significance of submerged archaeological sites and their relevance to world prehistory, in N C Flemming (ed) *Submarine prehistoric archaeology of the North Sea: research priorities and collaboration with industry*, CBA Res Rep **141**. York: Council for British Archaeology and English Heritage, 3–10

Bailey, G & Milner, N, 2002 Coastal hunter-gathers and social evolution marginal or central? *Before Farming: the archaeology of Old World hunter-gatherers*, **3–4**(1), 1–15

Bailey, G & Spikins, P (eds), 2008 *Mesolithic Europe.* Cambridge: Cambridge University Press

Baillie, M G L & Pilcher, J R, 1973 A simple cross-dating program for tree-ring research, *Tree Ring Bulletin*, **33**, 7–14

Bang-Anderson, S, 2003 Encircling the living space of early Postglacial reindeer hunters in the interior of Southern Norway, in H Kindgren, K Knutsson, D Loeffler & A Åkerlund (eds) *Mesolithic on the Move*. Oxford: Oxbow Books, 193–204

Barber, K E & Clarke, M J, 1987 Cranes Moor, New Forest: palynology and macrofossil stratigraphy, in K E Barber (ed) *Wessex and the Isle of Wight*. Cambridge: Quaternary Research Association Field Guide, 33–44

Barton, R N E, 1992 *Hengistbury Head, Dorset, vol. 2. The Late Upper Palaeolithic and Early Mesolithic sites*, Oxford Univ Comm Archaeol monogr **34**. Oxford

Basford, H V, with contributions by Insole, A N, Tomalin, D J, Scaife, R G and Motkin, D L, 1980 *The Vectis report: a survey of Isle of Wight archaeology*. Isle of Wight County Council

Bates, M R, 2001 The meeting of the waters: raised beaches and river gravels of the Sussex Coastal Plain/Hampshire Basin, in F F Wenben-Smith & R T Hosfield (eds) *Palaeolithic Archaeology of the Solent River*, Lithic Stud Soc Occ Pap **7**. London: Lithic Studies Society, 27–45

Battarbee, R W, 1986 Diatom analysis, in B E Berglund (ed) *Handbook of Holocene Palaeoecology and Palaeohydrology*. Chichester: John Wiley & Sons, 527–70

Bayliss, A & Tyers, I, 2004 Interpreting radiocarbon dates using evidence from tree rings, *Radiocarbon*, **46**(2), 957–64

Bayliss, A, Groves, C, McCormac, G, Baillie, M, Brown, D & Brennard, M, 1999 Precise dating of the Norfolk timber circle, *Nature*, **402**, 479

Bell, M, 2007 *Prehistoric Coastal Communities: The Mesolithic in western Britain*, CBA Res Rep **149**. York: Council for British Archaeology

Bennett, K D, Whittington, G & Edwards, K J, 1994 Recent plant nomenclatural changes and pollen morphology in the British Isles, *Quaternary Newsletter*, **73**, 1–6

Binford, L R, 1980 Willow smoke and dogs' tails: hunter-gatherer settlement systems and archaeological site formation, *American Antiquity*, **45**, 4–20

Birks, H J B, Deacon, J & Peglar, S 1975 Pollen maps for the British Isles 5000 years ago, *Proc Royal Soc London*, **B189**, 87–105

Bjerck, H B, 2008 Norwegian Mesolithic trends: a review, in G Bailey & P Spikins (eds) *Mesolithic Europe*. Cambridge: Cambridge University Press, 60–106

Bowens, A (ed), 2009 *Underwater Archaeology: the NAS Guide to Principles and Practice*, 2nd edn. Chichester: Blackwell

Brennand, M & Taylor, M, 2003 The Survey and Excavation of a Bronze Age Timber Circle at Holme-next-the-sea, Norfolk, 1998–9, *Proc Prehist Soc*, **69**, 1–84

Bridgland, D R & D'Olier, B, 1995 The Pleistocene evolution of the Thames and Rhine drainage systems in the southern North Sea Basin, in R. C. Preece (ed) *Island Britain: a Quaternary perspective*, Geological Society Special Pub **96**. London: Geological Society, 27–45

Bridgland, D R & D'Olier, B, 2001 The Pleistocene evolution and Palaeolithic occupation of the Solent River, in F F Wenben-Smith & R T Hosfield (eds) *Palaeolithic Archaeology of the Solent River*, Lithic Stud Occ Pap **7**. London: Lithic Studies Society, 15–25

Bronk Ramsey, C, 1995 Radiocarbon calibration and analysis of stratigraphy, *Radiocarbon*, **36**, 425–30

Bronk Ramsey, C, 1998 Probability and dating, *Radiocarbon*, **40**, 461–74

Bronk Ramsey, C, 2001 Development of the radiocarbon calibration program, *Radiocarbon*, **43**, 355–63

Bronk Ramsey, C, Higham, T & Leach, P, 2004 Towards high precision AMS: progress and limitations, *Radiocarbon*, **46**(1), 17–24

Brown, A, 2007 Dating the onset of cereal cultivation in Britain and Ireland: the evidence from charred cereal grains, *Antiquity*, **81**, 1042–52

Bruce, P, 1993 *Solent Tides*. Freshwater: West Island Printers

Buck, C E, Cavanagh, W G & Litton, C D, 1996 *Bayesian Approach to Interpreting Archaeological Data*. Chichester: Wiley

Bullock, P, Fedoroff, N, Jongerius, A, Stoops, G & Tursina, T, 1985 *Handbook for Soil Thin Section Description*. Wolverhampton: Waine Research Publications

Butler, C, 2005 *Prehistoric flintwork*. Stroud: Tempus

Camidge, K, Johns, C & Rees, P, 2006 Royal Anne Galley, Lizard Point, Cornwall: marine environmental assessment, Phase 1, desk-based assessment. Truro: Cornwall Historic Environment Unit/ English Heritage

Care, V, 1979 The production and distribution of Mesolithic axes in Southern Britain, *Proc Prehist Soc*, **45**, 93–102

Casati, C & Sørensen, L, 2009 The settlement patterns of the Maglemose culture on Bornholm, Denmark. Some preliminary results and hypotheses, in S B McCartan, R Schulting, G Warren & P Woodman (eds) *Mesolithic Horizons*. Oxford: Oxbow Books, 248–54

Cederland, C O, 2004 *Monitoring, Safeguarding and Visualizing North-European Shipwreck Sites: Final Report*, National Board of Antiquities. Helsinki, Finland

Christensen, K, 1997 Wood from fish weirs: forestry in the Stone Age, in L Pedersen, A Fischer & B Aaby (eds) *The Danish Storebaelt since the Ice Age: man, sea and forest*. Copenhagen: The Storebaelt Publications, 147–56

Churchill, D M, 1965 The kitchen midden site at Westward Ho!, Devon, England: Ecology, age and relation to changes in land and sea level, *Proc Prehist Soc*, **31**, 74–84

Clapham, A R, Tutin, T G & Moore, D M, 1987 *Flora of the British Isles*, 3rd edn. Cambridge: Cambridge University Press

Clark, J G D, 1972 *Star Carr: a Case Study in Bio-archaeology*. Reading, MA: Addison-Wesley

Clarke, J G D, 1954 *Excavations at Star Carr*. Cambridge: Cambridge University Press

Clarke, M J & Barber, K E, 1987 Mire development from the Devensian Lateglacial to present at Church Moor, Hampshire, in K E Barber (ed) *Wessex and the Isle of Wight*. Cambridge: Quaternary Research Association Field Guide, 23–32

Coles, B, 1998 Doggerland: a speculative survey, *Proc Prehist Soc*, **64**, 45–82

Coles, B, 2000 Doggerland: the cultural dynamics of a shifting coastline, in K Pye & J R L Allen (eds) *Coastal and Estuarine Environments: sedimentology, geomorphology and geoarchaeology*, Geological Society of London Special Publications **175**. London: Geological Society of London, 393–471

Coles, B & Coles, J, 1989 *People of the Wetlands*. London: Thames and Hudson

Conneller, C, 2009 Death, in C Conneller & G Warren (eds) *Mesolithic Britain and Ireland: New Approaches*. Stroud: The History Press, 139–64

Cope, S N, Bradbury, A P & Gorczynzka, M, 2008 *Solent Dynamic Coast Project: Summary Report*. Available: http://www.channelcoast.org/reports/ Accessed: 20 July 2010

Cowell, R W & Innes, J B, 1994 *The wetlands of Merseyside*, North West wetland survey monogr **1**, Lancaster imprints **2**. Lancaster: University of Lancaster Archaeological Unit

Crombé, P Y, Perdaen, J, Sergant, J-P, Van Roeyen, M & Van Strydonck, M, 2000 The Mesolithic–Neolithic transition in the sandy lowlands of Belgium: new evidence, *Antiquity*, **76**, 699–706

Crombé, P Y, Perdaen, J & Sergant, J, 2003 The site of Verrebroek 'Dok' (Flanders, Belgium): spatial organisation of an extensive Early Mesolithic settlement, in H Kindgren, K Knutsson, D Loeffler & A Åkerlund (eds) *Mesolithic on the Move*. Oxford: Oxbow Books, 205–15

Crossman, M & Simm, J, 2004 *Manual on the Use of Timber in Coastal and River Engineering*. London: Thomas Telford

Dark, P, 2000 Revised 'absolute' dating of the early Mesolithic site of Star Carr, North Yorkshire, in the light of changes in the early Holocene tree-ring chronology, *Antiquity*, **74**, 304–7

DCMS, 2008 *Draft Heritage Protection Bill*. London: TSO

Dean, J M, 1995 Holocene paleo-environmental reconstruction for the nearshore Newton area, Isle of Wight. Unpubl BSc thesis, University of Southampton

Devoy, R J, 1979 Flandrian sea level changes and vegetational history of the lower Thames Estuary, *Philosophical Transactions of the Royal Society of London. B* **285**, 355–407

Devoy, R J, 1982 Analysis of the geological evidence for Holocene sea-level movements in southeast England, *Proc Geol Ass*, **93**, 65–90

Devoy, R J, 1987 The estuary development of the western Yar, Isle of Wight: sea level changes in the Solent region, in K E Barber (ed), *Wessex and the Isle of Wight*. Cambridge: Quaternary Research Association Field Guide, 115–22

Dimbleby, G W, 1985 *The palynology of archaeological sites*. London: Academic Press

Dimbleby, G W & Bradley, R J, 1975 Evidence of pedogenesis from a Neolithic site at Rackham, Sussex, *J Archaeol Sci*, **2**, 179–86

Dix, J, 2000 A geological and geophysical investigation of the submerged cliff at Bouldnor, in R McInnes, D J Tomalin & J Jakeways (eds) *Coastal change, climate and instability: final technical report vol 2*, European Commission Life Project **97**, ENV/UK/000510. Ventnor: Isle of Wight Centre for the Coastal Environment, 5–13

Dix, J, 2001 The geology of the Solent river system, in F F Wenban-Smith & R T Hosfield (eds) *Palaeolithic Archaeology of the Solent River*, Lithic Stud Soc Occ Pap **7**. London: Lithic Studies Society, 7–14

Draper, J C, 1951 Stone age industries from Rainbow Bar, Hants, *Archaeological Newletter*, **3**(9), 147–9

Draper, J C, 1968 Mesolithic distributions in SE Hampshire, *Proc. Hampshire Fld Club Archaeol Soc*, **23**, 110–19

Druce, D, 2000 Mesolithic to Romano-British archaeology and environmental change of the Severn Estuary, England. Unpub PhD thesis, University of Bristol

Durrance, E M & Laming, D J C, 1982 *The geology of Devon*. Exeter: University of Exeter

Dyer, K R, 1969 Some aspects of coastal and estuarine sedimentation. Unpub PhD thesis, Depatment of Oceanography, University of Southampton

Dyer, K R, 1975 The buried channels of the 'Solent River' Southern England, *Proc Geol Ass London*, **86**(23), 9–246

English Heritage, 1996 *England's Coastal Heritage:* a statement on the management of coastal archaeology. London: English Heritage

English Heritage, 1998 *Dendrochronology: guidelines on producing and interpreting dendrochronological dates*. London: English Heritage

English Heritage, 2008a *Heritage At Risk*. London: English Heritage

English Heritage, 2008b *Protected Wreck Sites at Risk: A risk management handbook*. Portsmouth: English Heritage

Evans, C & Hodder, I, 2006 *A Woodland Archaeology – Neolithic Sites at Haddenham*. Cambridge: McDonald Institute for Archaeological Research

Everard, C E, 1954 The Solent River: a geomorphological study, *Trans Inst Brit Geogr*, **20**, 41–58

Ferrari, B & Adams, J, 1990 Biogenic Modifications of Marine Sediments and their Influence on Archaeological Material, *Int J Naut Archaeol*, **19**(2), 139–51

Fischer, A, 1997 People and the sea – settlement and fishing along the Mesolithic coasts, in L Pedersen, A Fischer & B Aaby (eds) *The Danish Storebaelt since the Ice Age: man, sea and forest*. Copenhagen: The Storebaelt Publications, 63–77

Fischer, A, 2004 Submerged Stone Age—Danish examples and North Sea potential, in N C Flemming (ed) *Submarine prehistoric archaeology of the North Sea: research priorities and collaboration with industry*, CBA Res Rep **141**. York: English Heritage and Council for British Archaeology, 23–36

FitzPatrick, E A, 1993 *Soil Microscopy and Micromophology*. Chichester: Wiley

Flemming, N (ed), 2004 *Submarine prehistoric archaeology of the North Sea, Research priorities and collaboration with industry*, CBA Res Rep **141**. York: English Heritage and Council for British Archaeology

Fox, W E, 1862 How and when was the Isle of Wight separated from the mainland? *Geologist* 5, 452

Fulford, M, Champion, T & Long, A, 1997 *Englands's coastal heritage: a survey for English Heritage and the RCHME*. London: EH/RCHME

Gaffney, V, Thompson, K & Fitch, S (eds), 2007 *Mapping Doggerland: The Mesolithic Landscapes of the Southern North Sea*. Oxford: Archaeopress

Galimberti, M, Bronk Ramsey, C & Manning, S, 2004 Wiggle-match dating of tree-ring sequences, *Radiocarbon*, **46**, 917–24

Gardiner, J, 2000 Worked flint, in J Allen & J Gardiner (eds) *Our changing coast: a survey of the intertidal archaeology of Langstone Harbour*, CBA Res Rep **124**. London: Council for British Archaeology

Geikie, J, 1881 *Prehistoric Europe: a geological sketch*. London: Edward Stanford

Gelfand, A E & Smith, A F M, 1990 Sampling approaches to calculating marginal densities, *J American Statistical Ass*, 85, 398–409

Gilks, W R, Richardson, S & Spiegelhalther, D J,

1996 *Markov Chain Monte Carlo in practice*, London: Chapman and Hall

Glimmerveen, J, Mol, D, Post, K, Reumer, J W F, Plicht, H, Vos, J, Geel, B, Reenen, G & Pals, J P, 2004 The North Sea Project: the first palaeontological, palynological and archaeological results, in N C Flemming (ed) *Submarine prehistoric archaeology of the North Sea: research priorities and collaboration with industry*, CBA Res Rep **141**. York: English Heritage and Council for British Archaeology, 38–43

Godwin, H, 1940 Pollen Analysis and Forest History of England and Wales, *New Phytologist* **39**(4), 370–400

Godwin, H, 1975 *The history of the British Flora*, 2nd edn. Cambridge: Cambridge University Press

Godwin, H & Godwin, M E, 1940 Submerged peat at Southampton: data for the study of post-Glacial history V, *New Phytol*, **39**, 303–7

Gooder, J, 2007 Excavation of a Mesolithic House at East Barns, East Lothian, Scotland: An Interim View, in C Waddington & K Pedersen (eds) *Mesolithic Studies in the North Sea Basin and Beyond: Proceedings of a Conference held at Newcastle in 2003*. Oxford: Oxbow Books, 49–59

Green, J W, 1963 Wood cellulose, in R L Whistler (ed) *Methods in Carbohydrate Chemistry*. New York: Academic Press, 9–20

Greig, J R A, 1982 Past and present lime woods of Europe, in M Bell & S Limbrey (eds) *Archaeological Aspects of Woodland Ecology*, Assoc. Environ. Arch. Symposia **2**, BAR Int Ser **146**. Oxford: BAR, 23–55

Grøn, O, 2003 Mesolithic dwelling places in south Scandinavia: their definition and social interpretation, *Antiquity*, **77**, 685–708

Gupta, S, Collier, J, Parmer-Felgate, A, Dickinson, J, Bushe, K & Humber, S, 2004 *Submerged Palaeo-Arun River: Reconstruction of Prehistoric Landscapes and Evaluation of Archaeological Resource Potential Final Report*. London: Imperial College on behalf of English Heritage

Guyot, A, 1998 Trouvailles en grès, *Les Outils*, Bulletin **3**, 1–6

Hack, B, 1998 Stone tools from Rainbow Bar, Hillhead, *Proc Hampshire Fld Club Archaeol Soc*, **53**, 219–21

Hack, B, 1999 More stone tools from Rainbow Bar, Hillhead, *Proc Hampshire Fld Club Archaeol Soc*, **54**, 163–71

Hack, B, 2000 Rainbow Bar; some observations and thoughts, *Lithics*, **21**, 34–44

Hamblin, R J O & Harrison, D J, 1989 *Marine aggregate survey, Phase 2: South Coast*, British Geological Survey. Nottingham: Keyworth

Hampshire County Council, 1995 *The Langstone Harbour archaeological survey project: second interim report, 1994*. Winchester: Hampshire County Council

Harding, J & Healy, F, 2007 *A Neolithic and Bronze Age Landscape in Northamptonshire*. Swindon: English Heritage

Harding, P, Thomsen, M H & Wakefield, E, 2004 *Artefacts from the sea: Catalogue of the Michael White collection*, Wessex Archaeology for English Heritage and the Aggregate Levy Sustainability Fund, Ref 51541.05a–b, 2 vols. Salisbury

Harff, J, Lemke, W, Lampe, R, Lüth, F, Lübke, H, Meyer, M & Tauber, F, 2007 The Baltic Sea coast – a mode of interrelations between geosphere, climate, and anthroposphere, in J Harff, W W Hay & D M Tetzlaff (eds) *Coastline changes: interrelation of climate and geological processes*, Geological Society of America Special Paper **426**. Bouldner, CO: Geological Society of America, 133–42

Hartley, B, 1986 Check list of British Diatoms, *J Marine Biological Ass*, **66**, 530–610

Hartley, B, 1996 *An Atlas of British Diatoms*, arranged by B Hartley, based on illustrations by H G Barber & J R Carter, ed P A Sims. Bristol: Biopress Ltd

Haskins, L E, 1978 The Vegetational History of South-East Dorset. Unpub PhD thesis, University of Southampton

Haslett, S K, 2001 Report on Foraminifera from samples collected at Minehead, Somerset. Appendix III, in J Jones, H Timsley & R R J McDonnel (eds) *Palaeoenvironmental Analysis from Intertidal Deposits. Volume II Minehead Sea Defence Scheme*, Environmental Agency Archaeological Report. Exeter

Healey, M G, 1995 The lithostratigraphy and biostratigraphy of a Holocene coastal sequence in Marazion Marsh, west Cornwall, U.K. with reference to relative sea-level movements, *Marine Geology*, **34**, 237–52

Hedges, R E M, Bronk, C R & Housley, R A, 1989 The Oxford Accelerator Mass Spectrometry facility: technical developments in routine dating, *Archaeometry*, **31**, 99–113

Heyworth, A & Kidson, C, 1982 Sea level changes in southwest England and Wales, *Proc Geol Ass*, **93**, 91–111

Hinout, J, 1989a Tardenoisien et facies Mauregny dans la Bassin Parisien, in J-P Mohen (ed) *Le temps de la prehistoire*, tome 1. Dijon: Societé Préhistorique Française, 346–7

Hinout, J, 1989b Le Sauveterrien au sud de la Sein, in J-P Mohen (ed) *Le temps de la prehistoire*, tome 1. Dijon: Societé Préhistorique Française, 348–9

Hodson, F & West, I M, 1972 Holocene Deposits of Fawley, Hampshire, and the Development of Southampton Water, *Proc Geol Ass*, **83**, 421–42

Hookey, T P, 1952 A Thames pick from Shorwell, *Proc Isle Wight Natur Hist Archaeol Soc*, **4**, 268

Hosfield, R T, 2001 The Lower Palaeolithic of the Solent: site formation and interpretive frameworks, in F F Wenban-Smith & R T Hosfield (eds) *Palaeolithic Archaeology of the Solent river*, Lithic Stud Soc Occ Pap **7**. London: Lithic Studies Society, 85–98

HWTMA (Hampshire and Wight Trust for Maritime

Archaeology), 2002/2003 *A Year in Depth*, The Annual Report of Hampshire and Wight Trust for Maritime Archaeology. Wickham: Studio 6

HWTMA (Hampshire and Wight Trust for Maritime Archaeology), 2006 *Quantifying the Hazardous Threat: An assessment of site monitoring data and environmental data sets*. HWTMA/ English Heritage, unpublished project report

Innes, J, Blackford, J & Rowley-Conwy, P, 2003 The start of the Mesolithic–Neolithic transition in North-West Europe – the palynological contribution, *Antiquity*, **77(297)**, 647–52

Jacobi, R M, 1980 The Early Holocene settlements of Wales, in J A Taylor (ed) *Culture and Environment in Prehistoric Wales*, BAR Brit Ser **76**. Oxford: BAR, 131–206

Jacobi, R M, 1981 The last hunters in Hampshire, in S J Shennan & R T Schadla Hall (eds) *The archaeology of Hampshire*, Hampshire Fld Club Archaeol Soc Monogr **1**. Hambleton: Hampshire Field Club and Archaeological Society, 10–25

James, H, 1847 On a section exposed by the excavation at the new steam basin in Portsmouth Dockyard, *Quarterly J. Geol Soc*, **3**, 249–51

Jennings, S C & Smythe, C, 1990 Holocene evolution of the gravel coastline of East Sussex, *Proc Geol Ass*, **101**, 213–24

Johns, C, Camidge, K, Charman, D, Muville, J & Rees, R, 2007 *The Lyonesse Project, Isles of Scilly: Project Design*, Truro: Historic Environment Service

Johnstone, P, 1988 *The Sea-craft of Prehistory*, London: Routledge

Jorgensen, S, 1985 *Tree Felling with Original Flint-axes in Draved Wood*. Copenhagen: National Museum of Denmark

Kayser, O, 1989 L'Epipaléolithique et le Mésolithique en Bretagne, in J-P Mohen (ed) *Le temps de la prehistoire*, tome 1. Dijon: Societé Préhistorique Française, 350–52

Ke, X & Collins, M, 2002 Saltmarshes in the West Solent (southern England): their morphodynamics and evolution, in T Healy, Y Wang & J A Healy (eds), *Muddy Coasts of the World: Processes, Deposits and Function*. New York: Elsevier Science BV, 411–40

Keatinge, T, 1982 Influence of stemflow on the representation of pollen of *Tilia* in soils, *Grana*, **21**,171–4

Keatinge, T, 1983 Development of pollen assemblage zones in soil profiles in southeastern England, *Boreas*, **12**, 1–12

Keefe, P A M, Wymer, J J & Dimbleby, G W, 1965 A Mesolithic site on Iping Common, Sussex, England, *Proc Prehist Soc*, **31**, 85–92

Kloet, G S & Hincks, W D, 1977 *A check list of British insects: part 3 Coleoptera and Strepsiptera*, 2nd edition (revised), Royal Entomological Society of London; Handbook for the Identification of British Insects 11. London: Royal Entomological Society

Lambeck, K, 1995 Late Devensian and Holocene shorelines of the British Isles and North Sea from models of glacio-hydro-isostatic rebound, *J Geol Soc London*, **152**, 437–48

Lambeck, K & Chappell, J, 2001 Sea Level Change through the last Glacial Cycle, *Science*, **292**, 679–86

Larsonneur, C, Bouysee, P & Auffret, J-P, 1972 The superficial sediments of the English Channel and its Western Approaches, *Sedimentology*, **29**, 851–64

Larsson, L, 1980 Some aspects of the Kongemose Cultur in Southern Sweden, *Meddelanden från Lunds universitets historiska museum 1979–1980*, 13–39

Larsson, L, 1983 Mesolithic settlement on the sea floor of the Strait of Oresund, in P M Masters & N C Flemming (eds) *Quaternary coastlines and marine archaeology: towards the prehistory of land bridges and continental shelves*. London: Academic Press, 283–302

Lidén, K, Eriksson, G, Nordquist, B, Gotherstom, A. & Bendixen, E, 2004 The wet and the wild followed by the dry and the tame – diet in Mesolithic and Neolithic southern Sweden, *Antiquity*, **78**, 22–33

Loader, R, 1999 An assessment of the lithics from Bouldnor Cliff. Unpubl report for the Hampshire and Wight Trust for Maritime Archaeology

Loader, R, 2007 Isle of Wight: Upper Palaeolithic and Mesolithic Resource Assessment. Contributory section for the Solent – Thames Regional Research Framework. Available: http://www.buckscc.gov.uk/assets/content/bcc/docs/archaeology/A_ST_IOW_2_Isle_of_Wight_Upper_Palaeolithic_Mesolithic2.pdf Accessed: 14 August 2010

Loader, R, forthcoming, Lithic scatters and findspots, in D J Tomalin, R D Loader & R G Scaife, *Coastal archaeology in a dynamic environment: Wootton-Quarr, a Solent case study*

Loader, R, Westmore, I and Tomalin, D, 1997 *Time and Tide: An Archaeological Survey of the Wootton-Quarr Coast*. Isle of Wight: Isle of Wight Council

Long, A J 1992 Coastal response to change in sea level in the East Kent fens and southeast England, UK, over the last 7500 years, *Proceedings of the Geologists Association*, **103**, 187–199

Long, A J & Innes, J B, 1993 Holocene sea-level changes and coastal sedimentation in Romney Marsh, southeast England, UK, *Proc Geol Ass*, 104, 223–37

Long, A J & Innes, J B, 1995 A palaeoenvironmental investigation of the 'Middle Sand' and associated deposits at the Middle Church Bank, Romney Marsh, in J. Eddison (ed) *Romney Marsh: The Debatable Ground*, Oxford University Committee for Archaeology Monogr **41**. Oxford: Oxford University Committee for Archaeology, 37–50

Long, A J & Scaife, R G, 1996 *Pleistocene and Holocene Evolution of Southampton Water and its tributaries*, Report of Environmental

Research Centre, Department of Geography, University of Durham

Long, A J & Scaife, R G, in press The Solent sea-level record, in D J Tomalin, R Loader & R G Scaife *Wootton Haven: Coastal and port archaeology in a dynamic environment*. English Heritage

Long, A J & Tooley, M J, 1995 Holocene sea-level and crustal movements in Hampshire and Southeast England, United Kingdom, *J Coastal Res* Special Issue **17**, 299–310

Long, A J, Plater, A J, Waller, M P and Innes, J B, 1996 Holocene coastal sedimentation in the eastern English Channel: new data from the Romney Marsh region, United Kingdom, *Marine Geology*, **136**, 97–120

Long, A J, Scaife, R G & Edwards, R J, 1999 Pine pollen in intertidal sediments from Poole Harbour, U.K; implications for late-Holocene sediment accretion rates and sea level rise, *Quaternary International*, **55**, 3–16

Long, A J, Scaife, R G & Edwards, R G, 2000 Stratigraphic architecture, relative sea level and models of estuarine development in southern England: new data from Southampton Water, in K Pye & J R L Allen (eds) *Coastal and estuarine environments: sedimentology, geomorphology and geoarchaeology*, Geological Society Special Publication **175**. Bath: Geological Society, 253–79

Longin, R, 1971 New method of collagen extraction for radiocarbon dating, *Nature*, **230**, 241–2

Louwe Kooijmans, L P, 2003 The Hardinxveld sites in the Rhine/Meuse Delta, The Netherlands 5500–4500cal BC, in L Larsson (ed) *Mesolithic on the Move*. Oxford: Oxbow Books, 608–24

Lübke, H, 2009 Hunters and fishers in a changing world. Investigations on submerged Stone Age sites off the Baltic coast of Mecklenburg-Vorpommern, Germany, in S B McCartan, R Schulting, G Warren & P Woodman (eds) *Mesolithic Horizons*. Oxford, Oxbow Books, 556–63

Lynch, A, 1981 *Man and environment on south-west Ireland 4000BC–AD800: a study of man's impact on the development of soil and vegetation*, BAR Brit Ser **85**. Oxford: BAR

Maarleveld, T J & Peeters, H, 2004 The inundated landscapes of the Western Solent, in N Flemming (ed) *Submarine Prehistoric Archaeology of the North Sea: research priorities and collaboration with industry*, CBA Res Rep **141**. York: English Heritage and Council for British Archaeology, 102–12

McGrail, S, 1978 *The logboats of England and Wales*, BAR Brit Ser **51**. Oxford: BAR

McGrail, S, 1998 *Ancient boats of North-West Europe. The archaeology of water transport to 1500*. London and New York: Longman

McVean, D N, 1953 Account of Alnus glutinosa (L) Gaertn. for the Biological Flora of the British Isles, *J Ecol*, **41**(2), 447–66

McVean, D N, 1956 Ecology of *Alnus glutinosa* (L) Gaertn. VI Post-glacial history, *J Ecol*, **44**, 331–3

Maitland, P S & Campbell, R N, 1992 *Freshwater Fishes of the British Isles*, New Naturalist Series. London: Harper Collins

Mannino, M A & Thomas K D, 2009 The tradegy of the shoreline? Social ecology of Mesolithic coastal subsistence, with reference to the site at Culverwell, Portland (southern England), in S B McCartan, R Schulting, G Warren & P Woodman (eds) *Mesolithic Horizons*. Oxford, Oxbow Books, 146–51

Mellars, P & Dark, P, 1998 *Star Carr in Context*, McDonald Institute Monograph. Cambridge: McDonald Institute for Archaeological Research

Mellars, P & Reinhardt, S C, 1978 Patterns of Mesolithic land-use in Southern Britain: a geological perspective, in P Mellars (ed) *The early post-glacial settlement of Northern Europe*. London: Duckworth, 720–31

Milner, M & Bailey, G, 2003 Coastal hunter-gathers and social evolution marginal or central? *Before Farming: the archaeology of Old World hunter-gatherers* **3–4**(1), 1–15

Milner, N, Craig, O E, Bailey, G N, Pedersen, K & Andersen, S H, 2003 Something fishy in the Neolithic? A re-evaluation of stable isotope analysis of Mesolithic and Neolithic coastal populations, *Antiquity*, **78**, 9–22

Milner, N, Craig, O & Bailey, G (eds), 2007 *Shell Middens in Atlantic Europe*. Oxford: Oxbow Books

Mithen, S J, 2004 The Mesolithic experience in Scotland, in A Saville (ed) *Mesolithic Scotland: The Early Holocene Prehistory of Scotland and its European Context*. Edinburgh: Society of Antiquaries of Scotland, 243–60

Momber, G, 2000 Drowned and deserted: a submerged prehistoric landscape in the Solent, England, *Int J Naut Archaeol*, **29**(1), 86–99

Momber, G, 2004 Drowned and deserted: a submerged prehistoric landscape in the Solent, England, in N. Flemming (ed) *Submarine Prehistoric Archaeology of the North Sea. The inundated landscapes of the Western Solent*, CBA Res Rep **141**. York: English Heritage and Council for British Archaeology, 37–42

Momber, G & Campbell, C, 2005 Stone Age Oven under the Solent, *Int J Naut Archaeol*, **34**(1), 148–9

Momber, G & Geen, M, 2000 The application of the Submetrix ESIS 100 Swath Bathymetry system to the management of underwater sites, *Int J Naut Archaeol*, **29**(1), 154–62

Momber, G, Draper, S & Rackley, A, 1994 *New Forest Coast Archaeological resource*, unpubl report by The Hampshire and Wight Trust for Maritime Archaeology for New Forest District Council

Mook, W G, 1986 Business meeting: Recommendations/Resolutions adopted by the Twelfth International Radiocarbon Conference, *Radiocarbon*, **28**, 799

Moore, P D & Webb, J A, 1978 *An Illustrated Guide to Pollen Analysis*. London: Hodder & Stoughton

Moore, P D, Webb, J A & Collinson, M E, 1991 *Pollen Analysis*, 2nd edn. Oxford: Blackwell Scientific

Morales, A & Rosenlund, K, 1979 *Fish Bone Measurements*. Copenhagen: Steenstrupia

Mowat, R J C, 1996 *The Logboats of Scotland, with notes on related artefact types*. Oxbow Monogr ser 68. Oxford: Oxbow Books

Munro, M A R, 1984 An improved algorithm for crossdating tree-ring series, *Tree Ring Bulletin*, **44**, 17–27

Murray, J W, 1991 *Ecology and palaeoecology of Benthic Foraminifera*. London: Longmans

Murton, J B & Lautridou, J P, 2003 Recent advances in the understanding of Quaternary perigalcial features of the English Channel coastlands, in P L Gibbard & J P Lautridou (eds) The Quaternary History of the English Channel, *J Quaternary Sci* Special Issue, **18**, 301–8

Nayling, N & Manning, S, with contributions by Kromer, B, Bronk Ramsey, C, Pearson, C L & Talamo, S, 2007 Dating the submerged forests: dendrochronology and radiocarbon 'wiggle-match' dating, in M Bell (ed) *Prehistoric Coastal Communities: The Mesolithic in western Britain*, CBA Res Rep **149**. York: Council for British Archaeology

Nichols, R J & Clarke, M J, 1986 Flandrian peat deposits at Hurst Castle Spit, *Proc Hampshire Fld Club Archaeol Soc*, **83**, 421–41

Nowell, D A G, 1995 Faults in the Purbeck–Isle of Wight Monocline, *Proc Geol Ass*, **106**, 145–50

Oakley, K P, 1943 A note on the post-Glacial submergence of the Solent margin, *Proc Prehist Soc*, **9**, 56–9

Okorokov, A. V, 1995 'Archaeological finds of ancient dugouts in Russia and the Ukraine', *Int J Naut Archaeol*, 24(1), 33–45

Palma, P, 2005 Monitoring of Shipwreck Sites, *Int J Naut Archaeol*, **34**(2), 323–31

Palmer, S, 1972 The Mesolithic industries of Mother Siller's Channel, Christchurch and neighbouring areas, *Proc Hampshire Fld Club Archaeol Soc*, **27**, 9–32

Palmer, S, 1977 *Mesolithic cultures of Britain*. Poole: Dolphin

Palmer, S, 1990 Culverwell – unique opportunities for studying the intra-site structure of a Mesolithic habitation site in Dorset, England, in P M Vermeersch & P Van Peer (eds) *Contributions to the Mesolithic in Europe*. Leuven: Leuven University Press, 87–91

Pedersen, L, 1997 Settlement and subsistence in the late Mesolithic and early Neolithic, in L Pedersen, A Fishcher & B Aaby (eds) *The Danish Storebaelt since the Ice Age: man, sea and forest*. Copenhagen: The Storebaelt Publications, 109–15

Peeters, J H M, 2007 *Hoge Vaart-A27 in Context: Towards a model of Mesolithic–Neolithic land use dynamics as a framework for archaeological heritage management*. Amersfoot: RACM

Poole, H F, 1928 Natural history and archaeological notes, *Proc Isle Wight Natur Hist Archaeol Soc*, **1**, 609

Poole, H F, 1929 Stone axes found in the Isle of Wight, *Proc Isle Wight Natur Hist Archaeol Soc*, **1**, 652–8

Poole, H F, 1936 An outline of the Mesolithic flint cultures of the Isle of Wight, *Proc Isle Wight Natur Hist Archaeol Soc*, **2**, 551–81

Poole, H F, 1938 The Stone Age in the Isle of Wight, *Proc Isle Wight Natur Hist Archaeol Soc*, **3**, 33–47

Poole, H F, 1940 Stone Age implements found during 1940, *Proc Isle Wight Natur Hist Archaeol Soc*, **3**, 234–6

Rankine, W F, 1940 Mesolithic sites in Hampshire: some notes on flints from Beaulieu, *Proc Hampshire Fld Club Archaeol Soc*, **14**, 230

Rankine, W F, 1952 A Mesolithic Chipping Floor at The Warren, Oakhanger, Selborne, Hants, *Proc Prehist Soc*, **18**, 21–35

Rankine, W F, 1953 Mesolithic research in East Hampshire, *Proc Hampshire Fld Club Archaeol Soc*, **18**, 157

Rankine, W F, 1956 *The Mesolithic of Southern England*, Surrey Archaeol Soc Res Pap **4**. Guildford: Surrey Archaeological Society

Reid, C, 1905, The island of Ictis, *Archaeologia*, **59**, 281–8

Reid, C, 1913 *Submerged Forests*. Cambridge: Cambridge University Press

Reimer, P J, Baillie, M G L, Bard, E, Bayliss, A, Beck, J W, Bertrand, C J H, Blackwell, P G, Buck, C E, Burr, G S, Cutler, K B, Damon, P E, Edwards, R L, Fairbanks, R G, Friedrich, M, Guilderson, T P, Hogg, A G, Hughen, K A, Kromer, B, McCormac, G, Manning, S, Bronk Ramsey, C, Reimer, R W, Remmele, S, Southon, J R, Stuiver, M, Talamo, S, Taylor, F W, van der Plicht, J & Weyhenmeyer, C E, 2004 IntCal04 Terrestrial radiocarbon age calibration, 0–26 Cal Kyr BP, *Radiocarbon*, **46**, 1029–58

Reynier, M, 2000 Thatcham revisited: spatial and stratigraphic analysis of two subassemblages from Site III and its implications for Early Mesolithic typo-chronology in Britain, in R Young (ed) *Mesolithic lifeways: current research from Britain and Ireland*. Leicester Univ Archaeol Monogr **7**. Leicester: University of Leicester, 33–46

Richards, M P & Schulting, R J, 2003 Characterising subsistence in Mesolithic Britain using stable isotope analysis, in L Bevan & J Moore, *Peopling the Mesolithic in a Northern Environment*, BAR Int Ser **1157**. Oxford: Archaeopress, 119–28

Rowley-Conwy, P, 1983 Sedentary hunters: the Ertebolle example, in G Bailey (ed) *Hunter-gatherer economy in prehistory: a European perspective*. Cambridge: Cambridge University Press, 111–26

Sass-Klaassen, U, Kooistra, M, Kooistra, L, Hanraets, E, van Rijn, P & Leuschner, H H, 2004 How did bog oaks grow? Excavation of past woodland at Zwolle-Stadshagen, The Netherlands, in E Jansma & H Gaertner (eds) *TRACE, Tree Rings in Archaeology, Climatology and Ecology* **2**, 112–15

Scaife, R G, 1980 Late-Devensian and Flandrian palaeoecological studies in the Isle of Wight. Unpub PhD thesis, University of London, King's College

Scaife, R G, 1982 'Late Devensian and early Flandrian vegetational changes in southern England', in S Limbrey & M Bell (eds) *Archaeological Aspects of Woodland Ecology*, Assoc. Environ. Arch. Symposia **2**, BAR Int Ser **146**. Oxford: BAR, 57–74

Scaife, R G, 1987 The Late-Devensian and Flandrian vegetation of the Isle of Wight, in K E Barber (ed) *Wessex and the Isle of Wight*. Cambridge: Quaternary Research Association Field Guide, 156–80

Scaife, R G, 1988 The *Ulmus* decline in the pollen record of South East England and its relationship to early agriculture, in M Jones (ed) *Archaeology and the flora of the British Isles*. Oxford: Oxbow Books, 21–33

Scaife, R G, 1992 Plant macrofossils, in F Healy, M Heaton & S J Lobb, Excavations of a Mesolithic site at Thatcham, *Proc Prehist Soc*, **58**, 64–6

Scaife, R G, 1998 Mountbatten Park, Southampton: Pollen analysis of the Holocene peat and sediment sequence. Unpubl report for Southampton City Council

Scaife, R G, 2000a Palaeo-environmental investigations of the submerged sediment archives in the West Solent at Bouldnor and Yarmouth, in R McInnes, D J Tomalin & J Jakeways (eds) *Coastal change, climate and instability: final technical report vol 2*, European Commission Life Project **97**, ENV/UK/000510. Ventnor: Isle of Wight Centre for the Coastal Environment, 13–26

Scaife, R G, 2000b Grasping the Holocene timetable of coastal change, in R McInnes, D J Tomalin & J Jakeways (eds) *Coastal change, climate and instability: final technical report vol 2*, European Commission Life Project **97**, ENV/UK/000510. Ventnor: Isle of Wight Centre for the Coastal Environment, 54–61

Scaife, R G, 2003a Testwood, Rownhams: Pollen analysis, palaeo-environmental history and vegetational history. Unpubl report for Wessex Archaeology

Scaife, R G, 2003b North West Solent BCIV: Tanners Hard Pitts Deep, Lymington. Unpubl report for the Hampshire and Wight Trust for Maritime Archaeology

Scaife, R G, 2003c The palaeoecological background, in C Pope, L Snow, D Allen *The Isle of Wight Flora*. Wimborne: Dovecote Press and Isle of

Wight Natural History and Archaeological Society, 19–31

Scaife, R G, 2004a Bouldnor 2003: A pollen assessment of the monolith profiles. Unpubl report for the Hampshire and Wight Trust for Maritime Archaeology

Scaife, R G, 2004b BCIV: Pollen analysis and vegetation history of monolith MS10. Unpubl report for the Hampshire and Wight Trust for Maritime Archaeology

Scaife, R G, 2005 Bouldnor 2004: Pollen analysis of sites BCV04 BCV05. Unpubl report for the Hampshire and Wight Trust for Maritime Archaeology

Scaife, R G, forthcoming The changing vegetation and environment, in D J Tomalin, R Loader & R G Scaife *Wootton Haven: Coastal and port archaeology in a dynamic environment*. English Heritage

Scaife, R G & Long, A J, 2001 Section 10 The Western Solent: a summary discussion on change in the Holocene environment'. Section 11 'Biostratigraphical markers and their application to coastal sedimentary dynamics, in R McInnes, D J Tomalin & J Jakeways (eds) *Coastal change, climate and instability: final technical report vol 2*, European Commission Life Project **97**, ENV/UK/000510. Ventnor: Isle of Wight Centre for the Coastal Environment, 26–8

Schulting, R, 2009 Worm's Head and Caldey Island (south Wales, UK) and the question of Mesolithic territories, in S B McCartan, R Schulting, G Warren & P Woodman (eds) *Mesolithic Horizons*. Oxford: Oxbow Books, 354–61

Schweingruber, F H, 1978 *Microscopic wood anatomy*. Zug, Switzerland: Zürcher

Scott, E M (ed), 2003 The Third International Radiocarbon Intercomparison (TIRI) and the Fourth International Radiocarbon Intercomparison (FIRI) 1990–2002: results, analysis, and conclusions, *Radiocarbon*, **45**, 135–408

Semenov, S A, 1964 *Prehistoric technology: an experimental study of the oldest flint tools and artefacts from traces of manufacture and wear*. London: Cory Adams & Mackay

Sergant, J, Crombé, P & Perdaen, Y, 2006 The invisible hearths: a contribution to the discernment of Mesolithic non-structured hearths, *J Archaeol Sci*, **33**, 999–1007

Serjeantson, D, Wales, S & Evans, J, 1994 Fish in Later Prehistoric Britain, in D Heinrich (ed) Archaeo-Ichthyological Studies, Papers presented at the 6th meeting of the I.C.A.Z. Fish Remains Working Group, *Offa*, **51**, 332–9

Sharples, J, 2000 Water Circulation in Southampton Water and the Solent, in M B Collins & K Ansell (eds) *Solent Science: a review*. Amsterdam: Elsevier, 45–53

Shennan, I, Lambeck, K, Flather, R, Horton, B P, McArthur, J J, Innes, J B, Lloyd, J M, Rutherford, M M & Wingfield, R, 2000 Modelling western North Sea palaeogeographies and tidal changes during the Holocene, in I Shennan & J Andrews (eds) *Holocene Land–Ocean Interaction and Environmental Change around the North Sea*, Geological Society Special Publication **166**. Bath: Geological Society Publishing House, 299–319

Shore, T W, 1893 Hampshire mudflats and other alluvium, *Proc Hampshire Fld Club*, **2**, 181–200

Shore, T W & Elwes, J W, 1889 The new dock extension at Southampton, *Proc Hampshire Fld Club*, **1**, 43–56

Simmons, I, 1996 *The Environmental Impact of Later Mesolithic Cultures*. Edinburgh: Edinburgh University Press

Simmons, I G, and Innes, J B, 1996 Disturbance Phases in the Mid-Holocene Vegetation at North Gill, North York Moors: Form and Process, *J Archaeol Sci*, **23**, 183–91

Simmons, I, Dimbleby, G W & Grigson, C, 1981 The Mesolithic, in I Simmons & M Tooley *The Environment in British Prehistory*. London: Duckworth, 82–124

Skaarup, J & Grøn, O, 2004 *Møllegabet II. A submerged settlement in southern Denmark*, BAR Int Ser **1328**. Oxford: Archaeopress, 41–73

Slota, Jr P J, Jull, A J T, Linick, T W & Toolin, L J, 1987 Preparation of small samples for 14C accelerator targets by catalytic reduction of CO, *Radiocarbon*, **29**, 303–6

Sparks, B, Momber, G & Satchell, J, 2001 A decade of diving, delving and dissemination: Hampshire and Wight Trust for Maritime Archaeology 1991–2001, *Nautical Archaeology: The NAS Newsletter* **02**(1), 11

Stace, C, 1991 *New Flora of the British Isles*. Cambridge: Cambridge University Press

Stockmarr, J, 1971 Tablets with spores used in absolute pollen analysis, *Pollen et Spores*, **13**, 614–21

Stuiver, M & Kra, R S, 1986 Editorial comment, *Radiocarbon*, **28**(2B), ii

Stuiver, M & Polach, H A, 1977 Reporting of 14C data, *Radiocarbon*, **19**, 355–63

Stuiver, M & Reimer, P J, 1986 A computer program for radiocarbon age calculation, *Radiocarbon*, **28**, 1022–30

Stuiver, M & Reimer, P J, 1993 Extended 14C data base and revised CALIB 3.0 14C age calibration program, *Radiocarbon*, **35**, 215–30

Tarrête, J, 1977 *Le Montmorencien*, Xe Supp. Gallia Prehistoire. Paris: CRNS

Tarrête, J, 1989 Le Montmorencien, in J-P Mohen (ed), *Le temps de la prehistoire*, tome 1. Dijon: Societé Préhistorique Française, 344–5

Taylor, K C, Mayewski, P A, Alley, R B, Brook, E J, Gow, A J, Grootes, P M, Meese, D A, Saltzman, E S, Severinghaus, J P, Twickler, M S, White, J W C, Whitlow, S, Zielinski, G A, 1997 The Holocene–Younger Dryas Transition Recorded at Summit, Greenland, *Science*, **278**(5339), 825–7

Taylor, M, 1998 Wood and bark from the enclosure ditch, in F Pryor *Etton: Excavations at a Neolithic causewayed enclosure near Maxey, Cambridgeshire 1982–7*. London: English Heritage

Taylor, M, 2010 Big Trees and Monumental Timbers, in F Pryor and M Bamforth *Excavation and Research at Flag Fen, Peterborough 1995–2007*. Oxford: Oxbow Books

Thompson, K, 2006 Quaternary channels of Poole and Christchurch bays and the existence of the Palaeo-Solent. Unpub research article, University of Birmingham

Tolan-Smith, C, 2008 Mesolithic Britain, in G Bailey & P Spikins (eds) *Mesolithic Europe*. Cambridge: Cambridge University Press, 132–57

Tomalin, D J, 1993 Maritime archaeology as a coastal management issue, in *Proceedings of the Standing Conference on Problems Associated with the Coastline: seminar on regional coastal groups – after the House of Commons Report*, SCOPAC. Isle of Wight County Council, 93–112

Tomalin, D, J, 2000a Geomorphological evolution of the Solent seaway and the severance of Wight: a review, in M B Collins & K Ansell (eds) *Solent Science: a review*. Amsterdam: Elsevier, 9–19

Tomalin, D J, 2000b Wisdom of hindsight: palaeo-environmental and archaeological evidence of long-term processual changes and coastline sustainability, in M B Collins & K Ansell (eds) *Solent Science: a review*. Amsterdam: Elsevier, 71–83

Tomalin, D J, 2000c Palaeo-environmental investigations of submerged sediment archives in the West Solent study area at Bouldnor and Yarmouth, in R McInnes, D J Tomalin & J Jakeways (eds) *Coastal change, climate and instability: final technical report vol 2*, European Commission Life Project **97**, ENV/UK/000510. Ventnor: Isle of Wight Centre for the Coastal Environment, 13–45

Tomalin, D J & Scaife, R G, 1979 A Neolithic flint assemblage and associated palynological sequence at Gatcombe, Isle of Wight, *Proc Hampshire Fld Club Archaeol Soc*, **36**, 25–34

Tomalin, D J, Loader, R D & Scaife, R G, 1998 *Coastal archaeology in a dynamic environment: a Solent case study*, draft report for English Heritage

Tomalin, D J, Loader, R & Scaife, R G, forthcoming *Coastal archaeology in a dynamic environment: Wootton-Quarr, a Solent case study*

Trowbridge, T, 1936 A Mesolithic village in Hampshire, *Antiq J*, **16**, 200–202

Tyers, I, 1999 *Dendro for Windows program guide*, 2nd edn. ARCUS Rep, **500**

Vairo, C P 1997 *Los Yamana: nuestra única tradición naval marítima autóctona*. Buenos Aires: Zagier & Urruty

Valentin, B, Fosse, G & Billard, C, 2004 Aspects et rythmes de l'Azilianisation dans le Bassin Parisien, *Gallia Préhistoire*, **46**, 171–209

Van de Noort, R, Ellis, S, Taylor M & Weir, D, 1995 Preservation of archaeological sites, in R Van de Noort & S Ellis *Wetland Heritage of Holderness: an archaeological survey*, Humber

Wetlands Project. Kingston upon Hull: University of Hull

Van der Werff, H & Huls, H, 1958–1974 *Diatomeenflora van Nederland*, 8 parts. Published privately: De Hoef, the Netherlands

Vaughan, D, 1987 The plant macrofossils, in N D Balaam, M G Bell, A E U David, B Levitan, R I Macphail, M Robinson & R G Scaife, Prehistoric and Romano-British sites at Westward Ho!, Devon. Archaeological and palaeo-environmental surveys 1983–1984, in N D Balaam, B Levitan & V Straker (eds) *Studies in palaeoeconomy and environment in South West England*, BAR Brit Ser **181**. Oxford: BAR, 233–8

Velegrakis, A, 1994 Aspects of morphology and sedimentology of a trangressional embayment system: Poole Harbour and Christchurch Bay, Southern England. Unpub PhD thesis, University of Southampton

Velegrakis, A, 2000 Geology, geomorphology and sediments of the Solent system, in M B Collins & K Ansell (eds) *Solent Science: a review*. Amsterdam: Elsevier, 21–34

Velegrakis, A F, Dix, J K & Collins, M B, 1999 Late Quaternary evolution of the upper reaches of the Solent river, Southern England, based upon marine geophysical evidence, *J Geol Soc London*, **156**, 73–87

Verron, G, 2000 *Préhistoire de la Normandie*. Rennes: Editions Ouest-France

Volmar, M, nd *The Dugout Canoe Project* Available: http://www.fruitlands.org/media/Dugout_Canoe_Article.pdf Accessed: 14 August 2010

Waddington, C, 2007a Rethinking Mesolithic Settlement and a Case Study from Howick, in C Waddington & K Pedersen (eds) *Mesolithic Studies in the North Sea Basin and Beyond*, Proceedings of a conference held at Newcastle in 2003. Oxford: Oxbow Books, 101–13

Waddington, C (ed), 2007b *Mesolithic Settlement in the North Sea Basin: A Case Study from Howick, North-east England*. Oxford: Oxbow Books

Waller, M, 1994 Paludification and pollen representation: the influence of wetland size on *Tilia* representation in pollen diagrams, *The Holocene*, **4**, 430–34

Ward, G K & Wilson, S R, 1978 Procedures for comparing and combining radiocarbon age determinations: a critique, *Archaeometry*, **20**, 19–31

Ward, I, Larcombe, P & Lillie, M, 2006 The dating of Doggerland: post-Glacial geochronology of the southern North Sea, *Environmental Archaeol*, **11**(2), 207–18

Wenban-Smith, F F & Hosfield, R T (eds), 2001 *Palaeolithic Archaeology of the Solent River*, Lithic Stud Soc Occ Pap **7**. London: Lithic Studies Society, 112

Wessex Archaeology, 2003 Artefacts from the sea. Aggregate Levy Sustainability Fund Report. Prepared on behalf of English Heritage maritime division

Wessex Archaeology, 2008 *Selection Guide: Prehistoric Landsurfaces and Deposits*. Draft document. Aggregate Levy Sustainability Fund/ English Heritage

West, I, 1980 Geology of the Solent Estuarine System, in J D Burton and I M West *The Solent Estuarine System: an assessment of present knowledge*, NERC Publications, Series C, **22**. Swindon: Natural Environment Research Council, 6–19

West, I M, 2008 Hurst spit Barrier Beach of the West Solent Hampshire: Geology of the Wessex Coast. Available: http://www.soton.ac.uk/~imw/Hurst-Castle-Spit.htm Accessed: 14 August 2010

West, I & Harvey, D, 2005 *Chesil Beach pebbles, Geology of the Dorset Coast*. Available: http://www.soton.ac.uk/~imw/chesil.htm Accessed: 21 July 2010

Wheeler, A, 1978 *Key to the Fishes of Northern Europe*. London: Warne

Wickham-Jones, C R, 1990 *Rhum: Mesolithic and later sites at Kinloch: excavations 1984–86*, Soc Antiq Scotl Monogr Ser **7**. Edinburgh: Society of Antiquaries of Scotland

Wickham-Jones, C R, 2009 Them bones: midden sites as a defining characteristic of the Scottish Mesolithic, in S B McCartan, R Schulting, G Warren & P Woodman (eds) *Mesolithic Horizons*. Oxford, Oxbow Books, 478–84

Williams, C T, 1985 *Mesolithic exploitation patterns in the central Pennines: a palynological study of Soyland Moor*, BAR Brit Ser **139**. Oxford: BAR

Winder, T, 1924 Submerged forest in Bigbury Bay, at Thurlestone Sands, S. Devon, *Trans Devon Ass*, **56**, 120–23

Woodman, P C, 1985 *Excavations at Mount Sandel 1973–77*, Northern Ir Archaeol Monogr **2**. Belfast: Her Majesty's Stationery Office

Woodman, P C, 2000 Getting back to basics: transitions to farming in Ireland and Britain, in T D Price (ed) *Europe's first farmers*. Cambridge: Cambridge University Press, 219–59

Woodman, P C, Andersen, E & Finlay, N, 1999 *Excavations at Ferriter's Cove, 1983–95: last foragers, first farmers in the Dingle Peninula*. Bray: Wordwell

Wymer, J, 1977 *Gazetteer of Mesolithic sites in England and Wales*, CBA Res Rep **20**. London: Council for British Archaeology

Wymer, J, 1991 *Mesolithic Britain*. Princes Risborough: Shire Publications

Xu, S, Anderson, R, Bryant, C, Cook, G T, Dougans, A, Freeman, S, Naysmith, P, Schnabel, C & Scott, E M, 2004 Capabilities of the new SUERC 5MV AMS facility for 14C dating, *Radiocarbon*, **46**, 59–64

Yesner, D R, 1980 Maritime hunter-gatherers: ecology and prehistory, *Current Anthropology*, **21**, 33–60

Zvelebil, M, 1994 Plant use in the Mesolithic and its role in the transition to farming, *Proc Prehist Soc*, **60**, 35–74

Index

Entries in bold refer to the figures

194   *Bouldnor Cliff*

erosion xxvii, xxxi, 15, 16, 37, 81, 120, 127, 129, 135,
    136, 139, 140, 156, 167–8
    monitoring of 21–4, 139
    of protective deposits 6, 12, 13, 66, 94, 105, 168,
        175
Ertebølle culture 173
Etton, Neolithic causewayed enclosure
    (Cambridgeshire) 87, 88
eustatic change 115, 116, 118 see *also* sea levels
experimental archaeology 87, 152

Fareham (Hampshire) 158
fen 44, 63, 96, 112, 116, 119, 128 see *also* woodland
fish
    Esox lucius (pike) 52, 63
Fishbourne Beach, Isle of Wight 52
Flandrian chronozones 41, 44, 74, 96, 99, 118
Flandrian Transgression xxv, 11 see *also* marine
    transgression
floodplains 74, 92, 98, 116, 118, 128, 133, 136, 155,
    156, 158, 161
fluvial environments 63, 98, 116
fluvial pathways see drainage systems
foraminifera 46–8, 64, 96, 98, 99–100, 116, 133
Foxhole Cave (Derbyshire) 52
Freshwater Bay, Isle of Wight **126**, 130, 131, **131**,
    143
freshwater conditions 42, 44, 46, 47, 64, 91, 92, 98,
    116, 118, 119, 121, 122, 128, 131, 133, 134,
    157
funding 4, 28, 76, 78, 94

Gatcombe Withy Bed, Isle of Wight 98, 112, 115,
    117, 118, 152
geology 123–4, **124**
Global Positioning Systems (GPS) 15, 21, 94, 94,
    106, 107
Goldcliff, Severn estuary 104, 173
groundwater tables 42, 64, 96, 112, 116, 132

Haddenham, Neolithic long barrow
    (Cambridgeshire) 89, 93
Hamble estuary 120
Hampshire and Wight Trust for Maritime
    Archaeology (HWTMA) 4, 5, 6, 11
Hampshire Basin xxvi, **xxvii**, 123, 124
Hawker's Lake (Hampshire) 9
Hayling Island (Hampshire) 158
Hengistbury Head (Dorset) xxvi, 145, 147, 159
Holme, Bronze Age timber circle (Norfolk) 87
Holocene 128
    early 74
    middle (Atlantic) 44, 74, 89, 92, 98, 99, 109, 115,
        116, 117, 121
human migration xxvi, 125, 127, 128, 172
Humber Wetlands Project 85
hunter-gatherer lifestyles 116, 118, 123, 136, 158,
    159, 173, 174
Hurst Castle **xxix**
Hurst Deep 127
Hurst Narrows **126**, 127, 128, 135, 156
Hurst Spit xxvi, 9, 127, 128, 129

Hythe Bay, Southampton Water 120
Hythe Marshes, Southampton Water 120

ice ages 124
Iping Common (Sussex) 115
Isle of Wight 44, 158
    Archaeological Committee 4
    County Archaeological Unit 4
    County Council 4
        Maritime Sites and Monuments Record 4
    Trust for Maritime Archaeology 4
isostatic rebound 173

Jones, Mike 3

Keyhaven Marshes (Hampshire) xxvi, 9, 128
Kongemose culture 173

Langstone Harbour (Hampshire) xxvi, 119, 158,
    159, 161, 173
lime migration 41, 92, 96, 117
lithic industries 140, 156, 158, 162–3
    in France 160
lithic types 141
    blades 146, 149, 150
    bladelets 146, 149–51
    chips/spalls 151
    cores 144, **144**, **145**
    core rejuvenation flakes 145, **145**
    flakes 147–9, 153–4
    hammerstones **142**, 143, 144, **144**
    microburins 147
    microliths 146, **146**, 147, **147**
    picks 159, 160, 161, 162, **162**, 163, 179, 182
    pièces tronquée **146**, 147, 152
    tranchet axes/adzes 89, 145, 152, 158–9, 160,
        162, **162**, 163, 179, 182
    tranchet flakes 145, **145**
lithics 115, 158, 159, 162 see *also* burnt flint
    condition of 141–2, **142**
    contexts of 139–40, 155
    debitage 151
    distribution of 158–9, 162, **162**
    examination of 141–2
    gloss **140**, 145, 146, **152**, 153–4, **153**
    in situ 27, 42, 43, 139
    knapping techniques 147, 148–50, 152, 159,
        162
    of Neolithic type 140
    raw materials 142–3, 144, 160, 162
        sources of 143–4
    recovery of 158
    retouch 146, **146**, 147, 152
    in secondary contexts 12, 19–20, 168
    use for cooking 142, 143
    use of 145, 146, 152, 153, 154, 162–3
    worked 13, 19, 20, 40, 51, 63, 74, 80, **81**, 94, 115,
        139, 143, 173
lobster burrows 13, 19, **20**, 24, 139, 168
lobster fishing 16, 170
log boats 89, 93, 174, 175
Lymington River 8, 9, 129, 130, 131